Applicable Law in International Arbitration –
The Experience of ICSID and Iran-United States Claims Tribunal

Studien zum vergleichenden und internationalen Recht - Comparative and International Law Studies

Herausgeber: Bernd von Hoffmann (†), Erik Jayme, Heinz-Peter Mansel, Christine Budzikiewicz, Michael Stürner, Karsten Thorn und Marc-Philippe Weller

Band 199

PETER LANG

Niki Nozari

Applicable Law in International Arbitration – The Experience of ICSID and Iran-United States Claims Tribunal

PETER LANG

Bibliografische Information der Deutschen Nationalbibliothek
Die Deutsche Nationalbibliothek verzeichnet diese Publikation in der Deutschen Nationalbibliografie; detaillierte bibliografische Daten sind im Internet über http://dnb.d-nb.de abrufbar.

Zugl.: Köln, Univ., Diss., 2018

D 38
ISSN 0930-4746
ISBN 978-3-631-77504-2 (Print)
E-ISBN 978-3-631-77556-1 (E-PDF)
E-ISBN 978-3-631-77557-8 (EPUB)
E-ISBN 978-3-631-77558-5 (MOBI)
DOI 10.3726/b14975

Peter Lang – Berlin · Bern · Bruxelles · New York · Oxford · Warszawa · Wien

Dieses Buch wurde vor Erscheinen peer reviewed.

www.peterlang.com

Contents

Introduction

Current trends in international dispute resolution are all rooted in the booming concept of globalization. When we think profoundly of every single desirable characteristic in any available means of international dispute settlement, we could easily acknowledge that the factors that create the attractiveness of these novel means reflect our today's world. Time efficiency, for example, has gained great importance, which perfectly mirrors the present-day reality not only in the field of international law or business and legal matters in general but also in our real day-to-day life.

International arbitration as one of the most utilized means of dispute resolution would continue to evolve only when it can meet the demands of the contemporary world. With that being said, flexibility in this method would become a vital element for a variety of reasons.

Arbitration or any other method should be capable of satisfying the expectations of two parties. Expectations that as a matter of fact are not in line with one another.

Notwithstanding the method of dispute settlement, applicable substantive law as the basis of deciding disputes, and its determination as one of the preliminary steps of every legal procedure are of great importance. In this research, we are about to look at this issue throughout the experience of two arbitral institutions.

The two institutions that we are going to analyze are ICSID and Iran-United States Claims Tribunal. There are a variety of reasons behind choosing these two institutions. It should however be noted that the comparison may still be of great importance, even where it seems at the outset that the subjects of it, are not of identical goals and purposes, such as the case with the two institutions compared in this study. To that end, at the beginning we should take into account that these two tribunals have several discrepancies, to name a few, their origins, procedural rules and jurisdictional scopes. Even though their differences are distinct, they cover extensive common legal issues that are of the utmost importance particularly in connection with international investment arbitration.

This study comprises two main chapters. The first chapter is dedicated to ICSID tribunals, which begins with a brief background and purposes of ICSID's establishment. The primary intentions of the drafters will be considered in order to perceive the elements that were vital at the time in order to meet the expectations of the fast-growing sphere of international investment.

Subsequently, we will review the jurisdictional scope of ICSID Convention. Although our main study focuses on applicable law issues, reviewing the key jurisdictional issues even briefly seems indispensable given the fact that the essence of a comparative study relies on the comprehension of the scope, under which two institutions are functioning. To that end, we also end the Jurisdiction section by analyzing the correlation between the scope of jurisdiction and applicable law.

The main part of our first chapter deals with various aspects of applicable substantive law in accordance with the ICSID Convention. Firstly, we will define the principle of party autonomy, which is considered as a cornerstone of determination of the applicable law, not only under the ICSID Convention but also in many other arbitration rules. The further step would be analyzing Article 42 of the Convention and its key features. To that end, we need to examine the situations that the Convention has stipulated as to whether the parties have selected the governing law and what would be the consequences of each situation. We continue the research by reviewing each matter in the light of Tribunal's caseload.

The focus will be further drawn to the role of international law along with national laws and whether one has primacy over the other and what are the consequences. General principles of law recognized by civilized nations as a source of international law will be taken into account, given its vital role in meeting the expectations of the players of today's globalized investment transactions.

Another approach of ICSID Convention on applicable law in case of an existing agreement of parties is whether the choice is explicit. The ICSID tribunals diligently examine the requirements for an implicit choice to be considered as eligible.

Our study would not be complete without taking other alternative methods into consideration. *Ex aequo et bono* is a method consistent with today's necessities. We all share the opinion that arbitration is aiming to facilitate the settlement of disputes by bringing them out of the national legal systems in order to provide the parties with an unbiased settlement procedures, while all these advantages and what makes them attractive is the distrust that parties share of each other's national courts system along with national laws. Therefore, setting the case free of the legal boundaries might practically advance the arbitration procedures; however, there are some inconsistencies regarding this theory.

We will sum up the first chapter by reviewing the annulment proceedings by ICSID *ad hoc* committees to reflect how the controversial issues with respect to applicable law have been dealt with at these committees. We try to demonstrate the possible arguments, under which the parties have brought up their challenges in connection with applicable law before the committees, since the grounds provided by Article 52 of the Convention, based on which the parties may request annulment of the award are limited, observing the cases on this matter would be of essence.

The objective of the second chapter of this research is reviewing the rules concerning substantive applicable law and the relevant experience of the Iran-United States Claims tribunal.

The Iran-US Tribunal is a unique institution mainly given to its background, history and the political setting, in which the tribunal was established. The Tribunal is rooted in a historical event early after the Islamic Revolution in Iran. The upheaval caused by Iranian students capturing the United States' Embassy in Tehran and taking its personnel as hostage, demanding the United States to return the Shah to Iran. The political repercussions of this event have led to a very complicated circumstance between Iran and the United States, which ultimately resulted in two declarations known as Algiers Accords issued by the Government of Algeria as the official intermediary. Alongside with the General declaration, the "Declaration of the Government of Democratic and Popular Republic of Algeria concerning the Settlement of Claims by the Government of the United States of America and the Government of the Islamic Republic of Iran" was the agreement to establish the Iran-United States Claims Tribunal. The General Declaration ensured the release of American nationals detained in the U.S. Embassy in Tehran and the return of Iranian assets. In addition, following the termination of the pending cases against Iran in United States courts, the General Declaration provided for the establishment of a security account to secure and pay the claims against Iran, which were to be submitted to the newly born Tribunal.

Given the challenges that the Tribunal had to face, it issued a remarkable amount of awards and decisions. As many commentators agree, the Tribunal's awards have been acknowledged as one of the most influential and important bodies of international arbitration jurisprudence. The Tribunal's workload does not only cover an extensive variety of legal issues, but also they stand out given their persuasive power, which is an essential character for an award to be considered as precedent. It is noteworthy that ICSID has the most references to Iran-United States Claims Tribunal's awards and decisions among other arbitral institutions.

After explaining the Tribunal's history, which in order to conceive its jurisprudence seems inevitable, we lay the groundwork by describing the Tribunal's structure and scope of jurisdiction. Reviewing the provisions of the Claims Settlement Declaration concerning the jurisdiction of the Tribunal is necessary given the discrepancies between them and the ICSID rules on jurisdictional matters. Under this section, we also analyze legal issues such as identifying government-controlled entities and dealing with dual nationals in depth as they are an area of significant activity for the Tribunal.

The Tribunal's jurisdiction over claims based on contracts containing choice of forum clauses has been also a controversial issue. Choice of forum clauses were common in Iran's prerevolutionary contracts, and we will discuss the existing arguments whether such clauses in certain contracts were enforceable.

The substantive applicable law under the Claims Settlement Declaration is set out by Article V, which gives the decision makers a great freedom in determination of the applicable law. Due to this Article, which is not similar to the applicable law provisions that we typically see, the arbitrators have a great discretion in determining the governing law, which leads to divergent arguments. Similar to what we examine under ICSID, here again we try to find out the relation between national and international law, the tendency of the Tribunal toward each choice, whether the Tribunal gives priority to one source over another and the role of general principles of international law.

1. Applicable substantive law and the ICSID Convention

I) Background

After more than ten years debate in various organs of the United Nations over the relationship between developing countries and multinational corporations, the General Assembly of the United Nations passed a resolution concerning the matter of permanent sovereignty over natural resources. This resolution was the first step toward the establishment of ICSID.[1]

This was the time of decolonization when a large number of previously colonized nations became sovereign countries. In their desire to develop, many of these newly independent countries were wished to attract foreign investment but unfortunately there were various factors that made the investors reluctant.

On the one hand the developing countries needed fund, technical assistance and know-how from the multinational corporations. On the other hand, the investors did not have enough protection.

From the point of view of foreign investors, factors that provide a favorable climate for investment include economic stability, a well-developed legal and regulatory framework, including favorable tax and labor codes, investment laws, property laws, the protection of intellectual property rights, a sufficient infrastructure and overall political stability.[2] Most of these countries were lacking in many of these areas.

At the root of the major problem concerning the paucity of foreign investment was the lack of appropriate international mechanisms to stimulate the international investment. In the absence of international mechanisms, dispute settlement between a State and foreign investor has to take place in the host state's court, which would not be desirable for the investors. The reasons are clear. The domestic courts of the host state usually do not have the specialized knowledge, which is necessary to settle the international investment disputes in a proper way. Moreover, they are bound to apply domestic law even when it fails to protect

---

1 Lowenfeld, Andreas F., "The ICSID Convention: Origins and Transformation", Georgia Journal of International and Comparative Law., Vol. 38, (2009), p. 47.

2 Rowat, Malcolm D., "Multilateral Approaches to Improving the Investment Climate of Developing Countries: The Cases of ICSID and MIGA", Harvard International Law Journal, Vol. 33, (1992), p. 104.

the investor's rights. Above all was the investor's suspicion about the lack of partiality of these courts.

The only method available to the foreign investors prior to the creation of ICSID was to pursue their claims through diplomatic protection by the investor's country of nationality against the host state. However, this method proved to be inadequate and was riffed with difficulties. Firstly, before pursuing diplomatic protection may be given, the investor was obliged to exhaust all local remedies in the host state. Secondly, there was no certainty that diplomatic protection would be granted. Besides, in this method the investor does not have a direct control over its claim. Lastly, pursuing the diplomatic protection route could lead to political tensions between the states. Therefore, overall this method was not an attractive choice.

Therefore, the problem to find an appropriate system to promote the private international investment is still persisted.

Finally, after the drafting phase of the Convention on the Settlement of Investment Disputes between States and Nationals of other States between 1961 and 1965 through the framework of the International Bank for Reconstruction and Development (IBRD), the text of the convention was adopted by IBRD's directors and entered into force on 14 October 1966.

The ICSID Convention is universally considered to be the "major arbitration treaty with worldwide effects."[3] The founders of ICSID believed that the "creation of an institution designed to facilitate the settlement of disputes between states and foreign investors can be a major step toward promoting an atmosphere of mutual confidence and thus stimulate a larger flow of private international capital into those countries which wish to attract it."[4]

In order to "depoliticize" the settlement of investment disputes, Article 27[5] of the ICSID Convention suspends the right of Contracting States to exercise

---

3 De Vries, H.P., "International Commercial Arbitration: A Contractual Substitute for National Courts", Tulane law Review, Vol. 57, (1982), pp. 42–56.

4 Report of the Executive Directors on the Convention on the Settlement of Investment Disputes between States and Nationals of Other States, Mar. 18, 1965, reprinted in ICSID, Convention on the Settlement of Investment Disputes Between States and Nationals of Other States, Documents Concerning the Origin and the Formulation of the Convention, vol. II, part 2, 1069, 1073 (1968).

5 Article 27 of ICSID Convention:

> No Contracting State shall give diplomatic protection, or bring an international claim, in respect of a dispute which one of its nationals and another Contracting State shall have consented to submit or shall have submitted to arbitration under this

diplomatic protection of nationals, who have consented to ICSID arbitration.[6] At the present time, ICSID is the most important institution to settle the international investment disputes and has registered nearly 400 cases.

Millions of arbitration cases until now have proved that this method is one of the most effective means of dispute settlement in the field of international investment arbitration.[7] There are numerous reasons why parties choose arbitration as their preferred means. Beside the confidentiality, fast proceeding, flexibility and adaptability, parties' ability to designate both the forum and the arbitrators and many others, one could not deny the amount of party autonomy this method provides.[8]

ICSID arbitration has been successful because of numerous advantages for both investors and host states. It offers standard clauses, provides an institutional support for the arbitration proceedings and assures the non-frustration of the process of arbitration. The investor could gain direct access to an effective international forum and it helps the host state by improving its investment situation.

This background will demonstrate the great role of dispute settlement mechanisms and the contributions of ICSID to this field. In the arbitration proceedings, the matter of "Applicable Law" has been always a critical issue which its wrong or correct determination could bring practical, legal and psychological effects on arbitration proceedings and their outcome. The autonomy of the parties is reflected in their effective role to determine the applicable law of their dispute, which has been already raised or may be raised in future.

Therefore, this chapter concentrates on the precedent of ICSID and its rules and regulations to determine the applicable law.

Convention, unless such other Contracting State shall have failed to abide by and comply with the award rendered in such dispute.

Diplomatic protection, for the purposes of paragraph (1), shall not include informal diplomatic exchanges for the sole purpose of facilitating a settlement of the dispute.

6 Rowat, Malcolm D., "Multilateral Approaches to Improving the Investment Climate of Developing Countries: The Cases of ICSID and MIGA", Harvard International Law Journal, Vol. 33, (1992), p. 107.

7 Engle, Rachel, "Party Autonomy in International Arbitration: Where Uniformity Gives Way to Predictability", The Transnational Lawyer, Vol. 15, (2002), p. 324.

8 Silberman, Linda; Ferrari, Franco, "Getting to the Law Applicable to the Merits in International Arbitration and the Consequences of Getting It Wrong", Conflict of Laws in International Arbitration, Vol. 7, (2010), pp. 73–121.

Before discussing the applicable law issues, it's important to look at the distinction between Jurisdiction and applicable law. These two issues are usually not separable but are not always coextensive.[9]

II) ICSID jurisdiction

Any party to an investment agreement can submit a dispute to ICSID arbitration by fulfillment of three conditions. Before all, one should always consider that the jurisdiction of the Center rests upon a strictly voluntary basis.[10] At the outset, we provide a general view on ICSID's jurisdictional system. The next part would be devoted to a deeper analysis of the surrounding issues.

Article 25 of the Convention deals with the issue of Jurisdiction. The first paragraph of this article states:

> "(1) The jurisdiction of the Centre shall extend to any legal dispute arising out of an investment, between a Contracting State (or any constituent subdivision or agency of a Contracting State designated to the Centre by that State) and a national of another Contracting State, which the parties to the dispute consent in writing to submit to the Centre. When the parties have given their consent, no party may withdraw its consent unilaterally."

This article outlines the main three conditions for a claim to fall within the ICSID's jurisdiction. The first condition outlined in Article 25 of the ICSID Convention requires the dispute to be arisen "between a Contracting State (or any constituent subdivision or agency of a Contracting State designated to the Center by that State) and a national of another Contracting State."[11] Second, the parties to the dispute must "consent in writing to submit the dispute to the Center."[12] The convention, however, does not mention the type of instrument, in which parties' consent may be expressed. Such consent may stem from a provision stipulated in an investment agreement or from any other contractual agreement between investors and Contracting States. Third, the dispute must "arise directly out of an investment."[13]

---

9 Schreuer, Christoph, "Jurisdiction and Applicable Law in International Treaty Arbitration", McGill Journal of Dispute Resolution, (2014), Vol. 1, Issue. 1, p. 2.

10 Delaume, Georges R., "Convention on the Settlement of Investment Disputes between States and Nationals of Other States", International Lawyer, Vol. 1, No. 1, (1966), p. 67.

11 Art. 25(1) of the ICSID Convention.

12 Art. 25(1) of the ICSID Convention.

13 Art. 25(1) of ICSID Convention.

There are two important issues in relation to the first requirement. One is the definition of "constituent subdivision or agency of the Contracting State". Firstly, based on the ICSID Convention, a subdivision or agency of state must have the State's approval before consenting to ICSID jurisdiction.[14] Further issue would be the answer to the question of how to determine that the investor is a national of another Contracting State. Based on many domestic law systems, an investment should be carried out through a locally incorporated entity. However, ICSID has still jurisdiction when the incorporated entity is foreign-controlled and the parties have agreed that the company "should be treated as a national of another Contracting State for the purpose of the Convention."[15] It is though obvious that intergovernmental disputes and disputes wholly between private parties are not included in the jurisdiction of the Center.

The system of double consent has been established by ICSID to ensure the validity of parties' consent to ICSID jurisdiction. First, a host state should become a Contracting State and assent to the ICSID Convention by ratifying the treaty. The voluntary nature of the Convention was of a great importance to the drafters, which is clearly envisaged in the Preamble stating that the mere fact of ratification, acceptance or approval of the Convention does not establish an obligation of a government to submit any particular case to the Center. Obligation does not occur until the state has specifically agreed to submit to the ICSID arbitration a particular dispute or class of disputes. Another way to consent to ICSID jurisdiction is that the state adopts its investment law effectively in line with ICSID provisions or enters to a BIT which submits the disputes to ICSID. Inclusion of an ICSID arbitration clause into the agreements also assures the state's consent. These could affect, however, when the tribunal is to decide such inclusion and whether the choice was expressed or implied.

For example, in *Antoine Goetz v. Burundi*, the Tribunal had to determine whether the applicable law clause in the BIT between Burundi and Belgium should be considered as an express choice of law under Article 42(1) of the ICSID Convention. Consequently, the Tribunal said: "Undoubtedly, the applicable law has not been determined here, strictly speaking, by the parties to this arbitration (Burundi and the investors), but rather by the parties to the Bilateral Treaty (Belgium and Burundi). As was the case with the consent of the parties [to the arbitration], the Tribunal deems nevertheless that Burundi accepted the applicable law as determined in the above provision of the Bilateral Treaty by

14 Art. 25(3) of ICSID Convention.
15 Art. 23(2)(b) of ICSID Convention.

becoming a party to this Treaty, and that claimants did the same by filing their request for arbitration based on the Treaty."[16] Therefore, in this case and many other cases, in spite of the fact that the parties to the dispute are a State and investors from another State, but not two States, the applicable law has been well chosen originally by the two States through the BIT negotiations. Later the parties to the dispute by reference to that BIT as a whole have also effectively chosen their choice of law. Therefore, in this case the parties have not opted for any applicable law in course of negotiations or also after the rise of dispute. However, they have referred to a BIT which includes a choice of law clause and in the above case the Tribunal employed a broader view and concluded that insofar that the parties have not otherwise selected any applicable laws, the selection of the certain BIT can be taken as the incorporation of that BIT including its terms on applicable law in the contract.

The abovementioned system also applies to the investor's side. The investor's home country should ratify the Convention as well and express its acceptance by including an ICSID arbitration clause or by giving permission for ICSID arbitration at the time a dispute arises.[17] This method ensures that all three parties, namely, investor, host state and investor's state, have all consented to ICSID arbitration.

There would be a possibility that one party has not yet ratified the Convention. At this situation an ICSID arbitration clause has its effect only at the time when both Contracting States have ratified the Convention.

Given the last condition, three individual issues are to be checked by the Tribunal. ICSID Convention requires that a "legal" dispute must arise "directly" out of an "investment". Consequently, there should be a direct link between the dispute and an investment. The other requirement is the legal nature of the dispute, which is to exclude political and other conflicts from the jurisdiction of ICSID. However, this condition has led to numerous awards and comments signaling different approaches. To this end, the definition of investment itself and interpretation of the phrase "directly out of an investment" has become a challenge and at the same time provided the parties plenty of room for maneuver. As we mentioned before, one of the aims of the Center is providing a depoliticized

16 Antoine Goetz, et al. v. The Republic of Burundi, Award, ICSID Case No. ARB/95/3, (10 February 1999), in Albert Jan van den Berg (ed.), Yearbook Commercial Arbitration, Vol. 26, (2001), para. 39.

17 Jacob, Kenneth S., "Reinvigorating ICSID with a New Mission and with Renewed Respect for Party Autonomy", Virginia Journal of International Law, Vol. 33, (1992), p. 129.

forum to settle the pure legal investment disputes. Furthermore, the notion of investment is not defined by the Convention, which is intentional. Many scholars believe that it's more appropriate to leave the parties free to define it based on their relations, since narrowing and widening the scope of this notion could have its own risks. For example, it could lead to impossibility of submitting a case to the ICSID arbitration. Therefore, it appeared more appropriate to remove any definition of "investment" from the text of the Convention through its finalization.[18]

Given these requirements, there are numerous awards that have discussed said issues in order to clarify tribunal's jurisdictional scope, some of which will be explained later in this section. First of all, the tribunals have to determine the existence of a legal dispute under Article 25 of the Convention. As the Convention does not define "legal dispute" the tribunals have generally interpreted it as to referring either to disputes concerning the existence or scope of a legal right or obligation or to disputes regarding the means of needed reparation for breach of a legal obligation.[19] In other words, ICSID tribunals examine at their own discretion what may constitute a legal dispute according to the said article.[20] For example, the Tribunal in *El Paso Energy v. Argentina* refers to the definition of the Permanent Court of International Justice, which has been later confirmed by the ICJ:

> "For this Tribunal, the notion of dispute generally has been accurately defined by the Permanent Court of International Justice (PCIJ) in the *Mavrommatis* case (Greece v. Great Britain), Judgment of 30 August 1924, PCIJ, Series A, No. 2, where the court said (p. 11) that '[a] dispute is a disagreement on a point of law or fact, a conflict of legal views or interests between two persons'. The above definition was recently confirmed by the ICJ in the *East Timor* case... It covers all 'disputes', legal or political, national or international. 'Legal' disputes have generally been defined as 'controversies in which

18 Delaume, Georges R., "Convention on the Settlement of Investment Disputes Between States and Nationals of Other States", International Lawyer, Vol. 1, No. 1, (1966), p. 70.

19 Reed, Lucy; Paulsson, Jan; Blackaby, Nigel, "Guide to ICSID Arbitration", Kluwer Law International, (2004), p. 15; Abaclat and Others (Case formerly known as Giovanna A Beccara and Others) v. The Argentine Republic, Decision on Jurisdiction and Admissibility, ICSID Case No.ARB/07/5, (4 August 2011), para. 255; AES Corporation v. The Argentine Republic, Decision on Jurisdiction, ICSID Case No. ARB/02/17, (26 April 2005), paras. 43–44; Alpha Projektholding GMBH v. Ukraine, Award, ICSID Case No. ARB/07/16, (8 November 2010), paras. 246–249; Jan de Nul N.V., Dredging International N.V. v. Arab Republic of Egypt, Decision on Jurisdiction, ICSID Case No. ARB/04/13, (16 June 2006), para. 74.

20 Daimler Financial Services AG v. Argentine Republic, Award, ICSID Case No. ARB/05/1, (22 August 2012), paras. 62–82.

> the Parties are in disagreement over a right'... Regarding the International level, one may recall, for example, Article 1 of the 1925 Locarno Arbitration Conventions between Germany, on the one hand, and Belgium, France, Poland and Czechoslovakia, on the other hand ('disputes with regard to which the parties are in conflict as to their respective rights'). What matters here is whether the pretensions of the Claimant (and the arguments of the Respondent) are formulated as being based on terms of existing law. The answer is of the ICJ (see above, § 60), 'a matter for objective determination.' "[21]

Next issue with regard to our above discussion would be the definition of "Investment". As we mentioned, the Convention does not provide any definition with respect to the notion of investment. Tribunals mainly tend to deliver a broad meaning. The Tribunal, for example, in *Tokios Tokelės v. Ukraine* mentions the "broad discretion".[22] Then the Tribunal refers to CMS and Fedax cases and concludes since the Convention does not define "investment", it intended to provide parties with a large measure of discretion to determine for themselves whether their transaction constitutes an investment for the purpose of the Convention.[23] Given these explanations, absence of a definition of investment in the ICSID Convention is a fact recognized by many awards and decisions,[24]

---

21 El Paso Energy International Company v. The Argentine Republic, Decision in Jurisdiction, ICSID Case No. ARB/03/15, (27 April 2006), para. 61.

22 Tokios Tokelės v. Ukraine, Decision on Jurisdiction, ICSID Case No. ARB/02/18, (29 April 2004), para. 19.

23 Tokios Tokelės v. Ukraine, Decision on Jurisdiction, ICSID Case No. ARB/02/18, (29 April 2004), para. 73; Fedax N.V. v. The Republic of Venezuela, Decision of the Tribunal on Objections to Jurisdiction, ICSID Case No. ARB/96/3, (11 July 1997), paras. 21–22; CMS Gas Transmission Company v. The Republic of Argentina, Decision of the Tribunal on Objections to Jurisdiction, ICSID Case No. ARB/01/8, (17 July 2003), para. 51.

24 Ambiente Ufficio S.P.A. and Others (Case formerly known as Giordano Alpi and Others) v. The Argentine Republic, Decision on Jurisdiction and Admissibility, ICSID Case No. ARB/08/9, (8 February 2013); Philip Morris Brands SÀRL, Philip Morris Products S.A. and Abal Hermanos S.A. v. Oriental Republic of Uruguay, Decision on Jurisdiction, ICSID Case No. ARB/10/7, (2 July 2013), para. 197; Fedax N.V. v. The Republic of Venezuela, Decision of the Tribunal on Objections to Jurisdiction, ICSID Case No. ARB/96/3, (11 July 1997), paras. 21–22; Ceskoslovenska Obchodni Banka, A.S. (CSOB) v. The Slovak Republic, Decision of the Tribunal on Objections to Jurisdiction, ICSID Case No. ARB/97/4, (24 May 1999), para. 63; Salini Costruttori S.P.A and Italstrade S.P.A v. Kingdom of Morocco, Decision on Jurisdiction, ICSID Case No. ARB/00/4, (23 July 2003), para. 51; Mihaly International Corporation v. Democratic Socialist Republic of Sri Lanka, Individual Concurring Opinion by Mr. David Suratgar, ICSID Case No. ARB/00/2, (7 March 2002), para.2; Parkerings-Campagniet A.S. v. Republic

which leads to employing a broad meaning of investment in determining the jurisdiction of the Center.

Once the three conditions are fulfilled, each party to the investment could send a request for arbitration to the Secretary-General of ICSID and if it is proper, it is registered and the arbitration process begins.

III) Jurisdiction and applicable law

The scope of the tribunal's jurisdiction could influence the applicable law and vice versa.

In investment treaty arbitration, the offer of consent to an investment treaty, which is made by States, is the base of jurisdiction and the commencement of arbitration proceedings by investor reflects the acceptance of the offer; therefore, the investor may rely on the substantive standards guaranteed by the treaty. Thus, the presumption would be fair that jurisdiction and applicable law are always linked and even one step further, one could assume that since the tribunal's jurisdiction derives from a particular treaty; therefore, the applicable law is necessarily made up of that treaty's substantive standards of protection.[25]

1) Scope of jurisdiction

The scope of tribunal's jurisdiction depends on treaties. One treaty may grant a wide jurisdiction to a tribunal, while the other grants rather a limited one and it is not governed by the law applicable to the merits of the case. In fact, the tribunal's jurisdiction is governed by its own system, which is defined by the instruments containing the parties' consent to jurisdiction.

In many cases, tribunals have held that the question of jurisdiction is not to be answered by the law applicable to the merits of the case. The arbitral practice and

---

of Lithuania, Award, ICSID Case No. ARB/05/8, (11 September 2007), para. 249; Millicom International Operations B.V. and Sentel GSM SA v. The Republic of Senegal, Decision on the Jurisdiction of the Arbitral Tribunal, ICSID Case No. ARB/08/20, (16 July 2010), para. 80; Deutsche Bank AG v. Democratic Socialist Republic of Sri Lanka, Award, ICSID Case No. ARB/09/02, (31 October 2012), para. 294; Abaclat and Others v. Argentina, Dissenting Opinion of Georges Abi-Saab, ICSID Case No. ARB/07/5, (28 October 2011), para. 38.

25 Schreuer, Christoph, "Jurisdiction and Applicable Law in International Treaty Arbitration", McGill Journal of Dispute Resolution, Vol. 1, Issue. 1, (2014), p. 2.

the insights of ICSID tribunals with respect to this issue could be well observed in *Siemens A.G. v. The Argentina Republic* case.[26]

In this case, under applicable law section, the Argentina Republic refers to the Treaty clause on applicable law, which states that the dispute shall be decided "on the basis of the present treaty, and if applicable on the basis of other treaties in force between the parties, the local law of the Contracting Party in which territory the investment was made, including its rules on conflict of laws and on the general principles of international law."[27]

Based on the Respondent's view, the dispute is governed largely by Argentine law, which is applicable to contractual issues as well as to those concerning the status of the investor in an Argentine corporation underlying Siemens' claim.[28]

On the contrary, the Claimant argues, "It is a well-established principle that jurisdictional questions should be decided on the basis of the Treaty and international law only. Decisions on jurisdiction are governed solely by Article 25[29] of the

---

26 Siemens A.G. v. The Argentina Republic, ICSID Case No. ARB/02/8, Decision on Jurisdiction, (3 August 2004), paras. 29–31.

27 Siemens A.G. v. The Argentina Republic, ICSID Case No. ARB/02/8, Decision on Jurisdiction, (3 August 2004), para. 29.

28 Siemens A.G. v. The Argentina Republic, ICSID Case No. ARB/02/8, Decision on Jurisdiction, (3 August 2004), paras. 29.

29 Article 25 of ICSID Convention:
(1) The jurisdiction of the Centre shall extend to any legal dispute arising directly out of an investment, between a Contracting State (or any constituent subdivision or agency of a Contracting State designated to the Centre by that State) and a national of another Contracting State, which the parties to the dispute consent in writing to submit to the Centre. When the parties have given their consent, no party may withdraw its consent unilaterally.
(2) "National of another Contracting State" means:
(a) any natural person who had the nationality of a Contracting State other than the State party to the dispute in the date on which the parties consented to submit such dispute to conciliation or arbitration as well as on the date on which the request was registered pursuant to paragraph (3) of Article 28 or paragraph (3) of Article 36, but does not include any person who on either date also had the nationality of the Contracting State party to the dispute; and
(b) any judicial person which had the nationality of a Contracting State other than the State party to the dispute on the date on which the parties consented to submit such dispute to conciliation or arbitration and any judicial person which had the nationality of the Contracting State party to the dispute on that date and which, because of foreign control, the parties have agreed should be treated as a national of another Contracting State for the purposes of this Convention.

ICSID Convention and the pertinent provisions of the Treaty, as lex specialis."[30] None of these provisions is affected by any provision of Argentine law to the contrary. Furthermore, the Treaty is also an international law instrument and international law applies alongside the Treaty. The Claimant also pointed out that the law applicable to the dispute shall not be considered at this stage as a jurisdictional matter but through the merits phase of the proceedings.[31]

Moreover, the distinction between the rules governing jurisdiction and the rules, which govern applicable law, shall be noted. As in *CMS v. Argentina*[32] the Tribunal stated:

> "Article 42 [of the ICSID Convention] is mainly designed for the resolution of disputes on the merits and, as such, it is in principle independent from the decision on jurisdiction, governed solely by Article 25 of the [ICSID] Convention and those other provisions of the consent instrument which might be applicable, in the instant case the Treaty provisions."[33]

In order to answer the abovementioned question whether jurisdiction determines the applicable law, we should take the scope of jurisdiction into account, which is determined by treaty clauses providing for consent to arbitration. From one treaty to another, the scope of jurisdiction varies. Some treaties provide for a wide jurisdiction while under some other treaties the scope of jurisdiction is defined narrower and limited to disputes arising out of the interpretation and application of the treaty's substantive standards. For example, Article 17(1) of the Japan-Cambodia BIT provides for jurisdiction over a dispute concerning "an

---

(3) Consent by a constituent subdivision or agency of a Contracting State shall require the approval of that State unless that State notifies the Centre that no such approval is required.

(4) Any Contracting State may, at the time of ratification, acceptance or approval of this Convention or at any time thereafter, notify the Centre of the class or classes of disputes which it would or would not consider submitting to the jurisdiction of the Centre. The Secretary General shall forthwith transmit such notification to all Contracting States. Such notification shall not constitute the consent required by paragraph (1).

30 Siemens A.G. v. The Argentina Republic, ICSID Case No. ARB/02/8, Decision on Jurisdiction, (3 August 2004), para. 30.

31 Siemens A.G. v. The Argentina Republic, ICSID Case No. ARB/02/8, Decision on Jurisdiction, (3 August 2004), paras. 30.

32 CMS Gas Transmission Company v. The Argentine Republic, ICSID Case No. ARB/01/8, Decision on Jurisdiction, (17 July 2003).

33 CMS Gas Transmission Company v. The Argentine Republic, ICSID Case No. ARB/01/8, Decision on Jurisdiction, (17 July 2003), para. 88.

alleged breach of any right conferred by this Agreement."[34] This approach could also be seen in multilateral treaties like NAFTA under which the scope of the consent to arbitration is limited to claims arising from alleged breaches of the NAFTA itself.[35]

On the contrary, there are also treaties granting broader jurisdictional scope to the tribunal by stipulating phrases such as "disputes concerning an investment"[36] or "all dispute concerning investments". For instance, Germany's Model BIT refers to "disputes concerning investments". [37] By providing such a broad scope of jurisdiction, the tribunal goes beyond the interpretation and application of the BIT itself and disputes that arise from a contract and other rules of law in connection with the investment could also be submitted to the tribunal.[38]

Between these wide and narrow approaches, some BITs offer consent to arbitration for "disputes with respect to investments". In this phrase, there are two points of views. Based on the first view as it could be seen in *SGS v. Pakistan*, the tribunal held that the consent phrase in the BIT between Switzerland and Pakistan is only descriptive of the factual subject matter of the dispute and does not relate to the legal basis of the claims or cause of action asserted in the claims. Thus, the tribunal does not have jurisdiction with respect to contract claims, which did not constitute breaches of the BIT's substantive standards. The tribunal held:

---

34 Agreement between Japan and the Kingdom of Cambodia for the Liberalization, Promotion and Protection of Investment, (14 June 2007), Art. 17(1).

35 Article 1116 NAFTA:
"An investor of a Party may submit to arbitration under this Section a claim that another Party has breached an obligation under:
Section A or Article 1503(2) (State Enterprises), or
Article 1502(3) (Monopolies and State Enterprises) where the monopoly has acted in a manner inconsistent with the Party's obligations under Section A,
and that the investor has incurred loss or damage by reason of, or arising out of, that breach.
2) An investor may not make a claim if more than three years have elapsed from the date on which the investor first acquired, or should have first acquired, knowledge of the alleged breach and knowledge that the investor has incurred loss or damage."

36 Agreement on encouragement and reciprocal protection of investments between the Government of the People's Republic of China and the Government of the Kingdom of the Netherlands, (2001), Article 10(1).

37 German Model Treaty, (2008), Article 10(1).

38 Schreuer, Christoph, "Jurisdiction and Applicable Law in International Treaty Arbitration", McGill Journal of Dispute Resolution, Vol. Issue. 1, (2014), p. 8.

> "... We do not see anything in Article 9 or in any other provision of the BIT that can be read as vesting this Tribunal with jurisdiction over claims resting *ex hypothesi* exclusively on contract."[39]

Some other tribunals held that this clause is general and encompasses the submission of all investment disputes and even contractual disputes.

In *SGS v. Republic of the Philippines*, the arbitral tribunal held:

> "[t]he term 'dispute with respect to investments' is not limited by reference to the legal classification of the claim that is made. A dispute about an alleged expropriation contrary to Article VI of the BIT would be a 'dispute with respect to investments' "[40]

Similarly in *Perkings-Compagniet AS v. Republic of Lithuania*, the tribunal held as follows:

> "The phrase 'any dispute [...] in connection with investment' as provided by Article IX (1) of the BIT is a general provision that provides the basis for an international Arbitral Tribunal's competence over any disputes related to an investment."[41]

Given the above examples and the notes made on the notion of "investment" and its definition under the convention, it has been observed that the views are not entirely consistent. However, the general view is that Article 25 of the Convention provides some objective meanings for this term and includes certain outer limits to the jurisdiction of the Center which are not at the disposition of the parties. Even though it reflects the main view, not all the commentators accept that. Alongside the objectivist movement, the subjectivist movement concentrates more on the will of the parties rather than certain outer limits provided by the Convention. However, what both groups are trying to determine is the extent to which, the term "investment" is supposed to be given objective significance.[42]

---

39 SGS Société Générale de Surveillance S.A. v. Islamic Republic of Pakistan, Decision of the Tribunal on Objections to Jurisdiction, ICSID Case No. ARB/01/13, (6 August 2013), para. 161.

40 SGS Société Générale de Surveillance S.A. v. Republic of the Philippines, Decision of the Tribunal on Objection to Jurisdiction, ICSID Case No. ARB/02/6, (29 January 2004), para. 131.

41 Perkings-Compagniet AS v. Republic of Lithuania, Award, ICSID Case No. ARB/05/8, (11 September 2007), para. 261.

42 Timmer, Laurens J. E., "The Meaning of 'Investment' as a Requirement for Jurisdiction Ratione Materiae of the ICSID Centre", Journal of International Arbitration, Kluwer Law International, Vol. 29, Issue. 4, (2012), p. 364.

2) Applicable law rules in treaties

After reviewing various forms of provisions with respect to jurisdiction under treaties, at this section the provisions on applicable law will go under examination and the potential relation between these subjects will be demonstrated. Since the main topic in this chapter has its focus on ICSID, this section above all begins with exploring ICSID provisions on applicable law.

Under Article 42(1) of ICSID Convention, the primary choice of law is granted to the parties. Subsequently, the Convention refers to host state law and applicable rules of international law. This Article covers most of the elements, which are mainly used in other treaties.

Some BITs have their own rules on applicable law. Such rule incorporated in a treaty that offers consent to arbitration becomes part of the arbitration agreement and the investor's acceptance includes the acceptance of the clause on applicable law. Many tribunals have considered these types of clauses as the basis for an agreement of applicable law between the host state and the investor.[43] Some of those treaties have a more elaborate clause on applicable law and the others contain a simpler formula and refer only to the treaty itself and relevant international law rules. Therefore, the only typical difference between such clauses is the absence of the law of host state, which is not covered by some treaties.

As an example for the simple formula, the Canada Model FIPA states:

> "A Tribunal established under this section shall decide the issues in dispute in accordance with this agreement and applicable rules of international law."[44]

This rule does not contain the law of the host state and refers only to the agreement and applicable rules of international law.

More elaborate clauses such as the BIT between Argentina and Italy in Article 8(7) provide:

> "The arbitration tribunal will decide on the basis of the laws of the Contracting Party involved in the dispute-including its rules on the conflict of laws-and of the provisions of the Agreement, of clauses of any particular agreements relating to the investment, as well as on the basis of the applicable principles of international law."[45]

---

43 Schreuer, Christoph, "Jurisdiction and Applicable Law in International Treaty Arbitration", McGill Journal of Dispute Resolution, Vol. Issue. 1, (2014), p. 12.

44 Canadian Model Foreign Investment Protection Agreement (FIPA), (2004), Article 40(1).

45 Agreement between Italy and Argentine Republic for the Promotion and Protection of Investment, (1990), Article 8(7).

This clause contains the law of the host state, even its rules on the conflict of laws, the agreement itself and the relevant rules of international law.

3) The correlation between the scope of jurisdiction and applicable law

So far two types of clauses with respect to applicable law and jurisdiction demonstrating the narrower view on the one hand and the boarder one on the other have been observed. At first glance, one could presume that due to the interlocking nature of these forms, a correlation is beyond doubt. In other words, one could take this as a logical theory that the simpler formula of applicable law in treaties also offer a narrower scope of jurisdiction, for instance, jurisdiction only for claims based on the treaty itself, while more detailed applicable law clauses would go hand in hand with the jurisdictional clauses which grant jurisdiction for all investment disputes. In a treaty which offers jurisdiction for all investment disputes, one would expect rather more comprehensive choice of law provision.[46]

This correspondence, however, does not exist in all treaties. There are examples of treaties which offer a wide jurisdiction and at the same time provide for a very simple choice of law clause that refers only to the treaty itself and international law.

For instance, in the BIT between Italy and Argentina, although the jurisdictional clause is limited to claims based on violation of its substantive standards, as we have seen before, Article 8(7) of the BIT offers a comprehensive choice of law formula, which also contains the law of the host state.

This is not a consistent approach adopted by all treaties. Numerous model and actual treaties, which grant a wide jurisdiction does not even offer any guidance on applicable law.[47] In this case, under ICSID arbitration, it comes to applying the residual rule of Article 42(1) of the ICSID Convention, which leads the tribunal to deciding based on the law of the host state.

---

46 Schreuer, Christoph, "Jurisdiction and Applicable Law in International Treaty Arbitration", McGill Journal of Dispute Resolution, Vol. 1, Issue.1, (2014), p. 13.

47 See Article 10 of Germany's Model BIT; Article 8 of French Model BIT; Article 8 of Russia's Model BIT; Article 8 of United Kingdom Model BIT; Article VIII of the Switzerland-Philippines BIT; Article 9 of the Switzerland-Pakistan BIT; Article 7 of the Czech Republic-Israel BIT.

Moreover, sometimes in situations involving inter-temporal questions, the applicable law would be completely outside the treaty establishing jurisdiction.[48] It is possible that in some cases a treaty provides for jurisdiction over disputes that have been arisen from events occurred before the treaty's entry into force. At this time, the law in force at the time of the relevant events should be applied to the merits of the case not the treaty establishing jurisdiction.[49] It's called the principle of contemporaneity, which is well known in arbitral practice.[50]

When jurisdiction of a tribunal extends to events that had occurred before the entry into force of the treaty, the applicable law could not be found in that treaty. In this case, tribunals have done separate examinations of their jurisdiction *ratione temporis* and the law applicable to the relevant facts.

In *Impregilo v. Pakistan* case, Pakistan refers to the basic rule of non-retroactivity of treaties incorporated into Article 28 of the 1969 Vienna Convention, which states:

> "Unless a different intention appears from the treaty or is otherwise established, its provisions do not bind a party in relation to any act or fact which took place or any situation which ceased to exist before the date of the entry into force of the treaty with respect to that party."[51]

After mentioning this Article, Pakistan contends that the BIT[52]:

> "... Can have no application in respect of conduct relied upon by Impregilo taking place before 22 June 2001, and similarly that the Tribunal can have no jurisdiction in respect of alleged breaches concerning acts and omissions occurring prior to that date." Pakistan added "Impregilo has sought to avoid the basic rule on non-retroactivity of

48 Schreuer, Christoph, "Jurisdiction and Applicable Law in International Treaty Arbitration", McGill Journal of Dispute Resolution, Vol. Issue. 1, (2014), p. 20.

49 Schreuer, Christoph, "Jurisdiction and Applicable Law in International Treaty Arbitration", McGill Journal of Dispute Resolution, Vol. Issue. 1, (2014), p. 20.

50 The Principle of Contemporaneity means that the legality of the state's conduct must be assessed in light of the law that was in force at the time of its conduct. Judge Huber in the Island of Palmas case was expressed this principle as follows:

"A juridical fact must be appreciated in the light of the law contemporary with it, and not of the law in force at the time when a dispute in regard to it arises or falls to be settled".

51 Impregilo S.p.A v. Islamic Republic of Pakistan, Decision on Jurisdiction, ICSID Case No. ARB 03/3, (22 April 2005), paras 292–314.

52 Agreement between the Government of the Islamic Republic of Pakistan and the Government of the Italian Republic on the Promotion and Protection of Investments, (1997), entry into force 22.06.2001.

> treaties by (I) failing to plead the specific dates of alleged breaches and (II) asserting that the breaches it alleges are continuing in character."

Impreglio contends on the other hand that all of its claims directly arise out of the same subject matter, therefore, constitute a single continuing dispute. It stressed that the dispute "deals with a systematic and continuous pattern of conduct that has resulted subsequent to the BIT's entry into force, in the current and continuing breach of the BIT." Thus, the Tribunal has jurisdiction over such dispute and the application of the BIT is not at odds with the principle of non-retroactivity of treaties.

Article 9(1) of the BIT, which entered into force on 22 June 2001, applies to "… any dispute arising between a contracting party and the investors of the other."

The language of the Article and the absence of specific provision for retroactivity infer that disputes that may have arisen before the entry into force of the BIT are not covered by its provisions.

In the Tribunal's view, care must be taken to distinguish between (1) the jurisdiction *ratione temporis* of an ICSID tribunal and (2) the applicability *ratione temporis* of the substantive obligations contained in a BIT. To that end, one should take into account that Article 1(1) of the BIT does not give the substantive provisions of the Treaty any retrospective effect. Therefore, the normal principle stated in Article 28 of the Vienna Convention on the Law of Treaties applies, and the provisions of the BIT:

> "… Do not bind the Party in relation to any act of facts which took place or any situation which ceased to exist before the date of entry into force of the Treaty."

Impregilo also complains a number of acts for which Pakistan is said to be responsible. The legality of such acts must be determined, in each case, according to the law applicable at the time of their performance. As the BIT entered into force on 22 June 2001, it covers merely acts that took place until this specific date.

This analysis therefore compels the conclusion that the provisions of the BIT do not bind Pakistan in relation to any act that took place, or any situation that ceased to exist, before 22 June 2001 and the jurisdiction of the Tribunal *ratione temporis* is limited accordingly.

After this discussion regarding the relationship between jurisdiction and applicable law, firstly we should emphasize that matters concerning jurisdiction are predominantly determined by reference to the legal instruments establishing jurisdiction and general international law and not by the law applicable to the merits of a case, but some issues related to jurisdiction, such as the nationality of the investor, the existence of property rights and the notion of investment itself, are governed by domestic law.

As mentioned above, there are various types of provisions on both jurisdiction and choice of law issues which are sometimes but not always in the same direction and seem to correspond. Such correspondence could lead one to believe that there is always a direct relation between jurisdiction and applicable law but we saw numerous examples, which prove the contrary.

This analysis facilitate the understanding of the applicable law in general and clarify the distinction between applicable law and jurisdiction to lay the ground work for us to begin with our focus on the applicable law issues under ICSID Convention in the following section.

IV) General rules of applicable law in ICSID Convention

In the context of applicable law, there are four layers of law applicable in a dispute subject to arbitration: the law governing the substantive contract or dispute, the law governing the agreement to arbitrate and the performance of arbitration, the law governing the conduct of the arbitration and the conflict of laws rules applicable to the each of the above layers.[53] The most important layer is the substantive law applicable to the merits of the dispute, which has been also defined as the "proper law of the contract". In order to render an award, the arbitrators should rely on some substantive rules of law, which are applicable in a particular case before the tribunal. In this study, we focus on this layer of the applicable law.

ICSID Convention, like most other conventions, does not provide those substantive rules directly, but it builds a framework with which the tribunal will be able to determine the applicable substantive law.

ICSID provides this framework in Article 42:

> *"The Tribunal shall decide a dispute in accordance with such rules of law as may be agreed by the parties. In the absence of such agreement, the Tribunal shall apply the law of Contracting State party to the dispute (including its rules on the conflict of laws) and such rules of international law as may be applicable.*
> *The Tribunal may not bring in a finding of non liquet on the ground of silence or obscurity of the law.*
> *The provisions of paragraphs (1) and (2) shall not prejudice the power of the Tribunal to decide a dispute ex aequo et bono if the parties so agree."*

This article is the core element of this chapter. The first part of this Article explains two situations.

---

53 Engle, Rachel, "Party Autonomy in International Arbitration: Where Uniformity Gives Way to Predictability", The Transnational Lawyer, Vol. 15, (2002), p. 329.

First sentence of article 42(1) describes the situation where the parties designate a choice of law in their agreement. There are few possibilities for them to express their choice; therefore, we study the choice of law varieties after we explain the principle of party autonomy, which is the foundation of this article and almost all laws and regulations regarding the matter of applicable law. It is also the great incentive for the parties to choose arbitration among the other means of dispute resolution. Parties often include a choice of law clause in their agreement to combat uncertainty in arbitration proceedings.

The second sentence of article 42(2) provides rules, when there is no choice of law agreed upon by the parties. As there is a great number of BITs, which do not provide for any choice of law, the second sentence of Article 42(1) gains considerable importance. By this rule, the arbitrators will be guided through the decision on the applicable law.

It should be mentioned that this article does not govern the applicable law to procedural matters and jurisdiction.

The nationality of the parties is not also governed by the convention and this is one of the situations where we resort to the domestic law. Such law also governs the parties' status and legal capacity; however, the matters in connection with jurisdiction are governed by Article 25.

In light of the abovementioned issue, *Amco v. Indonesia* case can well serve as an example.[54]

In this case, the Republic of Indonesia objected to the jurisdiction ratione personae of Amoco Asia because it was dissolved on 27 December 1984, one month after the original award was rendered.

It was agreed by both parties that the law, which governs the dissolution of Amco Asia was the law of the state of Delaware. However, Indonesia drew a distinction between the dissolution of Amco Asia and the legal effect of such dissolution on the holder of rights and duties under an agreement to arbitrate. Indonesia contended that in the facts and circumstances of the present case, Article 42(1) of the ICSID Convention provided the guide to determine the appropriate applicable law, based on which Indonesian law should be the only law to be applied. Indonesia stated, "Under Indonesian law, once a limited liability corporation is dissolved, it ceases to exist for any purpose."[55]

---

54 Amco v. Republic of Indonesia, Decision on Jurisdiction (Resubmitted case), ICSID Case No. ARB/81/8, (10 May 1988), paras. 99–109.

55 Amco v. Republic of Indonesia, Decision on Jurisdiction (Resubmitted case), ICSID Case No. ARB/81/8, (10 May 1988), para. 102.

The tribunal, however, does not believe that the distinction put forward by Indonesia can possibly lead to the conclusion that Indonesian law should apply. Nor does the tribunal find it necessary to pronounce upon the respective place of Indonesian law and international law in Article 42(1) of the ICSID Convention.

When a company enters into an agreement with a foreign legal person, the legal status and capacity of that company is determined by the law of the state of incorporation. Similarly, one should apply the law of the state of incorporation to answer the question whether such a company, though dissolved, is still an existing legal entity for any specified legal purpose.

The dissolution of Amco Asia was governed by the law of the state of Delaware. According to Delaware general corporation law, all corporations, whether they expire by their own limitation or dissolve by other means, shall be continued for the term of three years from such expiration or dissolution. The provisions further state that with respect to any action, suit or proceeding, such action shall not abate by reason of the dissolution and the corporation continues solely for the purpose of such action, suit or proceeding until any judgments, orders or decrees therein is fully executed.[56] Therefore, in light of said law, law Amco Asia remains a juridical entity for purposes of any action, suit or proceeding which is begun by Amco or brought against it, prior to or within the years of dissolution or until such action, suit or proceeding is completed, and any judgment, order or decree therein is executed.

The tribunal, therefore, finds that it continues to have jurisdiction *ratione personae* over the dissolved Amco Asia.[57]

The Tribunal shall first of all in accordance to the first sentence of Article 42(1) determine if the parties have chosen a particular rules or legal systems to govern their case, if not then the tribunal may take the second sentence of Article 42(1) into account. The process of determination will be analyzed in the following sections.

---

56 State of Delaware General Corporation Law, Subchapter X, Section 278.

57 Amco v. Republic of Indonesia, Decision on Jurisdiction (Resubmitted case), ICSID Case No. ARB/81/8, (10 May 1988), para. 108.

V) The autonomy of the parties

1) Background and definition

The principle of party autonomy has been characterized as "perhaps the most widely accepted private international rule of our time."[58] Almost all arbitration rules have accepted this principle and recognize it as binding to avoid the application of any unfavorable or inappropriate rules.[59] This principle has been widely recognized both in common law and civil law. Most of the civil law codes recognize as well the choice of law by the parties, and few countries, which have not explicitly provided for party autonomy in their codes, have introduced the doctrine of party autonomy through case law development.[60] To that end, party autonomy has been excluded in number of countries including in the Middle East. A partial rejection of this concept can be found, for instance, in Article 968 of the Iranian Civil Code, where the freedom of the parties to choose the applicable law has been limited to cases where the contracting parties are foreign nationals and have expressly or implicitly subjected the contract to another law. Consequently, this fact counts as another motivation for the parties to opt for arbitration at the first place mainly because of this freedom of choice of law.[61]

Originally, national law was the only basis of autonomy of the parties and its limitations, but it has evolved further since then. The principle of party autonomy is not a new concept. However, it is a matter of doubt when exactly the doctrine of party autonomy was born. Some writers deem that it originated from the writings of Dumoulin, a French scholar of the sixteenth century who is also known as "the father of party autonomy".[62] He believed that the will of the parties is sovereign and should be respected. The will of the parties is also the most important element in determining the governing law.[63] He also stated that

---

58 Weintraub, Russel J., "Functional Developments in Choice of Law for Contracts", Académie de droit international, recueil de cours, M. Nijhoff, (1984), p. 239.

59 Arbitration Rules of the United Nations Commission on International Trade Law (UNCITRAL), 1976; International Chamber of Commerce (ICC) Rules of Conciliation and Arbitration.

60 Croff, Carlo, "The Applicable Law in an International Commercial Arbitration: Is it Still a Conflict of Laws Problem?", The International Lawyer, Vol. 16, (1982), p. 615.

61 Engle, Rachel, "Party Autonomy in International Arbitration: Where Uniformity Gives Way to Predictability", The Transnational Lawyer, Vol. 15, (2002), p. 334.

62 Lorenzen, Ernest G., "Validity and Effects of Contracts in the conflict of Laws (Part 1), Yale Law Journal, Vol. 30, (1920–21), p. 573.

63 Lorenzen, Ernest G., "Validity and Effects of Contracts in the conflict of Laws (Part 1), Yale Law Journal, Vol. 30, (1920–21), p. 573.

in the silence of the parties' agreement we should try to extract the true intention of them because the will of the parties is not always expressed.[64]

Prior to that time, the approach of *Lex loci contractus* was prevailed over all other possible solutions, including *lex loci solutionis.*[65] This approach was based on the thoughts of Bartolus, who believed that the law of the place of contract governs all questions regarding the form and substance of the contract. Bartolus and his followers saw a contract like a person that is subjected to the law of the place of its origin. According to their opinion, *lex loci* governs the contract regardless the will of the parties.[66] This approach was different from Dumoulin, since the latter deemed the will of parties as sovereign and viewed the contract separate from its birthplace.

But as mentioned, Dumoulin pointed out arguments against the *Lex loci* approach that when the parties enter into a contract they might stipulate the law concerning their relations. At the time party autonomy had at least two functions. First, the intention of the parties could be either expressed or implied and second, that intention governed both validity and effects of the contracts. Moreover, the principle applied also to the whole contract.[67]

In the nineteenth century, classical liberalism was the dominant ideological force in the West. Based on this worldview, states should interfere as little as possible with the economy. The theory of "Freedom of Contracts" which formed the "party autonomy" principle, was based on this ideology. In better words, party autonomy reflects the fundamental inherent principle of freedom of contract.[68] It is an attempt to reduce the role of the government as possible in the marketplace and to emphasize individual choices as well as personal freedom.[69] That was the reason that, for example, in 1860 the United Kingdom courts stated that the law

64 Zhang, Mo, "Party Autonomy and Beyond: An International Perspective of Contractual Choice of Law", Emory International Law Review, Vol. 20, (2006), p. 517.

65 Lew, Julian D. M., "Applicable Law in International Commercial Arbitration – A Study in Commercial Arbitration Awards", Oceana Publications, INC., (1978), p. 73.

66 Lorenzen, Ernest G., "Validity and Effects of Contracts in the conflict of Laws (Part 1), Yale Law Journal, Vol. 30, (1920–21), p. 573.

67 Zhang, Mo, "Party Autonomy and Beyond: An International Perspective of Contractual Choice of Law", Emory International Law Review, Vol. 20, (2006), p. 518.

68 Juenger, Friedrich K., "Conflict of Laws, Comparative Law and Civil Law: The Lex Mercatoria and Private International Law", Louisiana Law Review, Vol. 60, (2000), p. 1141.

69 Chukwumerije, Okezie, "Choice of Law in International Commercial Arbitration", Quorum Books, (1994), p. 108.

applicable to the contracts is the law by which the parties intend their case to be governed.[70] This approach is also introduced by German and French legal systems.[71] Even though the scope of freedom in various systems may be different, the principle of party autonomy is the mutual point.

There is a difference in the scope of this principle at Dumoulin's time and in the nineteenth century. Earlier it was merely about the intention of parties on determining the law governing the validity of the contract but then it expands also to determination of the rights and obligations of the parties to the contract.[72]

Speaking of the scope of party autonomy, we should consider the evolution of this principle also in other aspects. The other evolution with respect to the scope of party autonomy is the doctrine of *dépaçage*.[73] Under this doctrine, it's allowed for the parties to choose more than one law governing each part of their contract. In other words, parties may split their contract to different parts and choose a particular applicable law for each part.

The parties could choose the substantive law of a certain country or they may choose its "whole law". Choosing the latter option would lead to the problem of "remission", which is commonly known as *renvoi*. The parties' choice of law will encompass the conflict of laws rules of that national law. This happens when the forum applies the conflict of laws, rules of the law chosen by the parties to select a different law from which the parties have designated. Presently, there are various approaches on the acceptance of *renvoi*.

The origin of party autonomy is twofold; one is national law and the other the parties' agreement. According to the traditional view and Bartolus views as explained above, the national law determines the conditions and the limitations of this principle and many states have recognized it. The other view is based on the contractual relationship. Based on this view, in line with Domulin's viewpoint stated before, a contract is seen as private law between the two parties so that their agreement functions like a binding law between them. The parties in a private contractual dispute should be free to choose every element of their agreement, including the applicable law, and this choice should be respected. The purported autonomy of parties primarily relates to various points such as

70 See P&O SN Co. v. Shand (1856) 3 Moo NS 272; Lloyd v. Guibert (1865) LR. 1 QB 115.

71 See Triebel, Volker, "The Choice of Law in Commercial Relations: A German Perspective", International and Comparative Law Quarterly, Vol. 37, (1988), p. 935; French (Napoleonic) Civil Code (1804), ss 1107–34.

72 Zhang, Mo, "Party Autonomy and Beyond: An International Perspective of Contractual Choice of Law", Emory International Law Review, Vol. 20, (2006), p. 519.

73 Derived from the French verb dépecer, which means to slice thinly.

appointment of arbitrators, the choice of the forum and the governing law, appointment of experts, the determination of the timetable, especially in *ad hoc* arbitrations, and the choice of the language of the proceedings.[74] They can also choose their witnesses and experts where necessary.

This principle has numerous advantages. It allows the parties to feel safe and choose their favorable applicable law and consequently avoid inappropriate interpretations. As a result, they would know their expectations from each other precisely, which leads to more predictability.[75] Certainty, predictability and uniformity are three crucial factors in the field of international arbitration. Party autonomy does guarantee these three factors for the parties. It keeps the contract from being regulated by an ambiguous or unfavorable law, while the consequences and potential matter with respect to the contract would become more predictable. Additionally, it ensures a uniform solution to certain disputes, notwithstanding the nature of the Tribunal and the seat of it.

Although, it is important to mention that this principle is effectively exercised by the lawyers acting on behalf of their parties and it nevertheless offers a degree of psychological satisfaction to them that they may have chosen the best arbitrators, forum and the governing law. The parties may feel that it is their arbitration and the proceedings would be the way they planned.[76] They can also abandon the proceedings according to this rule at any stage.

However, this principle as the basis of conflict of laws rules and is universally accepted by many regional and international conventions, has limitations similar to other principle.

The party autonomy doctrine is not free from criticisms and objections. Some scholars have discussed that if parties are permitted to avoid mandatory national laws or national courts may not review awards concerning public policy or national laws, "arbitration is given primacy over the law."[77]

The first and perhaps one of the most debated objections to the principle of party autonomy is with respect to the State sovereignty. Some believe that allowing the parties to choose the applicable law involves delegation of sovereign

---

74 Chetterjee, Charles, "The Reality of The Party Autonomy Rule In International Arbitration", Journal of International Arbitration, Vol. 20, (2003), p. 540.

75 Chukwumerije, Okezie, Choice of Law in International Commercial Arbitration, Quorum Books, (1994), p. 108.

76 Chetterjee, Charles, "The Reality of The Party Autonomy Rule In International Arbitration", Journal of International Arbitration, Vol. 20, (2003), p. 540.

77 Sever, Jay R., "The Relaxation of Inarbitrability and Public Policy Checks on U.S. and Foreign Arbitration: Arbitration Out of Control?" 65 TUL. L. REV. (1991), p. 1694.

powers to private individuals.[78] The arguments manifested that the freedom of choice of law and the selection of an applicable law irrespective of an objective connecting factor would count as an impairment of sovereignty.[79] However, the conception has evolved so that especially based on the theory that State sovereignty can also be attributed to the will of the individual, the exercise of such will no longer infringe the sovereignty of the State.[80] Given this arguments, this principle was not as strong as it is today at earlier times. It has evolved by the time and reached its strength in our era to that extent that in most cases no one would question its validity.

The second category of the objections which is still in some sense related to the former objection (sovereignty) would be the choice of law's ability to set aside the *ordre public*. Opposing such objections the fact shall be taken into account that the concept of *ordre public* has evolved greatly through time and can now be divided into domestic and international; each subject to certain rules. As an example, it is in the meantime accepted for territorial limitations to be imposed on international *ordre public* in many cross-border cases. With respect to domestic *ordre public*, it is also widely accepted that this set of rules, which is basically all the mandatory laws of a legal system is of a controlling virtue in all domestic cases and valid irrespective of the applicable law.[81] Another sensitive point throughout this stream of objections to party autonomy is with regard to domestic contacts. Firstly, it shall be taken into account the distinction between negative and positive international *ordre public*. Based on this subdivision, positive *ordre public* can be defined as "rules and principles which – *tels quels* – unconditionally demand implementation inclusive of those cases having foreign contacts."[82] On the other hand, negative international ordre public comprises

78 Lorenzen, Ernest G., "Validity and Effects of Contracts in the Conflict of Laws (Part 2)", Yale Law Journal, Vol. 30, (1921), p. 658.

79 Basedow, Jürgen, "The Law of Open Societies: Private Ordering and Public Regulation of International Relations: General Course on Private International Law", Leiden, Boston, Martinus Nijhoff Publishers, (2013), pp. 178–179.

80 Basedow, Jürgen, "The Law of Open Societies: Private Ordering and Public Regulation of International Relations: General Course on Private International Law", Leiden, Boston, Martinus Nijhoff Publishers, (2013), pp. 182–183.

81 Basedow, Jürgen, "The Law of Open Societies: Private Ordering and Public Regulation of International Relations: General Course on Private International Law", Leiden, Boston, Martinus Nijhoff Publishers, (2013), pp. 183–184.

82 Basedow, Jürgen, "The Law of Open Societies: Private Ordering and Public Regulation of International Relations: General Course on Private International Law", Leiden, Boston, Martinus Nijhoff Publishers, (2013), p. 184.

rules and principles which are not required to be implemented unconditionally. Deviating of such rules, however, shall remain in certain limited margin.[83] With respect to invocation of both positive and negative *ordre public*, sufficient domestic connection shall be manifested. The extent of such connection can strongly depend on relevant provisions and legal principles. Therefore, it can be concluded that with the evolution of the concept of *ordre public*, the arguments against party autonomy may not have as strong grounds as before, since as explained there are several instances and situations where *ordre public* cannot be infringed regardless of the parties' choice of law.

Among other objections to the principle of party autonomy is the understanding that contracts are of no binding effects outside the legal order. Based on this theory for any private accord to be given a legal effect, it is required to be within the framework of the applicable law. Even though such law does not have to be the forum State's law, it shall be resulted from the application of the objective factors laid down within the forum State's private international law. However, in response to this theory it shall be distinguished between differences existed through different legal systems on the one hand, and the shared principles of law, on the other hand. The latter too produces a binding effect. Therefore, where two parties agree to subject their contract to certain law, such agreement produce a legally binding effect, details of which however might ultimately fall within a particular legal order.[84]

Another objection pointed to the principle of party autonomy is aimed to protect the weaker parties. It may seem as a quite convincing argument especially in instances where the imbalance of the parties (the position of the stronger party) has not been subject to any regulatory rules such as rules set out by competitive market forces. But it shall be taken into account that this objection may go under question where competition functions in an effective manner. In addition, in reality, the interests of the weaker parties in choosing the applicable law in the contract is much less, if any, to those of the suppliers.[85]

Against this background it can be concluded that the objections course to the principle of party autonomy rest on rather shaky ground. This fact, however, can by no means leads to the unrestricted deployment of freedom of choice.

---

83 *Ibid*, p. 184.
84 *Ibid*, p. 188.
85 *Ibid*, pp. 190–191.

The widest scope of party autonomy allows the parties to choose a non-national standard[86] to rule their contract in addition or in lieu of a national law. These standards are such as international law, international customs or usages, transnational law, *Lex Mercatoria*, supranational law, international conventions and general principles of law. While using these non-national sources, parties may use the conflict of laws rules in addition to reaffirm the applicable law. Since generally the non-national rules are not mandatory body of rules therefore their specific application to a dispute is limited to situations where the parties already have an agreement calling for their application.

In the context of investment treaty, two types of party autonomy exist. On one hand, the State parties' autonomy is exercised once they formulate terms of the treaty, which includes the arbitration mechanism to which any Claimant should adhere for submitting a claim. On the other hand, the autonomy of the parties to a specific dispute as they agree upon how any future dispute will be settled under the said treaty. Choices related to applicable law generally result from the exercise of the States' autonomy rather than of the disputing parties' perception of the applicable law when the State parties have not designated the applicable law.[87]

Apart from the origin and objections to the freedom of choice principle are the theories in favor of this principle and the more recent understandings of the proper foundations of this concept.

Currently in hand with the modern conflicts theory which stems from the economic analysis of law, party autonomy is praised for the efficiency that it provides. This is reflected in many issues including less legal uncertainty, which could have been prevailed in absence of such theory, suitability of the chosen law to the type of contract and its convenience with respect to specific dispute settlement bodies. Consequently, invalidation of the agreed applicable law might in some instances negatively influence business in certain countries.[88]

The other theoretical basis for party autonomy falls within freedom and natural will, which in legal theory are in fact foundations to justify the binding

---

86 Croff, Carlo, "The Applicable Law in an International Commercial Arbitration: Is it Still a Conflict of Laws Problem?", The International Lawyer, Vol. 16, (1982) (defines a non-national standard as a "set of rules that do not have their origin in any national law").

87 Thomas, J. Christopher, "Applicable Law under International Investment Treaties", Singapore Academy of Law Journal, Vol. 26, (2014), p. 977.

88 Basedow, Jürgen, "The Law of Open Societies: Private Ordering and Public Regulation of International Relations: General Course on Private International Law", Leiden, Boston, Martinus Nijhoff Publishers, (2013), pp. 193–196.

effects of contracts. In addition, it shall be taken into account that choice of law agreements are of special nature, which is distinct from other type of contracts in which certain promises and mutual performances are at stake. Consequently, choice of law agreements can be viewed as self-fulfilling contracts and a result of parties' natural freedom.[89] Additionally, more recently, the principle of party autonomy is also attributed to natural law as well as human rights.[90]

In conclusion, depending what theoretical basis is chosen, one might face difficulties to justify certain aspects of interaction of choice of law and objective law. For instance, certain theories such as pre-governmental right of individuals to subject themselves to certain positive legal order would justify party autonomy in international scene and with respect to cross-border matters but not in solely domestic matters.[91]

Greater approval of party autonomy in recent times are undeniable in special sectors such as issues relating to *in rem* rights and there is definitely a growing tolerance with respect to private arrangements in applicable law. This is also partially indebted to activities of several international organization and especially the European Union.[92]

2) Party autonomy and the first sentence of Article 42(1) of the ICSID Convention

A glance at the first sentence of article 42(1) of ICSID Convention reflects that party autonomy is also the primary rule to determining the law applicable to the dispute.

In accordance with Article 42(1) first sentence, an ICSID tribunal

> "…Shall decide a dispute in accordance with such rules of law as may be agreed by the parties."

According to this article, the parties could agree to any substantive rules that they prefer at any time. There is no time limitation for their agreement. When the parties have chosen the applicable law, the arbitrators should apply such law and nothing but such law. Only in absence of such agreement, arbitrators may have a degree of discretion in determining the applicable law.

---

89 *Ibid*, p. 200.
90 *Ibid*, p. 203.
91 *Ibid*, p. 205.
92 *Ibid*, pp. 211–212.

Article 42(1) refers to "rules of law" rather than systems of law. Therefore, the parties are not obligated to accept a complete legal system of law but are free to combine rules of diverse origins; therefore, the choice of law clauses may refer to various legal systems simultaneously.[93] The parties are also free to set aside certain parts of a chosen legal system from its application.

This choice could reflect in a direct agreement, in the contract, or the parties could agree on the option even after the case has been registered to the arbitration proceeding or in the course of the arbitration proceeding. If no choice of law has been made by direct agreement, legislation or treaty by the time the arbitration is instituted, nothing precludes a subsequent agreement by the parties on applicable law. *Benvenuti & Bonfant v. Congo* is one of the most cited cases in the field of ICSID arbitration that we discuss in this part merely to refer a matter, in which the agreement upon applicable law was discussed during the arbitral proceedings.[94]

On 15 December 1977 the Italian firm of Ltd. Benvenuti & Bonfant (B and B) addressed to the Secretary-General of the ICSID, a request for arbitration dated 12 December 1977 accompanied by a protocol of agreement dated 16 April 1973 between B and B and the Government of the People's Republic of Congo containing an arbitration clause referring to the ICSID Convention. B and B in the course of arbitration proceeding decided to submit to the Government a proposal to confer on the Tribunal of the power to decide the dispute ex aequo et bono, in accordance with Article 42(3) of the Convention.

Despite the wide acceptance of the principle of party autonomy there has been always a parallel application of international law in the precedent of international investment arbitration. Even though the tribunals have always taken into account the applicable law chosen by the parties, they also emphasized the complementary and corrective role of international Law. This matter will be discussed precisely in next parts regarding the role of national and international law in accordance with the second sentence of Article 42(1).

A glance at the Tribunal's explanations in *Letco v. Liberia* case could help to get a preliminary view on this approach.[95] The Concession Agreement of

---

93 Broches, Aron, "Convention on the Settlement of Investment Disputes between States and Nationals of Other States of 1965 Explanatory Notes and Survey of its Application, Albert Jan van den Berg (ed.), Yearbook Commercial Arbitration, Vol. 18, (1993), p. 666.

94 Benvenuti & Bonfant v. People's Republic of the Congo, 1982, Award, ICSID Case No. ARB/77/2, (8 August 1980), paras. 4.1–4.8.

95 Liberian Eastern Timber Corporation (LETCO) v. The Government of the Republic of Liberia, ICSID Case No. ARB/83/2, Award, (31 March 1986).

12 May 1970 made between the Government of Liberia and LETCO states at its outset that the Concession Agreement is made "under the General Business Law, Title 15 of the Liberian Code of Laws of 1956."[96] This appears to indicate an express choice by the parties of the law of Liberia as the law governing the Concession Agreement.

Tribunal maintained since no other rules or systems were opted by the parties, it can be concluded that there was no explicit choice of law made by the parties and even in the absence of the opening words of the Concession Agreement, Liberian law was to apply.[97]

Further, the Tribunal asks the question, whether Liberian law is to be applied on its own (as the law chosen by the parties) or in conjunction with applicable principles of public international law. According to the ICSID Convention, in the absence of any agreement between the parties as to the rules of law by which a dispute is to be decided "…the Tribunal shall apply the law of the Contracting State party to the dispute (including its rules of the conflict of laws) and such rules of international law as may be applicable."[98]

This provision of the ICSID envisages that, in the absence of any express choice of law by the parties, the Tribunal must apply a system of concurrent law. The law of the contracting state is recognized as paramount within its own territory, but is nevertheless subjected to control by international law. The role of international law as a "regulator" of national systems of law has been much discussed, with particular emphasis on the problems that are likely to arise if there is divergence on a particular point between national and international law.

Another view is reflected in *SPP v. EGYPT* case.[99] The case is mainly with regards to the Respondent's obligations and incurred duties according to the Heads of Agreement of September 1974 entered into by the member of its Government concerning the Investment of Arab and Foreign Funds and Free Zones.[100]

---

96 Liberian Eastern Timber Corporation (LETCO) v. The Government of the Republic of Liberia, ICSID Case No. ARB/83/2, Award, (31 March 1986), para. 53.

97 Liberian Eastern Timber Corporation (LETCO) v. The Government of the Republic of Liberia, ICSID Case No. ARB/83/2, Award, (31 March 1986), para. 55.

98 Article 42 of ICSID Convention.

99 Southern Pacific Properties (Middle East) v. Arab Republic of Egypt, Award, ICSID Case No. ARB/84/3, (20 May1992).

100 Southern Pacific Properties (Middle East) v. Arab Republic of Egypt, Award, ICSID Case No. ARB/84/3, (20 May1992), para. I(1).

In this case, the Respondent contends that the parties have implicitly agreed to apply Egyptian law in accordance with the first sentence of Article 42(1). As mentioned, the choice of law need not be expressed; and in this case, this choice stemmed from the preamble of the Heads of Agreement, which refers to Egyptian Laws No. 1 and No. 2 of 1972 and Law No. 43 of 1974.[101]

According to the Respondent, the second sentence of Article 42(1) is not applicable because it applies only in the absence of an agreement. Therefore, the Respondent states that international law should not be applied in this case because the role of international law is limited through those rules and principles incorporated in Egyptian law. In other words, based on the Respondent's view since the role of international is limited to instances, where it is in line with domestic law, it can only be applied indirectly through incorporation in Egyptian law.[102] To the contrary, the Claimant believed that there is no agreement between the parties; therefore, there is only room for applying the second sentence of Article 42(1), where the Tribunal is bound to apply the law of the Contracting State party and such rules of international law as may be applicable.[103]

Even though the Tribunal is of the view that this issue would bring not a significant practical difference, it states that even accepting the Respondent's view that the parties have implicitly agreed to apply Egyptian law, such an agreement cannot entirely exclude the direct applicability of international law in certain situations.[104]

VI) Limitations of party autonomy

The basic idea of party autonomy at the Dumoulin's time was to freely honor the intention of the parties. Through the evolution of this principle, it turns out that the free will of the parties cannot be endless. It should be identified how far the intention of the parties to choose the applicable law could go.

Therefore, this widely accepted principle has its own limitations similar to almost every other principle. However, some believe that the choice of the parties

101 Southern Pacific Properties (Middle East) v. Arab Republic of Egypt, Award, ICSID Case No. ARB/84/3, (20 May1992), para. II(44).

102 Southern Pacific Properties (Middle East) v. Arab Republic of Egypt, Award, ICSID Case No. ARB/84/3, (20 May1992), para. III(76).

103 Southern Pacific Properties (Middle East) v. Arab Republic of Egypt, Award, ICSID Case No. ARB/84/3, (20 May1992), para. III(77).

104 Southern Pacific Properties (Middle East) v. Arab Republic of Egypt, Award, ICSID Case No. ARB/84/3, (20 May1992), para. III(80).

should always be followed in order to maintain certainty and predictability in international arbitration. On the contrary, other scholars believe that parties' choice despite its importance should be ignored when it comes to those limitations.[105] In other words, public policy has an overriding effect over the party autonomy rule. The limitations could vary from one to another country but the law systems are almost agreed on some primary situations, which the parties' choice in their agreement will be disregarded.

1) Public policy

Public policy, or *ordre public*, refers to the grounds on which a receiving court may vacate an arbitral award that is contrary to the laws or standards of the court's jurisdiction.[106] Sometimes tribunals should avoid application of the laws that may be incompatible with the public policy of the forum.[107] To that end, if the chosen applicable law violates the strongest moral convictions or appears profoundly unjust at the forum, its application should be avoided.[108]

Public policy is defined in domestic, international and transnational fields. On the one hand, domestic public policy is defined by legislative enactments, constitutional constraints, or judicial practice within individual states. Therefore, domestic courts may disallow arbitration agreements or awards, which has been made within their jurisdiction in situations where their enforcement would violate the forum state's basic notions of morality and justice.[109] So, public policy, as used in many conventions, is limited to the public policy of the forum.[110]

---

105 Engle, Rachel, "Party Autonomy in International Arbitration: Where Uniformity Gives Way to Predictability", The Transnational lawyer, Vol. 15, (2002), p. 341.

106 Sever, Jay R., "Comment: The Relaxation of Inarbitrability and Public Policy Checks on U.S. and Foreign Arbitration: Arbitration Out of Control?", Tulane Law Review, Vol. 65, (1991), p. 1664.

107 Levin, Morris J, "Party Autonomy: Choice-of-Law Clauses in Commercial Contracts", The Georgetown Law Journal", Vol. 46, (1957–58), p. 264.

108 Paulsen, Monrad G.; Sovern, Michael I., "Public Policy in the Conflict of Laws", Columbia Law Review, Vol. 56, No. 7, (1956), p. 1015.

109 Sever, Jay R., "Comment: The Relaxation of Inarbitrability and Public Policy Checks on U.S. and Foreign Arbitration: Arbitration Out of Control?", Tulane Law Review, Vol. 65, (1991), p. 1664.

110 For example see:

Article 16 of the Convention on the Law Applicable to Contractual Obligations (Rome Convention), (1980): "The application of a rule of law of any country specified by this Convention may be refused only if such application is manifestly incompatible with the public policy ('ordre public') of the forum."

On the other hand, international public policy refers to the laws, standards and principles by which states rule international arbitration. The need for coherence and predictability in international arbitration is a reason for more liberal state's laws on international arbitration, which are less limiting than those governing domestic arbitration.

Moreover, an arbitration agreement or award may contravene transnational public policy. These are agreements or awards that violate universal standards and international rules. In other words, it is the most extreme forms of human conduct that offend public morals such as piracy, bribery, corruption, smuggling and genocide.[111]

The notion of public policy varies from one state to the other. For example, an agreement fully accepted in Germany may violate a public policy standard in Indonesia and be disallowed.

Public policy is a limit not only to the party autonomy principle but it could also be a limit to the enforcement of an award. There are some cases that we could examine how the arbitral tribunals react to this notion.

One of the cases is *World Duty Free Company Limited v. The Republic of Kenya* case.[112]

In this case, Kenya contends that the 1989 Agreement was procured by paying a bribe to the then president of Kenya, Daniel arap Moi, and the payment of such a bribe is criminal therefore the resulting contract is neither valid nor enforceable, and the claims cannot be heard as a matter of public policy and as a matter of applicable law. Furthermore, the contract is voidable and has been validly avoided by Kenya. Kenya believes that the claims should be dismissed with prejudice.[113]

Therefore, initially the Tribunal should examine the existence of the bribe and whether the Agreement has been procured as a result of such a payment. Then the Tribunal has to examine the consequences of the bribe on the legality and enforceability of the Agreement under international public policy and respective applicable laws.[114]

---

111 Bray, Devin; Bray, Heather L., "International Arbitration and Public Policy", JurisNet LLC, (2014), p. 27.

112 World Duty Free Company Limited v. The Republic of Kenya, Award, ICSID Case No. ARB/00/7, (4 October 2006).

113 World Duty Free Company Limited v. The Republic of Kenya, Award, ICSID Case No. ARB/00/7, (2006), para. 128.

114 World Duty Free Company Limited v. The Republic of Kenya, Award, ICSID Case No. ARB/00/7, (2006), para. 129.

After the statements made by parties at the Tribunal, the Tribunal maintains with no doubt that the payments could not be viewed as a personal donation for public purposes and they were made not only in order to obtain an audience with President Moi (as submitted by the Claimant), but mainly to obtain the agreement of the president on the contemplated investment and therefore the payments must be considered as a bribe in order to obtain the conclusion of the 1989 Agreement.[115]

Based on Kenya's submissions, as a matter of international public policy, as well as Kenyan and English law, the 1989 Agreement does not have force of law; thus, the World Duty Free's claims must be dismissed.[116]

According to this award, the concept of public policy (*ordre public*) is rooted in most, if not all, legal systems and violation of the enforcing State's public policy is one of the main grounds for refusing recognition or enforcement of foreign judgments and awards. This principle is also to be seen in a number of Conventions and Model laws recommended by the General Assembly of the United Nations. Numerous legislatures and courts have decided that a narrow concept of public policy should apply to foreign awards, which is known as "international public policy" (*ordre public international*). In fact, it is nothing more than domestic public policy applied to foreign awards. This term also has another meaning, which is an international consensus to universal standards and accepted norms of conduct that must be applied in all fora. This concept is referred to as "transnational public policy" or "truly international public policy".[117]

While domestic courts generally refer to their own international public policy, arbitral tribunals have more often based their decisions on universal values in using various formulations such as "good morals", "ethics of international trade" or "transnational public policy". Similarly, in this case, the Tribunal's first statement was that bribery is sanctioned by criminal law in almost all countries and also a number of international and regional conventions.[118]

115 World Duty Free Company Limited v. The Republic of Kenya, Award, ICSID Case No. ARB/00/7, (2006), para. 136.

116 World Duty Free Company Limited v. The Republic of Kenya, Award, ICSID Case No. ARB/00/7, (2006), para. 137.

117 World Duty Free Company Limited v. The Republic of Kenya, Award, ICSID Case No. ARB/00/7, (2006), paras. 138–139.

118 Inter-American Convention against Corruption (1996); Convention on Combating Bribery of Foreign Public Officials in International Business Transactions (1997); Criminal Law Convention on Corruption (1999); African Union Convention on Preventing and Combating Corruption (2003); United Nations Declaration against

Furthermore, domestic courts and arbitral tribunals have considered corruption and bribery contrary to the international public policy. The Tribunal refers to many instances as examples of employing international public policy especially in issues regarding corruption. The Tribunal then among others referred to Legergren in ICC case No. 1110 para. 20 where he held that "although these commissions were not to be used exclusively for bribes, a very substantial part of them must have been intended for such use. Whether one is taking the point of view of good government or that of commercial ethics it is impossible to close one's eyes to the probable destination of amounts of this magnitude, and to the destructive effect thereof on the business pattern with consequent impairment of industrial progress. Such corruption is an international evil; it is contrary to good morals and to an international public policy common to the community of nations."[119] And then he concluded: "After weighing all the evidence I am convinced that a case such as this, involving such gross violation of good morals and international public policy, can have no countenance in any court either in the Argentine or in France, or, for that matter in any other civilized country, nor in any arbitral tribunal. Thus, jurisdiction must be declined in this case. It follows from the foregoing, that in concluding that I have no jurisdiction, guidance has been sought from general principles denying arbitrators to entertain disputes of this nature rather than from any national rules on arbitrability. Parties who ally themselves in an enterprise of the present nature must realize that they have forfeited any right to ask for assistance of the machinery of justice (national courts or arbitral tribunals) in settling their disputes."[120]

The Tribunal moreover turned to numerous mainly ICC awards in connection with corruption and bribery and eventually in light of domestic laws and international conventions and awards rendered in this matter by courts and arbitral tribunals, the tribunal was convinced that bribery is well in contradiction with the international public policy of most, if not all, States or, in other words, to transnational public policy, thus, claims based on contracts connected with corruption cannot be upheld by this Arbitral Tribunal.[121]

Corruption and Bribery in International Commercial Transactions (1996); United Nations Convention against Corruption (2003).

119 World Duty Free Company Limited v. The Republic of Kenya, Award, ICSID Case No. ARB/00/7, (2006), para. 148.

120 World Duty Free Company Limited v. The Republic of Kenya, Award, ICSID Case No. ARB/00/7, (2006), para. 148.

121 World Duty Free Company Limited v. The Republic of Kenya, Award, ICSID Case No. ARB/00/7, (2006), para. 157.

Then, as required by Article 42(1) of the ICSID Convention, the tribunal turns to the applicable laws chosen by the parties in the 1989 Agreement, which called for application of English law by any arbitral tribunal shall constitute based on the Agreement. The Agreement now before the Tribunal also stipulated that it shall be construes and governed by the law of Kenya.[122] Although these two provisions are apparently inconsistent, but as there is no substantive difference on the matters relating to contract between position at common law in England and Kenya it does not lead to any difficulty yet.[123] In Tribunal's view, the place of bribery in the common law is historically significant, as the common law has traditionally abhorred the corruption by bribery of officers of state, ranking its offense next to high treason. It does not even depend upon any financial loss and neither does it require an immediate victim.[124] The Tribunal, therefore, dismisses the Claimant's submission that the bribe was an independent collateral transaction or at least severable from the 1989 Agreement.[125]

In conclusion, based on the public policy both under English and Kenyan law which are materially identical and based on the specific facts of this case, the Tribunal held that the Claimant is not legally entitled to maintain any of its pleaded claims in these proceedings on the ground of *ex turpi causa non oritur* action. These claims all sound or depend upon the 1989 Agreement and no other claim is pleaded, including any non-contractual proprietary or restitutionary claim.[126]

2) Mandatory provisions of the host state's law

At first, one may believe that the party autonomy principle is generally accepted in almost all countries and consider it as an unlimited freedom. The limit of this freedom has resulted in lengthy debates, which are also related to the application of mandatory rules of law. The question is how to distinct the border between party

122 World Duty Free Company Limited v. The Republic of Kenya, Award, ICSID Case No. ARB/00/7, (2006), para. 158.
123 World Duty Free Company Limited v. The Republic of Kenya, Award, ICSID Case No. ARB/00/7, (2006), paras. 158–159.
124 A World Duty Free Company Limited v. The Republic of Kenya, Award, ICSID Case No. ARB/00/7, (2006), para. 173.
125 World Duty Free Company Limited v. The Republic of Kenya, Award, ICSID Case No. ARB/00/7, (2006), para. 174.
126 World Duty Free Company Limited v. The Republic of Kenya, Award, ICSID Case No. ARB/00/7, (2006), para. 179.

autonomy and the protection of states' interests.[127] Even though arbitration has provided a great range of freedom and actually this is why it is one of the most appropriate means of dispute resolution, it cannot ignore the mandate of states. Mandatory rules are existed because states need to apply certain rights and obligations regardless of the wishes of private parties.[128]

There are several definitions of mandatory rules. According to Pierre Mayer, a mandatory rule is an imperative provision of law, which must be applied in an international relationship irrespective of the law that governs that relationship.[129]

These rules can limit both parties and arbitrators. They limit the ability of the arbitrators to give full effect to the parties' choices to exclude those rules.[130]

While an investment is being implemented, there is wide range of laws that should be applied. Among those, some are classified as mandatory laws and could neither be excluded by a term in a contract nor be overridden.[131] Sometimes it depends on the host state's policies, which may tend to limit the foreign participation in some strategic sectors or culturally or socially sensitive areas such as media.[132] There is no exhaustive list of these imperative rules. Typically, they are incorporated in fields including but not limited to foreign exchange controls, environmental regulation, competition law, securities law, company law, embargoes, blockades or boycotts.[133]

---

127 Waincymer, Jeff, "International Commercial Arbitration and the Application of Mandatory Rules of Law", Asian International Arbitration Journal, Vol. 5, Issue. 1, (2009), p. 1.

128 Waincymer, Jeff, "International Commercial Arbitration and the Application of Mandatory Rules of Law", Asian International Arbitration Journal, Vol. 5, Issue. 1, (2009), p. 5.

129 Mayer, Pierre, "Mandatory Rules of Law in International Arbitration", Arbitration International, Vol. 2, (1986), p. 274.

130 Bjorklund, Andrea K, "Mandatory Rules of Law and Investment Arbitration", American Review of International Arbitration, Vol. 18, (2007), p. 179.

131 See The Convention on the Law Applicable to Contractual Obligations (Rome Convention), (opened for signature on 19 June 1980).

Article 3(3): The fact that the parties have chosen a foreign law, whether or not accompanied by the choice of a foreign tribunal, shall not, where all the other elements relevant to the situation at the time of the choice are connected with one country only, prejudice the application of rules of the law of that country which cannot be derogated from by contract, hereinafter called "mandatory rules".

132 Diehl, Alexandra, "The Core Standard of International Investment Protection-Fair and Equitable Treatment", Kluwer Law International, (2012), p. 277.

133 Bjorklund, Andrea K, "Mandatory Rules of Law and Investment Arbitration", American Review of International Arbitration, Vol. 18, (2007), p. 179.

Moreover, the other objective behind this limitation is to protect the weaker party by taking away the parties' right to choose, where there is an inequality of bargaining power in the contract. An example could be the employee or consumer contracts.[134]

Generally, there are various aims that the governments need to protect. As Blessing stated:

> "Some are aimed solely at protecting certain monetary interests of the State, such as exchange control regulations or transfer restrictions;
> some are of a merely policing nature;
> others are aimed at safeguarding certain vital interests of a State and its people's welfare; and, in particular
> others are aimed at protecting the free trade and the functioning of an effective market, such as competition laws."[135]

Additionally, in many countries there is some conflict of law rules that limit that freedom. For example, in the English system, in which party autonomy is of great importance, choice of law by the parties should be "bona fide and legal" otherwise it has no effect. This rule is derived from *Vita Food Products Inc v. Unus Shipping Co Ltd*, where Lord Wright considered lack of bona fides a factor that may invalid a choice of law. This case will be reported briefly at this section. Mandatory law issue in connection with applicable law has been also formulated by Dicey & Morris in the comment of Rule 145 Sub-rule I:

> "No court, is submitted, will give effect to a choice of law (whether English or foreign) if the parties intended to apply it in order to evade the mandatory provisions of that legal system with which the contract has its most substantial connection and which, for this reason, the court would, in the absence of an express or implied choice of law, have applied."

Therefore, the English system has also accepted the freedom of choice of law with certain qualifications.

American system also has its own limitations to this principle. The American Law Institute, provides in Section 186 of Restatement of the Law 2nd:

> "Issues in contract are determined by the law chosen by the parties."

---

134 Livingstone, Mia Louise, "Party Autonomy in International Commercial Arbitration: Popular Fallacy or Proven Fact?", Journal of International Arbitration, Vol. 25, Issue. 5, (2008), p. 532.

135 Blessing, Marc, "Mandatory Rules of Law versus Party Autonomy in International Arbitration", Journal of International Arbitration, Vol. 14, Issue. 4, (1997), p. 26.

This approach shows the general acceptance of the party autonomy doctrine; however, section 187 subject this freedom to limitations:

The law of the state chosen by the parties to govern their contractual rights and duties will be applied if the particular issue is one which the parties could have resolved by an explicit provision in their agreement directed to that issue.

The law of the state chosen by the parties to govern their contractual rights and duties will be applied, even if the particular issue is one which the parties could not have resolved by an explicit provision in their agreement directed to that issue, unless either the chosen states have no substantial relationship to the parties or the transaction and there is no other reasonable basis for the parties choice, or application of the law of the chosen state would be contrary to a fundamental policy of a state which has a materially greater interest than the chosen state in the determination of the particular issue and which, under the rule of 188, would be the state of the applicable law, that is, the absence of an effective choice of law by the parties.

Thus, the American system also has some limitations to this principle. For example, parties could not endow themselves with contractual capacity or dispense with contractual requirements, which could not be obtained under the law that has the closest relation with the contract, by choosing another applicable law.[136]

In the civil countries, this principle used to be free of limitations but recently some European countries have subjected this freedom to certain limitations. They have held that the parties' choice of law applies only when it is consistent with the conflict of laws rule of the forum or those of the site of the arbitration.[137]

Vita Food Products Inc v. Unus Shipping Co Ltd[138] case is considered important regarding questions on carriage of goods and as well on conflicts of law; therefore, it will be summarized as to the extent relevant to this study. In this case, an express choice by the parties of the proper or governing law of a contract will be given effect provided that the choice is bona fide and legal and not contrary to forum public policy.[139]

136 Croff, Carlo, "The Applicable Law in an International Commercial Arbitration: Is it Still a Conflict of Laws Problem?", The International Lawyer, Vol. 16, (1982), p. 616.

137 Engle, Rachel, "Party Autonomy in International Arbitration: Where Uniformity Gives Way to Predictability", The Transnational lawyer, Vol. 15, (2002), p. 336.

138 A leading decision of the Judicial Committee of the Privy Council on the conflict of laws, 1939.

139 See also Tetley, William Q.C., "Vita Food Products Revisited (Which Parts of the Decision Are Good Law Today?)", McGill Law Journal, (1992), p. 292.

The defendant, a Nova Scotia corporation, was the owner of the ship *Hurry On*, which was registered in Nova Scotia. The plaintiff, a New York corporation, was the owner of a cargo of herrings, which was loaded on the *Hurry On* for carriage from Newfoundland to New York. Due to negligent navigation, the ship ran aground in Nova Scotia and the cargo of herrings was damaged. In respect of this loss, the plaintiff commenced an action for damages against the defendant in the Supreme Court of Nova Scotia.

The contract between the plaintiff and the defendant for the carriage of the cargo (which comprised three bills of lading in identical terms) contained a term, valid under English law, which exempted the defendant from liability for a loss due to negligence. The contract also provided that it shall be governed by English law.

The plaintiff's action was dismissed by the primary judge and decision was affirmed by the Supreme Court of Nova Scotia En Banc.

Subsequently, the Privy Council dismissed the plaintiff's appeal. The express choice of English law as the proper or governing law of the contract should be given effect even although the parties and the contract had no connection with England except that the insurers were "likely to be English." Accordingly, the contractual exemption of liability for a loss due to negligence precluded the plaintiff's claim.

It is objected that this is too broadly stated and that some qualifications are necessary. But where the English rule that intention is the test applies, and where there is an express statement by the parties of their intention to select the law of the contract, it is difficult to see what qualifications are possible, provided the intention expressed is bona fide and legal, and provided there is no reason for avoiding the choice on the ground of public policy. There is, in their Lordships' opinion, no ground for refusing to give effect to the express selection of English law as the proper law in the bills of lading. In other words, there is an unwarranted extension given to the intent of parties' doctrine.[140]

After taking a look at these cases, we should mention that the issue of mandatory national laws is controversial because its application is based on some views in contrary to the nature of arbitration. As a private means of resolving dispute, arbitration is a preferred type which is often considered transnational or outside the jurisdiction of any one country. Therefore, the possibility that country's law can influence on the applicability the parties' choice of law is problematic. In

140 William Q.C., "Vita Food Products Revisited (Which Parts of the Decision Are Good Law Today?)", McGill Law Journal, (1992), p. 300.

some cases, however, arbitrators may feel obligated to follow a law contrary to the parties' choice. At the same time, parties to a contract specifying arbitration need to have a degree of certainty that their agreement will be followed.

3) Reasonable connection

Another area, which limits the parties' free choice of law, is the requirement of reasonable connection. As the definition of this concept, Levin stated: "The theory which has always demanded that there be a substantial connection between the contract and the place whose law is designated as controlling is based upon the formalistic view that parties, and their contracts, are creatures of the state wherein they reside and act, and that they cannot avoid the consequences of the local law by stipulating for a foreign law."[141]

The further step in this section and with respect to the substantive connection is the reasonable connection, which means the parties' choice of law may have a certain level of relationship with the parties or the transaction itself.[142] To that end, there is more chance for the law chosen by the parties to be compatible with the law of the countries connected with the contract. It means that the possibility of imposing the limiting power of mandatory rules will be reduced. There are many connections that may be acceptable to the tribunals such as the place of performance, the place of the domicile of one or both of the parties, the rules that are well known to a particular profession, the place with an integral interest and connection with the contract.[143]

Nowadays, this limitation does not have its effect as before. In the era of globalization and through the more complicated transactions, it is not as unlikely as before not to find any of this connections. According to many international Conventions, there is a "no relation" or "no interest" rule and none of the conventions stipulated any requirement for "reasonable relation" between the chosen applicable law and the parties or their transactions.[144] Unlike domestic legal systems, in which a choice of law without any connection to that law

---

141 Levin, Morris J, "Party Autonomy: Choice-of-Law Clauses in Commercial Contracts", The Georgetown Law Journal", Vol. 46, (1957–58), p. 263.

142 Zhang, Mo, "Party Autonomy and Beyond: An International Perspective of Contractual Choice of Law", Emory International Law Review, Vol. 20, (2006), p. 527.

143 Levin, Morris J, "Party Autonomy: Choice-of-Law Clauses in Commercial Contracts", The Georgetown Law Journal", Vol. 46, (1957–1958), p. 264.

144 Zhang, Mo, "Party Autonomy and Beyond: An International Perspective of Contractual Choice of Law", Emory International Law Review, Vol. 20, (2006), p. 548.

would be irrational, such a choice in international arbitration would be deemed rational and even attractive in many situations. Therefore, the parties could choose the applicable law, as they desire. Under the ICSID Convention, reasonable connection of the transaction to the law chosen by the parties is not required.[145]

Ultimately, and to sum up, it can be asserted that the limitations of party autonomy can be categorized to different forms. One instance would be, where party autonomy is generally excluded in a certain area of the law and it may only be implemented in marginal sectors of that area. The motivation of such exclusion and limitation is high degree of public reliance on a uniform system, for example, in field of *in rem* rights.[146]

Other categories of limitations are in the form of basic admission subject to a list of restrictive eligible laws. This reflects the compromise virtue of conflict rules, which allow party autonomy, and are agreed upon in international bodies.[147]

VII) Choice of law varieties

1) Direct agreement between the parties

The direct agreement between the parties may be reached before or after the institution of proceedings. This agreement is normally stated in the initial investment agreement between the host state and the investor.

The 1993 ICSID Model Clauses offer the following sample for a direct agreement on choice of law:

> "Clause 10
> Any arbitral Tribunal constituted pursuant to this agreement shall apply specification of system of law [as in force on the date on which this agreement is signed]/[subject to the following modifications: . . .]."[148]

---

145 Schreuer, Christoph, "The ICSID Convention- A Commentary", Cambridge University Press, Second Edition, (2009), p. 564.

146 Basedow, Jürgen, "The Law of Open Societies: Private Ordering and Public Regulation of International Relations: General Course on Private International Law", Leiden, Boston, Martinus Nijhoff Publishers, (2013), pp. 212–214.

147 *Ibid.*

148 ICSID Model Clauses, available at: http://icsidfiles.worldbank.org/icsid/icsid/staticfiles/model-clauses-en/7.htm, (last seen 16.05 2017).

The parties may choose various rules of law in their agreement, such as domestic law, international law or a combination of both. Parties can also choose various laws as the governing law of their relationship. This process is called "dépeçage".

It is discussed that the parties should have the freedom to set aside any national law and internationalize their relationship by referring to general principles of international law and the like.

It has also been argued that parties may choose their contract or any other instrument among them as the sole applicable law.[149] Under all these circumstances, the parties' choice has to be clear and identifiable.[150]

a) The law of the host state

One of the potential choices of the parties in their agreement may be the law of the host state. This choice is widely supported by developing countries.[151] This option has been frequently used with respect to a contractual relationship concerning an investment. It is a pertinent choice because it has the closest connection to the activity being exercised in the host state; or in other words, the contract has its most substantial connection with the host state's national law. The other ground of application of the law of the host state is that it is presumed that the foreign investor by entering into an investment contract has consented to the application of the law of the host state.[152] It also argues that each contract, which is not between States in their capacities as subjects of international law, is necessarily based on the national law of some country.[153] This approach is also rooted in the political self-affirmation of developing countries as stated in United Nations resolution on the Charter of Economic Rights and Duties of States (CERDS), which affirms the view that foreign investment should be exclusively regulated by municipal law.[154]

---

149 Broches, Aron, "The Convention on the Settlement of Investment Disputes between States and Nationals of Other States", Collected Courses of the Hague Academy of International Law, Vol. 136, Brill Nijhoff, Leiden Boston, (1972).

150 See Santa Elena v. Costa Rica, ICSID Case No. ARB/96/1, Award, (17 February 2000).

151 Atsegbua, Lawrence, "International Arbitration of Oil Investment Disputes: The Severability Doctrine and Applicable Law Issues Revisited", African Journal of International and Comparative Law, Vol. 5, Issue. 3, (1993), p. 645.

152 Cherian, Joy, "Investment Contracts and Arbitration, The World Bank Convention on the Settlement of Investment Disputes", A. W. Sijthoff, (1975), p. 19.

153 Atsegbua, Lawrence, "International Arbitration of Oil Investment Disputes: The Severability Doctrine and Applicable Law Issues Revisited", African Journal of International and Comparative Law, Vol. 5, Issue. 3, (1993), p. 645.

154 Charter of Economic Rights and Duties of States, (12 December 1974).

At the present time, the law of the host state has been opted infrequently because this option usually and sometimes unnecessarily privileges the host state. Therefore, the other party, that is, the investors are reluctant to accept it as the only applicable law. They would rather subject that choice to a stabilization clause or apply it together with international law. The financial risks associated with some investment contracts are considerable and the application of the law of the host state may represent a further risk for the investor. These contracts with such choice of law clause are vulnerable to the possible unilateral changes by the exercise of legislative sovereignty by the host state. Another argument would be that by the application of the law of the host state, there is no room for international law to be applied and the investor could not seek to provide remedy by this means. Therefore, it would not be the best choice for the foreign investor. The investor seeks to escape the dangers of this choice and safeguards its investment by numerous means such as internationalization.

Further argument, which stands against this choice of law, is the lack of a well-developed municipal legal system regarding investment contracts in developing countries.[155] But this argument can no longer be taken into account since most developing countries have nowadays a well-developed municipal law system. Unfamiliarity and the possible prejudice and other sensitivities arising from this choice of law could have further reasons.[156]

b) The law of the investor's home country or of third state

Reference to the law of the investor or third state in investment arbitration is not frequent and is unlikely for a host state to accept such choice. When the investment activities take place within the host state, any choice of law other than of that state's legal system could lead to difficulties. That plus other issues such as close connection between those activities and the legal system of the host state like tax law and administrative law may prove this choice impractical even for the investor.

The choice of a third state or a neutral legal system is more frequent but it could create the same problems. Sometimes in the field of loan or licensing agreements, a third state becomes an important financial center and its legal system acquires a close connection to the case. Given the fact that the governing

155 Cherian, Joy, "Investment Contracts and Arbitration, The World Bank Convention on the Settlement of Investment Disputes", A. W. Sijthoff, (1975), pp. 24–25.

156 Diehl, Alexandra, "The Core Standard of International Investment Protection-Fair and Equitable Treatment", Kluwer Law International, (2012), p. 258.

law of a loan relationship or a licensing agreement is naturally the law of the lender's country or the law of the licensor's home country, the choice of a third state may be appropriate.

Regardless of the considered option, it should have been extracted from the stipulation of the parties. In the absence of such stipulation the tribunal may apply the second sentence of Article 42(1).

Another instance, where the applicable law could be the law of a third state are numerous cases, where Swiss law has been opted as a neutral law.[157]

c) *Investment agreement as a self-contained legal system*

Another method to choose the governing law is viewing the agreement as a sole legal system apart from any other. This method may bring difficulties when the agreement is not detailed enough and the tribunal could not find any appropriate guidance regarding an issue in the agreement because naturally the agreement itself could not answer all the questions which may arise in the dispute. In such a situation and in accordance with the Article 42(2) (Prohibition of a Non Liquet), the only way remaining for the tribunal is to refer to the second sentence of Article 42(1) and apply the law of the Contracting State and such rules of international law as may be applicable.

When this method is chosen, the best way to avoid problems is to employ international law or domestic law together with the agreement as the applicable law. For example, in the Khemco agreement of 1966 between Amoco and NPC (National Petrochemical Company controlled by the Government of Iran) such a compound provision could be seen:

> "Article 30
> 'Applicable Law'
> This Agreement shall be construed and interpreted in accordance with the plain meaning of its terms, but subject thereto, shall be governed and construed in accordance with the laws of Iran.
> The provisions of any current laws and regulations which may be wholly or partially inconsistent with the provisions of this Agreement shall, to the extent of any such inconsistency, be of no effect in respect of the provisions of this Agreement."

In this agreement, the first choice of the parties with respect to applicable law is the Khemco agreement, which is supplemented by reference to Iranian Law.

157 Gouran, Hafiz; Khosla, Aditi, "The Choice of Law in ICSID Arbitration in Relation to Investment Disputes", Vindobona Journal of International Commercial Law & Arbitration, Vol. 16, (2012), p. 36.

d) International law

In the field of international investment, the investors seek protection and one of the best methods to reach this aim is to internationalize the agreement by adopting international law as the law applicable to the merits of the case.

The origin of the theory of "internationalization", especially in the field of oil investment contracts, *inter alia* is to be found in the disputes arising from petroleum concessions in the Middle East.

The principal proponents of this theory in the field of investment contracts include Dupuy F. A. Mann and P. Weil, who held that investment contracts may be governed by the principle and rules of public international law.[158] This theory contends that the outcome of an investment contract by a State with a foreign private investor is not necessarily divergent from the conclusion of a treaty as an act that creates legal obligation.

The parties may choose international law alone or in conjunction with another legal system such as the law of the host state.

aa) International law alone as the law chosen by the parties

Choosing international law as the sole applicable law by the parties, reflects internationalization of their relationship.

This choice would not be optimal given the fact that some of the activities with respect to foreign investment are significantly intertwined with the law of the host state. To that end, international law probably would not be able to cover all the questions and challenges that may arise.[159] However, some multilateral treaties providing for ICSID arbitration such as NAFTA[160] and the Energy Charter Treaty, refer merely to the treaty and international law.

For example, Article 1131 of NAFTA states:

> "A Tribunal established under this Section shall decide the issues in dispute in accordance with this Agreement and the applicable rules of international law."

---

158 Mann, Francis, "The Proper Law of Contracts Concluded by International Persons", British Year Book of International Law, Vol. 35, (1959), pp. 34–75.

159 Schreuer, Christoph, "The ICSID Convention: A Commentary", Cambridge University Press, Second Edition, (2009), p. 562.

160 The North American Free Trade Agreement

bb) Compound choice of law

The more practical and realistic method of applying rules of international law and providing the protection needed by the investors is to employ a compound choice of law clause containing the rules of international law together with the law of the host state. The investment activities take place in host state; therefore, the choice of its law is logical and appropriate. At the same time the applicability of international rules will guarantee that the minimum standards of international law will not be violated. However, there are two different approaches on this matter. Some commentators support the view of mutability of investment contracts and believes the presence of both public and private interests in investment contracts offers that the sanctity of contract principle should be taken broader and less rigid in the context of the international law of contracts.[161] While others suggest that an international contract is withdrawn from the host country's legislative influence and is stabilized.[162]

Such clauses can be seen in both recent and older investment agreements. An example of such clause is the Agreement of 1974 in *AGIP v. Congo*[163]:

> "Article 15:
> The law of the Congo, supplemented if need be by any principles of international law, will be applicable."[164]

cc) International minimum standards

Even in the absence of reference to international law, the minimum standards of international law should be taken into account. One may think that in some situations the tribunal should totally exclude the application of international law. This would lead to such an extreme situation. Since the legislative sovereignty of a state is quasi unlimited, this would mean that even a manifest denial of justice, discriminatory or arbitrary measure of the host state should be upheld by

161 Peter, Wolfgang, "Arbitration and Renegotiation of International Investment Agreements", Kluwer Law International, (1995), p. 96.

162 Atsegbua, Lawrence, "International Arbitration of Oil Investment Disputes: The Severability Doctrine and Applicable Law Issues Revisited", African Journal of International and Comparative Law, Vol. 5, Issue. 3, (1993), p. 647.

163 AGIP SPA v. People's Republic of the Congo, Award, ICSID Case No. ARB/77/1, (30 November 1979).

164 AGIP SPA v. People's Republic of the Congo, Award, ICSID Case No. ARB/77/1, (30 November 1979), Agreement of 2 January 1974, Art. 15.

the tribunal.[165] That would be even in contradiction with the aim of the ICSID Convention. The minimum standards such as the prohibition of denial of justice and the discriminatory taking of property have an obligatory nature and therefore could not be violated by the parties.

e) *Transnational law and* Lex Mercatoria

As the title suggests, transnational law includes all types of law, be it national or international that applies to all persons, businesses and governments that perform or have influence across state lines. Many definitions have been given with respect to transnational law such as "all law which regulates actions or events that transcend national frontiers..."[166] This approach is arisen from the inability of traditional international law to cope with the complex and interdependent nature of modern international relations and instances which by applying those laws merely would have been left uncovered.

Pursuant to the delocalization movement in the field of international arbitration especially the law governing the arbitration, the extent of the party autonomy expands and includes even non-legal standards that are generally a part of *Lex Mercatoria* today. Many scholars and practitioners have criticized this notion based on various grounds, most important of which is the vagueness of this concept that leads to uncertainty.[167] It is difficult to find a degree of uniformity on its definition, whereas some common elements could be derived from those definitions. For example, *Lex Mercatoria* is not based on any legal system but contains international commercial rules, general principles of law, standards, and trade usages.[168] There have been also attempts to make *Lex Mercatoria* more specific by making a list of the principles and the updates.[169]

In practice, it would be more preferred to have a list of laws, which are accessible rather than referring to *Lex Mercatoria*. The same approach can be seen in

---

165 Fenyvesi, Jósef Bulcsú, "Application of International Law as Applicable Law under the First Sentence of Ast 42(1) of the ICSID Convention", Jura: A Pecsi Tudomanyegytem Allam- es Jogtudomanyi Karanak tudomanyos lapja, Vol. 2005, issue. 1, (2005), p. 64.
166 Koh, Harold Hongju, "Why Transnational Law Matters", Penn State International Law Review, Vol. 24, Issue. 4, (2006), p. 745.
167 Moses, Margaret L., "The Principles of International Commercial Arbitration", Cambridge University Press, Second Edition, (2012), p. 64.
168 Moses, Margaret L., "The Principles of International Commercial Arbitration", Cambridge University Press, Second Edition, (2012), p. 65.
169 See www.trans-lex.org.

view of some arbitrators that are reluctant to base their decision on transnational law or *Lex Mercatoria* and tend to refer to general principles of law.[170]

f) General principles of law

In investment contracts, if the parties do not choose any particular legal system, then their contract should be governed by the general principle of law recognized by civilized nations.[171]

In order to apply this principle, two points should be taken into account. First, the fact that many host countries do not own a law system yet, under which they could deal with this particular type of transaction; second, the parties do not specify the applicable law but they only agree to submit their disputes to arbitration.

Today, the first point is no longer tenable because most of the developing countries have a well-developed law system to rule the investment contracts and deal with the foreign investment. Another difficulty is to define these "general principles of law recognized by civilized nations."[172]

2) Applicable law chosen in treaty or legislation

Sometimes the legislation or treaty providing for ICSID's jurisdiction includes a provision on applicable law. Such choice might be reflected in various forms which will be discussed below.

a) Choice of law in domestic legislation

Some national investment laws provide for a provision determining the jurisdiction of ICSID or some other forum of dispute settlement for States and investors. Once the investor accepts the jurisdiction, its action also infers acceptance of that provision regarding the applicable law which equals to an agreed choice of law but it could not be taken as a choice of host state's law merely because the jurisdiction is based on a provision of the law of the host state.[173]

---

170 Moses, Margaret L., "The Principles of International Commercial Arbitration", Cambridge University Press, Second Edition, (2012), p. 66.

171 Peter, Wolfgang, "Arbitration and Renegotiation of International Investment Agreements", Kluwer Law International, (1995), p. 10.

172 Peter, Wolfgang, "Arbitration and Renegotiation of International Investment Agreements", Kluwer Law International, (1995), pp. 6–10.

173 Schreuer, Christoph, "The ICSID Convention: A Commentary", Cambridge University Press, Second Edition, (2009), p. 570.

Moreover, single reference to a matter in the host state's law could not be seen as an explicit choice of the law of that state. It proves the application of some parts of the host state's law but not the general application thereof.[174] The more frequent situation is in the absence of the parties' agreement on applicable law due to the rarity of the explicit choice of law clauses in national investment laws.[175]

b) *Choice of law in treaties*

Another method that mirrors the parties' freedom to choose the applicable law is the "applicable law clauses" in investment treaties. Some treaties providing for ICSID's jurisdiction have their own rules on applicable law; however, not all the treaties contain such a clause. When the investor accepts the offer to consent to jurisdiction, it contains also the acceptance of the applicable law clause. This acceptance could be expressed by simply pursuing the arbitration proceedings.

Many BITs and multilateral treaties contain choice of law clauses, which refer only to the treaty itself or add the reference to the law of the Contracting State and the rules of international law and/or general principles of law. This clause usually appears as a compound clause, which refers to at least two sources of law.[176] For example, Germany-China BIT provides:

"The arbitral tribunal shall reach its award in accordance with the provisions of this Agreement and the principles of international law recognized by both Contracting Parties."[177]

Where a treaty is the basis for the arbitral jurisdiction and, for example, provides for ICSID's jurisdiction, its clause on applicable law is the agreed choice of law made by the parties.

A clause on governing law stipulated in the Canada/Tanzania BIT of 2013, which provides:

---

174 See LETCO (Liberian Eastern Timber Corporation) v. Republic of Liberia, Award, ICSID Case No. ARB/83/2, (31 March 1986).

175 Diehl, Alexandra, "The Core Standard of International Investment Protection-Fair and Equitable Treatment", Kluwer Law International, (2012), p. 269.

176 Diehl, Alexandra, "The Core Standard of International Investment Protection-Fair and Equitable Treatment", Kluwer Law International, (2012), p. 265.

177 Art. 8(5) of the Agreement between the People's Republic of China and the Federal Republic of Germany on the Encouragement and Reciprocal Protection of Investment, 1 December 2003.

> "Article 32 – Governing Law
> A Tribunal established under this Section shall decide the issues in dispute in accordance with this Agreement and applicable rules of international law. A joint interpretation by the parties of a provision of this Agreement shall be binding on a Tribunal established under this Section, and any award under this Section shall be consistent with such interpretation."[178]

Moreover, some treaties contain a four-source clause which refers to the law of the host state (including its conflict of law rules), BIT itself, the rules and principles of international law and to any special investment agreement concluded between the host state and the investor. The Sweden-Argentina BIT of 1991 is an example:

> "The arbitration tribunal shall decide in accordance with the provisions of this Agreement, the law of the Contracting Party involved in the dispute, including its rules of conflict laws, the terms of any specific agreement concluded in relation to such an investment and the principles of international law."[179]

On the contrary, a rare amount of BITs refer only to the law of the host state, as the Romanian-Sri Lanka BIT which reads as follows:

> "Application of National Laws
> All investments made by the investor of one Contracting Party in the territory of the other Contracting Party shall, subject to this Agreement, be governed by the laws in force in the territory of the Contracting Party in which such investments are made."[180]

Some multilateral treaties such as NAFTA, ECT and the Colonia Investment Protocol of MERCOSUR contain applicable law clauses.

As an example for the choice of law in multilateral treaties, ECT provides:

> "A tribunal established under paragraph (4) shall decide the issues in dispute in accordance with this Treaty and applicable rules and principles of international law."[181]

---

178 Agreement between the Government of Canada and the Government of the Unites Republic of Tanzania for the Promotion and Reciprocal Protection of Investments, 2013.

179 Agreement between the Government of the Kingdom of Sweden and the Government of the Republic of Argentina on the Promotion and Reciprocal Protection of Investments, (22 November 1991).

180 Art. 10 of the Romania and Sri Lanka Agreement on the Mutual Promotion and Guarantee of Investments, (9 February 1981).

181 The Energy Charter Treaty (ECT), (17 DEC 1994), Article 26(6).

NAFTA in this regard provides:

> "A tribunal established under this section shall decide the issues in dispute in accordance with this Agreement and applicable rules of international law."[182]

VIII) Implied choice of law

There is a great importance to answer this question whether in order to bind the arbitrator the agreement should result from an express clause or whether it can be implied from other indications. Much of the effectiveness of Article 42 depends on the respond to this question. In the absence of an explicit choice of law the tribunal may act in two ways. It may search to find the true intention of the parties or may treat that there is no agreement on applicable law at all. The attempt of the tribunals to identify the implicit choice of law shows the possibility of such an agreement.

The theory of implied choice of law has evolved given the fact that the parties do not always choose the applicable law explicitly but their choice of law could be perceived by certain actions, which envisage their intention to have their relationship regulated by a particular legal system. The most common example of this theory is the principle that the choice of arbitral seat implies the law of the seat as the applicable law. English, French and German courts have applied this view.[183] This approach is rooted in the notion of consent in arbitration on one hand. As generally consent is an important element in arbitration, arbitrators should identify it precisely. Since determining the applicable law is part of the arbitral proceedings, thus it establishes a part of the parties' consent, so the tribunal should attempt to identify the possible implicit agreements. On the other hand, the provisions incorporated in authorizing instruments rarely demand an explicit choice of law or even in writing.[184]

In ICSID arbitral proceedings, it is still an open question whether the choice of law by the parties must only be expressed or it may also be implicit. It has been said by the principal drafter of the ICSID Convention that the agreement of the parties on the issue of applicable law must be explicit in accordance with the first paragraph of Article 42.[185]

---

182 North American Free Trade Agreement (NAFTA), (1 Jan 1994), Article 1131(1).

183 Chukwumerije, Okezie, "Choice of Law in International Commercial Arbitration", Quorum Books, (1994), pp. 122–123.

184 Diehl, Alexandra, "The Core Standard of International Investment Protection-Fair and Equitable Treatment", Kluwer Law International, (2012), p. 270.

185 Broches, Aron, "Convention on the Settlement of Investment Disputes Between States and Nationals of Other States of 1965: Explanatory Notes and Survey of its

On the one hand, it has been argued that an insistence on an express agreement may lead a tribunal to not take the desirable choice of the parties into account. On the other hand, seeking an implicit agreement as a first step could lead to the imputation of an agreement where none was in reality formed,[186] and it is likely to undermine the residual rule of the second sentence of Article 42.[187]

Under this article, it has not been stated that the parties' agreement should be in writing or even that it should be stated expressly but one should bear in mind that the implicit choice of law, even accepted, should be clearly evidenced "with reasonable certainty" by the terms of the parties' contract or the circumstances of the case.[188] As clearly stated in the European Convention on the Law Applicable to Contractual Obligations (Rome Convention):

"A contract shall be governed by the law chosen by the parties. The choice must be expressed or demonstrated with reasonable certainty by the terms of the contract or the circumstances of the case."[189]

The Compañía del desarrollo de santa elena, *S.A v. The Republic of Costa Rica* would reflect this issue.[190]

In this case, the Claimant believes that, since there is no agreement on the applicable law governing the dispute, the second sentence of Article 42(1) should be applied. Thus it submits:

i) the Tribunal must apply the law of Costa Rica to the issues in dispute;
ii) rules of international law are to be applied only in the event of *lacuna* in Costa Rican law or if such law is inconsistent with the international law principles of good faith and *pacta sunt servanda.*

Application", Yearbook Commercial Arbitration, Kluwer Law International, (1993), Vol. 18

186 Shihata, Ibrahim F. I.; Parra, Antonio R., "Applicable substantive law in disputes between states and private foreign parties: the case of arbitration under the ICSID Convention", ICSID Review (1994), pp. 183–213.

187 Schreuer, Christoph, "The ICSID Convention: A Commentary", Cambridge University Press, Second Edition, (2009), p. 570

188 Shihata, Ibrahim F.I.; Parra, Antonio R., "Applicable substantive law in disputes between states and private foreign parties: the case of arbitration under the ICSID Convention", ICSID Review (1994), p. 190

189 Art. 3(1) of the European Convention on the Law Applicable to Contractual Obligations (Rome Convention), opened for signature on 19 June 1980.

190 Compañía Del Desarrollo de Santa Elena, S.A. v. The Republic of Costa Rica, Final Award, ICSID Case No. ARB/96/1, (17 February 2000).

iii) In the present case, there is no such inconsistency, with the result that the Tribunal should apply Costa Rican law. But the results would be the same if principles of international law were applied."[191]

Respondent contends that international law applies to the merits of the dispute by virtue of the parties' agreement to that effect. Even though the agreement, although not in writing nor even stated expressly, finds its sources, according to Respondent, in Costa Rica's 24 March 1995 consent to ICSID jurisdiction and Claimant's 15 May 1995 request for arbitration.[192]

Then it has referred to Article 42(1) of the ICSID Convention which does not require the parties' agreement to be reflecting the applicable law in writing or even that it shall be stated expressly.[193] However, for the Tribunal to find that such an agreement was implied, it had to begin with determining whether the substance of the agreement, irrespective of its form, is clear. After having reviewed and considered Respondent's oral and written argument on this question and analyzed the documents to which it has been referred, the Tribunal was not satisfied that the parties have ever reached a clear and unequivocal agreement based on which their dispute would be decided solely in accordance with international law.[194]

In addition, in the typical current international development agreements, the parties often do not clearly stipulate a certain legal systems but particular elements of the contractual provisions as a whole merely infer the parties' intention to connect the agreement to one system or to exclude the application of another.[195] Since these type of agreements are very common, if the interpretation of Article 42 always required an express manifestation of intent, in most cases the residual rule of Article 42 had to be applied, which is consequently the application of the law of the Contracting State.

191 Compañía Del Desarrollo de Santa Elena, S.A. v. The Republic of Costa Rica, Final Award, ICSID Case No. ARB/96/1, (17 February 2000), p. 190, para. 61.

192 Compañía Del Desarrollo de Santa Elena, S.A. v. The Republic of Costa Rica, Final Award, ICSID Case No. ARB/96/1, (17 February 2000), p. 190, para. 62.

193 Compañía Del Desarrollo de Santa Elena, S.A. v. The Republic of Costa Rica, Final Award, ICSID Case No. ARB/96/1, (17 February 2000), p. 190, para. 63.

194 Compañía Del Desarrollo de Santa Elena, S.A. v. The Republic of Costa Rica, Final Award, ICSID Case No. ARB/96/1, (17 February 2000), p. 190, para. 63.

195 Kahn, Phillipe, "The Law Applicable to Foreign Investments: The Contribution of the World Bank Convention on The Settlement of Investment Disputes", Indiana Law Journal, Vol. 44, No. 1, (1968), p. 8.

ICSID Convention did not clearly stipulate how the parties should express their choice of law. Bearing in mind that the substantive law of investment is controversial and uncertain and so are the factors that may lead to its application. It could be an explanation with much more precision regarding this issue. As we can see such an explanation was made in 1964 Uniform Law Convention on the International Sale of Goods. During the drafting phase of this Convention, the question arose whether the buyer could choose a legal system other than that instituted by the Convention, and if so, in what manner the choice should be stipulated. During the preparation of the Convention's preliminary draft it was proposed that the parties should be able to exclude application of the uniform law provided they are quoted in the contract of the foreign rules agreed upon or indicates precisely. It was also stated that the reference should be expressly stipulated by a clause or clearly distinguishable from the provisions of the contract. This was the system adopted by the Hague Convention of 15 June 1955 on the law applicable to international sales.[196] The next version rejected the earlier view and permits it to be either explicit or implicit.[197] This evolution could clearly reveal the effect of the unambiguous setting of rules on this matter. Therefore, as Kahn well pointed out, "It can only be regretted that the drafters of the Convention on the Settlement of Investment Disputes did not indicate with greater precision how the parties should express their choice of law."[198]

There are some methods, however, to distinguish and eventually clarify the implicit agreements on choice of law, the applicability of which we analyze through the following section.

---

196 Article 2 of the Convention on the Law Applicable to International Sales of Goods (1955):

"A sale shall be governed by the domestic law of the country designated by the Contracting Parties.

Such designation must be contained in an express clause, or unambiguously result from the provisions of the contract.

Conditions affecting the consent of the parties to the law declared applicable shall be determined by such law."

197 Article 3 of the Uniform Law on the International Sale of Goods (1964):
"The parties to a contract of sale shall be free to exclude the application of the present law either entirely or partially. Such exclusion may be express or implied."

198 Kahn, Phillipe, "The Law Applicable to Foreign Investments: The Contribution of the World Bank Convention on The Settlement of Investment Disputes", Indiana Law Journal, Vol. 44, No. 1, (1968), p. 10.

1) Reference to international arbitration

Where the parties agree to refer their dispute to an international arbitration, they also implicitly agree that their dispute will be resolved by the international law as the applicable substantive law. Investment arbitration genuinely has an international character given the parties coming from different states. However, any dispute between the nationals of different states even in the national courts is tend to have this character but no one would think of international law as the law applicable. At the same time, investment disputes have a public character because of the role of sovereign states but no one questions the applicability of private law rules in such disputes. Therefore, the choice of international arbitration for settling the investment disputes would not be assumed as an exact agreement of applying the international law.[199]

2) Choice of the place of arbitration

An argument would be that the choice of the place of arbitration leads not only to the choice of the procedural law but also to the applicable substantive law. However, this is not the case in ICSID arbitration because the ICSID Convention has clearly pointed out that the choice of the place of arbitration has no impact on the proceedings. As mentioned before, the ICSID system is a self-contained and delocalized system with no reliance on the place of arbitration.

In non-ICSID arbitrations, however, the place of arbitration influences on the proceedings. For instance, in the case of ICC or ICSID Additional Facility Arbitration, any mandatory provisions of the law that govern the arbitration are to be taken into account. The only exception is where the State party has a right to expect immunity from the jurisdiction of domestic courts at the seat of the arbitration.

Therefore, in general, we should note that the choice of the place of arbitration could not be considered as an automatic implicit choice of law.

3) Choice of law by reference to domestic legislation

As mentioned above, sometimes the national investment laws providing for ICSID's jurisdiction contain a provision on the applicable law. The acceptance of the offer to jurisdiction by the investor could include that provision. But solely

199 Diehl, Alexandra, "The Core Standard of International Investment Protection-Fair and Equitable Treatment", Kluwer Law International, (2012), p. 271.

a reference to a part of the domestic legal system could not be taken as general. The arbitral tribunal could not find it a sufficient evidence to apply a system of law entirely because such references do not show the intention of the parties to choose an entire legal system as applicable law to their relationship.

4) Parties' submissions and the circumstances of the case

In the submissions of the parties during the arbitral proceedings they may imply a choice of law, which shows their intention for that law as the law governing to their relationship. Moreover, the terms of the contract and the circumstances of the case could lead the tribunal to find the implicit choice of law. While discussing the corrective role of international law in previous parts, we went through some aspects of the LETCO case.[200] This case is of great importance also in analyzing of the practice of tribunals to identify an implicit choice of law out of the terms of the contract. This ICSID case is arisen from the revocation of Libya of the concession Agreement of 1970 before the expiration date of the Agreement. At the first paragraph of the Agreement was stated that it was made under the General Business Law, Title 15 of the Liberian Code of Laws of 1956.

The parties weren't agreed upon whether they have an explicit choice of law or not. At one time, Claimant expressed that there had been no explicit choice of law; therefore, the international law should apply in accordance with the second sentence of the Article 42 of the ICSID Convention. But later it stated that the Liberian law was probably applicable.

The tribunal consequently stated that there is no doubt on the application of the Liberian law. This phrase was based on the first paragraph of the agreement, which refers to a part of the Liberian law and not the Liberian law in general. So in this case, the tribunal assumed Liberian law as the law applicable just because of a single reference to a domestic law statute and saw it as an implicit choice of law.

Tribunals have sometime identified the implied choice of law from the parties' submissions during the proceedings. Submissions of the parties could be taken as an implied choice of law on itself, but sometimes it is just a confirmation for the choice that the tribunal has made through its own determination.

200 See LETCO (Liberian Eastern Timber Corporation) v. Republic of Liberia, Award, ICSID Case No. ARB/83/2, (31 March 1986).

a) Choice of law derived from parties' submissions

When the parties argue their case before a tribunal on the basis of a particular law, even though they had not agreed on that law, the tribunal could perceive it as an implied choice of law agreed by the parties.[201]

This issue is envisaged in *AAPL v. Sri Lanka Case.*[202] In this case, which is also referred to as "Prawn Farm Case". Asian Agriculture Company was a shareholder in a Sri Lankan company. The case was arisen pursuant to the destruction of the Serendib shrimp farm by Sri Lankan Security Forces. The dispute was brought to ICSID under the provisions of the Sri Lanka-UK BIT.[203] The treaty did not contain a choice of law clause. Therefore, the Tribunal concluded that the parties were given no opportunity to exercise their right to choose the governing law with respect to different aspects of their future disputes in advance.[204]

The Tribunal added: "Under these special circumstances, the choice-of-law process would normally materialize after the emergence of the dispute, by observing and construing the conduct of the Parties throughout the arbitration proceedings."[205]

On one hand, AAPL argued that the Sri Lanka-UK BIT "should be considered tantamount to" an agreement between the two parties as to the applicable rules of law, within the context of Article 42 of the ICSID Convention.[206] In addition, the Claimant believes in the applicability of customary international law rules.[207]

---

201 Silberman, Linda; Ferrari, Franco, "Getting to the Law Applicable to the Merits in International Arbitration and the Consequences of Getting It Wrong", Conflict of Laws in International Arbitration, Vol. 7, (2010), pp. 73–12.

202 Asian Agricultural Products LTD. (AAPL) v. Republic of Sri Lanka, Award, ICSID Case No. ARB/87/3, (27 June 1990).

203 Agreement between the Government of the United Kingdom of Great Britain and Northern Ireland and the Government of the Democratic Socialist Republic of Sri Lanka for the Promotion and Protection of Investments, (13 February 1980).

204 Asian Agricultural Products LTD. (AAPL) v. Republic of Sri Lanka, Award, ICSID Case No. ARB/87/3, (27 June 1990), para. 19.

205 Asian Agricultural Products LTD. (AAPL) v. Republic of Sri Lanka, Award, ICSID Case No. ARB/87/3, (27 June 1990), para. 20.

206 Asian Agricultural Products LTD. (AAPL) v. Republic of Sri Lanka, Award, ICSID Case No. ARB/87/3, (27 June 1990), ICSID Review-Foreign Investment Law Journal, Vol. 6, (1991), p. 529, para. 9.

207 Asian Agricultural Products LTD. (AAPL) v. Republic of Sri Lanka, Award, ICSID Case No. ARB/87/3, (27 June 1990), ICSID Review-Foreign Investment Law Journal, Vol. 6, (1991), p. 533, para. 23.

On the other hand, the Respondent is of the opinion that the Sri Lankan law was the law applicable to the dispute and the application of the BIT as the source of the governing law was only permitted to the extent that it had been incorporated into the Sri Lankan law.

The tribunal held that the parties' acts reflect their mutual consent to consider the Sri Lanka-UK BIT as the primary source for applicable law.[208]

When the parties have not chosen the applicable law to their relationship, but in their submissions have referred constantly to a particular law then from the view of the majority of the tribunal this manner could be taken as an implicit choice of law.

However, sometimes it may undermine the second sentence of Article 42(1) and the application of the host state and international law. This approach could be seen in the dissenting opinion of Samuel K. B. Asante.[209] He states that the argument of the Claimant that considers the mutual submission to the S.L.-U.K Treaty as tantamount to the agreement envisaged in Article 42 is superficially attractive but not acceptable. He emphasizes the distinction between jurisdiction and the issues concerning applicable law.[210] The parties have submitted the case to the jurisdiction of ICSID tribunal but this fact would not imply that they have agreed on the applicable law.

The first part of the dissenting opinion based on the explanation of Bowett reads as follows:

> "Prima facie an arbitration clause affects jurisdiction, not choice of law, and there is no inherent reason why arbitrators should not apply the local law. Such an inference as to the displacement of the local law can only properly be drawn in those cases where the arbitration tribunal must be assumed to be applying international law. Thus, choice of arbitration under the World Bank Convention on the Settlement of Disputes 1965 would involve the application of Article 42(1) of the Convention by the parties, to apply the law of international law as may be applicable."[211]

---

208 Asian Agricultural Products LTD. (AAPL) v. Republic of Sri Lanka, Award, ICSID Case No. ARB/87/3, 27 June 1990, ICSID Review-Foreign Investment Law Journal, Vol. 6, (1991), p. 533, para. 20.

209 AAPL v. Sri Lanka, Dissenting Opinion of Samuel K.B. Asante, ICSID Case No. ARB/87/3, ICSID Review-Foreign Investment Law Journal, Vol. 6(2), (1991).

210 For a general view of the relation of jurisdiction and applicable law see: Schreuer, Christoph, "Jurisdiction and Applicable Law in Investment Treaty Arbitration", McGill Journal of Dispute Resolution, (2014), Vol. Issue. 1.

211 Bowett, Derek W., "State Contracts with Aliens", British Yearbook of International Law, Vol. 59, (1988), p. 49.

He further argues that the parties to this dispute are not the same as the parties to the S.L.-U.K. Treaty. If they want to invoke the provisions of this treaty as the applicable law, they have to show that either the treaty authorized it or the parties have expressly agreed that the provisions of the treaty are their choice of law.

Then he explains another reason based on which the decision of the tribunal seems to be unconvincing.

> "... In adversarial proceedings such as those before this Tribunal, it is usually the best interest of each party to respond to all the substantive legal points raised by the other. Thus, where points of substance based on the Treaty were advanced by the Claimant, it was to be expected that the Respondent would address those particular points and vice versa; for the party which ignores this course of action may find ultimately that it has lost the opportunity to present its views on individual issues to the Tribunal."[212]

Therefore, he concludes that there was no real agreement between the parties on the issue of applicable law and the Tribunal according to the second sentence of Article 42(1) should have applied the Sri Lankan law and international law and according to article 157 of the Constitution of Sri Lanka,[213] the provisions of treaty are incorporated into the Sri Lankan law.

With respect to submissions of parties as a proof of implicit choice of law, we will take a look at *Wena Hotels Ltd. v. Arab Republic of Egypt* case.[214]

The dispute arose out of long-term agreements between Wena Hotels and the Egyptian Hotels Company (EHC), which is an Egyptian public sector company to lease and develop two hotels in Luxor and Cairo, Egypt.

---

212 AAPL v. Sri Lanka, Dissenting Opinion of Samuel K.B. Asante, ICSID Case No. ARB/87/3, ICSID Review-Foreign Investment Law Journal, Vol. 6(2), (1991), The Applicable Law.

213 Article 157 of the Constitution of Sri Lanka: "Where Parliament by resolution passed by not less than two-thirds of the whole number of Members of Parliament (including those not present) voting in its favor, approves as being essential for the development of the national economy, any Treaty or Agreement between the Government of Sri Lanka and the Government of any foreign State for the promotion and protection of the investments in Sri Lanka of such foreign State, its nationals, or of corporations, companies and other associations incorporated or constitutes under its laws, such Treaty or Agreement shall have the force of law in Sri Lanka, and otherwise than the interests of national security no written law shall be enacted or made, and no executive or administrative action shall be taken, in contravention of the provisions of such Treaty or Agreement."

214 Wena Hotels Limited v. Arab Republic of Egypt, Award, ICSID Case No. ARB/98/4, (8 December 2000).

ICSID jurisdiction was established under the Egypt-UK BIT.[215] So this case turns on an alleged violation by the Arab Republic of Egypt of the agreement for the promotion and protection of investments (IPPA) that was entered into in 1976 between the United Kingdom and the Arab Republic of Egypt. Under Article 2(1) of the IPPA, Egypt and the United Kingdom promise to "encourage and create favorable conditions for nationals or companies of other Contracting Party to invest capital in its territory."[216] Additionally, they guaranteed that investments of national or companies of either Contracting Party shall at all times be accorded fair and equitable treatment and they shall enjoy full protection and security in the territory of the other Contracting Party. Moreover, Egypt and the United Kingdom agreed "investments of nationals or companies of either Contracting Party shall not be nationalized, expropriated or subjected to measures having effect equivalent to nationalization or expropriation…in the territory of the other Contracting Party except for a public purpose related to the internal needs of the Party and against prompt, adequate and effective compensation."[217]

On 8 August 1989, Wena and EHC, entered into a 21 year, 6 month "Lease and Development Agreement" for the Luxor Hotel in Luxor, Egypt. According to this agreement, Wena should operate and manage the Hotel exclusively for the original or extended period of the Lease, to develop specification of the Egyptian Ministry of Tourism or upgrade it to a five-star hotel if Wena so elects. The agreement also provided that EHC shall not interfere in management and/or operation of the Hotel or interfere with the enjoyment of the lease by Wena and that disputes between the parties should be settled through arbitration. One year later, Wena and EHC entered into another almost identical, 25-year agreement for the El Nile Hotel in Cairo, Egypt.[218]

The dispute arose shortly after entering into these agreements, when Claimant, Wena Hotels Limited, filed a request against Respondent, the Arab Republic of

---

215 Agreement between the Government of the United Kingdom of Great Britain and Northern Ireland and the Government of the Arab Republic of Egypt for the Promotion and Protection of Investments, (11 June 1975), entered into force on 24 February 1976.

216 Wena Hotels Limited v. Arab Republic of Egypt, Award, ICSID Case No. ARB/98/4, (8 December 2000), Part. II. A. 16.

217 Wena Hotels Limited v. Arab Republic of Egypt, Award, ICSID Case No. ARB/98/4, (8 December 2000), Part. II. A. 16.

218 Wena Hotels Limited v. Arab Republic of Egypt, Award, ICSID Case No. ARB/98/4, (8 December 2000), Part. II. B. 18.

Egypt, and claimed that it has suffered enormous losses leading to the almost total collapse of its business because of Egypt's expropriation and failure to protect Wena's investment in Egypt.[219] As EHC seized the two hotels and placed them under its own management, Wena claimed that the expropriation was without providing prompt, adequate and effective compensation, and by failing to accord Wena's investments in Egypt fair and equitable treatment and full protection and security.[220] In turn, Egypt claimed that Wena failed to pay rent to EHC and EHC in return liquidated the performance security posted by Claimant.

Initially, the tribunal had to consider the applicable law governing the case. The tribunal firstly mentioned that both parties agreed that the case concerned an alleged violation of the BIT by Egypt. Subsequently, based on the parties' submissions the tribunal concluded that the BIT (IPPA) is the primary source of applicable law for this arbitration.

The tribunal stated that "However, the IPPA is a fairly terse agreement of only seven pages containing thirteen articles. The parties in their arguments have not treated it as containing all the rules of law applicable to their dispute, and this is also the view of the Tribunal. In particular, Egypt has relied on Egyptian law, namely, the Egyptian Code to raise its first defense—that Wena's claims are time barred. In its response to that defense, Wena has taken the position that both Egyptian law and international law are applicable to the dispute."[221]

Then the tribunal refers to Article 42(1) of the ICSID Convention and mentioned that there are no other agreements than the provisions of IPPA between the parties on the rules of law applicable to the dispute. But, the pleadings of both parties indicate that, aside from the provisions of the IPPA, the tribunal should apply both Egyptian law (i.e., "the law of the Contracting State party to the dispute") and "such rules of international law as may be applicable." The Tribunal pointed out that the provisions of the IPPA would in any event be the first rules of law to be applied by the Tribunal, both on the basis of the agreements of the parties and as mandated by Egyptian law as well as international law.

After determining the applicable law, the Tribunal began to examine the merits of the case. As noted before, Wena raised two claims against Egypt. At first, it claims that Egypt's actions constitute an unlawful expropriation without

---

219 Wena Hotels Limited v. Arab Republic of Egypt, Award, ICSID Case No. ARB/98/4, (8 December 2000), Part. I. 1

220 Wena Hotels Limited v. Arab Republic of Egypt, Award, ICSID Case No. ARB/98/4 (8 December 2000),, Part. II. B. 17.

221 Wena Hotels Limited v. Arab Republic of Egypt, Award, ICSID Case No. ARB/98/4, (8 December 2000), Part. III. A. 79.

"prompt, adequate and effective" compensation, which is at odds with Article 5 of the IPPA, as well as Egyptian law and other international law. Then, Wena argued that Egypt has violated Article 2(2)[222] of the IPPA, and other international norms, when it failed to accord Wena's investments "fair and equitable treatment" and "full protection and security".

In turn, Egypt denied both allegations, contending "that the Claimant has no legitimate grievance against the Respondent, who neither authorized nor participated in the repossession of the Luxor and Nile Hotels on April 1, 1991 or most of the subsequent events of which the Claimant complains."

Tribunal disagrees the Respondent since in the view of the Tribunal, "There is substantial evidence that, even if Egyptian officials other than officials of EHC did not participate in the seizures of the hotels on April 1, 1991, 1) Egypt was aware of EHC's intentions to seize the hotels and did nothing to prevent those seizures, 2) the police, although responding to the seizures, did nothing to protect Wena's investments; 3) for almost one year, Egypt (despite its control over EHC both before and after April 1, 1991) did nothing to restore the hotels to Wena; 4) Egypt failed to prevent damage to the hotels before their return to Wena; 5) Egypt failed to impose any substantial sanctions on EHC (or its senior officials responsible for the seizures), suggesting its approval of EHC's actions; and 6) Egypt refused to compensate Wena for the losses it suffered."[223]

After long discussions, the Tribunal compelled the conclusion that according to Article 2(2) of the IPPA Egypt has violated its obligation and consequently has failed to accord Wena's investments "fair and equitable treatment" and "full protection and security".

Regarding the Claimant's second contention on the matter of expropriation without "prompt, adequate and effective" compensation, the Tribunal also agrees with Wena and recognizes it as a violation of Article 5 of the IPPA.[224] Then the

---

222 Article 2(2) of the IPPA: "Investments of nationals or companies of either Contracting Party shall at all time be accorded fair and equitable treatment and shall enjoy full protection and security in the territory of the other Contracting Party. Each Contracting Party shall ensure that the management, maintenance, use, enjoyment or disposal of investments in its territory of nationals or companies of the other Contracting Party is not in any way impaired by unreasonable or discriminatory measures. Each Contracting Party shall observe any obligation it may have entered into with regard to investments of nationals or companies of the other Contracting party."

223 Wena Hotels Limited v. Arab Republic of Egypt, Award, ICSID Case No. ARB/98/4, Part. III. A. 79, (8 December 2000).

224 Article 5(1) of the IPPA: "Investments of nationals or companies of either Contracting Party shall not be nationalized, expropriated or subjected to measures having effect

Tribunal refers to the cases and writings to demonstrate the principles of constitution of an expropriation under international law. As well as in ICSID tribunals, Chamber two of the Iran-US Claims Tribunal observed in the Tippets case that "deprivation or taking of property may occur under international law through interference by a state in the use of that property or with the enjoyment of its benefits, even where legal title to the property is not affected."[225]

Against this background, the Tribunal concluded that Egypt also violated its obligation under Article 5 of the IPPA, by failing to provide Wena with "prompt, adequate and effective compensation" for the losses it suffered as a result of the seizures of the Luxor and Nile Hotel.

After examining the Claimant's contentions, the Tribunal began to discuss the Respondent's claims. Egypt argued that Wena's claims are time barred under Article 172(i) of the Egyptian Civil Code.[226] Moreover, it contends that if Egyptian law is not to be applied, it would be reasonable to take into account the principles common to both of the Contracting Parties to the IPPA, that is, in this case, the United Kingdom and noted that the statute of limitation, under the English Limitation Act 1980, for breach of Contract or tortious behavior is six years.[227] But the Tribunal believed that there was "no legal or equitable reason to bar Wena's claim" and noted that the "municipal statutes of limitation do not

---

equivalent to nationalization or expropriation (hereinafter referred to as 'expropriation') in the territory of the other Contracting Party except for a public purpose related to the internal needs of the Party and against prompt, adequate and effective compensation. Such compensation shall amount to the market value of the investment expropriated immediately before the expropriation itself or before there was an official Government announcement that expropriation would be effected in the future, whichever is the earlier, shall be made without delay, be effectively realizable and be freely transferable. The national or company affected shall have a right under the law of the Contracting Party making the expropriation to prompt review, by a judicial or other independent authority of that Party, of whether the expropriation is in conformity with domestic law and of the valuation of his or its investment in accordance with the principles set out in this paragraph."

225 Tippets, Abbett, McCarthy, Stratton v. TAMS-AFFA Consenting Engineers of Iran et al., Iran-U.S. Claims Tribunal, Award No. 141-7-2, (22 June 1984), p. 225.

226 Article 172)(i) of the Egyptian Civil Code: "A case filed for damages claimed for an illegal act fall by prescription by lapse of three years from the day the wronged person learns of the damage taking place and of the person who is responsible for it, in all events the case shall fall with the lapse of 15 years from the day the illegal act takes place."

227 Wena Hotels Limited v. Arab Republic of Egypt, Award, ICSID Case No. ARB/98/4, Part III. B. 100, (8 December 2000).

necessarily bind a claim for a violation of an international treaty before an international tribunal."[228] The Tribunal discussed that this principle is recognized a long time ago according to international precedents.

Another issue upon which the Tribunal was not agreed was the argument of Egypt which provided that Article 42(1) of the ICSID Convention mandates that the Tribunal must apply Article 172(i)'s three-year statute of limitation. The second sentence of Article 42(1) provides that a tribunal shall apply domestic law "and such rules of international law as may be applicable." Wena had correctly noted before the decision of the Tribunal in the Amco Asia case explained that situation, where a tribunal should apply rules of international law, namely when the regulatory feature of international law plays a role and tends to protect the international law norms when they are not in line with such norms. As explained, it was also an identical situation in this case in which application of Article 172(i)'s three-year limit, even if applicable, would collide with a general and well-recognized international principle.[229]

Additionally, as mentioned before, the Tribunal pointed out that the principal source of substantive law is the IPPA itself and even though the IPPA's provisions do not contain detailed procedure for bringing an arbitration, article 8(1) expressly provides that if a dispute should arise and agreement cannot be reached within three months between the parties to this dispute through pursuit of local remedies, through conciliation or otherwise, then, may a party institute ICSID proceedings.[230] Therefore, the Tribunal concluded that Wena's claim was not time barred.

Studying this case compels the conclusion that the Tribunal discovers an implied agreement on the BIT as the primary source of law and accepts it as a legitimate choice of law. Moreover, based on the parties' submissions, host state's law and international law are also to be applied. The more complex issue here is to clarify whether the tribunal base its analyze on the first or the second part of the Article 42(1). It shall be taken into account that the implicit choice of law is still a choice of law and lies under the first sentence of the Article 42(1), while the second sentence of this article namely the application of the

228 Wena Hotels Limited v. Arab Republic of Egypt, Award, ICSID Case No. ARB/98/4, Part III. B. 106, (8 December 2000).

229 Wena Hotels Limited v. Arab Republic of Egypt, Award, ICSID Case No. ARB/98/4, Part III. B. 106–107, (8 December 2000).

230 Wena Hotels Limited v. Arab Republic of Egypt, Award, ICSID Case No. ARB/98/4, Part III. B. 108, (8 December 2000).

international law applies when there is no agreement either explicit or implicit on the applicable law.

b) Parties' submissions as confirmation of the chosen law

In other situations, the Tribunal may reach an independent decision while using parties' submissions as a confirmation of its own determination.

As already described before in the case of *Amco v. Indonesia*, the Tribunal found that, since the parties had not expressed an agreement as to rules of applicable law, Indonesian law as well as rules of international law were to be applied. The Tribunal found confirmation for this finding in the fact that both parties had not just failed to deny the applicability of these two systems of law but had, in fact, constantly referred to both of them.

IX) Stabilization clauses

One of the most important questions in the field of contemporary international investment is how to balance between the competing needs of making a reasonable policy space for host states and giving foreign investors the ability to plan their operations in advance. These points show the significant tension between flexibility and predictability in international investment relations, in other words the states' need of regulating flexibility and the investors' need for legal predictability. Foreign investors should know and plan their further steps in advance but unexpected changes in the domestic law of the host state could gravely affect their operations and moreover could frustrate their expectations. International investment law has recognized the importance of predictability for the foreign investors.

The ICSID tribunal has referred to Max Weber and provided that:

"In an effort to develop an operational method for determining the existence on non-existence of fair and equitable treatment, arbitral tribunals have increasingly taken into account the legitimate expectations that a host country has created in the investor and the extent to which conduct by the host government subsequent to the investment has frustrated those expectations. When an investor undertakes an investment, a host government through its laws, regulations, declared policies and statements creates in the investor certain expectations about the nature of the treatment that it may anticipate from the host state. The resulting reasonable and legitimate expectations are important factors that influence initial investment decisions and afterwards the manner in which the investment is to be managed. The theoretical basis of this approach no doubt is found in the work of the eminent scholar Max Weber, who advanced the idea that one of the main contributions of law to any social system is to make economic life more calculable and also argued that capitalism arise in Europe because European law demonstrated a high degree of calculability."[231]

At the same time, governments should be able to react to the constantly changing circumstances in both domestic and international environments. Moreover, imposing limitations on the freedom of the host states could extremely undermine their ability to fulfill their fundamental commitment to develop the general situation of their inhabitants.[232] Therefore, this is not only the right of the governments to regulate their affairs but also it's a duty of them. Tribunals have also recognized the legitimate right of the host state to pass legislation. For example, the Tribunal in the *Perkerings v. Lithuania* award held that:

> "It is each State's undeniable right and privilege to exercise its sovereign legislative power. A State has the right to enact, modify or cancel a law as its own discretion."[233]

The tribunals have tried to reach the balance between those needs. Thus, again the Tribunal in *Suez v. Argentina* case stated:

> "Thus in interpreting the meaning of fair and equitable treatment to be accorded to investors, the Tribunal must balance the legitimate and reasonable expectations of the Claimants with Argentina's right to regulate the provision of vital public service."[234]

In this section, we will see to what extent these contradictory needs can go hand in hand.

1) Stabilization clause and the risk of subsequent changes in law

Once parties opt for the law of the host state as applicable law, there would always come to an issue if that State subsequently changes its laws, and those changes may adversely affect the legal terms of the relationship. Subsequent changes in

---

231 Suez, Sociedad General de Aguas de Barcelona S.A., and Vivendi Universal S.A. v. The Argentine Republic, Decision on Liability, ICSID Case No. ARB/03/19, (30 July 2010), para. 222.

232 Hirsh, Moshe, "Between Fair and Equitable Treatment and Stabilization Clause: Stable Legal Environment and Regulatory Change in International Investment Law", Journal of World Investment & Trade, Vol. 12, Issue. 6, (2011), p. 783.

233 Perkerings-Compagniet AS v. Republic of Lithuania, Award, ICSID Case No. ARB/05/8, (11 September 2007), para. 332.

234 Suez, Sociedad General de Aguas de Barcelona S.A., and Vivendi Universal S.A. v. The Argentine Republic, Decision on Liability, ICSID Case No. ARB/03/19, (30 July 2010), para. 236.

the applicable law may have a severe impact on the investment and may go as far as the termination of the contract and the expropriation of the investor's property.

Not only the changes in the applicable law but also changes in domestic regulations such as changes in taxation, environmental standards, and minimum wages may also have a strong impact on the investment relationships.

However, investors could shield themselves against these alterations by inserting a stabilization clause within the investment contract. The State may still change the law, but this clause establishes a promise not to apply any adverse changes to the investor's operations or a promise to compensate the investor for any extreme consequences of such a change. In other words, the law becomes frozen from the investor's perspective at the time of the contract.

The aim of the stabilization clauses is to make the regulatory changes inapplicable to the certain investment projects, otherwise the investor should be compensated for the cost of compliance with them.[235]

There is no precise legal definition of stabilization clauses and the effects thereof. Based on one view, any changes of the law applicable to the contract will be a violation of a stabilization clause, while the other view which protects the sovereignty of the state contends that any change is allowed but will be accompanied by a duty to compensate the investor.[236]

The stabilization clauses are more common in long-term investments in the extractive industries and also in private contracts for public infrastructure. The most important point of the stabilization clause is the removal of the government's right to unilaterally change the investor's rights by changing its municipal law.

The concession contract between the parties in *Liamco v. Libya* sets a good example of a stabilization clause. It states as follows:

> "The Government of Libya, the Commission and the appropriate provincial authorities will take all steps necessary to ensure that the Company enjoys all the rights conferred by this Concession. The contractual rights expressly created by this Concession shall not be altered except by mutual consent of the parties.
>
> This Concession shall throughout the period of its validity be construed in accordance with the Petroleum Law and the Regulations in force on the date of execution of the Agreement of Amendment by which this paragraph was incorporated into this

235 Hirsh, Moshe, "Between Fair and Equitable Treatment and Stabilization Clause: Stable Legal Environment and Regulatory Change in International Investment Law", Journal of World Investment & Trade, Vol. 12, Issue. 6, (2011), p. 787.

236 Dolzer, Rudolf; Schreuer, Christoph, "Principles of International Investment Law", Oxford University Press, (2008), p. 75.

> Concession Agreement. Any amendment to or repeal of such Regulations shall not affect the contractual rights of the Company without its consent."[237]

The first paragraph states that mutual consent of the parties is required to change the contractual rights secured by concession and the second paragraph makes clear that the municipal law is fixed as of a certain date, therefore, subsequent legislation cannot unilaterally infringe upon the company's contractual rights.[238]

Another example of the stabilization clause, which has been addressed in the ICSID award in the *Duke v. Peru* case, provides:

> "Three- By virtue of this Agreement, the STATE, and as long as it remains in effect, in connection with the investment referred in clause two, the STATE guarantees legal stability for Duke Energy International, according to the following terms:
> Stability of the tax regime with respect to the Income Tax, as stipulated in … of Article 10 of Legislative Decree No. 662 …Neither the remittances sent abroad of amounts corresponding to Duke Energy International for any of the items contemplated in this subsection are taxed pursuant to the aforementioned law…."[239]

This case the stabilization clause targets domestic regulations, namely the taxation system.

Atlantic v. Triton provides also a stabilization clause. In this case, the applicability of the host state's law was also subject to stabilization clause. Article 14 of their Agreement provides:

> "The term 'law' in the present Agreement refers to Guinean law. However, Guinean law will be applicable only insofar as it is not incompatible with the terms of the present Agreement, and where it is not more restrictive than the law in force at the date of entry into force of the present Agreement."[240]

There are two basic types of stabilization clauses namely, Freezing clauses and Economic equilibrium clauses. The freezing clause functions exactly as its title

---

237 Libyan American Oil Company (LIAMCO) v. Government of Libyan Arab Republic, Award, (1977).

238 Comeaux, Paul E.; Kinsella, N. Stephen, "Reducing Political Risk in Developing Countries: Bilateral Investment Treaties, Stabilization Clauses, and MIGA & OPIC Investment Insurance", New York Law School Journal of International and Comparative Law, Vol. 15, (1994), p. 24.

239 Clause Three of the DEI Bermuda LSA cited in Duke Energy International Peru Investments No. 1, LTD. v. Republic of Peru, Decision on Jurisdiction, ICSID Case No. ARB/03/28, (1 February 2006), para. 85.

240 Atlantic Triton Company Limited v. People's Revolutionary Republic of Guinea, ICSID Case No. ARB/84/1, Award, (21 April 1986), under part II section 2: The Management Agreement of 12 August 1981.

implies. It freezes the law at the time period of the investment project. There are few methods to stabilize a contract. First method is by incorporating the State law into the contract and freezing it as of a stipulated date. In other words, the law becomes part of the contract. Second method is freezing the contract by stipulating that any further legislation or regulation cannot materially affect the rights and obligations of the parties in relation to the investment. Any further changes may only be allowed through a mutual agreement between the host state and the investor. Third type of freezing stabilization clauses are identified by a provision stating that any further legislation or alteration should be inapplicable in case of its inconsistency with the contract. It is inapplicable even where the subsequent laws are not necessarily inconsistent but it has a grave effect on the contract.[241]

The second type of stabilization clause is divided into two varieties itself. A rigid equilibrium clause permits changes in the law but the host state should indemnify the investor for its compliance with the new legislation. Under a more flexible version of equilibrium clause or a negotiating clause, the host state and the investor will commit to conducting future negotiations with the ultimate aim of adjusting the allocation of risks or losses/gains, based on the altered version of the regulatory rules.[242]

There is no consensus on the success and effectiveness of these provisions but some scholars suggest the idea of replacing freezing clauses with negotiation clauses. The point is that it seems not to be a significant difference between the final effects of these varieties. While freezing clauses prevent the changes to affect the investors and their project by preventing states from applying the new laws, negotiation clauses allow the changes but the host state has the obligation to compensate the effects on the investor. Moreover, there is no need for the investor to demonstrate the existence of faults or expropriations or any other kind of taking in order to be compensated. Still many of the negotiation clauses are not fully effective and they only establish a constant payment routine for the host state.[243]

241 Chukwumerije, Okezie, "Choice of Law in International Commercial Arbitration", Quorum Books, (1994), pp. 144–145.

242 Nelson, Annalise, "Investments in the deep freeze? Stabilization clauses in investment contracts", Kluwer Arbitration Blog, (2011).

243 Martin, Antoine P., "Stability in Contemporary Investment Law: Reconsidering the Role and Shape of Contractual Commitments in Light of Recent Trends", Manchester Journal of International Economic Law, Vol. 10, Issue. 1, (2013), p. 40.

2) Non-comprehensive stabilization clauses

Stabilization clauses need not to be always comprehensive and general. They may only cover one specific area, for example, a "no further tax" clause in *Kaiser Bauxite Company v. Jamaica or Revere Copper* case.[244]

In this case, which arose from a concession agreement for the mining of bauxite by a subsidiary of the Revere Copper company with the government of Jamaica, there was a stabilization clause which stated that taxes and other financial liabilities on the part of the foreign company would remain as agreed for the duration of the company.

3) Absence of stabilization clauses

When there is not any stabilization clause incorporated in the contract, the chosen law will be applied normally and consequently normal changes in the host state's regulatory system will also be applied to the investment relationships. For example, changes of labor law and normal adjustments in the field of taxation and so on.

However, changes that reflect the will of defeating previous undertakings are contrary to international law. If the changes result in a situation under which the investor could no longer operate, they will become inapplicable, since the host state's freedom to legislate is limited by the minimum standards of protection mandated by international law.

In fact, after a long debate during the drafting phase of the Convention, reference to international law finally became one of the drafters' solutions for cases, in which a State would change its law. Even though there were initially some views, under which some governments did not wish for international law to be applied, the vote in the legal committee was clearly in favor of such application. It was one of the main reasons of the delegates, who were in favor of the application of international law and not merely national law. It is however quite logical that in such cases, where a State has changed its law, international law merely applies. In other words, international law could not question the act of legislation in that State or try to undo it, but can recognize the liability of that State. This issue was also stated in a clear language in the memorandum of the meeting of the committee of the whole, which reads as follows:

> "As to the issue national versus international law, the vote in the Legal Committee had been very clearly in favor of permitting the tribunal to apply international law

---

244 Revere Copper and Brass Inc. v. Overseas Private Investment Corporation, AAA, Award, (24 August 1978).

particularly in order to take account of cases where a State changes its own law to the detriment of an investor and in violation of an agreement not to do so. In such a case international law would not question the power of the sovereign State to change its law, but could hold that State liable in damages to the investor whose rights it had violated through an act inconsistent with international law."[245]

X) Absence of agreement on the applicable law

Arbitral practice has shown that in numerous cases, there was no choice of law provision in arbitrations based on a bilateral investment treaty. In many cases, the parties have made no choice of law in respect of the merits of the dispute.[246] There could be many reasons in connection with lack of parties' choice of law. Though it should not be necessarily attributed to the carelessness of parties since they sometimes willingly choose to not mention the applicable law at all.[247] It would be easily imaginable that at a particular time they could not agree on certain laws or merely believed that the arbitral Tribunal would be best qualified to deal with the question of applicable law.[248] Since the parties come from different countries with divergent economic and political backgrounds, it may be not an easy task to come up with a mutual choice regarding applicable law and eventually they may prefer to leave this part open rather than not to conclude any contract.[249] One of the most representative examples of such situation will be discussed in the next chapter under Iran-United States Claims Tribunal.

The majority of BITs entered into force by countries such as the United States, the United Kingdom, Germany, or France do not contain an applicable law clause. For example, a clause on applicable law can be found only in 12 out of

245 Document 132 (SID/65-5), "Memorandum of the Meeting of the Committee of the Whole", (23 February 1965), History of ICSID Convention, ICSID Publication, Volume. II, Part. II, (2006), p. 985.

246 See Cable Television of Nevis, Ltd., Cable Television of Nevis Holdings, Ltd. V. Federation of St. Kitts and Nevis, Award, ICSID Case No. ARB/95/2, para. 6.02. The Tribunal stated:
"The Agreement is silent on the matter of applicable law and, in the circumstances, in accordance with Article 42(1) of the Convention the law of the Federation and applicable international law will apply".

247 Croff, Carlo, "The Applicable Law in an International Commercial Arbitration: Is it Still a Conflict of Laws Problem?", The International Lawyer, Vol. 16, (1982), p. 623.

248 Cherian, Joy, "Investment Contracts and Arbitration-The World Bank Convention on the Settlement of Investment Disputes", A.W. Sijthoff-Leyden, 1975, p. 76.

249 Croff, Carlo, "The Applicable Law in an International Commercial Arbitration: Is it Still a Conflict of Laws Problem?", The International Lawyer, Vol. 16, (1982), p. 624.

91 BITs concluded by France and also in only 6 out of 91 BITs concluded by the United Kingdom.[250]

In the abovementioned cases, the arbitrators need to determine the law or rules according to which the dispute can be resolved. Determination of the applicable law in these cases depends on the arbitration rules. Under almost all of the arbitration rules, there are provisions regarding the absence of agreed choice of law, which lies down possible mechanism(s) to determine the law applicable to the dispute. Among these various rules we will discuss the ICSID rules on this matter under Article 42(1) of the ICSID Convention.

1) Examining the absence of the agreed choice of law

Before the tribunal turns into applying the residual rule of the authorizing instrument, it should examine whether the agreed choice of law is lacking. In such a situation, the tribunal may proceed based on various methods.

For example, in *Benvenuti & Bonfant v. Congo*, the Tribunal held that there is no agreed choice of law under the parties' contract and as a result the Tribunal should apply the Congolese law and international law. Regarding the issue of applicable law, the Tribunal said:

> "4.2. These Articles do not contain any provision regarding the law applicable. In this case, according to Article 42(1) of the Convention, the Tribunal applies the law of the contracting State, which is a party to the dispute as well as the principles of international law in the matter.
> 4.3. Congolese law applies to civil and commercial matters French law as it existed at the time of the accession of the country to independence (1960). This body of rules, and in particular the French civil Code, has the force of the law by virtue of Article 23 of the French decree of 28 September 1897. This legislation falls within the framework of the Constitution of the People's Republic of Congo of 24 June 1973 and the 'Fundamental Act of the Military Committee of the Party' of 5 April 1977, which amended certain provisions of the Constitution."[251]

So, after examining the contract concluded between the parties, the Tribunal has determined the absence of an agreed choice of law. Additionally, in this case there is also a third source for the Tribunal. According to Article 42(3) of the

250 Banifatemi, Yas, "The Law Applicable in Investment Treaty Arbitration", in Katia Yannaca-Small (ed.), Arbitration under International Investment Agreements, A Guide to the Key Issues, Oxford University Press, (2010), p. 200.

251 Benvenuti & Bonfant v. People's Republic of the Congo, 1982, Award, ICSID Case No. ARB/77/2, (8 August 1980), paras. 4.2.,4.3.

Convention, the Tribunal has the power to decide based on equity. It should be noted that the Tribunal also examines whether there is an implicit choice of law. In such case, similar to instances where an explicit choice of law exists, the residual rule does not come into effect.

2) General view of the second sentence of Article 42(1) – The residual rule

Article 42(1) of the ICSID Convention is the key to resolve matters regarding the law applicable to the merits of the case. First, part of this Article consists of two sentences. The first sentence, which we explained earlier, introduces the party autonomy principle and how the parties may agree on the applicable law. On the other hand, the second sentence of this Article turns in when there is no agreement on the applicable law and provides a method for the arbitrators to determine the law that is to be applied.

From the beginning of the drafting phase of the ICSID convention, this matter was of a great importance and long debates have been contributed to this issue. It was one of the most challenging parts of the convention for the directors to sum up all the viewpoints and come to the final provision. Since this topic extremely influence the outcome of the case and the amount of predictability for each party to the dispute, and as each party has its own interests and expectations, the applicable law issue became one of the most challenging issues during working on the earlier drafts of the convention. It was undoubtedly not an easy task for the directors to establish a rule, which could balance the sometimes-contradictory interests of the parties. During four consultative meetings of the directors envisaged in the ICSID documents, the delegations pointed out their governments' standpoint by making comments and objections to the preliminary draft of October 1963.

A glance at the history of the ICSID Convention demonstrates that the issue of determining the applicable law in the absence of parties' agreement has been initially discussed in section 4(1) of Article IV of the preliminary draft.[252] The next version can be seen in Article 45(1) of the first draft of the

252 Document 24 (COM/AF/WH/EU/AS/1), "Preliminary Draft of a Convention on the Settlement of Investment Disputes between States and Nationals of Other States", (15 October 1963), History of ICSID Convention, ICSID Publication, Volume. II, Part. I, (2006), p. 184.

convention.[253] The final versions were the revised draft[254] and the Convention (Article 42(1)).

The second sentence of Article 42(1) gains importance, since as before mentioned, in the most frequent number of BITs there is no choice of law provision and in the absence of such provision, the law applicable to the merits of the dispute should be the law of the host state and international law, according to the second sentence of Article 42(1), unless the parties agree otherwise during the course of arbitration.

The second sentence of Article 42(1) contains a compound choice of law, which reads as follows:

> "... In the absence of such agreement, the Tribunal shall apply the law of the Contracting State party to the dispute (including its rules on the conflict of laws) and such rules of international law as may be applicable."[255]

Therefore, in an ICSID arbitration case, in the absence of choice of law by the parties, the Tribunal should apply to two sources: the national law of the contracting country, where the investment had taken place (including its conflict of law rules) and the applicable rules of international law. This article eliminates the confusion with respect to the fundamental question that what law is the applicable law for the arbitration in the absence of an agreed choice of law between a foreign investor and a Contracting State.[256]

The Tribunal's duty is therefore to determine the respective roles of the law of the host state and international law and this act has its own practical and symbolic consequences.[257]

Practically, this issue might affect the case to that extent that it determines the winner. Moreover, the primacy given to the law of the host state functions as a

---

253 Document 43 (Z 12), "Draft Convention on the Settlement of Investment Disputes between States and Nationals of Other States", (11 September 1964), History of ICSID Convention, ICSID Publication, Volume. II, Part. I, (2006), p. 610.

254 Document 123 (Z-13), "Revised Draft of Convention on the Settlement of Investment Disputes between States and Nationals of Other States", (11 December 1964), History of ICSID Convention, ICSID Publication, Volume. II, Part. II, (2006), p. 911.

255 Art 42(1) of the ICSID Convention.

256 Cherian, Joy, "Investment Contracts and Arbitration-The World Bank Convention on the Settlement of Investment Disputes", A.W. Sijthoff-Leyden, (1975), p. 76.

257 Gaillard, Emmanuel; Banifatemi, Yas, "The Meaning of "and" in Article 42(1), Second Sentence, of the Washington Convention: The Role of International Law in the ICSID Choice of Law Process", ICSID Review-Foreign Investment Law Journal, Vol. 18, (2003), p. 380.

symbolic guarantee for the importing States that their law, which they assume to be the most favorable, will also be applied.[258] But it is, however, never obvious that this law would be favorable for the host state and unfavorable for the investor as it is never obvious that the application of international law would always be desirable for the investor. These are matters, which would be different from one case to another.

3) Application of the host state's law

According to Article 42(1) of the ICSID Conventions, the application of the law of the host state in case of absence of choice of law is mandatory.

First of all, we should discuss the appropriateness of this law and why this choice leads to the best results and what are the justifications behind it.

There are various justifications for applying the law of the Contracting State. Every single justification might not seem convincing enough by itself but as a whole it would certainly establish a strong argument favoring the law of the Contracting State.

It has long been acknowledged in theory and also by the permanent court of international justice that in contracts between States and private parties, there is a postulation in favor of the law of the Contracting State. There are some arguments based on the notion of State sovereignty, which leads eventually to some opposition based on mainly two grounds. Firstly, the notion of State sovereignty is obsolete and should be restricted to the defense of essential State interests. Secondly, international commerce needs more flexibility. However, this theory is still defended by some scholars.[259]

In addition to the theoretical view, there are practical justifications in favor of the application of the law of the Contracting State. The most important issue among these arguments is the capability of the parties to choose a legal system, which covers their expectations in a fair manner. Predictability gains great important, where due to whatever reason, the parties were not able to reach an agreement on a legal system. At this point, we can argue that the law of the Contracting State is the one, which is mostly known to both parties. But it has to

258 Gaillard, Emmanuel; Banifatemi, Yas, "The Meaning of "and" in Article 42(1), Second Sentence, of the Washington Convention: The Role of International Law in the ICSID Choice of Law Process", ICSID Review-Foreign Investment Law Journal, Vol. 18, (2003), p. 380.

259 See, Kahn, Phillipe, "The Law Applicable to Foreign Investments: The Contribution of the World Bank Convention on The Settlement of Investment Disputes", Indiana Law Journal, Vol. 44, No. 1, (1968), pp. 21–24.

be mentioned that reference to the law of the Contracting State must permit the application of international law where needed.[260]

Article 42(1) of the ICSID Convention came a long way to become what it eventually is. The earlier drafts of this article show that at first the approaches through this issue were strikingly different.

The preliminary draft, which was submitted to regional consultative meetings of Government representatives, reads as follows[261]:

> "In the absence of agreement between the parties concerning the law to be applied, and unless the parties shall have given the Tribunal the power to decide *ex aequo et bono*, the Tribunal shall decide the dispute submitted to it in accordance with rules of law, whether national or international, as it shall determine to be applicable."[262]

Article 45(1) of the preliminary draft also provides:

> "In the absence of agreement between the parties concerning the law to be applied, the Tribunal shall decide the dispute submitted to it in accordance with such rules of national and international law as it shall determine to be applicable. The term 'international law' shall be understood in the sense given to it by Article 38 of the Statute of the International Court of Justice."[263]

This wording of the earlier drafts was to let the tribunal find the proper law by applying generally accepted principles of the conflict of laws or private international law.[264] However, logically in most cases it will lead to application of the law of the host state due to the significant connection of the transaction with the host country.

260 Kahn, Phillipe, "The Law Applicable to Foreign Investments: The Contribution of the World Bank Convention on The Settlement of Investment Disputes", Indiana Law Journal, Vol. 44, No. 1, (1968), p. 24.

261 See, Cherian, Joy, "Investment Contracts and Arbitration-The World Bank Convention on the Settlement of Investment Disputes", A. W. Sijthoff-Leyden, (1975), p. 78.

262 ICSID Convention Preliminary Draft, Article IV, Section 4(1).

263 Article 38(1) of the Statute of the International Court of Justice provides:
"1. The Court, whose function it is to decide in accordance with international law such disputes as are submitted to it, shall apply:
international convention, whether general or particular, establishing rules expressly recognized by the contesting states; international custom, as evidence of a general practice accepted as law the general principles of law recognized by civilized nations; and subject to the provisions of Article 59, judicial decisions and the teachings of the most highly qualified publicists of the various nations, as subsidiary means for the determination of rules of law."

264 Schreuer, Christoph, "The ICSID Convention- A Commentary", Cambridge University Press, Second Edition, (2009), p. 594.

Capital-importing countries were more willing to solely apply the law of the host state in the absence of any agreement on applicable law, for example, the Spanish Government had brought up in one of the early meetings of executive directors that the determination of the applicable law in the proceedings of the center is of a great importance and if the litigation involved private investors in a foreign country, the internal law of such country should apply.[265] Insisting on these views resulted in redrafting the article and directing the tribunal to apply the law of the host state including its rules on conflict of laws, which is reflected in the final draft of the Convention.

The other comments regarding the "national law", which was stipulated in the preliminary draft, was about the meaning of this term. For example, Bilgen (Turkey) said that there is a need to clarify the term "national law" because "this term could be construed as referring possibly to the national law of the capital-exporting country. In fact only the national law of the capital-importing country applied."[266] The chairman has answered that "the choice of national law would be a matter for the tribunal to decide in accordance with the appropriate rules of private international law. In most cases, proper law would indeed be the national law of the capital-importing country. However, in certain cases—such as licensing and know-how agreements—there might be a question as to what law applied."[267] But from another perspective, it seems that the representative of Turkey was intended to explain that this term could be stipulated in a more clear way. This comment was repeated during working on the revised draft. Turkey said one more time that the national law stated by the draft could be only the national law of the capital-importing country. This was the opinion which is also given by the delegations of Spain, Iran, India, Thailand and China.[268] The outcome of those comments was that in the final draft of the Convention the term "national law" was substituted by "Contracting State".

265 Document No. 5, (M 62–68), "Memorandum of Meeting of Executive Directors on the Subject of Settlement of Investment Disputes", (13 March 1962), History of ICSID Convention, ICSID Publication, Volume. II, Part. I, (2006), p. 13.

266 Document 29 (Z9), "Settlement of Investment Disputes Consultative Meeting of Legal Experts", Geneva, (17–22 February 1964), History of ICSID Convention, ICSID Publication, Volume. II, Part. I, 2006, p. 418.

267 Document 29 (Z9), "Settlement of Investment Disputes Consultative Meeting of Legal Experts", Geneva, (17–22 February 1964), History of ICSID Convention, ICSID Publication, Volume. II, Part. I, 2006, p. 418.

268 Document 45 (SID/LC/5), "Comments and Observations of Member Governments on the Draft Convention", (23 November 1964), History of ICSID Convention, ICSID Publication, Volume. II, Part. II, 2006, p. 663.

It is also necessary to mention that the words at the end of sentence "as may be applicable" do not refer to the law of the host state; therefore, it doesn't make this choice contingent on some particular circumstances.[269]

The law of the host state has a great role in the residual rule of Article 42(1), but actually because of its close connection to the investment, at the same time it is the most likely option that it would be made by the conflict of law rules anyway. But in a case there is a stronger connection with another State, the conflict of law rules may provide for *renvoi* to the law of that State.

Beside the residual rule of the second sentence of Article 42(1), there is always a possibility for parties to agree on another law based on the first sentence of this article. Especially where the result of applying the residual rule is undesirable or inappropriate.

Even though the wording of the second sentence of Article 42(1) implies the application of both national and international law, there are some cases, in which the Tribunal has only applied the law of the host state.

As an example the Tribunal in *SOABI v. Senegal* has applied only the Senegalese law and said:

> "... In the Tribunal's view, in the absence of agreement between the parties, the national law applicable to the relations of two Senegalese parties in respect of a project that was to take place in Senegal, can only be Senegalese law. The Tribunal is of the opinion that the agreements in question must be characterized as 'government contracts', the effect and execution of which are governed primarily by the Code of Governmental Obligations (C.G.O.). It appears from the position of the Government stated in its Counter-Memorial (p. 11) and that of SOABI contained in its Reply (p. 7) that both parties agree that the applicable law is Senegalese administrative law."[270]

Another example would be in *Genin v. Estonia* case. The Tribunal holds that:

> "According to Article 42(1) of the Convention 'the Tribunal shall decide a dispute in accordance with such rules as may be agreed by the parties. In the absence of such agreement, the Tribunal shall apply the law of the Contracting State party to the dispute (including its rules on the conflict of laws) and such rules of international law as may be applicable.' In the present case, in the absence of any agreement by the parties to the contrary, it is the law of the Republic of Estonia that applies. Moreover, neither party has argued otherwise nor contended that particular rules of international law (other than set out in the BIT and the Convention) shall apply, therefore there is no basis on which

269 Schreuer, Christoph, "The ICSID Convention- A Commentary", Cambridge University Press, Second Edition, (2009), p. 595.

270 Société Ouest Africaine des Bétons Industriels v. Senegal, Award, ICSID Case No. ARB/82/1, (25 February 1988), para. 5.02

> to conclude that the application of rules of international law would effect a result any different than that reached on the basis of Estonian law."[271]

Likewise in *MCI v. Ecuador* the Tribunal analyzes:

> "From the supporting documentation supplied by the parties during the proceedings, the Tribunal finds no evidence of any agreement on the law applicable to this dispute. Therefore, the Tribunal considers that it must respect the provisions of the second part of Article 42(1) of the ICSID Convention, i.e., in the absence of an agreement, the Tribunal shall apply Ecuadorian law, including its rules of private international law and such rules of international law as may be applicable."[272]

As we will discuss further, according to the second sentence of Article 42(1) the law of the host state is not to apply solely but there is always turn for international law when it comes to any inconsistency between the law of the host state and international law. Inconsistency is not the only situation, where international law comes to effect. We discuss the role of international law in the next part.

a) Limits on the application of the host state's law

There are some situations under which the law of the contracting State in accordance with the second sentence of Article 42(1) does not apply. Those instances will be discussed in the following.

aa) Application of international law

One of the most important limitations to the application of host state's law is the applicable international rules. There are various circumstances, under which international law prevails over the domestic law. These cases will be explained mainly in the next section under the title of application of international law. Distinguishing the role of international law and national law and their relationship is one of the most complicated topics in the field of ICSID arbitration. This topic has created one of the greatest and perhaps longest parts of debates among the drafters of the Convention and other scholars regarding applicable law.

Additionally, as mentioned before, there are some limitations to the principle of party autonomy such as public policy. Such limitations affect the application

---

271 Alex Genin, Eastern Credit Limited, Inc. and A.S. Baltoil v. The Republic of Estonia, Award, ICSID Case No. ARB/99/2, (25 June 2001), para. 350.

272 M.C.I. Power Group L.C. & New Turbine, Inc. v. Republic of Ecuador, Award, ICSID Case No. ARB/03/6, (31 July 2007), para. 217.

of the host state's law, whether it was roosted in parties' intention or was a result of the residual rule of Article 42(1).

bb) The state's capacity to submit to arbitration

Under some legal systems, there are limitations on the capacity and status of the State and its agencies in order to enter into arbitration agreements. Therefore, submitting a case to arbitration by a State or State's agency or taking part in an arbitral proceeding could be subjected to some limitations or conditions.[273]

Therefore, in case of unconditional acceptance of the host state's law, the State could always resort to those parts of the host state's law, which recognize the submission to ICSID arbitration as invalid.[274]

These limitations have not to be explicit. They might be implicit in the general scheme of the state's constitutional or administrative structure.[275]

One practicable solution regarding this matter would be adding a clause to the agreement between the parties excluding the application of any limiting provision in the host state's law, which could restrict the capacity of the State to submit to arbitration.

From the other angle, this is an issue also related to international law and its relation to national law. It's quite contrary to fundamental principles of international law such as the principles of good faith and of estoppel, if a State would rely on its own law to release itself from contractual commitments to the investor.[276]

Furthermore, Article 25(1) of the Convention provides:

> "The jurisdiction of the Center shall extend to any legal dispute arising directly out of an investment, between a Contracting State (or any constituent subdivision or agency of a Contracting State designated to the Center by that State) and a national of another Contracting State, which the parties to the dispute consent in writing to submit to the Center. When the parties have given their consent, no party may withdraw its consent unilaterally."

Therefore, in accordance with this Article, the State cannot withdraw its consent unilaterally.

---

273 Delaume, George R., "How to Draft an ICSID Arbitration Clause", ICSID Review-Foreign Investment Law Journal, Vol. 7, (1992), pp. 168–169.

274 Schreuer, Christoph, "The ICSID Convention: A Commentary", Cambridge University Press, Second Edition, (2009), p. 598.

275 Alvik, Ivar, "Contracting with Sovereignty: State Contracts and International Arbitration", Hart Publishing, (2011), p. 106.

276 Schreuer, Christoph, "The ICSID Convention: A Commentary", Cambridge University Press, Second Edition, (2009), p. 599.

As an example, in *Autopista v. Venezuela*, Venezuela contends that based on Venezuelan law any issues related to the termination of the Concession Agreement shall be reserved to the Venezuelan courts. Specifically, according to Article 10 of Decree Law No. 138 this law allows a concession agreement to be submitted to arbitration regarding matters relating to interpretation or performance of a concession contract, but not termination of such a contract.[277]

The Tribunal did not accept the argument of the State and held:

> "... Moreover, a jurisdictional challenge based on an alleged exclusive jurisdiction of a Venezuelan authority would also violate the well-established principle of international law pursuant to which a state cannot rely on its own domestic legislation to renege on a contractual obligation to resort to arbitration."[278]

Another emphasis could be seen at paragraph 207 of the award, which reads as follows:

> "Further, it is a well settled principle of international law that a state cannot rely on a provision of its domestic law to defeat its consent to arbitration. It is further a well-accepted practice that the national law governing by virtue of a choice of law agreement (pursuant to Article 42(1) first sentence of the ICSID Convention) is subject to correction by international law in the same manner as the application of the hos state law failing an agreement (under the second sentence of the same treaty provision). As a result, Venezuela's defense based on national law is no bar to Aucoven's claim of a breach of Clause 64."[279]

cc) The investor's legal status

Along with the issues regarding the capacity of State and its agencies, legal status of the investor may also play a role to limit the application of the host state's law.

The capacity and legal status of the investor are issues governed by the law of the State of incorporation. Therefore, they are not necessarily under control of the host state's law.

In *AMCO v. Indonesia*, we could clearly see the reflection of this limitation.

In this case, the applicable law was the Indonesian law, as it was the law of the host state. The Claimant in this case was a company registered in Delaware. This

277 Autopista Concesionada de Venezuela, C.A. v. Bolivarian Republic of Venezuela, Award, ICSID Case No. ARB/00/5, (23 September 2003), para. 89.

278 Autopista Concesionada de Venezuela, C.A. v. Bolivarian Republic of Venezuela, Award, ICSID Case No. ARB/00/5, (23 September 2003), para. 91.

279 Autopista Concesionada de Venezuela, C.A. v. Bolivarian Republic of Venezuela, Award, ICSID Case No. ARB/00/5, (23 September 2003), para. 207.

company was dissolved under the law of Delaware one month after rendering the first award. Indonesia argued that since the Indonesian law is applicable, based on this law a dissolved company ceases to exist for any purpose. The Tribunal did not accept Indonesia's argument:

> "When a company enters into an agreement with a foreign legal person, the legal status and capacity of that company is determined by the law of the state of incorporation. Similarly, one should apply the law of the state of incorporation to determine whether such a company, though dissolved, is still an existing legal entity for any specified legal purpose.
> The dissolution of Amco Asia was governed by the law of the state of Delaware. Under Delaware law Amco Asia remains a juridical entity for purposes of any action, suit or proceeding begun by or against it prior to or within three years of dissolution or until such action, suit or proceeding is completed and any judgment, order or decree therein is executed (Section 278, Delaware General Corporation Law)."[280]
> Another example indicating this matter is Scimitar v. Bangladesh case.

The Claimant was a company, which is established under the law of the British Virgin Islands. The Respondent contended that a non-competent person brings the dispute to the Tribunal. The Tribunal deemed that this observation is invalid, since it believes that application of the law of the British Virgin Islands is the mutual position of the parties and further reviews also do not provide the Tribunal with sufficient results to depart from this position. The Tribunal also finds it in line with Article 42(1) of the ICSID Convention.[281] Against this background and with regards to the parties' legal status, the Tribunal examined the question of corporate authorization under the law of the British Virgin Islands, which is that proceedings initiated by a corporation without proper corporate authority or authorization are invalid.[282]

4) Rules on the conflict of laws

The history of the ICSID Convention shows that prior to the revised draft of the Convention on 11 December 1964 there was no reference to the conflict

---

280 Amco Asia Corporation, Pan American Development Limited, PT Amco Indonesia v. Republic of Indonesia, Resubmitted Case: Decision on Jurisdiction, ICSID Case No. ARB/81/1, Section D: Jurisdiction Ratione Personae.

281 Scimitar Exploration Limited v. Republic of Bangladesh; Bangladesh Oil, Gas and Mineral Corporation, Award declining jurisdiction over the dispute, ICSID Case No. ARB/92/2, (4 May 1994), para.26.

282 Scimitar Exploration Limited v. Republic of Bangladesh; Bangladesh Oil, Gas and Mineral Corporation, Award declining jurisdiction over the dispute, ICSID Case No. ARB/92/2, (4 May 1994), para. 28.

of law rules of the Contracting State's law. In the earlier drafts, the law of the Contracting State was not even mentioned. Those drafts simply provided for such rules of national and international law as the Tribunal determines to be applicable. Pursuant to the persistent arguments made by the capital-importing countries, the draft was eventually changed. The developing countries based their arguments on that host state is where the investment is made so its law should be the applicable law and this result would be reached in any event by the application of conflict rules.[283] The modified draft encompasses the private international law of the host state either. The process is called *renvoi*.

This is logical for the Tribunal to apply a system of law which has a stronger contact to the transaction and by this means this Article was to prevent the automatic application of the law of the Contracting State in the cases which are not the most appropriate options. In loan contracts or similar financial arrangements between private investors and foreign public entities, the law of that country would be the proper law.[284]

On the one hand, because of the emphasis on the conflict of law rules in the second sentence of Article 42(1), some believe that there is a difference between the first sentence of this article and the second on this matter. Therefore, in the first sentence, where the parties agree on a choice of law there is possibly no room for the application of the private international law of that legal system. In other words, by application of the conflict of laws rules under the circumstances of the first sentence, the emphasis on the reference to such laws according to the second sentence becomes meaningless. Therefore, it seems logical that *renvoi* is not contemplated under the first sentence. The other indication that leads us to this conclusion is employing "rules of law" instead of "system of law" in the first sentence. Because we could expect the conflict of law rules merely in a system of law.[285]

---

283 Broches, Aron, "Convention on the Settlement of Investment Disputes between States and Nationals of Other States of 1965 Explanatory Notes and Survey of Its Application", Albert Jan van den Berg (ed.), Yearbook Commercial Arbitration, Vol. 18, (1993), p. 667, para. 115.

284 Delaume, George R., "Convention on the Settlement of Investment Disputes Between States and Nationals of Other States", International Lawyer, Vol. 1, Issue. 1, (1966–1967), p. 79.

285 Schreuer, Christoph, "The ICSID Convention- A Commentary", Cambridge University Press, Second Edition, (2009), p. 568.

On the other hand, Broches' explanations lead us toward the chance of applicability of the conflict of laws rules even in the case under the first sentence of Article 42(1).

He words the question this way:

> "Does the express reference in the second sentence of Art. 42(1) to conflict of laws provisions and the application of international law, and the silence on these points of the first sentence necessarily exclude their application when the parties have chosen a given national law under the first sentence?"[286]

Answering this question, in the first instance he said that an affirmative answer might be in order. He added that understanding would be correct only when that sentence had been framed in terms of a choice of national law. But since in this case the sentence states "rules of law," which may not necessarily be of a national system of law, a reference to conflict of laws provisions would therefore not be in order. At the end he added:

> "In the circumstances, it seems to me at least arguable that the choice of a given national law does not exclude its conflict provisions."[287]

Same as other rules the *renvoi* clause is also subject to variation or exclusion by agreement of the parties.[288]

5) Application of international law

According to the second sentence of Article 42(1), application of international law has been prescribed in addition to the application of the host state's law. Since

---

286 Broches, Aron, "Convention on the Settlement of Investment Disputes between States and Nationals of Other States of 1965 Explanatory Notes and Survey of Its Application", Albert Jan van den Berg (ed.), Yearbook Commercial Arbitration, Vol. 18, (1993) p. 667, para. 118.

287 Broches, Aron, "Convention on the Settlement of Investment Disputes between States and Nationals of Other States of 1965 Explanatory Notes and Survey of Its Application", Albert Jan van den Berg (ed.), Yearbook Commercial Arbitration, Vol. 18, (1993), p. 668, para. 120.

The author makes an example that if this result was desired, as in Art. 28(1) of the UNCITRAL Model Law it was expressly stated:

"...Any designation of the law or legal system of a given State shall be construed, unless otherwise expressed, as directly referring to the substantive law of that State and not to its conflict of laws rules."

288 Schreuer, Christoph, "The ICSID Convention- A Commentary", Cambridge University Press, Second Edition, (2009), p. 602.

the preliminary draft of the Convention, international law was part of the applicable law rules. At first, Article IV of the preliminary draft provided that:

> "…, the Tribunal shall decide the dispute submitted to it in accordance with rules of law, whether national or international, as it shall determine to be applicable."[289]

During the Regional Meeting the majority found this article acceptable; however, there were also some comments objecting the reference to international law. The objection was mainly based on the presumption that making an investment in a host country normally implied that the investor had already given consent to the jurisdiction of the national law of the host state and its applicability in all aspects of contract. Hence, the tribunal should apply the law of the Contracting State and not international law. During the Bangkok consultative meeting, Mr. China proposed an amendment to section 4(1) of Article IV, which provided:

> "In the absence of agreement between the parties concerning the law to be applied, unless the parties shall have given the tribunal the power to decide *ex aequo et bono*, the tribunal shall decide the dispute submitted to it in accordance with such rules of law, whether national or international, as it shall determine to be applicable; provided, however, that the act of investment implies the investor's consent to the application of law of the host country in the absence of a written declaration to the contrary made prior to the investment."[290]

Therefore, he believed that the fact of making an investment in the host state would imply the consent of the investor to both jurisdiction and the law of the host state, and any law other than the national law of the host country should not be applied, unless in case of a written declaration. China was insisted on this approach in its comments on the first draft as well. Thailand stated in sympathy with China "… national law applicable in Article 45 should be limited to municipal law of host State since act of investment in country implies consent of investors to application of law in host State."[291] Some other delegates were also in this favor that contracts between private persons and States should not be

289 Preliminary Draf of ICSID Convention, Art. IV.

290 Document 29 (Z9), "Settlement of Investment Disputes Consultative Meeting of Legal Experts", Geneva, (17–22 February 1964), History of ICSID Convention, ICSID Publication, Volume. II, Part. I, (2006), p. 513.

291 Document 45 (SID/LC/5), "Comments and Observations of Member Governments on the Draft Convention", (23 November 1964), History of ICSID Convention, ICSID Publication, Volume. II, Part. II, (2006), p. 660.

governed by international law.[292] Among them some contemplated that application of international law should be limited to cases in which the national law of the country provides for its application.[293] Broches however believed that insisting on application of the national law solely could be traced to historical roots in the regime of so-called capitulations. Some countries were apprehensive of not much of the application of international law to the transaction but of the national law of a foreign state. This could give rise to some difficulties. Based on this approach those countries do not wish to give the tribunal a great freedom in the issue of applicable law.[294]

Based on two main reasons Broches had to oppose this approach. Firstly, a tribunal involved with international cases could not be restrained from applying international law. Secondly, it is completely reasonable for the tribunal to apply international law, since the basic characteristic of the Convention is the establishment of an international jurisdiction. Some of the governments were in favor of application of international law such as Germany, as Bertram indicated, "There are many countries in which the national courts must apply national law as well as international law, and it would seem strange if a tribunal which was admittedly international would be precluded from the application of international law."[295] It was not just Germany in favor of application of international law. Other capital-exporting countries such as the United States, the United Kingdom and Austria were at the same page.

In the next draft of the Convention, the word "or" was replaced with the word "and". Article 45(1) of this draft said:

> "In the absence of agreement between the parties concerning the law to be applied, the Tribunal shall decide the dispute submitted to it in accordance with such rules of national and international law as it shall determine to be applicable. The term 'international law'

---

292 Document 81 (SID/LC/SR/14), "Comment of Mr. Wanasundera (Ceylon) in Summary Proceedings of the Legal Committee Meeting", (7 December 1964), History of ICSID Convention, ICSID Publication, Volume. II, Part. II, (2006), p. 801.

293 Document 81 (SID/LC/SR/14), "Comment of Mr. Ortiz (Peru) in Summary Proceedings of the Legal Committee Meeting", (7 December 1964), History of ICSID Convention, ICSID Publication, Volume. II, Part. II, (2006), p. 802.

294 Document 132 (SID/65-5). "Memorandum of the Meeting of the Committee of the Whole", (23 February 1965), History of ICSID Convention, ICSID Publication, Volume. II, Part. II, (2006), p. 985.

295 Document 81 (SID/LC/SR/14), "Summary Proceedings of the Legal Committee Meeting", (7 December 1964), History of ICSID Convention, ICSID Publication, Volume. II, Part. II, (2006), p. 801.

shall be understood in the sense given to it by Article 38 of the Statute of the International Court of Justice."

The replacement of the word "or" with "and" was intended to refute any inference that the Tribunal would have to choose between national and international law and not apply them together. Broches pointed out that "... It was quite clear that the laws of the host country would be of primary importance and that international law itself would in the first place refer to them. The principles of international law which might be brought into play would be such as pacta sunt servanda."[296] He also added that the revision made in the new draft by substitution of "national or international" by "national and international" was in order to avoid the impression that international law would always apply or that it was necessarily a question of alternatives.[297]

The debates regarding international law were not mainly about the exact role of it and whether it should be limited to a corrective or supplemental role or more. The focus of debates was also whether or not it should be applied at all. Some countries were extremely opposed to the application of international law, while some found it even a prerequisite. Therefore, we can say that omitting international law from this section is not logical and it is even in contrary to the essence of the Convention. The reference to international law was adopted by a majority of 24 to 6.[298]

Unfortunately, there is no uniformity about the role of international law yet. Even though, as previously mentioned, Broches pointed out more than once during the meetings that international law would not be applied in the first place, he said regarding the hierarchical order of national and international law that the order in which the two systems of law are mentioned, national law first and international law second, does not denote their hierarchical order.[299] He added that "The Tribunal will first look at the law of the host State and that law will in the

296 Document 81 (SID/LC/SR/14), "Summary Proceedings of the Legal Committee Meeting", (7 December 1964), History of ICSID Convention, ICSID Publication, Volume. II, Part. II, (2006), p. 800.

297 Document 81 (SID/LC/SR/14), "Summary Proceedings of the Legal Committee Meeting", (7 December 1964), History of ICSID Convention, ICSID Publication, Volume. II, Part. II, (2006), p. 800.

298 Document 81 (SID/LC/SR/14), "Summary Proceedings of the Legal Committee Meeting", (7 December 1964), History of ICSID Convention, ICSID Publication, Volume. II, Part. II, (2006), p. 804.

299 Broches, Aron, "The Convention on the Settlement of Investment disputes between States and Nationals of other States, Collected Courses of the Hague Academy of International Law, Vol. 136, (1972), p. 390.

first instance be applied to the merits of the dispute. Then the result will be tested against international law. That process will not involve confirmation or denial of the validity of the host State's law, but may result on not applying it where that law, or action taken under that law, violates international law. In that sense, as I suggested earlier, international law is hierarchically superior to national law under Article 42(1)."[300]

In the final revisions at the meeting of the committee of the whole, one more time we see some explanations regarding the primacy of national law over international law. The chairman used the term "in the first place" for national law and "secondly" for international law.[301] This shows the intention of the drafters to apply these laws not hand in hand but in an order. For this reason, the term "as may be applicable" was added to the end of the sentence. In order to explain that international law does not apply in an unlimited way.

Now that we had a short review on the history of the ICSID Convention and examined the intentions of the governments during the drafting phase, we should assess the role of international law. Does the international law go hand in hand with the law of the host state or does the law of the host state have primacy over international law?

There are few theories about this matter. According to the first theory, the application of international law is restricted only to situations where there are gaps in the law of the host state on certain issues or where the law of the host state is inconsistent with international law. In the first case international law would fill the gap and has only a complementary role and in the latter case international law will have a corrective role.[302] As it seems, this theory gives primacy to the law of the host state over international law.

---

300 Broches, Aron, "The Convention on the Settlement of Investment disputes between States and Nationals of other States, Collected Courses of the Hague Academy of International Law, Vol. 136, (1972), p. 392.

301 Document 132 (SID/65-5). "Memorandum of the Meeting of the Committee of the Whole", (23 February 1965), History of ICSID Convention, ICSID Publication, Volume. II, Part. II, (2006), p. 984.

302 The corrective role of international law and its role as a guidance for interpretation of the host State's law could be seen in:

Tradex Hellas S.A. v. Republic of Albania, ICSID Case No. ARB/94/2, Award, (29 April 1999), para. 68–69:

"An important limitation of this framework is that, in its Decision on Jurisdiction of 24 December 1996, The Tribunal found that it only had jurisdiction on the basis

Same as the first theory, the second theory is to give the law of the host state a maximum effect. Under this theory, the role of international law is limited only to the cases where certain rules of domestic law collide with fundamental norms of international law. This theory is even narrower than the first.

As the Tribunal in *Autopista v. Venezuela* stated:

> "The role of international law in ICSID practice is not entirely clear. It is well settled that international law may fill lacunae when national law lacks rules on certain issues (so called complementary function). It is also established that it may correct the result of the application of national law when the latter violates international law (corrective function)…"[303]

The Tribunal added:

> "Whatever the extent of the role that international law plays under Article 42(1) (second sentence), this Tribunal believes that there is no reason in this case, considering especially that it is a contract and not a treaty arbitration, to go beyond the corrective and supplemental functions of international law."[304]

Based on the third theory, international law has its own independency and need not to be filtered through the law of the host state.

A discussion about the various theories regarding the relationship between the law of the host state and international law is envisaged in *Goetz v. Burundi* case:

---

of the Albanian Law No. 7764 of 2 November 1993 on Foreign Investments (the 1993 Law).

Therefore, in its consideration of the merits the Tribunal is prevented from examining the claim on any other possible legal basis such as any other of the various investment laws issued in Albania, the Bilateral Investment Treaty between Albania and Greece, as well as other sources of international law. Although court and arbitral decisions and legal writings dealing with such other sources may be of relevance in interpreting the 1993 Law, it is this 1993 Law which the Tribunal will examine as to whether Tradex' claim is justified on the merits. This is in conformity with Art. 42(1) of the ICSID Convention according to which 'the Tribunal shall apply the law of the Contracting State party to the dispute (including its rules on the conflict of laws) and such rules of international law as may be applicable'. Accordingly the Tribunal will make use of sources of international law insofar as that seems appropriate for the interpretation of terms used in the 1993 Law, such as 'expropriation'…"

303 Autopista Concesionada de Venezuela, C.A. v. Bolivarian Republic of Venezuela, Award, ICSID Case No. ARB/00/5, (23 September 2003), para. 102.

304 Autopista Concesionada de Venezuela, C.A. v. Bolivarian Republic of Venezuela, Award, ICSID Case No. ARB/00/5, (23 September 2003), para. 102.

> "In the previous case-law the problem of the links between the various applicable sources of international law is posed in the context of the second sentence of Article 42, first paragraph, of the ICSID Convention, and it has received divergent responses, abundantly commented on in academic writings: hierarchal relationships according to some, domestic law applying first of all but being overborne where it contradicts international law; according to others, relationships based on subsidiarity, with international law being called upon only to fill lacunae or to settle uncertainties in national law; according to others again, complementary relationships, with domestic law and international law each having its own sphere of application."[305]

Considering only a subsidiary or corrective role for international law has been seen in cases such as *Klöckner* case.[306] This subsidiary role of international law, which is limited only in cases of a lacunae or inconsistency, may seem accepted at first glance but under this understanding the word "and" in the second sentence of Article 42(1) will be understood as "and, in case of *lacunae*, or should the law of the Contracting State be inconsistent with international law."[307]

One of the main justifications for this approach is the history of the ICSID Convention, in which the drafters' intention was to limit the role of international law to cases of *lacunae* or inconsistency, as Broches said that "... even an international tribunal would in the first place have to look at the national law, since the relationship between the investor and the host State is governed in the first instance by national law, and it would only be in those instances in which national law was in violation of international law that the tribunal would, in the application of international law, set aside national law."[308] He also pointed out that "... The remainder of Article 42(1) gives subsidiary rules for the case where the parties have failed to prescribe the applicable law. Under these subsidiary rules the tribunal may apply both national and international law. The history of the provision leaves no doubt, in my opinion, that the tribunal lay apply international law (i) where national law calls for its application; (ii) where the subject

305 Antoine Goetz and Others v. Republic of Burundi, Award, ICSID Case No. ARB/95/3, (10 February 1999), para. 97.

306 Klöckner Industrie-Anlagen GmbH v. United Republic of Cameroon, Société Camerounaise des Engrais, Award, ICSID Case No. ARB/81/2, (21 October 1983).

307 Gaillard, Emmanuel; Banifatemi, Yas, "The Meaning of "and" in Article 42(1), Second Sentence, of the Washington Convention: The Role of International Law in the ICSID Choice of Law Process", ICSID Review-Foreign Investment Law Journal, Vol. 18, (2003), p. 381.

308 Document 33 (Z11), "Chairman's Report on the Regional Consultative Meetings of Legal Experts", (9 July 1964), History of ICSID Convention, ICSID Publication, Volume. II, Part. I, (2006), p. 557.

matter is directly regulated by international law (a case which may not be easily distinguishable in practice from (i)); and (iii) where international law or action taken thereunder violates international law."[309] Kahn has also concludes that:

> "The text in its present formulation would indicate if taken literally, simultaneous application of the two laws, but the reference to the law of the State should counsel prudence to arbitrators and guide them to call on the more general rules of international law only where the State law is not well adapted to settlement of the dispute or in case of flagrant violation of the law of nations. Obviously, this supposes that the content of the principles of international law will permit such a construction."[310]

The question is now whether we should base our understanding of this article on some quotations from the history of the Convention or in other words does the history of the Convention come to an effect in the course of interpretation of this Article?

In order to answer this question, we should discuss the matter of interpretation of the ICSID Convention. Since it is an international convention, it should be interpreted in accordance with the rules of interpretation of international treaties. According to this issue, Article 31 of the Vienna Convention of 1969 on the Law of Treaties provides that "[a] treaty shall be interpreted in good faith in accordance with the ordinary meaning to be given to the terms of treaty in their context and the light of its object and purpose."

When the text is not clear enough then the supplementary rule of Article 32 of the Vienna Convention comes into effect, which reads as follows:

> "Recourse may be had to supplementary means of interpretation, including the preparatory work of the treaty and the circumstances of its conclusion, in order to confirm the meaning resulting from the application of article 31, or to determine the meaning when the interpretation according to article 31:
> Leaves the meaning ambiguous or obscure; or
> Leads to a result which is manifestly absurd or unreasonable."

After reading this rules, referring to the history of the Convention seems unnecessary because without referring to it, the article would not remain obscure or it wouldn't lead to an unreasonable result but the article is very clear and could be interpreted in accordance with its ordinary meaning.

---

309 Broches, Aron, "Selected Essays- World Bank, ICSID, and Other Subjects of Public and Private International Law", Martinus Nijhoff publishers, (1994), p. 184.

310 Kahn, Phillipe, "The Law Applicable to Foreign Investments: The Contribution of the World Bank Convention on The Settlement of Investment Disputes", Indiana Law Journal, Vol. 44, No. 1, (1968), p. 28.

Even if we look at the history of the Convention, we could admit that the debates were mostly about whether or not international law should be applied at all. But the text was eventually adopted in favor of the majority's opinion permitting the application of international law. Additionally, we should admit that the text of the Article 42(1) neither contains any explanation with regard to the relation of national and international rule nor it stipulated that the application of international law should be limited only in cases of *lacuna* or inconsistency. Therefore, this approach might be an interpretation beyond the soul of Article 42(1).

In contrary to the abovementioned conclusion, the precedent of ICSID tribunals has shown particularly in the klöckner and AMCO cases that international law could not be considered as an independent body of law but it only comes into effect in case of *lacunae* or inconsistency such as recognizing a gap in the national law. Therefore, the arbitral tribunal does not have free access to international law except considering the national law in advance.

In the annulment decision of the *ad hoc* Committee in *Klöckner v. Cameroon*, the Committee had to examine whether the Tribunal exceeded its powers due to a violation of Article 42(1). Since in this case the agreement of parties regarding applicable law was absent, the second sentence of Article 42(1) had come into effect, under which the law of the host state was applicable. According to the Claimant, the Tribunal ignored this principle and went beyond its powers by applying French law, which had been applied in the eastern part of Cameroon. The Tribunal stated, since the SOCAME factory project was situated in the eastern part of Cameroon, where French law is applicable, this law should also be the governing law in this case.

As the Committee cited, the Tribunal based its decision on two grounds. First, the Tribunal concludes that Klöckner violated its duty of full disclosure and as a result it is not entitled to the contract price and Cameroon has already paid enough.[311]

Furthermore, the tribunal stated that the decision is based "not on a principle of French law, but on a sort of declaration, as general as it is imprecise, of principles which are allegedly universally recognized." In fact, the Tribunal based its decision on such principle and explains:

311 Klöckner Industrie-Anlagen GmbH v. United Republic of Cameroon, Société Camerounaise des Engrais, Award, ICSID Case No. ARB/81/2, (21 October 1983), part VI, Section. B.

> "We take for granted that the principle according to which a person who engages in close contractual relations, based on confidence, must deal with its partner in a frank, loyal and candid manner is a basic principle of French civil law, as is indeed the case under other national codes which we know of. This is the criterion that applies to relations between partners in simple forms of association anywhere. The rule is particularly appropriate in more complex international ventures, such as the present one."[312]

From these statements, the *ad hoc* Committee concluded that the tribunal has based its decision on the general principles of law recognized by civilized nation, as that term is used in Article 38(1) of the Statute of the International Court of Justice. The Committee added that it's also possible that the Tribunal was tended to refer to "principles of international law as may be applicable," stipulated in Article 42(1).[313] The Committee deemed this conclusion unacceptable and analyze this article this way that:

> "Article 42 of the Washington Convention certainly provides that 'in the absence of agreement between the parties, the Tribunal shall apply the law of the Contracting State party to the dispute ... and *such principles of international law as may be applicable*.' This gives these principles (perhaps omitting cases in which it should be ascertained whether the domestic law conforms to international law) a dual role, that it, *complementary* (in the case of 'lacunae' in the law of the State), or *corrective*, should the State's law not conform on all points to the principles of international law. *In both cases*, the arbitrators may have recourse to the 'principles of international law' only after having inquired into and established the content of the law of the State party to the dispute (which cannot be reduced to *one* principle, even a basic one) and *after* having applied the relevant rules of the State's law.
> Article 42(1) therefore clearly does not allow the arbitrator to base his decision *solely* on the 'rules' or 'principles of international law.'"[314]

Therefore, by this approach the Committee has established a precedent under which the application of international law does not have an independent role and could be applied only in certain situations.

---

312 Klöckner Industrie-Anlagen GmbH v. United Republic of Cameroon, Société Camerounaise des Engrais, Award, ICSID Case No. ARB/81/2, (21 October 1983), part VI, Section. B.

313 Klöckner Industrie-Anlagen GmbH v. United Republic of Cameroon, Société Camerounaise des Engrais, Decision on Annulment, ICSID Case No. ARB/81/2, (3 May 1985), para. 69.

314 Klöckner Industrie-Anlagen GmbH v. United Republic of Cameroon, Société Camerounaise des Engrais, Decision on Annulment, ICSID Case No. ARB/81/2, (3 May 1985), para. 69.

It was not only the *Klöckner* case that evolved this view. In *AMCO* case we find a similar approach to this matter.

In this case, the Tribunal firstly stated that since the parties have not expressed an agreement as to the applicable law, the Tribunal have to on one hand apply the Indonesian law, which is the law of the Contracting State and on the other hand, such rules of international law as the Tribunal deems to be applicable.[315]

Additionally, the parties referred to both Indonesian and international law constantly at their pleadings.

On 18 March 1985, the Republic of Indonesia filed with the Secretariat of the International Center for the Settlement of Investment Disputes between States and Nationals of Other States an application for annulment, under Article 52 of the Convention.

One of the preliminary questions that the Committee had to deal with was the law governing the resolution of the dispute among the parties. The committee same as the Tribunal referred to Article 42(1) of the Convention. The same as in *Klöckner* case, "It seems to the *ad hoc* Committee worth noting that Article 42(1) of the Convention authorizes an ICSID tribunal to apply rules of international law only to fill up lacunae in the applicable domestic law and to ensure precedence to international law norms where the rules of the applicable domestic law are in collision with such norms."[316] It also states that this perspective on the role or relationship of international law norms and the law of the host state has been derived from a general evaluation of the system established by the Convention. The law of the host state is, in principle, the law to be applied in settling the dispute. Applicable norms of international law must also be complied with since every ICSID award has to eventually be recognized, and the pecuniary obligations imposed by such award enforced, by every Contracting State of the Convention (Art. 54(1), Convention). Moreover, the national state of the investor is precluded from exercising its normal right of diplomatic protection during and even after the ICSID proceedings, in respect of a Contracting State which complies with the ICSID award (Art. 27, Convention). Article 54(1) and of Article 27 of the Convention would only make sense under the supposition

---

315 Amco Asia Corporation, Pan American Development Limited, PT Amco Indonesia v. Republic of Indonesia, Award, ICSID Case No. ARB/81/1, (20 November 1984), para. 148.

316 Amco Asia Corporation, Pan American Development Limited, PT Amco Indonesia v. Republic of Indonesia, Decision on the Application for Annulment, ICSID Case No. ARB/81/1, (16 May 1986), para.20.

that the award involved does not violate applicable principles and rules of international law.[317]

Therefore, the Committee insisted on the supplemental and corrective role of international law with addressing the Decision of Annulment in *Klöckner* case and the comments and observations of Broches.[318]

This approach taken by the Committee and limiting the applicability of international law merely to certain cases is analogous to the debates about the history of ICSID, which we mentioned that the most important aim of that debate was omitting the reference to international law at all, which confronted with the majority's disapproval.

Viewing from another angle, there may well be some serious issues, in case of *lacunae* in national laws. The nature of the national laws as a legal order could be questioned under this view. For example, how could we assume a legal system as more complete than the other only because it foresaw some legal issues in a more detailed manner? It is possible that one legal system does not provide some rules in a very detail manner, as we could not see the answer of one legal problem at first instance, but in no way it implies that this legal system does not have a way to confront this issue. A specific concept sometimes does not exist in a legal system but this is not a reason that there is no solution to solve the problem under that legal system. There are always more general concepts, which encompass the detailed ones. For example, one legal concept may not recognize the concept of "turnkey contract". It may not recognize the concepts of "EPC (engineering procurement and construction) contract", of "design-and-build contract" of "contract for work by the job" either. But it most likely recognizes the concepts of contract, *pacta sunt servanda*, good faith, and so on.[319] Therefore, when the tribunal should take the national law of a certain country into account, and it does not find the detailed matching concept in the rules of that country, then the tribunal has to solve the problem relying on the general principles of that national law. In some cases, the tribunal failed to find such law because of

317 Amco Asia Corporation, Pan American Development Limited, PT Amco Indonesia v. Republic of Indonesia, Decision on the Application for Annulment, ICSID Case No. ARB/81/1, (16 May 1986), para. 21.

318 Amco Asia Corporation, Pan American Development Limited, PT Amco Indonesia v. Republic of Indonesia, Decision on the Application for Annulment, ICSID Case No. ARB/81/1, (16 May 1986), para. 22.

319 Gaillard, Emmanuel; Banifatemi, Yas, "The Meaning of "and" in Article 42(1), Second Sentence, of the Washington Convention: The Role of International Law in the ICSID

the lack of sufficient investigation through the national law. And therefore, it decided that there is a case of *lacunae*. Reisman clearly explained:

"The notion of addressing a problem must be understood broadly. Even the most developed of legal systems and even the most articulated code cannot anticipate and provide for every contingency and every possible legal dispute. Thus, the question for an ICSID tribunal under Article 42(1) is not whether the host State law provides a pre-packaged answer. If the host State's law provides a general analytical framework, it is up to the Tribunal to apply that framework to the statutes, judicial precedents, and general principles of that system ..."[320] The author emphasizes that "... the absence of a remedy is not necessarily a *lacunae*; it may represent a decision not to regulate a certain matter or to regulate it in a different way. A *lacunae*, or gap, in the law of a particular State may be said to exist only when the State engages in certain transactions for which its legal system has not yet considered regulations or remedies. In short, it exists in those circumstances in which there is a socio-legal lag."[321] So, based on his explanations every failure to provide a remedy for a particular matter is not necessarily a *lacunae*. It is also possible that there is a special system in the law of a Contracting State in case of *lacunae*. For example in some legal systems there is a judicial supplementation method, which is performed by referring to an earlier or more general system of law, such as Roman law.[322] In addition to supplementing, the law of the Contracting State should be examined to see what other procedures it provides for dealing with *lacunae*. When the law of the Contracting State has been properly scrutinized and there were no possible way for filling *lacunae*, the application of international law comes into effect. Additionally international law applies where inconsistency exists between national and international law but according to a view, it should be more than a mere difference. In those cases international law cannot prevail in the first instance. There should be in other words a veritable collision. Where this is not the case, by application of international law, Article 42(1) will lose its meaning. Therefore, the violation of something fundamental to international law should be proved.[323] These fundamental rules are characterized as international public

Choice of Law Process", ICSID Review-Foreign Investment Law Journal, Vol. 18, (2003), p. 394.

320 Reisman, W. Michael, "The Regime for Lacunae in the ICSID Choice of Law Provision and the Question of Its Threshold", ICSID Review- Foreign Investment Law Journal, Vol. 15, (2000), p. 371.

321 Reisman, W. Michael, "The Regime for Lacunae in the ICSID Choice of Law Provision and the Question of Its Threshold", ICSID Review- Foreign Investment Law Journal, Vol. 15, (2000), p. 371.

322 Reisman, W. Michael, "The Regime for Lacunae in the ICSID Choice of Law Provision and the Question of Its Threshold", ICSID Review- Foreign Investment Law Journal, Vol. 15, (2000), p. 374.

323 Reisman, W. Michael, "The Regime for Lacunae in the ICSID Choice of Law Provision and the Question of Its Threshold", ICSID Review- Foreign Investment Law Journal, Vol. 15, (2000), p. 375.

policy or Jus Cogens. As we mentioned before the arguments during the drafting phase would approve this view.

Aside from the role of international law in this provision, there were also arguments regarding the clarification of the term "international law" during working on the preliminary draft of the Convention at the consultative meetings, as the representative of Jamaica pointed out that section 4 of Article IV of this draft did not specify the type of international law that would be applicable. The chairman was also agreed to include some explanation as to the meaning of that term.[324] Such comments lead to insert the reference to Article 38(1) of the Statute of the International Court of Justice to the first draft.

Some delegations also suggested including some basic rules of international law that should be applied by arbitral tribunals, such as prohibition of discriminatory treatment, the obligation to act in good faith, and prohibition of measures contrary to international public policy or general principles of law. But the chairman pointed out in his report that these indications are not necessary and should not be included because the aim is to keep the Convention flexible in different situations. Therefore, the second sentence of Article 42(1), "and such rules of international law as may be applicable," should be understood as a body of substantive rules, which may be applicable to a specific issue, brought to an ICSID tribunal.

As Reisman suggested restricting the role of international law, another theory on the role of international law and its relationship with the law of the Contracting State could be discussed.[325] Under this view, the application of international law would be limited to some rare cases of fundamental violation of international law. This method insists on existence of a genuine collision between national and international law because it tends to give the law of the host state the most effective role. The arguable point is that it is hard to understand the reference of the second sentence of Article 42(1), "and such rules of international law as may be applicable" only to the rules of *jus cogens*. For an ICSID tribunal, as an international tribunal, giving effect to the rules of *jus cogens* needs no further emphasis. Even when there is no emphasis on taking the non-derogatory rules of international law into account, there is a prerequisite for any international tribunal to decide in favor of these rules. Under this analysis, therefore, the second

---

324 Document 27 (Z8), "Settlement of Investment Disputes Consultative Meeting of Legal Experts", Santiago, Chile, (3–7 February 1964), History of ICSID Convention, ICSID Publication, Volume. II, Part. I, (2006), p. 330.

325 See also Ajibo, Collins C., "The Governing Law in Investor-State Arbitration: The BIT, International Law, and Choice of Law Clause", International Arbitration Law Review, (2015).

sentence of Article 42(1) would be nothing more than an unnecessary emphasis, which hardly could be the true intention of the drafters. Another reason, under which the theory of Reisman could be questioned is the meaning of international law based on Article 38 of the Statute of the International Court of Justice. By applying that theory most of the rules of international law become inaccessible for an ICSID tribunal.[326] This approach could be in contrary to the purpose of the second sentence of Article 42(1).

However, there are different views regarding the role of international law in accordance with the second sentence of Article 42(1). Among others, the simple rule of the Vienna Convention with respect to the way of interpretation shall be taken into account. It seems that national and international law could properly function together; therefore, the conjunction "and" in Article 42(1) could simply mean and.

This is a view also approved by the *ad hoc* Committee in the *Wena v. Egypt* case. In the annulment procedure, the Committee had to examine the real role of international law and its place in Article 42(1) of the Convention. The Tribunal firstly summarized the arguments made by various scholars and also the experience of *AMCO* and *Klöckner* cases. The tribunals stated that the comments mostly gave a complementary role to international law and are aimed at restricting the role of international law and highlighting the law of the Contracting State at the same time and also based of a view that international law has a controlling function of domestic applicable law to the extent that there is a collision between such law and fundamental norms of international law characterized as *jus cogens*.[327] The Tribunal stated:

> "Further, the use of the word 'may' in the second sentence of this provision indicates that the Convention does not draw a sharp line for the distinction of the respective scope of international and of domestic law and, correspondingly, that this has the effect to confer on to the Tribunal a certain margin and power for interpretation."[328]

---

326 Gaillard, Emmanuel; Banifatemi, Yas, "The Meaning of "and" in Article 42(1), Second Sentence, of the Washington Convention: The Role of International Law in the ICSID Choice of Law Process", ICSID Review-Foreign Investment Law Journal, Vol. 18, (2003), p. 402.

327 Wena Hotels Limited v. Arab Republic of Egypt, Annulment Proceeding, ICSID Case No. ARB/98/4, (8 December 2000), para. 38.

328 Wena Hotels Limited v. Arab Republic of Egypt, Annulment Proceeding, ICSID Case No. ARB/98/4, (8 December 2000), para. 39.

The Tribunal employed a modern view and confirmed the equation of the roles of national and international law. So, it added:

> "What is clear is that the sense and meaning of the negotiations leading to the second sentence of Article 42(1) allowed for both legal orders to have a role. The law of the host State can indeed be applied in conjunction with international law if this is justified. So too international law can be applied by itself if the appropriate rule is found in this other ambit."[329]

Contrary to the former theories regarding the role of international law, this time the Tribunal acts in a very flexible manner. Based on the approach of the Committee in this case, one should not prevail one law to another in all cases but each case should be treated in its most appropriately suited way. National and international law are both accessible at the same time and the specific situations in each case would lead to the most appropriate choice. This choice is sometimes national law and sometimes international law.

The Tribunal said in opposition to the views that subordinate international law in all cases:

> "In particular, the rules of international law that directly or indirectly relate to the State's consent prevail over domestic rules that might be incompatible with them. In this context it cannot be concluded that the resort to the rules of international law under the Convention, or under particular treaties related to its operation, is antagonistic to that State's national interest."[330]

As we read the analysis of the Tribunal in this case, we can clearly see that the Tribunal's stance is completely inconsistent in the *AMCO* and *Klöckner* cases. The latter cases were predominantly in favor of subordinating international law, while the former tends toward the equation of the laws and recognizes an independent role for international law. In other words, the Tribunal in the *Wena* case believed that the rules of international law could be applied as the proper law in the same way as the law of the host state. These two sets of rules are equal and should be applied equally and the wording of Article 42(1) approves this view. In that case, there were neither a gap in the Egyptian law nor the Tribunal recognized an inconsistency.

This view is also approved by the Tribunal in *LG&E v. Argentina*. First, the Tribunal examined the precedent of ICSID tribunals and the scholar's approaches

---

329 Wena Hotels Limited v. Arab Republic of Egypt, Annulment Proceeding, ICSID Case No. ARB/98/4, (8 December 2000), para. 40.

330 Wena Hotels Limited v. Arab Republic of Egypt, Annulment Proceeding, ICSID Case No. ARB/98/4, (8 December 2000), para. 41.

on this matter and tried to find about the real intent behind the wording of the Convention:

> "If this contradiction does not exist, it is not an easy task to establish the relationship between international law and domestic law. In the original draft of the ICSID Convention, the conjunction 'and' was not present in the rule, but rather the conjunction 'or' was in its place, so that it read, 'The Arbitral Tribunal shall decide the dispute submitted to it in accordance with such rules of law, whether national or international as it shall determine to be applicable.' The intention in the language of the original draft was not to establish an order of preference, but rather to establish the possibility of alternatives. Initially, scholarly authorities and some ICSID Tribunals admitted that the conjunction 'and' meant that "and in case of lacunae, or should the law of the Contraction State be inconsistent with international law.'However, any limitation to the role of international law under these terms would imply accepting that international law may be subordinate to domestic law and would obviate the fact that there are growing number of arbitrations initiated on the basis of bilateral or multilateral investment treaties.' "[331]

The Tribunal, therefore, concludes that:

> "It is the Tribunal's opinion that 'and' means 'and', so that the rules of international law, especially those included in the ICSID Convention and in the Bilateral Treaty as well as those of domestic law are to be applied."[332]

Consequently, we conclude that in each case the Tribunal examines that under what rules it could reach the best results. This contemporary approach represents the freedom of ICSID tribunals to find in international law, as well as in the law of the host state, the most appropriate rules for the settlement of investment disputes.[333] The new approach tends to give both national and international law an autonomous and simultaneous role.[334]

---

331 LG&E Energy Corp., LG&E International, Inc. v. Argentine Republic, ICSID Case No. ARB/02/1, Decision on Liability, (3 October 2006), para. 95.

332 LG&E Energy Corp., LG&E International, Inc. v. Argentine Republic, ICSID Case No. ARB/02/1, Decision on Liability, (3 October 2006), para. 96.

333 Gaillard, Emmanuel; Banifatemi, Yas, "The Meaning of "and" in Article 42(1), Second Sentence, of the Washington Convention: The Role of International Law in the ICSID Choice of Law Process", ICSID Review-Foreign Investment Law Journal, Vol. 18, (2003), p. 411.

334 For more examples of this approach see also:

XI) Prohibition of a *non liquet*

The second paragraph of Article 42 of the ICSID Conventions provides:

> "The tribunal may not bring in a finding of *non liquet* on the ground of silence or obscurity of law."

According to this Article, the Tribunal cannot refuse to give a decision based on lacking clarity or insufficiency of the available laws.

This provision incorporated first time with Article IV, Section 4(2) of the Preliminary Draft and remained almost unchanged until the final draft of the Convention.[335]

In contrary to the first paragraph of Article 42, the third paragraph was not subject to long debates during the drafting phase of the Convention.

The intention of this Article is mainly reaching an award in every case, which is submitted to the Center. Genuinely, the drafters of the Convention based this provision on the Model Rules on Arbitral Procedure adopted by the International Law Commission in 1958, which reads as follows:

> "The tribunal may not bring in a finding of on liquet on the ground of silence or obscurity of international law or the compromise."[336]

This Convention, which was intended for proceedings between States, was based on the view that international law is a complete body of law, able to answer all questions in every dispute. Some scholars believe that the definition of international law stipulated in Article 38 of the Statute of the ICJ and recognizing "general principles of law" as a source of international law will make a great system of law which is unlikely to have gaps and *non liquet*. As Lauterpacht stated:

> "It has definitely removed the last vestige of the possibility of gaps conceived as a deadlock in the way of the settlement of a dispute."[337]

Sempra Energy International v. Argentine Republic, ICSID Case No. ARB/02/16, Award, (28 September 2007).

335 Article IV, Section 4(2) of the Preliminary Draft:
The Tribunal may not bring in a finding of non liquet on the ground of the silence or obscurity of the law to be applied.

336 Article 12 of the ILC Craft Convention, (1958).

337 Lauterpacht, Hersch, "The Function of Law in the International Community", Archon Books, (1966), p. 67.

He believes that the terms of Article 38 of the Statute, and in particular its third paragraph, are broad enough to be able to answer all the legal questions, which might be brought in every dispute.[338]

The prohibition of *non liquet* could be also found in many of the national legal systems. Most legal systems, either expressly or implicitly, have considered substitute jurisprudence for the circumstances, under which the law is either silent or unclear. Many national legal orders provide for filling the gaps through applying general principles of law.[339]

The second sentence of the Article 42(1) of the Convention refers to the law of the host state including its conflict of laws rules, therefore, it logically does not exclude any mechanism in this law, which comes into effect in order to fill the gaps.[340]

Prohibition of *non liquet* under the ICSID Convention does not depend on what law is to be applied. The second paragraph of Article 42 applies in both cases, whether the law is applicable based on the parties' agreement or is a result of the residual rule of Article 42(1).

We can conclude that when there is an agreed choice of law, the Tribunal should firstly resort to that law, including utilizing its gap-filling mechanisms. If it provides no answer, the Tribunal will resort to the residual rule of Article 42(1). Then it has a broad range of possibilities by putting national and international law together and by this way a *non liquet* would be near to unimaginable.[341]

The difference between using a gap-filling mechanism and being able to prove it and applying equity should always be considered. These are two wholly different methods. If the Tribunal apply a law without being able to explain the reason it has come up with that choice, its award could be in risk of annulment on the ground that the Tribunal exceeded its powers under Article 52(1)(b) of the Convention.[342]

---

338 Lauterpacht, Hersch, "The Function of Law in the International Community", Archon Books, (1966), p. 67.

339 Reisman, William M., "International Non-Liquet: Recrudescence and Transformation", International Lawyer, Vol. 3, Issue. 4, (1969), p. 770.

340 Shihata, Ibrahim F.I.; Parra, Antonio R., "Applicable substantive law in disputes between states and private foreign parties: the case of arbitration under the ICSID Convention." ICSID Review, (1994), p. 196.

341 Schreuer, Christoph, "The ICSID Convention: A Commentary", Cambridge University Press, Second Edition, (2009), p. 631.

342 Article 52(1) of the ICSID Convention:

XII) Decision ex aequo et bono

1) Definition

The third paragraph of Article 42 of the ICSID Convention permits the tribunal to decide based on equity, only where the parties have authorized it to do so. This paragraph reads as follows:

> "The provisions of paragraphs (1) and (2) shall not prejudice the power of the Tribunal to decide a dispute *ex aequo et bono* if the parties so agree."

The wording of this article is rooted in section 2 of Article 38 of the Statute of the International Court of Justice.[343]

Basically, the arbitrators are obliged to make decisions according to applicable substantive law but the aim of ICSID Convention is to liberate the arbitrators from the rigidities of positive law and to allow considerations of equity, justice and fairness where it seems to be required.[344] Therefore, in addition to applicable rules of law, the parties may also agree on settling their dispute on the basis of equity. This provision together with the party autonomy principle envisaged in Article 42(1) are the elements which provide flexibility.

This concept is also to be seen in many international arbitration rules such as ICC Rules of Arbitration, the UNCITRAL Arbitration Rules, and the ILC Model Rules on Arbitral Procedure.

Formerly, one of the most important reasons that arbitrators were eager to refer to equity was the perception of *lacunae* in international law. This was a method to fill the gaps and consequently avoid a *non liquet*. Therefore, it was appropriate for the settlement of non-justiciable disputes, or where one or both parties mistrust the law or its application to their particular dispute.[345]

"Either party may request annulment of the award by an application in writing addressed to the Secretary-General on one or more of the following grounds:
that the Tribunal was not properly constituted;
that the Tribunal has manifestly exceeded its powers;
that there was corruption on the part of a member of the Tribunal;
that there has been a serious departure from a fundamental rule of procedure; or
that the award has failed to state the reasons on which it is based."

343 "2. This provision shall not prejudice the power of the Court to decide a case ex aequo et bono, if the parties agree thereto."

344 Schreuer, Christoph, "Decisions Ex Aequo et Bono Under the ICSID Convention", ICSID Review- Foreign Investment Law Journal, Vol. 11, (1996), p. 37.

345 Trekman, Leon. "Ex Aequo et Bono: Demystifying an Ancient Concept", Chicago Journal of International Law, Vol. 8, (2007–2008), p. 623.

But in our case, settlement of a dispute *ex aequo et bono* is not resulted from *lacunae* in international law but it derives from the intention of the parties to make such a solution. In the extent of the ICSID Convention, this method of settlement is no longer specialized for settlement of non-justiciable disputes, because only legal disputes are within the jurisdiction of the Center.[346]

It should be mentioned that nowadays equity in international law or law in general could not be recognized as a precise equivalent for *ex aequo et bono*, since the former refers to a part of the overall legal system but the latter exists actually beyond law and requires specific party authorization.[347]

There are three terms of equity: *infra legem*, *praeter legem* and *contra legem*. *Infra legem*, which means within the law, is a part of the usual process of applying the law and is neither against nor outside the law. The second term means outside the law but not against it. The last term means against the law.

Since an investment is a long-term activity, decisions *ex aequo et bono* seem to be useful. The parties logically could not consider everything for a long period of time. There may be changes in economic, political and other areas, which cannot always be correctly assessed in advance. In some cases, the law may be inadequately developed or unsuitable to resolve complex disputes.[348] In such situations, a suitable decision may go beyond the legal framework and decision *ex aequo et bono* could facilitate further cooperation between the parties.[349]

2) The distinction between equity within the law and *ex aequo et bono*

Before considering the prerequisites for a decision *ex aequo et bono*, it would be appropriate to demonstrate the correlation between equity and *ex aequo et bono*. Some commentators treat them as two equivalent terms though they are not. The essences of these concepts are different. Equity is part of law while *ex aequo et bono* has an extra-legal realm. Adjudicators are deciding within the legal system

346 Broches, Aron, "Selected Essays-World Bank, ICSID, and Other Subjects of Public and Private International Law", Martinus Nijhoff publishers, (1994), p. 230.

347 Schreuer, Christoph, "Decisions Ex Aequo et Bono Under the ICSID Convention", ICSID Review- Foreign Investment Law Journal, Vol. 11, (1996), p. 38.

348 Trekman, Leon. "Ex Aequo et Bono: Demystifying an Ancient Concept", Chicago Journal of International Law, Vol. 8, (2007–2008), p. 621.

349 Schreuer, Christoph, "Decisions Ex Aequo et Bono Under the ICSID Convention", ICSID Review- Foreign Investment Law Journal, Vol. 11, (1996), p. 40.

while they are deciding based on equity since, it is also a part of an applicable legal system. On the contrary, notions of equity associated with *ex aequo et bono* are external to the law and could be moral, social or political.[350] This type of decision is the one that is decided in terms of fairness, equitability, or conscience notwithstanding the applicable law. This decision is not necessarily in contrary to the law, but it is more of an extra-legal decision.[351]

This distinction is also mentioned by the *ad hoc* Committee in *Amco v. Indonesia* case:

> "26. Neither does the *ad hoc* Committee consider that any mention of 'equitable consideration' in the Award necessarily amounts to a decision *ex aequo et bono* and a manifest excess of power on the part of the Tribunal. Equitable considerations may indeed form part of the law to be applied by the Tribunal, whether that be the law of Indonesia or international law…
> 28. The *ad hoc* Committee thus believes that invocation of equitable considerations is not properly regarded as automatically equivalent to a decision *ex* aequo *et bono* which, in view of the determination of the law applicable to the present case, would constitute a decision annullable for manifest excess of powers…"[352]

So, equity and *ex aequo et bono* are two distinct notions. When the case should be settled on the basis of equity, the existing law is still the starting point and should not be entirely disregarded, while an *ex aequo et bono* decision seems to be more unfettered.[353]

3) Amiable composition and *ex aequo et bono*

Alongside the reference to *ex aequo et bono*, some rules refer to amiable composition or even both at the same time. In some legal systems, they are even considered as synonyms. There are also differences in the way these two notions are interpreted. Based on one view, the allowance to decide the merits *ex aequo et bono*

350 Trekman, Leon. "Ex Aequo et Bono: Demystifying an Ancient Concept", Chicago Journal of International Law, Vol. 8, (2007–2008), p. 627.

351 Mason, Josephine K., "Arbitral & Judicial Decision: The Role of Ex Aequo Et Bono in International Border Settlement: A Critique of the Sudanese Abyei Arbitration", American Review of International Arbitration. Vol. 20, p. 530.

352 Amco Asia Corporation, Pan American Development Limited, PT Amco Indonesia v. Republic of Indonesia, ICSID Case No. ARB/81/1, Decision on the Application for Annulment, (16 May 1986).

353 Lauterpacht, Hersch, "The Function of Law in the International Community", Archon Books, (1966), p. 314.

does not equal to act as amiable compositeur and vice versa.[354] As Sammartano pointed out as a radical differentiation, acting as an amiable compositeur is different from deciding *ex aequo et bono*.[355] The term compositeur is derived from the word composition, which means agree or settle, rather than decide.[356] Therefore, amiable compositeur is kind of a quasi-settlement proceeding and an arbitrator is viewed as a representative authorized to resolve a dispute. The distinction between amiable compositeur and *ex aequo et bono* is also to be seen in the UNCITRAL Model Law (Article 28.3), which states:

> "The arbitral tribunal shall decide *ex aequo et bono* or as amiable compositeur only if the parties have expressly authorized it to do so."

The wording of this article and the use of "or" rather than "and" shows the distinction between these terms.

4) The agreement on a decision *ex aequo et bono* in ICSID arbitration

Normally, the agreement on a decision *ex aequo et bono* incorporates a provision in the initial arbitration agreement, which expresses the will of the parties to authorize the tribunal to decide *ex aequo et bono*.

ICSID has also prepared the following clause for this purpose:

> "Clause 11: Any Arbitral Tribunal constituted pursuant to this agreement shall have the power to decide a dispute *ex aequo et bono*."

An example could be the arbitration agreement in the *Atlantic Triton v. Guinea* case. Article 15 of the Agreement reads as follows:

> "Any dispute arising from the interpretation, application and execution of this Agreement shall be amicably settled.
> In case of disagreement, the parties accept to refer the arbitration of the "International Centre for Settlement of Investment Disputes Between States and Nationals of Other States" and the disagreement shall be settled *ex aequo et bono* in accordance with the

354 Belohlávek, Alexander J., "Application of Law in Arbitration, Ex aequo et Bono and Amiable Compositeur", Czech (& Central European) Yearbook of Arbitration, Vol. III, (2013), p. 27.

355 Rubino-Sammartano, Mauro, "Amiable Compositeur (Joint Mandate to Settle) and Ex Bono et Aequo (Discretional Authority to Mitigate Strict Law): Apparent Synonyms Revisited", Journal of International Arbitration, Vol. 9, Issue. 1, p. 14.

356 Belohlávek, Alexander J., "Application of Law in Arbitration, Ex aequo et Bono and Amiable Compositeur", Czech (& Central European) Yearbook of Arbitration, Vol. III, (2013), p. 30.

> provisions of Article 42(3) of the said Convention. The parties are bound to accept such a judgment and the government shall be precluded from invoking the exception of immunity..."[357]

The Agreement between the Minister of Fisheries for the Republic of Guinea and a Norwegian company, Atlantic Triton, in this case was for the conversion, equipping and operation of three fishing vessels in such a matter as to ensure efficient production and profitability. The company was to submit annually, for approval, a draft budget and production plan, while Guinea as ship owner undertook to provide funds for the running, provisioning and equipping of the vessels and to pay the company a monthly administration fee. As Guinea did not fulfill its obligations under the Agreement, Atlantic Triton was entitled to terminate the Agreement upon three months' notice. Under the Agreement, the disputes were to be settled *ex aequo et bono* in accordance with Article 42(3) of the ICSID Convention.[358] At the same time, the Guinean law is also applicable in accordance with Article 14 of the Management Agreement.[359] The parties have recognized and admitted that this law is identical to the French law in force prior to Guinea's independence in 1958.[360]

In January 1984, Atlantic Triton commences ICSID arbitration proceedings claiming payment of the amount of the second overrun and pecuniary and non-pecuniary damages for damage to its reputation.

In this award, the Tribunal decided *ex aequo et bono* and reduced the management fees on the basis of equity:

At first Atlantic Triton claimed payment of management fees for three quarters, namely from 1 October 1982 to 30 June 1983, that was a total of U.S. $344,444.[361] Guinea opposed this claim on the ground that the project was virtually stopped

---

357 Atlantic Triton Company Limited v. People's Revolutionary Republic of Guinea, Award, ICSID Case No. ARB/84/1, (21 April, 1986), Part. I.

358 Atlantic Triton Company Limited v. People's Revolutionary Republic of Guinea, Award, ICSID Case No. ARB/84/1, (21 April, 1986), Summary.

359 Article 14 – Law:

> The term "law" in the present Agreement refers to Guinean law. However, Guinean law will be applicable only insofar as it is not incompatible with the terms of the present Agreement, and where it is not more restrictive than the law in force at the date of entry into force of the present Agreement.

360 Atlantic Triton Company Limited v. People's Revolutionary Republic of Guinea, Award, ICSID Case No. ARB/84/1, (21 April, 1986), Introduction, Para. 9.

361 Atlantic Triton Company Limited v. People's Revolutionary Republic of Guinea, Award, ICSID Case No. ARB/84/1, (21 April, 1986), Part III, para. 2.2.

on August 1982 and the following months were devoted not to the management of the project. Therefore, Guinea requested that as it didn't receive any services, the management fees for that period should not be calculated.[362] So, the Tribunal considered that in the absence of any diligence during this period, it would not seem equitable to impose upon Guinea the payment of management fees for that quarter. The Tribunal stated:

> "However, the vessels not having been operated from the end of November 1982, even if Atlantic Triton continued to render certain services until 1 April 1983, their importance and nature would not justify that Atlantic Triton should be paid the totality of the fees prescribed for that period."[363]

Consequently, the Tribunal based on previous mentioned reasons, decided *ex aequo et bono* that it is equitable to reduce the lump sum of U.S. $100,000 the balance of the management fees owed by Guinea to Atlantic Triton by virtue of the execution of the contract of 12 August 1981.[364]

The Tribunal founded its award once again on equity, as it was considering the interest issue. Since the parties chose the American dollar as the monetary unit, the Tribunal judging equitably sets the interest rate at 9 % that was at that time the basic inter-bank interest rate in the United States. As we mentioned before, the Tribunal's decision was partly based on equity and partly on the law. The issues regarding the capitalization of interest decided in accordance with the provisions of Article 1154 of the French Civil Code.[365]

With respect to the parties' claims regarding arbitration fees and expenses, both parties requested reimbursement by the other party of its arbitration fees and expenses. This time again the Tribunal considered that based on equity, neither party having been shown to have acted in bad faith; therefore, each party should bear its own costs and as neither of the parties' claims have been accepted entirely, half of the arbitrator's fees, their expenses and the costs due for the use of ICSID's services should be borne by each party.[366] Relying on equity on this

362 Atlantic Triton Company Limited v. People's Revolutionary Republic of Guinea, Award, ICSID Case No. ARB/84/1, (21 April, 1986), Part III, para. 2.4.
363 Atlantic Triton Company Limited v. People's Revolutionary Republic of Guinea, Award, ICSID Case No. ARB/84/1, (21 April, 1986), Part III, para. 2.5.
364 Atlantic Triton Company Limited v. People's Revolutionary Republic of Guinea, Award, ICSID Case No. ARB/84/1, (21 April, 1986), Part III, para. 2.5.
365 Atlantic Triton Company Limited v. People's Revolutionary Republic of Guinea, Award, ICSID Case No. ARB/84/1, (21 April, 1986), Part III, para. 4.
366 Atlantic Triton Company Limited v. People's Revolutionary Republic of Guinea, Award, ICSID Case No. ARB/84/1, (21 April, 1986), Part V.

matter is somehow unclear because Article 61 of the ICSID Convention clearly provides that the Tribunal decides who should bear the costs and expenses for the proceedings.[367] In other words, when it is so said in the Convention that the arbitrators have discretion to decide on this matter, then how could it be meant as a reliance on the authorization to rule *ex aequo et bono*?[368] The possible interpretation could be that the Convention only authorize the arbitrators to decide how and by whom should the expenses be paid but the arbitrators could base their decision on equity, in cases that they are authorized to decide *ex aequo et bono*.

There is also a possibility for the parties to authorize the Tribunal to decide *ex aequo et bono* during the arbitral proceedings. Since a direct agreement between the parties is not the only way to resort to the ICSID arbitration and the jurisdiction of ICSID could also be established by a Bilateral Investment Treaty between the host state and the State of the investor's nationality or by national legislation in the host state. Therefore, ICSID arbitration could take place even without prior agreement with the host state. In such a situation, there is naturally no opportunity for the parties to the dispute to agree on a decision *ex aequo et bono* prior to the institution of the arbitral proceedings.[369] So, this decision could be made at an early or even later stage of the proceedings. Not only when the parties does not have an agreement at all but also when they did agree on the jurisdiction of ICSID but did not authorize the Tribunal to decide *ex aequo et bono*, it is possible for them to agree on such decision.

An example for the abovementioned situation is *Benvenuti and Bonfant v. Congo* case. In this case, the parties had agreed to refer the case to ICSID arbitration but there were no agreed applicable law. Therefore, the law of the Contracting State, together with the principles of international law in accordance with the residual rule of Article 42(1) applied. In June 1979, the parties asked the Tribunal for time in which to reach a settlement. If such a settlement

367 Article 61(2) of ICSID Convention: "In the case of arbitration proceedings the Tribunal shall, except as the parties otherwise agree, assess the expenses incurred by the parties in connection with the proceedings, and shall decide how and by whom those expenses, the fees and expenses of the members of the Tribunal and the charges for the use of the facilities of the Centre shall be paid. Such decision shall form part of the award."

368 Schreuer, Christoph, "Decisions Ex Aequo et Bono Under the ICSID Convention", ICSID Review- Foreign Investment Law Journal, Vol. 11, (1996), p. 49.

369 Schreuer, Christoph, "Decisions Ex Aequo et Bono Under the ICSID Convention", ICSID Review- Foreign Investment Law Journal, Vol. 11, (1996), p. 42.

was not concluded in that time they asked that an award be made as quickly as possible on the basis of judgment *ex aequo et bono*.[370] In a letter of 18 July 1979, Benvenuti and Bonfant informed the Tribunal that the negotiations with the Government had finally broken down, consequently, the tribunal decided *ex aequo et bono*.[371]

Bearing in mind, the clauses authorizing the Tribunal to decide *ex aequo et bono* are not always comprehensive; they could only cover particular matters and consequently the remaining issues are to be governed by rules of law. Therefore, we see the method of *dépeçage* here, which could ensure the flexibility. In other words, Article 42(3) does not preclude the application of law and parties could bring only certain defined issues to decision *ex aequo et bono*, while reserving others to be decided in accordance with law.[372] In *Benvenuti and Bonfant* case, the Tribunal applied law as well as equity. The Tribunal mentioned the applicability of Congolese law and the French Civil Code and added that:

> "In the present case, the Tribunal also has the power to rule "*ex aequo et bono*" in accordance with the agreement of the parties as authorized by Article 42(3) of the Convention. This agreement was signified to the Tribunal at the hearing of 6 June 1979 in Geneva. The Tribunal took cognizance of it in its procedural order of 7 June 1979."[373]

The Tribunal decided that the principle of compensation in case of nationalization is not only in line with the Congolese constitution but also one of the generally recognized principles of international law as well as of equity. Therefore, it ordered B&B to pay damages.[374]

In the same case, the Tribunal used its power to decide *ex aequo et bono* in order to adopt the rate of interest:

> "4.97. Following the provisional agreement between the parties, which was not ratified by the Government, B&B claimed interest at the rate of 15 % a year on all sums awarded to it.

370 Benvenuti and Bonfant SRL v. People's Republic of Congo, Award, ICSID Case No. ARB/77/2, (8 August 1980), p. 342.

371 Benvenuti and Bonfant SRL v. People's Republic of Congo, Award, ICSID Case No. ARB/77/2, (8 August 1980), para. 1.23.

372 Schreuer, Christoph, "The ICSID Convention: A Commentary", Cambridge University Press, Second Edition, (2009), p. 633.

373 Benvenuti and Bonfant SRL v. People's Republic of Congo, Award, ICSID Case No. ARB/77/2, (8 August 1980), para. 4.4.

374 Benvenuti and Bonfant SRL v. People's Republic of Congo, Award, ICSID Case No. ARB/77/2, (8 August 1980), paras. 4.64, 4.65.

> 4.98. The Tribunal does not consider it possible to uphold this claim seeing as the law applicable, Congolese law lays down a significantly lower rate of interest. The tribunal observes, however, that the Government, in its Memorial in Defense, suggested a rate of interest of 10 % in connection with its counterclaim. By virtue of its power to rule *ex aequo et bono*, the Tribunal considers it equitable to adopt this rate in relation to the compensation awarded to B&B."[375]

It seems that even if the tribunal in these cases had applied the law instead of equity, the outcome would not have been vastly different. In addition, it does not seem that applying the law would result in injustice in these two cases. In fact, the reference to *ex aequo et bono* by the Tribunal was mostly where it was to estimate the amounts of monetary compensation and the due interest. But it seems that applying the law on these points could have led to the same results.

The surprising fact is that even though we mentioned before that one of the most important advantages of deciding *ex aequo et bono* is the possibility to have a constant relationship in investment projects, which lasts usually for a long period of time, in both the cases, investment relationships had not lasted for too long and consequently there was no opportunity for an adjustment to change circumstances.[376]

Except the two abovementioned cases, there are not many situations in which the ICSID tribunals have been authorized to decide *ex aequo et bono*. Therefore, we cannot generalize the conclusions on this issue.

5) Absence of an authorization to decide *ex aequo et bono*

As discussed, decision *ex aequo et bono* is an extraordinary dimension of parties' freedom and could be implemented only when parties have agreed upon it and authorized the Tribunal to act so. In this section, the consequences of deciding *ex aequo et bono* in absence of an authorization will be examined.

When an ICSID tribunal decides *ex aequo et bono* without such authorization, the decision is always at risk of annulment. This act of the Tribunal creates an excess of powers or probably a failure to state the reasons on which the award is based.[377]

---

375 Benvenuti and Bonfant SRL v. People's Republic of Congo, Award, ICSID Case No. ARB/77/2, (8 August 1980), para. 4.97, 4.98.

376 Schreuer, Christoph, "Decisions Ex Aequo et Bono Under the ICSID Convention", ICSID Review- Foreign Investment Law Journal, Vol. 11, (1996), p. 50.

377 Schreuer, Christoph, "Decisions Ex Aequo et Bono Under the ICSID Convention", ICSID Review- Foreign Investment Law Journal, Vol. 11, (1996), p. 53.

According to Article 52 of the ICSID Convention, both of these situations could be a ground for a decision to be annulled.

A glance at the drafting phase of the ICSID Convention reveals that there were some suggestions on this issue to add "including failure to apply the proper law," but it was rejected. One of the comments was from the delegate of China, suggesting, "the clause 'the tribunal exceeded its power' could be improved if the words 'including failure to apply the proper law' were added. As the parties were entitled to agree on the applicable law, failure of the Tribunal to apply that law would frustrate that agreement."[378] The chairman explained that a mistake in applying the law does not qualify as a proper ground for annulment, while applying a different law, from which the parties have agreed upon could be a right ground the arbitrators had gone against the terms of the *compromis*.[379]

One of the examples of the annulment of the award on the abovementioned ground is *Klöckner v. Cameroon* case. Based on the parties' agreements, Klöckner Industrie-Anlagen GmbH, a German company together with its subsidiaries, was supposed to build a factory and manage it for a certain period of time. The Government was to provide a site for the factory and guarantee a loan arranged by Klöckner in order to cover the price of the factory.

On 10 April 1981, after a non-profitable period of time and cessation of the factory's operation by the Cameroonian Government, Klöckner delivered a request for arbitration against the United Republic of Cameroon claiming the balance of the price for the factory.[380] The Government also filed a counterclaim for the losses, which had incurred during the project.

Since the award was in favor of Cameroon, on 10 February 1984 Klöckner filed an application for annulment based on the Article 52 of the ICSID Convention and on the ground of manifest excess of powers because of the violation of Article 42(1) of the Convention.[381]

---

378 Document 43 (Z 10), "Summary Record of Proceedings, Bangkok Consultative Meetings of Legal Experts", (27 April- 1 May, 1964), History of ICSID Convention, ICSID Publication, Volume. II, Part. I, 2006, p. 518.

379 Document 43 (Z 10), "Summary Record of Proceedings, Bangkok Consultative Meetings of Legal Experts", (27 April- 1 May, 1964), History of ICSID Convention, ICSID Publication, Volume. II, Part. I, 2006, p. 518.

380 Klöckner Industrie-Anlagen GmbH v. United Republic of Cameroon, Société Camerounaise des Engrais, Award, ICSID Case No. ARB/81/2, (21 October 1983).

381 Klöckner Industrie-Anlagen GmbH v. United Republic of Cameroon, Société Camerounaise des Engrais. Decision on annulment, ICSID Case No. ARB/81/2, (3 May 1985).

In this case, the parties did not agree on a decision *ex aequo et bono*. Based on the Claimant's arguments, the Tribunal was required to apply the Cameroonian law based on French law, since the project was located in the eastern part of the country, where the French law normally applies. Therefore, the Claimant contended that the Tribunal exceeded its powers.

On this matter, the *ad hoc* Committee stated:

> "...excessive powers may consist, not only in deciding a question not submitted to the arbitrators, but also in misinterpreting the express provisions of the agreement in respect of the way in which they are to reach their decisions, notably with regard to the legislation or the principles of law to be applied.
> Excess of powers may consist of the non-application by the arbitrator of the rules contained in the arbitration agreement (*compromis*) or in the application of other rules. Such may be the case if the arbitrator (like Umpire Barge in the Orinoco case) applies rules of local law while the arbitration agreement prescribes that he decide on the basis of absolute equity, without regard ... to the provisions of local law, or if, conversely, he reaches a solution in equity while he is required to decide in law ..."[382]

Besides, there was another complaint against Klöckner contending that it had not dealt frankly with Cameroon. The Tribunal stated that it does not feel that Klöckner has dealt frankly with Cameroon and at some critical stages of the project Klöckner hid some vital information from its partner. The Tribunal also believed that, if the Cameroonian Government had known that information, maybe it could put an end to the venture and cancel the contract before the expenditure of the funds that now Klöckner seeks to obtain by means of an award.[383] The Tribunal emphasizes by mentioning where a partner in a complex financial situation fails to disclose matters and information of high importance to the other party and such failure leads to additional costs, the first partner has not acted frankly and locally *vis-à-vis* his partner.[384]

The point is, the Tribunal has not based its argument on any particular legal system, but the Tribunal's statement was very general:

---

382 Klöckner Industrie-Anlagen GmbH v. United Republic of Cameroon, Société Camerounaise des Engrais. Decision on annulment, ICSID Case No. ARB/81/2, (3 May 1985), para. 59.

383 Klöckner Industrie-Anlagen GmbH v. United Republic of Cameroon, Société Camerounaise des Engrais, Award, ICSID Case No. ARB/81/2, (21 October 1983), Part. VI, Section. B.

384 Klöckner Industrie-Anlagen GmbH v. United Republic of Cameroon, Société Camerounaise des Engrais, Award, ICSID Case No. ARB/81/2, (21 October 1983), Part. VI, Section. B.

"We take it for granted that the principle according to which a person who engages in close contractual relations, based on confidence, must deal with its partner in a frank, loyal and candid manner is a basic principle of French civil law, as is indeed the case under the other national codes which we know of. This is the criterion that applies to relations between partners in simple forms of association anywhere. The rule is particularly appropriate in more complex international ventures, such as the present one."[385]

Apparently, the Tribunal did not justify its argument by recourse to a particular national or even international law but it brought this issue as a general principle that is to be applied. On the one hand, the Tribunal maintained that it does not tend to apply exceptional legal principles to turn-key operations due to their influence on a one country's development.

On the other hand, the Tribunal believed that it is particularly important to apply universal requirements of frankness and loyalty in dealings between partners in cases such as this one, where a multinational company seeks and freely undertakes the obligation to supply an overall package of feasibility, analysis, design, management, bidding, construction and marketing for an industrial plant, and obtains in return the agreement of the Government to pay for the factory, whether or not it is profitable.[386]

Klöckner contended that the Tribunal was required to apply Cameroonian law but it based its decision "on a sort of declaration, as general as it is imprecise, of principles which are allegedly universally recognized."[387]

Therefore, the *ad hoc* Committee found it necessary to examine the award from this point of view. Firstly, the Committee argued whether the arbitrator's duty to apply the law of the Contracting State is or can be fulfilled by reference to one "basic principle" even without making any more precise reference.[388]

Moreover, the Committee pointed out that the reference to "other national codes which we know of", to the "particularly appropriate" character of the rule

385 Klöckner Industrie-Anlagen GmbH v. United Republic of Cameroon, Société Camerounaise des Engrais, Award, ICSID Case No. ARB/81/2, (21 October 1983), Part. VI, Section. B.

386 Klöckner Industrie-Anlagen GmbH v. United Republic of Cameroon, Société Camerounaise des Engrais, Award, ICSID Case No. ARB/81/2, (21 October 1983), Part. VI, Section. B.

387 Klöckner Industrie-Anlagen GmbH v. United Republic of Cameroon, Société Camerounaise des Engrais. Decision on annulment, ICSID Case No. ARB/81/2, (3 May 1985), para. 65.

388 Klöckner Industrie-Anlagen GmbH v. United Republic of Cameroon, Société Camerounaise des Engrais. Decision on annulment, ICSID Case No. ARB/81/2, (3 May 1985), para. 68.

"in more complex international ventures, such as the present one" and to the particular importance that "universal requirements of frankness and loyalty … be applied in cases such as this one" shows that the Tribunal has probably wanted to base its decision on the general principles of law recognized by civilized nations, as used in Article 38(3) of the Statute of the International Court of Justice. Therefore, maybe the Tribunal has wanted to refer to principles of international law in accordance with Article 42(1) of the ICSID Convention. But the Committee stated that these are not to be confused with "general principles" and therefore, such an interpretation is conjectural and could not be acceptable.[389]

From the Committee's point of view even if the principle of good faith is a basic principle of French civil law, it could not be unlimited:

> "It is true that the principle of good faith is 'at the basis' of French civil law, as of other legal systems, but this elementary proposition does not by itself answer the question. In Cameroonian or Franco-Cameroonian law does the 'principle' affirmed or postulated by the Award, the 'duty of full disclosure' exist? If it does, no doubt flowing from the general principle of good faith, from the obligation of frankness and loyalty, then how, by what rules and under what conditions is it implemented and within what limits? Is there a single legal system which contains such a broad obligation? These are a few of that questions that naturally come to mind and that the Award provides no basis for answering."[390]

So, the *ad hoc* Committee found that the Tribunal acted outside of its framework provided by Article 42(1), applying concepts and principles it probably considered equitable (acting as an amiable compositeur) and eventually concluded that the award should be annulled in its entirely.[391]

The Tribunal's award in *Klöckner* case has been also criticized from another angle for making equitable considerations and not referring to positive law when the Tribunal was examining the *exceptio non adimpleti contractus* principle. The defendant stated in its first written submission that the Cameroonian

---

389 Klöckner Industrie-Anlagen GmbH v. United Republic of Cameroon, Société Camerounaise des Engrais. Decision on annulment, ICSID Case No. ARB/81/2, (3 May 1985), para. 69.

390 Klöckner Industrie-Anlagen GmbH v. United Republic of Cameroon, Société Camerounaise des Engrais. Decision on annulment, ICSID Case No. ARB/81/2, (3 May 1985), para. 72.

391 Klöckner Industrie-Anlagen GmbH v. United Republic of Cameroon, Société Camerounaise des Engrais. Decision on annulment, ICSID Case No. ARB/81/2, (3 May 1985), para. 79.

Government undertook to substitute SOCAME as guarantor, though not unlimited, with respect to the repayment of the loan and payment of interest. Similar to other obligations the performance may be suspended by virtue of the *exceptio non adimpleti contractus* should Klöckner fail to implement its contractual obligations. Such failure by Klöckner eliminates the Cameroonian Government's financial obligations.[392]

As mentioned before, the Tribunal rejected both claim and counterclaim by pointing out that both parties had failed to perform their obligations properly. The Tribunal referred to the Doctrine in French law admitting that there is no mention of this principle in the French civil code.[393] Eventually, the Tribunal reached the following conclusion:

> "In the present case, taking into account, on the one hand, the significant payments effected by Defendant and, on the other hand, the significance of Claimant's failures to live up to contractual undertakings, it is appropriate to conclude that the amount paid corresponds equitably to the value of Klöckner's defective performance. There is a certain equilibrium, a certain relationship, as we have suggested above, between that which was paid and the approximate value of the components supplied by Klöckner in 1974-1975 and used by Defendant in the redesigned factory, which was restarted unsuccessfully in 1980. The two methods of analysis lead to results approximately equivalent, and we have thus concluded that Klöckner is entitled to what it has already received, but to nothing more."[394]

The *ad hoc* Committee did not accept the arguments held by the Tribunal and found that based on a sort of general equity rather than positive law.[395] The Committee adduced the Tribunal's argument as follows: "… This Section ends up with an attempt at an 'equitable valuation' of the 'quantitative comparison of the respective failure of performance' concluding that the amount

392 Klöckner Industrie-Anlagen GmbH v. United Republic of Cameroon, Société Camerounaise des Engrais, Award, ICSID Case No. ARB/81/2, (21 October 1983), Part. VI, Section. C.

393 Klöckner Industrie-Anlagen GmbH v. United Republic of Cameroon, Société Camerounaise des Engrais, Award, ICSID Case No. ARB/81/2, (21 October 1983), Part. VI, Section. C.

394 Klöckner Industrie-Anlagen GmbH v. United Republic of Cameroon, Société Camerounaise des Engrais, Award, ICSID Case No. ARB/81/2, (21 October 1983), Part. VI, Section. C.

395 Klöckner Industrie-Anlagen GmbH v. United Republic of Cameroon, Société Camerounaise des Engrais. Decision on annulment, ICSID Case No. ARB/81/2, (3 May 1985), para. 163.

already paid 'corresponds equitably to the value of Klöckner's defective performance'".[396]

The Committee found that "It is difficult to follow the Tribunal's thinking where different considerations, of fact and of law, are mixed together, with the same topics treated in ways that are now similar, now different. Nevertheless, it is possible to discern quite clearly a dominant concern, inspired by equity, which will ultimately send the parties back to square one each keeping what it already has, but each having its claim rejected, be it the principal claim for payment of the balance of the price or the counterclaim for damages. But it must also be recognized here that the Award is based more on a sort of general equity than on positive law (and in particular French civil law) or precise contractual provisions, such as Article 9 of the Turnkey contract."[397]

Therefore, using the words such as "fairness" and "equitable" could have led the *ad hoc* Committee to consider the Tribunal's award as a decision *ex aequo et bono*. But the annulment decision of the *ad hoc* Committee has also been criticized because it seems that the Committee has failed to remain in the realm of the annulment process and acted as in appeal process. It seems beyond doubt that there is a line between these processes. Annulment is limited to some significant procedural faults but there is no power for the Committee to examine the substance of the decision once again.[398]

On the one hand, the Committee strongly believes that the Tribunal has decided *ex aequo et bono* and not based on the applicable law. On the other hand, it is obvious at least for the Tribunal that it was applying the applicable law. It has kept referring specifically to the French civil law in its award and has never stated that it has power to decide *ex aequo et bono*.[399] Therefore, while it is clear that the reference to the French law was not enough throughout the award but it is not very clear if it could lead the award to nullity.[400] Furthermore, the

---

396 Klöckner Industrie-Anlagen GmbH v. United Republic of Cameroon, Société Camerounaise des Engrais. Decision on annulment, ICSID Case No. ARB/81/2, (3 May 1985), para. 161.

397 Klöckner Industrie-Anlagen GmbH v. United Republic of Cameroon, Société Camerounaise des Engrais. Decision on annulment, ICSID Case No. ARB/81/2, (3 May 1985), para. 163.

398 Schreuer, Christoph, "Decisions Ex Aequo et Bono Under the ICSID Convention", ICSID Review- Foreign Investment Law Journal, Vol. 11, (1996), p. 57.

399 Schreuer, Christoph, "Decisions Ex Aequo et Bono Under the ICSID Convention", ICSID Review- Foreign Investment Law Journal, Vol. 11, (1996), p. 57.

400 Schreuer, Christoph, "Decisions Ex Aequo et Bono Under the ICSID Convention", ICSID Review- Foreign Investment Law Journal, Vol. 11, (1996), p. 57.

terminology of the Tribunal using expressions such as "equitable," "certain equilibrium" seems not enough to charge that the Award is based more on equity than on positive law.[401]

This was the first annulment proceeding in the ICSID history. It has been largely debated whether the *ad hoc* Committee has done its job well or not. But generally, using some expressions associated with equity by the Tribunal while referring to Article 42(1) would not necessarily ruin the whole decision whenever the Tribunal refers to Article 42(1) of the ICSID Convention and determine the applicable law at the commencement of the proceeding, could not. There are situations, when the applicable law and equity norms overlap then referring to equity in order to temper the argument does not stand in contrast to being in the realm of applicable law.

Another example of annulment proceedings after the *Klöckner* case is *Amco v. Indonesia* case. The more moderate approach could be seen in this case stating that not every reference to "equity" or "justice" would amount to a decision *ex aequo et bono*. This was an investment case arose from agreements for the construction and management of a hotel in Indonesia. The Republic authorized the investment for a period of 30 years but in 1980 the Republic seized the investment in an armed, military action and cancelled its license. The arbitration proceedings were initiated on 15 January 1981 when Amco Asia Corporation, Pan American Development Limited and PT Amco Indonesia, as the claimants filed a request for arbitration against Republic of Indonesia.[402]

Chapter II of the award determining the applicable law is very clear. The Tribunal admits that it has no power to decide *ex aequo et bono* since the parties did not agree to such measures at any time as it is foreseen in para. 3 of Article 42 of ICSID Convention.[403]

Therefore, the Tribunal referred to the residual rule of Article 42(1), since the parties had not agreed on the governing law. The determination of the applicable law by the Tribunal reads as follows:

> "The parties having not expressed an agreement as to the rules of law according to which the disputes between them should be decided, the Tribunal has to apply Indonesian law,

401 Schreuer, Christoph, "Decisions Ex Aequo et Bono Under the ICSID Convention", ICSID Review- Foreign Investment Law Journal, Vol. 11, (1996), p. 57.

402 Amco Asia Corporation, Pan American Development Limited, PT Amco Indonesia v. Republic of Indonesia, Award, ICSID Case No. ARB/81/1, (20 November 1984).

403 Amco Asia Corporation, Pan American Development Limited, PT Amco Indonesia v. Republic of Indonesia, Award, ICSID Case No. ARB/81/1, (20 November 1984), para. 147.

which is the law of the Contracting State Party to the dispute, and such rules of international law as the Tribunal deems to be applicable, considering the matters and issues in dispute."[404]

Evidently, the Tribunal has decided based on Indonesian law and applicable international law and found that the revocation of Amco's investment license by Indonesia was in contradiction to both Indonesian law and to the general and fundamental principle of due process. More specifically, the Tribunal deemed that the procedure was in contradiction with Indonesian regulations regarding warnings that have to be given prior to revocation of an investment authorization. In addition and more generally the Tribunal believed that it is also at odds with the general principle of due process.[405]

While the decision seems to be rendered based on the applicable law, Indonesia claimed in the annulment process that it is based on equity. Therefore, the expression used by the Tribunal ("fundamental principle of due process") is one of the reasons for the annulment of the Award. Indonesia alleged that:

"...the general and fundamental principle of due process relied upon in the award (para. 201) has every appearance of being based on equity and not on the law prescribed to be applied by Article 42(1) of the Convention..."[406]

The *ad hoc* Committee did not accept Indonesia's allegations. It believes that there is no obligation for the Tribunal to preface each finding or conclusion with a specification of the Indonesian or international law rule on which such finding relies. The conclusions and findings of the Tribunal should be read only in their context.[407] The Committee adds that:

"Neither does the *ad hoc* Committee consider that any mention of 'equitable considerations' in the Award necessarily amounts to a decision *ex aequo et bono* and a manifest excess of power on the part of the Tribunal. Equitable considerations may

---

404 Amco Asia Corporation, Pan American Development Limited, PT Amco Indonesia v. Republic of Indonesia, ward, ICSID Case No. ARB/81/1, A (20 November 1984), para. 148.

405 Amco Asia Corporation, Pan American Development Limited, PT Amco Indonesia v. Republic of Indonesia, Award, ICSID Case No. ARB/81/1, (20 November 1984), para. 201.

406 Amco Asia Corporation, Pan American Development Limited, PT Amco Indonesia v. Republic of Indonesia, Decision on the Application for Annulment, ICSID Case No. ARB/81/1, (16 May 1986), para. 77.

407 Amco Asia Corporation, Pan American Development Limited, PT Amco Indonesia v. Republic of Indonesia, Decision on the Application for Annulment, ICSID Case No. ARB/81/1, (16 May 1986), para. 25.

> indeed form part of the law to be applied by the Tribunal, whether that be the law of Indonesia or international law …"[408]

In addition, Indonesia asserted that the International Court of Justice has applied equitable considerations only in the context of delimitation of maritime boundaries; therefore, it should remain only in this context. To this statement, the *ad hoc* Committee responded as follows:

> "… when the International Court of Justice looked into whether a claim for compensation was 'reasonable' in the Corfu Channel case (ICJ Cases, 1949, p. 249). The Court was in effect taking account of equitable considerations in a context not involving maritime boundaries delimitation. The Court did much the same thing in its judgment on the Merits in Barcelona Traction Case (ICJ Cases, 1970, p. 48, para. 92) and dealt directly with this problem in its Advisory Opinion of October 23, 1956 on Judgments of the Administrative Tribunal of the ILO upon complaints made against the UNESCO, (ICJ Reports, 1956, p. 100). The view that a tribunal applying international law may take account of equitable considerations in non-maritime boundaries cases, is fairly widely shared among scholars in international law…"[409]

After this considerations, the Tribunal concluded that invocation of equitable considerations is not necessarily equivalent to a decision *ex aequo et bono* which could have been a ground to lead the award to annulment. In other words, the Tribunal has not decided *ex aequo et bono*, consequently its nullity would not be a proper result. The *ad hoc* Committee annulled that award but not because of a decision *ex aequo et bono* or failure to apply the applicable law but based on other reasons.

Having discussed *Klöckner* and *Amco* cases, it is obvious that not every slight derogation of applicable law could lead to an annulment and not every equitable consideration could be considered as a decision *ex aequo et bono.* Every mistake in applying the law could not constitute a failure to apply that law.[410] The Klöckner's annulment proceeding has been criticized because it was oversensitive to the way the Tribunal cites the law or other resources. After a while in *Amco* case, the Tribunal shows that not every reference to equity should be

---

408 Amco Asia Corporation, Pan American Development Limited, PT Amco Indonesia v. Republic of Indonesia, Decision on the Application for Annulment, ICSID Case No. ARB/81/1, (16 May 1986), para. 26.

409 Amco Asia Corporation, Pan American Development Limited, PT Amco Indonesia v. Republic of Indonesia, Decision on the Application for Annulment, ICSID Case No. ARB/81/1, (16 May 1986), para. 27.

410 Schreuer, Christoph, "Decisions Ex Aequo et Bono Under the ICSID Convention", ICSID Review- Foreign Investment Law Journal, Vol. 11, (1996), p. 61.

taken as a decision *ex aequo et bono* and the *ad hoc* Committees should go slower where nullity of an award is on stake. At the same time, the experience of the *Klöckner* case could lead the Tribunals to be more sensitive with their wording in order to prevent the risk of nullity.

6) Limitations on decision *ex aequo et bono*

Similar to every other power, the power of a tribunal to decide *ex aequo et bono* has its own limitations too. However, the parties authorize the Tribunal to decide so this power is not unlimited. Under Article 48(3) of the ICSID Convention, the Tribunal is always obliged to state the reasons upon which its award is based.[411] This obligation in the case of decision *ex aequo et bono* could not be as rigorous as in decisions based on law.[412] However, a failure to provide any reasons for a decision *ex aequo et bono* may bring a risk of annulment under Article 52(1)(e).

Other fundamental principles of law such as international public policy, which were mentioned before, have also their limiting power on this case. For example, even where an award is based on *ex aequo et bono*, it still cannot violate or go beyond the basic and fundamental principles of law such as human rights.

The other question that could be made is that whether the law of the forum could limit the power to decide *ex aequo et bono*. The domestic law of some countries does not permit such decision. In this situation, we should pay attention that ICSID arbitration is a total international system, which is liberated from any national rules of law. The answer is also negative when the parties wish to combine their choice of law with an authorization to decide *ex aequo et bono*. There is no limitation for the parties to do so even when their chosen law prohibits an *ex aequo et bono* decision.[413] Article 42(3) confirms the answer as it states that the Tribunal's power to decide *ex aequo et bono* is not prejudiced by the selection of the proper law under Article 42(1).

XIII) Annulment of ICSID awards

In this section, rather than a detailed study on the annulment proceeding in ICSID arbitration the aim would be to study the points relevant to applicable

411 Article 48(3) of the ICSID Convention: "The award shall deal with every question submitted to the Tribunal, and shall state the reasons upon which it is based."

412 Schreuer, Christoph, "The ICSID Convention- A Commentary", Cambridge University Press, Second Edition, (2009), p. 638.

413 Schreuer, Christoph, "The ICSID Convention- A Commentary", Cambridge University Press, Second Edition, (2009), p. 638.

law as the main topic, and the situations where a mistake in applying the chosen law could lead to the nullity of an award. Before all we need to see the necessity of annulment proceedings and its distinction with the appeal process. Then we discuss some of the important cases to illustrate the issue even better.

1) Necessity of a review mechanism

Arbitration is considered as one of the most efficient means of resolving international investment disputes due to its extraordinary advantages, including expedition, economy and informality.[414] One other advantage is the finality of awards rendered by arbitral tribunals. Finality of an award ensures that arbitration could provide an expeditious and economical settlement of disputes.[415] The other goal in every means of dispute settlement is correctness, which is in contrast to finality, because in order to ensure the correctness of an award no one can guarantee a speedy manner and consequently an economical way. Therefore, in international arbitration especially under the ICSID Convention, the principle of finality has been given more weight than correctness in order to maintain the inducement of parties to choose arbitration as their preferred means of dispute settlement in place of litigation.

While the parties expect from an arbitral tribunal to act independent from the court and render an enforceable award in a speedy manner, they want also to have some control over it. It means a chance for the parties to object the Tribunal's decision in case they find deficiencies or drastic derogations from the prescribed rules. Similar to the national legislation where the parties could opt for an appeal, in the course of arbitration they should also have a right to want the award to be reviewed on an unbiased manner. In next part, we want to study the mechanisms provided by ICSID convention for reviewing an award without losing the great virtues of arbitration such as finality.

2) Annulment process by ICSID

In almost all non-ICSID arbitrations, the review of an award is split between several national jurisdictions, whether courts of the country in which the Tribunal had its seat or the courts charged with the task of enforcing the award. It is not easy for the parties when their agreement to arbitration finally results in both arbitration and litigation. The ICSID Convention has provided a unique

414 Feldman, Mark B., "The Annulment Proceedings and the Finality of ICSID Arbitral Awards", ICSID Review-Foreign Investment Law Journal, Vol. 2, (1987), p. 87.

415 Schreuer, Christoph, "ICSID Annulment Revisited", Legal Issues of Economic Integration, Vol. 30, (2003), p. 103.

solution for restricting the award to fall under the control of national courts. The review process under the ICSID Convention is a self-contained system, which constitutes a limited exception to the goal of finality.[416] An exhaustive list of the grounds, on which the parties can apply for the annulment of an award, is stated under Article 52(1) of the ICSID Convention. The next paragraphs of this article explain the formalities for an annulment application and the constitution of *ad hoc* Committees.[417] There is no permanent body for the review process; therefore,

---

416 Schreuer, Christoph, "From ICSID Annulment to Appeal Halfway Down the Slippery Slope", The Law and Practice of International Courts and Tribunals, Vol. 10, (2011), p. 211; See also Steindl, Barbara Helene, "ICSID Annulment vs. set aside by state courts-compared to ICSID ad hoc annulment Committees, is it the state courts that are now more hesitant to set aside awards?", Yearbook on International Arbitration, Vol. IV, (2015), pp. 181–206.

417 Article 52 of ICSID Convention:

Either party may request annulment of the award by an application in writing addressed to the Secretary-General on one more of the following grounds:

that the Tribunal was not properly constitutes;
that the Tribunal has manifestly exceeded its powers;
that there was corruption on the part of a member of the Tribunal;
that there has been a serious departure from a fundamental rule of procedure; or
that the award has failed to state the reasons on which it is based.

The application shall be made within 120 days after the date on which the award was rendered except that when annulment is requested on the ground of corruption such application shall be made within 120 days after discovery of the corruption and in any event within three years after the date on which the award was rendered.

On receipt of the request the Chairman shall forthwith appoint from the Panel of Arbitrators an ad hoc Committee of three persons. None of the members of the Committee shall have been a member of the Tribunal which rendered the award, shall be the same nationality as any such member, shall be a national of the State party to the dispute or the State whose national is a party to the dispute, shall have been designated to the Panel of Arbitrators by either of those States, or shall have acted as a conciliator in the same dispute. The Committee shall have the authority to annul the award or any part thereof on any of grounds set forth in paragraph (1).

The provisions of Articles 41–45, 48, 49, 53 and 54 and of Chapters VI and VII shall apply mutatis mutandis to proceedings before the Committee.

The Committee may, if it considers that the circumstances so require, stay enforcement of the award pending its decision. If the applicant requests a stay enforcement of the award in his application, enforcement shall be stayed provisionally until the Committee rules on such request.

IF the award is annulled the dispute shall, at the request of either party, be resubmitted to a new Tribunal constitutes in accordance with Section 2 of this Chapter.

inconsistency could be a risk in decisions rendered by *ad hoc* Committees, unless the Committees adopt a precedent-based system, which is apparently rejected in Amco decision.[418] At the same time, several *ad hoc* Committees have held that the annulment mechanism does not aim to bring consistency in international investment law. They believe that this is a task for the arbitral tribunals.[419]

Annulment committees should examine the grounds for annulment set out in Article 52 in a neutral and reasonable manner. The committees could not annul an award unless they are convinced that there has been a substantial violation of a rule based on Article 52.[420]

It should be stressed that the annulment process is fundamentally different in nature from an appeal. Appeal leads to the modification of an award, while a successful annulment results in invalidation of an award in whole or in part without replacing or amending it. If the plea for annulment is rejected, the decision will be left to stand. The other distinction between annulment and appeal is the aspects of the award, which are subject to review. In the annulment process, the focus is whether the decision is a result from a legitimate process and in contrast to appeal does not examine the substantive correctness of the decision.[421] The issues of legitimacy should be distinguished from the issues of substantive correctness. For example, legitimacy of process requires proper constitution of the deciding body and observation of fundamental rules of procedure, while the substantive correctness examines whether the decision reveals a correct determination of the facts and application of the law to those facts.[422] Bearing in mind that it's always possible that a substantively correct decision is not resulted from

418 Pinsolle, Philippe, "The Annulment of ICSID Awards", The Journal of World Investment & Trade, Vol. 1, Issue. 1, (2000), p. 243–244.

419 M.C.I. Power Group L.C., New Turbine Inc. v. Republic of Ecuador, ICSID Case No. ARB/03/6, Decision on Annulment, (19 October 2009), para. 24.

420 Ben Hamida, Walid, "Two Nebulous ICSID Features: The Notion of Investment and the Scope of Annulment Control – Ad Hoc Committee's Decision in Patrick Mitchell v. Democratic Republic of Congo", Journal of International Arbitration, Vol. 3, (2007), p. 302.

421 Timmer, Laurens J.E., "Manifest Excess of Powers as a Ground for the Annulment of ICSID Awards", The Journal of World Investment & Trade, Vol. 14, (2013), p. 780; Caron, David D., "Reputation and Reality in the ICSID Annulment Process: Understanding the Distinction Between Annulment and Appeal", ICSID Review-Foreign Investment Law Journal, Vol. 7, (1992), pp. 23–24.

422 Caron, David D., "Reputation and Reality in the ICSID Annulment Process: Understanding the Distinction Between Annulment and Appeal", ICSID Review-Foreign Investment Law Journal, Vol. 7, (1992), p. 24.

a legitimate process or, a substantively incorrect decision might be reached through an absolutely legitimate process. Therefore, the *ad hoc* Committees in charge of annulment procedures should act in accordance with their predefined framework and not be tempted to deal with the merits. This has become a ritual that the Committees stress their limited role at the beginning of their decisions and explain the distinction between annulment and appeal.[423]

There are plenty of examples demonstrating *ad hoc* Committees underlying their limited role such as in *MTD v. Chile*:

> "… at the same time the role of an *ad hoc* Committee in the ICSID system is a limited one. It cannot substitute its determination on the merits for that of the tribunal. Nor can it direct a tribunal on a resubmission how it should resolve substantive issue in dispute. All it can do is annul the decision of the tribunal: it can extinguish a *res judicata* but on a question of merits it cannot create a new one …"[424]

or in *Enron v. Argentina*:

> "An ICSID award is not subject to any appeal or to any other remedy except those provided for in the ICSID Convention. In annulment proceedings under Article 52 of the ICSID Convention, an *ad hoc* Committee is this not a court of appeal, and cannot consider the substance of the dispute, but can only determine whether the award should be annulled on one of the grounds in Article 52(1)."[425]

The Committee in Lucchetti similarly stated that:

> "…And in turn the task of the *ad hoc* Committee is to consider whether the manner in which the Tribunal approached and accomplished that task opened its Award to annulment under the Convention, as Lucchetti argues, or adequately met the requirements of the Convention, as the Republic of Peru responds. The word 'manner' is specifically used here in order to emphasize that it is no part of the Committee's function to review the decision itself which the Tribunal arrived at, still less to substitute its own views for those of the Tribunal, but merely to pass judgment on whether the manner in which the Tribunal carried out its functions met the requirements of the ICSID Convention."[426]

---

423 Schreuer, Christoph, "From ICSID Annulment to Appeal Halfway Down the Slippery Slope", The Law and Practice of International Courts and Tribunals, Vol. 10, (2011), p. 212.

424 MTD Equity Sdn Bhd. & MTD Chile S.A. v. Republic of Chile, ICSID Case No. ARB/01/7, Decision on Annulment, (21 March 2007), para. 54.

425 Enron Creditors Recovery Corporation (formerly Enron Corporation and ponderosa Assets L.P. v. Argentine Republic, Decision on the Application for Annulment of the Argentine Republic, ICSID Case No. ARB/01/3, (30 July 2010), para. 63.

426 Industria Nacional de Alimentos S.A. and Indalsa Perú S.A. v. Republic of Peru, Annulment Proceeding, ICSID Case No. ARB/03/4, (5 September 2007), para. 97.

However, as we mentioned before in the *Klöckner* case, ICSID annulment committees have been criticized for not considering this distinction at all times and acting as a court of appeal by giving a broad interpretation of their functions and the grounds for annulment listed in Article 52(1) of the ICSID Convention.

Sometimes it could be complicated to draw a line between annulment and appeal, especially where, for example, a decision is grossly incorrect that might be viewed as evidence of an illegitimate process.

Since the annulment committees should function only in the framework of ICSID Convention and consider the exhaustive list of Article 52(1) regarding the grounds for annulment, there is no room for them to examine the substantive correctness of the awards. That would also put the finality of awards at risk. Unlike national judiciaries, in case of arbitration, the parties almost always agree that the award will be final and binding upon them.

3) Manifest excess of powers

Manifest excess of powers is one of the most often invoked grounds in ICSID annulment processes. Article 52(1)(b) of the ICSID Convention allows either party to request for annulment of an award on the ground that the tribunal has manifestly exceeded its powers. There are several situations in which a tribunal can exceed its powers including a failure to apply the proper law. In the next parts, we will point out how the failure to apply the proper law would fit under this title and what are the limitations of the annulment Committees on considering them as nullifying. Furthermore, we are going to explain the meaning of the word "manifest" in the context of ICSID Convention and illustrate the issues regarding applicable law and the ICSID annulment process by reviewing various cases.

a) Non-application and misapplication of the applicable law

One of the grounds usually brought to the tribunals as a manifest excess of powers is failure to apply the proper law. Article 52(1) does not count a failure to apply the proper law itself as a ground for annulment. But there is no doubt that the provisions on applicable law are an essential element of the parties' agreement to arbitrate.[427] Therefore, the review of the applicable law is carried out through manifest excess of powers standard set out in Article 52 of the

427 Dolzer, Rudolf; Schreuer, Christoph, "Principles of International Investment Law", Oxford University Press, (2008), p. 282.

ICSID Convention.[428] Regarding this issue, the chairman also stated in the drafting phase of the Convention that:

> "...the drafters had intended by the words 'excès de pouvoir' to refer to the case where a decision of the tribunal went beyond the terms of the compromis or compromisory clause ..."[429]

He also added that in a case that the parties had agreed to the application of a particular law and the Tribunal had in fact applied a different law, "the award could be properly challenged on the ground that the arbitrators had gone against the terms of the compromis."[430]

Therefore, we could conclude that the application of the law other than the law that the parties have chosen will be considered as a manifest excess of powers. In other words, the parties' applicable law choice is a part of their agreement and tribunal's failure to give effect to that agreement may amount to a manifest excess of powers. However, a mere mistake in the application of the proper law could not be held as similar. This could be understood also from the debates during the drafting phase of the ICSID Convention, as we read in the drafting documents that:

> "The Chairman remarked that the draft Convention did not provide for an appeal against the award and in his opinion a mistake in the application of the law would not be a valid ground for annulment of the award. A mistake of law as well as a mistake of fact constitutes an inherent risk in judicial or arbitral decision for which appeal was not provided."[431]

Therefore, it is important for the *ad hoc* Committees to differ between a failure to apply the law agreed by the parties and a mere mistake in application of that law, since the latter could not lead to annulment of the award. Sometimes, the distinction between these two acts can become difficult and blurred. There were

---

428 Gaillard, Emmanuel, "The Extent of Review of the Applicable Law in Investment Treaty Arbitration", in: Annulment of ICSID Awards, E. Gaillard and Y. Banifatemi eds., (2004), p. 236.

429 Document 31, (Z10), "Summary Records of Proceedings, Bangkok Consultative Meetings of Legal Experts", (20 July 1964), History of ICSID Convention, ICSID Publication, Volume. II, Part. I, 2006, p. 517.

430 Document 31, (Z10), "Summary Records of Proceedings, Bangkok Consultative Meetings of Legal Experts", (20 July 1964), History of ICSID Convention, ICSID Publication, Volume. II, Part. I, 2006, p. 518.

431 Document 31, (Z10), "Summary Records of Proceedings, Bangkok Consultative Meetings of Legal Experts", (20 July 1964), History of ICSID Convention, ICSID Publication, Volume. II, Part. I, 2006, p. 518.

some situations in which the Tribunal states that it is applying the applicable law but in fact it applies different law. For example, the *ad hoc* Committee in *MTD v. Chile* stated trying to apply the law is not a pure subjective matter. In other words, the Committee would not only rely its decision on whether the correct law has been applied by examining the law which has been claimed to be applied, but it will assess which law has to be applied.[432]

Similarly, in *MINE v. Guinea* the Committee stressed this distinction after it considered that the Tribunal had not applied the applicable law:

> "Disregard of the applicable rules of law must be distinguished from erroneous application of those rules which, even if manifestly unwarranted, furnishes no ground for annulment."[433]

In this category, we can also mention an earlier decision by the *ad hoc* Committee in Amco I:

> "The law applied by the Tribunal will be examined by the *ad hoc* Committee, not for the purpose of scrutinizing whether the Tribunal committed errors in the interpretation of the requirements of applicable law or in the ascertainment or evaluation of the relevant facts to which such law has been applied. Such scrutiny is properly the task of a court of appeals, which the *ad hoc* Committee is not. The *ad hoc* Committee will limit itself to determining whether the Tribunal did in fact apply the law it was bound to apply to the dispute. Failure to apply such law, as distinguished from mere misconstruction of that law, would constitute a manifest excess of powers on the part of the Tribunal and a ground for nullity under Article 52(1)(b) of the Convention. The *ad hoc* Committee has approaches this task with caution, distinguishing failure to apply the applicable law as a ground for annulment and misinterpretation of the applicable law as a ground for appeal."[434]

In general, the misapplication of the applicable law cannot lead to annulment but at some points it could. When the misapplication of the proper law can be considered as equal to the non-application, then it may be an annullable error.[435]

---

432 MTD Equity Sdn Bhd. & MTD Chile S.A. v. Republic of Chile, Decision on Annulment, ICSID Case No. ARB/01/7, (21 March 2007), para. 47.

433 Republic of Guinea v. Maritime International Nominees Establishment ("MINE"), Decision on Annulment, ICSID Case No. ARB84/4, (22 December 1989), para. 5.04.

434 Amco Asia Corporation, Pan American development Limited, PT Amco Indonesia v. Republic of Indonesia, Decision on Annulment, ICSID Case No. ARB/81/1, (16 May 1986), para. 23.

435 Timmer, Laurens J.E., "Manifest Excess of Powers as a Ground for the Annulment of ICSID Awards", The Journal of World Investment & Trade, Vol. 14, (2013), p. 788; See also Guiguo, Wang, "The ICSID Annulment Mechanism: Practice, Problems and Alternatives", China Legal Science, Vol. 2, (2014), pp. 41–43.

The *ad hoc* Committee in *Soufraki v. United Arab Emirates* explains:

> "Misinterpretation or misapplication of the proper law may, in particular cases, be so gross or egregious as substantially to amount to failure to apply the proper law. Such gross and consequential misinterpretation or misapplication of the proper law which no reasonable person ('*bon père de famille*') could accept needs to be distinguished from simple error – even a serious error – in the interpretation of the law which in many national jurisdictions may be the subject of ordinary appeal as distinguished from, e.g., an extraordinary writ of *certiorari*. In the present annulment proceedings, both Claimant and Respondent have acknowledged during the oral hearing an egregiously wrong interpretation of the proper law – though nothing short of that – may amount to annullable error."[436]

Even though it seems so far that the awards in this field commonly and repeatedly explain the distinction between failure to apply the proper law and its misapplication and the consequents of these two, after a thorough search it could be seen that the word "manifest" could also play a role. The Committee in *MINE v. Guinea* has held that an error in the application of the applicable law, no matter how grave, could not lead to annulment. This approach does not give any place to the possible situations like the one explained by the Committee in *Soufraki* case. As the latter Committee stated, sometimes the error could not be taken as a mere mistake, since it turns to a non-application of the proper law. Giving a general rule in such situations is very difficult because the Convention itself has not stated the grounds leading to annulment very detailed; therefore, it is the task of the *ad hoc* Committees to try to conceive whether the error should be taken as manifest and consequently annullable.

On this matter, the annulment Committee in *Sempra v. Argentine* stated where incorrect application of law effectively disregard the applicable law, it may constitute a manifest excess of powers.[437]

> It seems essential to put an extra focus on the word "manifest". This word did not exist in the preliminary draft of the Convention. The preliminary draft was based on the ILC Model rules, which does not consider this word either. At the drafting phase the delegate of Germany suggested that:

436 Hussein Nuaman Soufraki v. United Arab Emirates, Decision of the Ad Hoc Committee on the Application for Annulment of Mr. Soufraki and a Separate Opinion and a Statement of Dissent by Omar Nabulsi, member of the ad hoc Committee, ICSID Case No. ARB/02/7, (5 June 2007), para. 86.

437 Sempra Energy International v. Argentine Republic, Decision on the Argentine Republic's Application for Annulment of the Award, ICSID Case No. ARB/02/16, (29 June 2010), paras. 163–164.

"...he had no objection in principle to the provisions of Section 13. There might, however, be some risk of frustration of awards in some cases and he was accordingly inclined to make the section more restrictive, for example, saying in paragraph (1): 'only on one or more of the following grounds'. And in sub-paragraph (a) of paragraph (1): 'that the Tribunal has manifestly exceeded its powers.' "[438]

So, this word was added in order to prevent from the frustration of awards and to make sure that not every single slight mistake could lead an award to nullification.[439] Regarding the meaning of "manifest," Schreuer has held an explanation which is also cited in the annulment decision in *AES v. Hungary*:

"Concerning the meaning of 'manifest', the Committee shares Schreuer's view that the term relates to the ease with which an excess of powers is perceived, rather than its gravity, and that such an excess must be able to 'be discerned with little effort and without deeper analysis'[440]. Such an approach is consistent with a manifest excess being one which is at once 'textually obvious and substantively serious.' "[441] [442]

In other words, as this point of view was accepted by other Committees such as the one in Wena Hotels, a classic example for manifest excess of powers would be where despite two possible boundary line submitted by the parties, the Tribunal chose a third. Excess of powers in this context shall be self-evident rather than an outcome of complex interpretations.[443]

---

438 Document 29, (Z 9), "Summary Record of Proceedings, Geneva Consultative Meetings of Legal Experts", (1 June 1964), History of ICSID Convention, ICSID Publication, Volume. II, Part. I, (2006), p. 423.

439 Broches, Aron, "Observation on the Finality of ICSID Awards", ICSID Review-Foreign Investment Law Journal, Vol. 6, (1991), p. 329.

440 Schreuer, Christoph, "The ICSID Convention- A Commentary", Cambridge University Press, Second Edition, (2009), p. 938.

441 Hussein Nuaman Soufraki v. United Arab Emirates, Decision of the Ad Hoc Committee on the Application for Annulment of Mr. Soufraki and a Separate Opinion and a Statement of Dissent by Omar Nabulsi, member of the ad hoc Committee, ICSID Case No. ARB/02/7, (5 June 2007), para. 40.

442 AES Summit Generation Limited and AES-Tisza Erömú Kft. V. Hungary, ICSID Case No. ARB/07/22, Decision on Annulment, (29 June 2012), para. 31.

443 Wena Hotels Limited v. Arab Republic of Egypt, Decision on Annulment, ICSID Case No. ARB/98/4, (5 February 2002), para. 25; See also Repsol YPF Ecuador, S.A. v. Empresa Estatal Petróleos del Ecuador (Petroecuador), Decision on Annulment, ICSID Case No. ARB/01/10, (8 January 2007), para. 36.; CDC Group PLC v. The Republic of Seychelles, Decision on Annulment, ICSID Case No. ARB/02/14, (29 June 2005), para. 41.

This approach is also called *Prima facie* test. In addition, there is another method called two-step methodological approach which has been adopted by *ad hoc* committees such as in *Vivendi* case.[444] In this sense, the Committee stated:

> "For all of these reasons, the Committee concludes that the Tribunal exceeded its powers in the sense of Article 52(1)(b), in that the Tribunal, having jurisdiction over the Tucumán claims, failed to decide those claims. Given the clear and serious implications of the decision for claimants in terms of Article 8(2) of the BIT, and the surrounding circumstances, the Committee can only conclude that that excess of powers was manifest. It accordingly annuls the decision of the Tribunal so far as concerns the entirety of the Tucumán claims."[445]

According to this method, the Committee first examines whether there is an excess of powers, then it determines whether it could be qualified as manifest.

The annulment decisions rendered by different *ad hoc* Committees reflect the variety of interpretations of their general functions and it seems that some committees construe their inquiries much broader than the other. This inconsistency makes the situation even more difficult for the future annulment proceedings. An even broader interpretation could be seen in the annulment decision in Vivendi II. In this case, the Committee initially heard the arguments as to whether the erroneous findings of law and fact qualify as grounds for annulment. To that end, the Tribunal stated that it would only be the case if they meet the standards stipulated in Article 52(1).[446]

It seems that the Committee believed that there must be a very exceptional situation, in which it could constitute an erroneous application of the proper law as a manifest excess of powers. But surprisingly, it stated also in the same decision that:

> "Although an improper application of the applicable law is not directly mentioned as ground for annulment under Article 52(1)(b), it is generally accepted that it may amount to an annulment ground under that Article and this issue needs therefore further consideration."[447]

---

444 Anzorena, Carlos Ignacio Suarez, "Vivendi v. Argentina: on the Admissibility of the Requests for Partial Annulment and the Ground of a Manifest Excess of Powers", in: Annulment of ICSID Awards, E. Gaillard and Y. Banifatemi eds., (2004), p. 170.

445 Compañía de Aguas del Aconquija S.A. and Vivendi Universal S.A. v. Argentine Republic, Decision on Annulment, ICSID Case No. ARB/97/3, (3 July 2002), para. 115.

446 Compañía de Aguas del Aconquija S.A. and Vivendi Universal S.A. v. Argentine Republic, ICSID Case No. ARB/97/3, Decision on the Argentine Republic's Request for Annulment of the Award, (10 August 2010), para. 251.

447 Compañía de Aguas del Aconquija S.A. and Vivendi Universal S.A. v. Argentine Republic, Decision on the Argentine Republic's Request for Annulment of the

These two statements by the annulment Committee just a few paragraphs apart can illustrate how narrow is the line between an error capable of nullifying an award and one without such impact.

b) Partial non-application of the applicable law

As pointed out, non-application or failure to apply the applicable law will lead to the nullification of the award. Now the question would be whether non-application of parts of the applicable law or merely a single provision of it could have the same effect.

It seems not defensible to claim that a partial non-application of the proper law could have the same effect as a failure to apply the law in its entirety and could consequently lead to annulment.

Regarding this matter, after reviewing a long debate in *Amco I* case, especially the arguments made by the *ad hoc* Committee, it would be fair to say that partial non-application of the proper law and its erroneous application are almost indistinguishable.[448]

The *Amco* case is one of the most-cited cases in the field of investment arbitration. We have already referred to this case in past sections. But as Reisman said: "the Amco case was in many ways the paradigmatic dispute about contemporary direct foreign investment."[449]; therefore, this time we take a look at this case from another angle to study deeper about the function of annulment Committees and the role of applicable law and correct application of it in accordance with Article 52(1).

In this case Amco, which was a U.S. company committed to build and manage a hotel complex in Jakarta. After the hotel was built and Indonesian government alleged non-payment of the capital sums, military personnel seized the hotel and expelled the management. The Indonesian government believed that Amco had not fulfilled its commitment and therefore it terminated Amco's license. Efforts to make a decision in Indonesian courts were not successful so Amco submitted a case in ICSID claiming nine million dollars plus interest. The dispute was about finding out two questions, one about expropriation and

---

Award, ICSID Case No. ARB/97/3, (10 August 2010), para. 260. See also AES Summit Generation Limited and AES-Tisza Erömú Kft. V. Hungary, Decision on Annulment, ICSID Case No. ARB/07/22, (29 June 2012), para. 33.

448 Schreuer, Christoph, "The ICSID Convention- A Commentary", Cambridge University Press, Second Edition, (2009), p. 964.

449 Reisman, W. Michael, "The Breakdown of the Control Mechanism in ICSID Arbitration", Duke Law Journal, No. 4, (1989), p. 770.

the other, breach of contract. Firstly, the Tribunal had to answer whether the act of taking can be attributed to the Indonesian government. The Tribunal did not find enough evidence that this act was due to a decision made by the Indonesian government. But the Tribunal found that act operated by the army as unlawful and in contradiction with international law. Regarding the second issue, the Tribunal found that the revocation of the license obviously constituted a breach of contract for which compensation was due under both Indonesian and international law.[450] The Tribunal believed that the revocation was unlawful because based on Indonesian law there was a lack of due process and also unjustified.[451] Regarding the alleged shortfall in the investment required from Amco, the Tribunal had calculated the total sum of actual investments at 2,472,490 U.S. dollars. But it concluded that the shortfall of 3,000,000 dollars is not material enough to justify the revocation of the license.[452] Eventually, the Tribunal awarded the Claimant 3,200,000 dollars plus 6% interest, which was considerably less than what Amco had claimed. Indonesia had counterclaimed and the Tribunal rejected it. Indonesia submitted an application for annulment. The *ad hoc* Committee found the calculation of the Tribunal wrong since under the relevant provisions of Indonesian law, only amounts recognized and registered by Indonesian authority were investments. Therefore, the Committee concluded that in line with Indonesian law, investments are only recognized and covered by the Foreign Investment Law, if they are registered by the competent Indonesian authority (Bank Indonesia) or a circular or an announcement of the Foreign Exchange Bureau of Bank Indonesia required investors to provide evidence that required amount of foreign capital originating from outside Indonesia had been invested in line with provisions of mentioned law.[453] The Committee deemed that Amco failed to acquire the Bank of Indonesia registration for the amounts

450 Amco Asia Corporation, Pan American Development Limited, PT Amco Indonesia v. Republic of Indonesia, Award, ICSID Case No. ARB/81/1, (20 November 1984), para. 172.

451 Amco Asia Corporation, Pan American Development Limited, PT Amco Indonesia v. Republic of Indonesia, Award, ICSID Case No. ARB/81/1, (20 November 1984), para. 242.

452 Amco Asia Corporation, Pan American Development Limited, PT Amco Indonesia v. Republic of Indonesia, Award, ICSID Case No. ARB/81/1, (20 November 1984), para. 241.

453 Amco Asia Corporation, Pan American development Limited, PT Amco Indonesia v. Republic of Indonesia, Decision on Annulment, ICSID Case No. ARB/81/1, (16 May 1986), para. 93.

invested in the project.[454] Therefore, it stated that Amco clearly failed to apply provisions of Indonesian law, thus the Tribunal had manifestly excessed its powers and the finding shall be annulled.

The Committee believed that the Tribunal had been so much preoccupied with the financing procedures that failed to seize the importance of a basic rule on the matter, which had been obscured by lengthy arguments that only approved and registered foreign capital inputs are investments within the contemplation of the Foreign Investment Law.[455]

The award rendered by the Tribunal in *Amco* case shows that the Tribunal has carefully examined the Indonesian law and also Foreign Investment law and applied it to the facts before it.[456] Therefore, there could not be a non-application of the proper law, which is distinguishable from an erroneous application and in such circumstances it becomes impossible to distinguish between non- and misapplication of the law.[457]

Some commentators relate this issue and the view of the *ad hoc* Committees regarding the way of their examination to two different approaches.[458] One approach is "technical discrepancy." Based on this approach, a Committee should announce nullification when there is a technical discrepancy from the Convention but the characteristic in this approach is that it is not important whether this discrepancy cause injury to the claiming party.

The second approach referred to as "material violation" is in contrast. Based on this point of view, a technical discrepancy will be ignored if it has not resulted in a grave and material violation of the standards of the Convention.[459] In the *Amco* case, we can say that the Committee was for the

---

454 Amco Asia Corporation, Pan American development Limited, PT Amco Indonesia v. Republic of Indonesia, Decision on Annulment, ICSID Case No. ARB/81/1, (16 May 1986), para. 94.

455 Amco Asia Corporation, Pan American development Limited, PT Amco Indonesia v. Republic of Indonesia, Decision on Annulment, ICSID Case No. ARB/81/1, (16 May 1986), para. 96.

456 Pirrwitz, Bjorn, "Annulment of Arbitral Awards under Article 52 of the Washington Convention on the Settlement of Investment Disputes between States and Nationals of Other States", Texas International Law Journal, Vol. 23, (1998), p. 108.

457 Schreuer, Christoph, "The ICSID Convention- A Commentary", Cambridge University Press, Second Edition, (2009), p. 965.

458 Reisman, W.Michael, "The Breakdown of the Control Mechanism in ICSID Arbitration", Duke Law Journal, No. 4, (1989), p. 776.

459 Reisman, W.Michael, "The Breakdown of the Control Mechanism in ICSID Arbitration", Duke Law Journal, No. 4, (1989), p. 777.

material violation approach because it concluded that the content of the international principle that the Tribunal had applied was materially the same as the Indonesian law. It was technically a violation of Article 52 but based on the testimony of the parties, the proper law would have the same result if it had been applied. Therefore, from one angle the Committee refrained to annul the award because of the failure of the application of the proper law and from another angle, which we pointed out before, not applying a section of Indonesian law led to nullification.[460] It may sometimes be almost impossible to decide whether a mistake would fit into Article 52 and become a ground for nullification. Looking at these cases made it clear that the Committees albeit the strict formulation of Article 52 have great discretion and sometimes it leads to inconsistency, which has not been the aim of the Convention and because of this we reviewed plenty of writings criticizing the ICSID's control system in this section.[461] However, more consistency can be seen in the decisions rendered after *Klöckner I*. As Broches said, *Klöckner I* was the result of the Committee's misconception of its function.[462] But this could not be considered as a failure of ICSID to act in its framework and consider annulment as a limited remedy, which was the wish of the drafters in order to

460 Amco Asia Corporation, Pan American development Limited, PT Amco Indonesia v. Republic of Indonesia, Decision on Annulment, ICSID Case No. ARB/81/1, (16 May 1986), paras. 58, 79.

461 See Feldman, Mark B., "The Annulment Proceedings and the Finality of ICSID Arbitral Awards", ICSID Review-Foreign Investment Law Journal, Vol. 2, (1987), pp. 85–110.; Reisman, W.Michael, "The Breakdown of the Control Mechanism in ICSID Arbitration", Duke Law Journal, No. 4, (1989), pp. 739–807.; Reisman, W.Michael, "Repairing ICSID's Control System: Some Comments on Aron Broches' "Observations on the Finality of ICSID Awards"", ICSID Review-Foreign Investment Law journal, Vol. 7, (1992), pp. 196–211.; Schatz, Sylvia, "The Effect of the Annulment Decision In Amco v. Indonesia and Klöckner v. Cameroon on the Future of the International Center for the Settlement of Investment Disputes", American University International Law Review, Vol. 3, No. 2, (1988), pp. 481–515.; Schwartz, Eric A., "Finality at what Cost? The Decision of the Ad Hoc Committee in Wena Hotels v. Egypt", in: Annulment of ICSID Awards, E. Gaillard and Y. Banifatemi eds., (2004), pp. 43–86.; Ben Hamida, Walid, "Two Nebulous ICSID Features: The Notion of Investment and the Scope of Annulment Control – Ad Hoc Committee's Decision in Patrick Mitchell v. Democratic Republic of Congo", Journal of International Arbitration, Vol. 3, (2007), pp. 287–306.

462 Broches, Aron, "On the Finality of Awards: A Reply to Michael Reisman", ICSID Review-Foreign Investment Law Journal, Vol. 8, (1993), p. 102.

non-frustration of awards. The next generation of annulment decisions did not follow the previous route but they re-established the annulment proceeding as it was meant to be under ICSID Convention.

c) *Substantiation of sources*

It is obvious that a tribunal should base its decision on the applicable law, which in ICSID's case would be in accordance with Article 42. In other words, the tribunal substantiates its decision with reference to the proper law. The question is if the Tribunal actually applies the proper law but fails to refer to the applicable law, will this decision be under risk of nullity? Or could the failure to cite specific legal authority amount to the failure to apply the law?

On the one hand, the aim of the Article 52(1) is to state the grounds based on which an award should be annulled. On the other hand, the wording of subparagraph (b) and the whole paragraph as an exhaustive list is to prevent the awards from frustration. It has also been mentioned in the debates during the drafting phase of the Convention. Therefore, it seems that the drafters leaned more toward the material violation approach. Since the finality of awards is an important characteristic in international arbitration, the awards could not be nullified just because the way the Tribunal substantiates the sources. The most important point is the outcome that should be in accordance with the applicable law.

This issue became bold as the *ad hoc* Committee in *Klöckner I* found the absence of adequate legal substantiation in the Tribunal's award unacceptable.[463] In the next annulment proceedings in *Amco* case, the Committee did not follow the previous view. The Committee believed that it's not necessary for the Tribunal to preface each finding or conclusion with a specification of the Indonesian or international law.[464]

463 Klöckner Industrie-Anlagen GmbH v. United Republic of Cameroon, Société Camerounaise des Engrais, Decision on annulment, ICSID Case No. ARB/81/2, (3 May 1985), paras. 71–79.

464 Amco Asia Corporation, Pan American development Limited, PT Amco Indonesia v. Republic of Indonesia, Decision on Annulment, ICSID Case No. ARB/81/1, (16 May 1986), para. 25; See also Republic of Guinea v. Maritime International Nominees Establishment ("MINE"), Decision on Annulment, ICSID Case No. ARB84/4, (22 December 1989), paras. 6.34–6.40; Hussein Nuaman Soufraki v. United Arab Emirates, Decision of the Ad Hoc Committee on the Application for Annulment

The annulment committees after Klöckner tend to focus more on examining what the tribunals have actually done and its result rather than how they substantiate their findings and it seems more compatible to the essence of ICSID Convention and in general international investment arbitration.

d) *Non-application of international law*

According to Article 42 of ICSID Convention, international law could be considered as the applicable law or at least it could be a part of it. There are various situations in which international law may serve as the proper law. First possibility is where parties choose international law as the applicable law alone or in conjunction with another law. International law could be the applicable law when it is incorporated in an investment protection treaty or in the law of a chosen domestic law. Even if the parties have not agreed upon the applicable law, international law would have been applicable under the second sentence of Article 42(1) along with the law of the host state. Now, the question is whether the non-application of international law and failure of its application may amount to an excess of powers and lead to the nullification of award.

As pointed out before, first step toward finding out whether the nullification would be fit is to distinguish a non-application from a mere mistake. Therefore, while a general failure to apply international law as the law applicable would lead to an excess of powers and put the award at risk of annulment, an erroneous application of international law would not have the same impact.[465]

In the previous part, it has been discussed that partial non-application could not lead to annulment. This is also true with regard to international law. The difference is when the non-applied parts of international law are considered as fundamental rules of international law. The fundamental rules of international law were described under the notion of public policy. Few examples of binding and peremptory rules of international law would be human rights, prohibition of terrorism, slavery and genocide. Furthermore, there are some other international rules, which are fundamental and basic though not considered as public policy such as denial of justice. It is complicated to examine whether the non-application

---

of Mr. Soufraki and a Separate Opinion and a Statement of Dissent by Omar Nabulsi, member of the ad hoc Committee, ICSID Case No. ARB/02/7, (5 June 2007), para. 128.

465 Schreuer, Christoph, "The ICSID Convention- A Commentary", Cambridge University Press, Second Edition, (2009), p. 975.

of these rules could lead to nullification of award. On the one hand, these rules are very fundamental in the field of international law that their non-application could amount to non-application of international law as a whole. On the other hand, such approach makes the difference between non-application and misapplication of international law even more opaque.[466]

In practice the problem has been mostly contrariwise. The most objections were not about the failure of application of international law, but its application in lieu of the law of the host state and it has produced long debates regarding the relationship of international law and host state law, which we discussed in detail before.

466 Schreuer, Christoph, "The ICSID Convention – A Commentary", Cambridge University Press, Second Edition, (2009), p. 976.

2. Applicable law and the Iran-United States Claims Tribunal

I) Background

From the early times Iran was always a strategic country in the Middle East due to its oil resources as well as its geographic situation. At the beginning of the Second World War in 1939, Iran declared its neutrality but the allies needed to use the Trans-Iranian Railway in order to ship the war supplies from Britain to Stalinist Russia. As at that time most of the Iranian foreign trade was with Germany, Reza Shah was to some extent under the pressure of Hitler and therefore he refused to keep his cooperation with the Allies. Thus, in 1941, the British imperialists and Russia invaded Iran.[467] After the Second World War and the forced replacement of Reza Shah Pahlavi with his son Mohammadreza, in the early 1950s, Mohammad Mosaddegh, Iranian prime minister, nationalized British and American oil operations. After the Shah did not approve this act, the mobs called for his removal and eventually he fled Iran. Again in 1953, the military of Iran with the support of CIA overthrew Mosaddegh and Shah came back to Iran and returned to power on 19 August 1953.[468]At that time the United States and Iran signed a Treaty of Amity.

In the 1960s and 1970s, Iran embarked on a development program with the purpose of economic and military growth. The oil revenues in Iran during these years increased steadily from 5 to 20 billion dollars a year.[469] During this time Iran was involved in great direct and large-scale investment programs with Western and especially American corporations. At that time Iran was open to foreign contractors, advisors and suppliers from both governmental and private sectors. Numerous projects were initiated in Iran by American companies to the point that by the end of the 1970s over 40,000 Americans were living in Iran.[470]

---

467 Dr. Zayar, "The Iranian Revolution Past, Present and Future", p. 9, available at www.iranchamber.com.

468 For a general overview see also: Wise, Krysta, "Islamic Revolution of 1979: The Downfall of American-Iranian Relations, Southern Illinois University Carbondale, Legacy, Vol. 11, Issue. 1, (2011).

469 Dr. Zayar, "The Iranian Revolution Past, Present and Future", p. 9, available at www.iranchamber.com.

470 Brower, Charles N., "The Iran-United States Claims Tribunal: its genesis, structure, organization, jurisdiction and history", Collected Courses of the Hague Academy of International Law, Vol. 224, (1990), p. 133.

Despite the beginning of many projects, which reflected a new development phase in Iran, not everyone was in favor of it. Some groups of people called it an unacceptable intervention of foreign countries, especially the United States in Iran's internal affairs.[471] In addition, the boom in oil revenues was accompanied by rapid inflation, housing shortage, large gap in the distribution of wealth and other problems, which led to revolutionary movements.

The people's disenchantments were also supported by Ayatollah Khomeini and other religious leaders. That time could be recognized as a beginning of a crisis. Ayatollah Khomeini was expelled from Iraq and ended up in France in October 1978. One month later, Shah fired his cabinet and installed a military government. Parallel to all these changes, Khomeini declared in Paris the possibility of formation of an Islamic republic in Iran. In January 1979, Shah left Iran and eventually Ayatollah Khomeini returned to Iran on 1 February as the Islamic Republic of Iran was declared.[472]

During the turbulence of the revolution in late 1978 and early 1979, most projects including those with American companies were disrupted. Consequently, contracts were terminated, American investments were expropriated and American nationals left Iran hastily leaving their personal belongings behind.[473]

The upheaval of the crisis was in November 1979, when Iranian students captured the United States' Embassy in Tehran and taking its personnel as hostage and demanded that the United States return the Shah to Iran.[474] This act had also the government's support as the day after Khomeini sent a support message for the students involved in the seizure of American embassy.

In response to the hostage crisis and an official Iranian announcement that Iran proposed to withdraw all its funds from the United States' banks, the United States froze the Iranian bank accounts in its banks and all their foreign branches

---

471 Mohebi, Mohsen, "The International Law Character of the Iran-United States Claims Tribunal", Kluwer Law International, (1998), p. 58.

472 Christopher, Warren; Mosk, Richard M., "The Iranian Hostage Crisis and the Iran-U.S, Claims Tribunal: Implications for International Dispute Resolution and Diplomacy", Pepperdine Dispute Resolution Law Journal, Vol. 7, (2007), p. 167.

473 Stewart. David P.; Sherman, Laura B., "Developments at the Iran-United States Claims Tribunal: 1981–1983", in The Iran-United States Claims Tribunal edited by Richard B. Lillich, University Press of Virginia, (1984), p. 2.

474 Hertz, Michael F., "The Hostage Crisis and Domestic Litigation: An Overview", in The Iran-United States Claims Tribunal edited by Richard B. Lillich, University Press of Virginia, (1984), p. 138.

based on an order issued by President Carter and announced that it would stop importing oil from Iran if Iran does not release the hostages.[475]

At that time, many American individuals and companies began filing cases against Iran in American courts and were about to obtain judicial attachments of Iranian properties in the United States.

Another response from the United States was its application to International Court of Justice against Iran demanding the release of hostages. However, after the death of Shah in Egypt on 7 April 1980, Khomeini declared that the hostages should remain in the control of the students at the embassy. This decision led to the severance of diplomatic relations between Iran and the United States and implementation of economic sanctions against Iran which didn't help to release the hostages and eventually the only option left for the United States was to launch an operation by its military to rescue the hostages. The attempt was not successful.

It was not an easy task for the parties to reach an agreement. Ayatollah Khomeini proposed four conditions in order to release the hostages. The first condition was that the United States must return the wealth of Shah and his family. Secondly, all the claims against Iran in the United States' courts should be cancelled. Thirdly, the United States must unfreeze the Iranian funds in the United States and as a last condition Iran demanded that the United States should guarantee that it would no longer interfere in Iran's affairs.[476]

As at that time the two countries did not communicate directly, Iran named Algeria as an intermediary for the hostage negotiations. The United States accepted Iran's conditions as "a basis for resolution of the crisis."

At first Iran demanded 24 billion dollars on 21 December 1980 for both assets and guarantees to be deposited in Algeria. The United States did not agree and eventually offered 7.9 billion dollars and the 10 billion dollars guarantee, to which Tehran agreed. At last an agreement was reached between Iran and the United States on 19 January 1981, which was the last day of President Carter's administration. Based on this agreement, Iran accepted to release the 52 American hostages and the United States agreed to return the Iranian assets and dismiss all the cases against Iran in American courts.

---

475 Brower, Charles N., "The Iran-United States Claims Tribunal: its genesis, structure, organization, jurisdiction and history", Collected Courses of the Hague Academy of International Law, Vol. 224, (1990), p. 134.

476 Warren, Christopher; Mosk, Richard M., "The Iranian Hostage Crisis and the Iran-U.S, Claims Tribunal: Implications for International Dispute Resolution and Diplomacy", Pepperdine Dispute Resolution Law Journal, Vol. 7, (2007), p. 168.

These agreements embodied in two declarations known as Algiers Accords issued by the government of Algeria, together with a number of technical implementing agreements. The first declaration, with the full official name of "Declaration of the Government of the Democratic and Popular Republic of Algeria" included the undertakings of each country and the other instrument with the full name of "Declaration of the Government of the Democratic and Popular Republic of Algeria concerning the Settlement of Claims by the Government of the United States of America and the Government of the Islamic Republic of Iran" was the agreement to establish an arbitral body – the Iran-United States Claims Tribunal – at The Hague in the Netherlands to hear and arbitrate all the claims by Unites States' nationals against Iran, Iran and by Iranian nationals against the United States and between the two governments.

In addition, the United States waived any right to further proceedings before ICJ or elsewhere regarding the hostages.

Based on the agreement, a large amount of Iranian funds went to pay American bank loans, some of them went into escrow accounts agreed to by Iran and one billion dollars went into a security account at the N.V. Settlement Bank of the Netherlands, a subsidiary of the Dutch Central Bank, to ensure the payment of awards against Iran at the Iran-United States Claims Tribunal, which was to be established by the second declaration.[477]

The Iran-United States Claims Tribunal is a very unique institution in many ways and is even described as "the most significant arbitral body in history."[478] This Tribunal has a complex nature. It is not an ordinary national court and at the same time it is not a tribunal based on a multilateral treaty such as ICJ or ICC. Furthermore, this Tribunal is not the same as other *ad hoc* tribunals, which are established for the resolution of one certain dispute. Therefore, it is a very special Tribunal with an enormous caseload.[479] It has been reported that by the date of the conclusion of Algiers Accords, there were about 2,150 cases pending against Iran in the United States' courts.[480] Those were the cases, which then

---

477 Declaration of the Government of the Democratic and Popular Republic of Algeria (General Declaration), 19 January 1981, para. 7.

478 Lillich, Richard B., Preface in "The Iran-United States Claims Tribunal 1981–1983", University Press of Virginia, (1984).

479 Crook, John R., "Applicable Law in International Arbitration: The Iran-U.S. Claims Tribunal Experience", The American Journal of International Law, Vol. 83, (1989), p. 279.

480 Mohebi, Mohsen, "The International Law Character of the Iran-United States Claims Tribunal", Kluwer Law International, (1998), p. 67.

should be filed with the Tribunal not later than one year after the entry into force of the agreement or six months after the date the president is appointed.[481] To date, the Tribunal has finalized over 3,900 cases.[482]

This was a short background of the crisis leading to the establishment of the Iran-United States Claims Tribunal. Our main focus in this chapter is to analyze the issues concerning the determination of applicable law by this Tribunal. As before mentioned, the Iran-United States Claims Tribunal is unique in many aspects. Among them is its background, its way of establishment and the tensed situation between two countries, which made the direct negotiation between the States almost impossible. That lasts until years when the two negotiators of Iran and the United States met informally in a hallway in The Hague during a Tribunal hearing.[483]

Reaching an agreement became hard in such tensed political atmosphere and absence of direct negotiation between parties and even harder was to reach an agreement concerning the more detailed issues such as applicable law.[484] Therefore, the Claims Settlement Declaration permits the Tribunal to look at wide range of sources to determine the applicable law. In this study, we will analyze the methods of the determination of applicable law that the Tribunal has been applied.

II) Structure of the Tribunal

The seat of the Tribunal according to Article VI of the Claims Settlement Declaration is The Hague, the Netherlands; however, the parties may agree upon any other place.[485] At the beginning, the arbitrators and the agents of both governments met in a room borrowed at the Peace Palace at The Hague. From April 1982, the Tribunal moved to its own place somewhere else at The Hague.[486]

---

481 Article III.4 of the Claims Settlement Declaration, 19 January 1981.

482 http://www.iusct.net, Accessed on 5 April 2016.

483 Warren, Christopher; Mosk, Richard M., "The Iranian Hostage Crisis and the Iran-U.S, Claims Tribunal: Implications for International Dispute Resolution and Diplomacy", Pepperdine Dispute Resolution Law Journal, Vol. 7, (2007), p. 168.

484 Drahozal, Christopher R.; Gibson, Christopher S., "Iran-United States Claims Tribunal Precedent in Investor-State Arbitration", Journal of International Arbitration, Vol. 23, Issue. 6, (2006), p. 522.

485 Claims Settlement Declarations, Article VI, para. 1, (19 January 1981).

486 Mohebi, Mohsen, "The International Law Character of the Iran-United States Claims Tribunal", Kluwer Law International, (1998), p. 73.

As provided by Article III, paragraph 1 of the Claims Settlement Declaration, the Tribunal consists of nine members or such larger multiple of three. They include three arbitrators chosen by Iran, three chosen by the United States, and three chosen by these six Party-appointed arbitrators. If the Party-appointed arbitrators could not reach an agreement, an "Appointing Authority" will appoint three arbitrators. The president of the Tribunal is one of the last three arbitrators who are commonly referred to as "third-country" arbitrators, because their nationality should be different from those of the States parties.

On 1 October 1981, based on the IR-US Presidential Order No. 1, the Tribunal was divided into three Chambers. Each Chamber consists of three arbitrators, one from Iran, one from the United States and the other from a third country. The third-country arbitrator is also the president of the Chamber. A Chamber may hear all cases submitted to the Tribunal, except that some disputes concerning the interpretation or application of the Claims Settlement Declaration, referred to as "A" cases or "interpretive disputes" should be decided by the full Tribunal (the Plenary Tribunal).[487] Besides, official claims of the United States and Iran against each other arising out of contractual arrangements between them for the purchase and sale of goods and services, known as "B" cases may be heard by a full tribunal. The same will apply, when a majority for a decision or an award cannot be found within a Chamber.[488]

Official languages of the Tribunal are Farsi and English and all the documents are to be submitted in both languages; therefore, a number of Tribunal's staff consists of translators and interpreters.

III) Jurisdiction of the Tribunal

Similar to many other international institutions, the Iran-United States Claims Tribunal was established in order to resolve certain classes of claims. Since this Tribunal is involved with different categories of disputes between two State parties and their nationals, it has a multi-jurisdiction system.[489] Like it is the case for every other Tribunal, there are limits to IR-US Tribunal's jurisdiction. Having in mind that international tribunals usually have more limitations than domestic

---

487 IR-US Presidential Order No. 1, para. 1, (1 October 1981), in Pieter Sanders (ed.), Yearbook Commercial Arbitration, Vol. 7, (1982), p. 260.

488 IR-US Presidential Order No. 1, para. 6(a), (1 October 1981), in Pieter Sanders (ed.), Yearbook Commercial Arbitration, Vol. 7, (1982), p. 261.

489 Mohebi, Mohsen, "The International Law Character of the Iran-United States Claims Tribunal", Kluwer Law International, (1998), p. 76.

tribunals, it shall be noted that despite the broad jurisdiction of the Tribunal, it has its own limitations set forth in the Algiers Accords.[490]

In order to study the Tribunal's Jurisdiction, we should divide the subject into personal and material jurisdiction.

1) The *Ratione Personae* jurisdiction of the Tribunal

The Ratione Personae of the Tribunal as well as its *Ratione Materiae* is set forth by Article II of the Claims Settlement Declaration.

In general, the right to submit a claim in an international tribunal is given to the States establishing that tribunal, but in this case this right is also given to the nationals of Contracting States to submit their claims directly to the Tribunal and not through diplomatic protection.

The basis of the *Ratione Personae* of the Tribunal could be found in Article II of the Claims Settlement Declaration and paragraph 2-B of the Undertakings.

First paragraph of Article II of the Claims Settlement Declaration provides:

> "An international arbitral Tribunal (the Iran-United States Claims Tribunal) is hereby established for the purpose of deciding claims of nationals of the United States against Iran and claims of nationals of Iran against the United States ..."

Second paragraph of the same Article states:

> "The Tribunal shall also have jurisdiction over official claims of the United States and Iran against each other arising out of contractual arrangements between them for the purchase and sale of goods and services."

So, in this part we study in detail that who are the eligible parties that have access to the proceedings.

a) *Private persons before the Tribunal*

Under the Claims Settlement Declaration, private persons have access to the arbitration proceedings in contradiction to the inter-state tribunals in which private persons could submit their claim normally through diplomatic protection procedures. Thus the State takes up the case on behalf of its national.

Paragraph 3 of Article III of the Claims Settlement Declaration states an exception to this rule and provides:

490 Aldrich, George H., "The Jurisprudence of the Iran-United States Claims Tribunal", Clarendon Press. Oxford, (1996), p. 44.

> "Claims of nationals of the United States and Iran that are within the scope of this agreement shall be presented to the tribunal either by claimants themselves or, in the case of claims of less than 250,000 U.S. Dollars by the Government of such national."

The word "national" is defined by Article VII of the Claims Settlement Declaration and based on the definition it consists not only the natural persons who are a citizen of Iran or the United States but also corporations or legal entities. They could appear directly before the Tribunal when they met the requirements pointed out in said Article. For any legal entity to be considered as an eligible national and allowed to appear directly before the Tribunal, it should meet two requirements. Firstly, it should be organized under the laws of Iran or the United States or any of its states or territories, the District of Columbia or the Commonwealth of Puerto Rico. Secondly, natural persons, who are citizens of such country, must hold, directly or indirectly, an interest in such an entity equivalent to 50% or more of its capital stock.

There are also another group of corporations that are subsidiaries and therefore do not meet the before-mentioned conditions. In this case, the parent corporation could bring the claim on behalf of its subsidiaries, provided that the ownership interests of such nationals, collectively, were sufficient at the time the claim arose to control the corporation or other entity.[491] This mechanism established by the Claims Settlement Declaration is called indirect claims. Therefore, we could conclude that the claims brought by the corporations could be divided into two types: direct and indirect.

b) *States versus nationals*

The Algiers Accords recognizes the claims asserted by nationals of Iran or the United States against the other State Party or by either State Party against the other. Therefore, these types of Claims are not admissible: Claims by a national of either State Party against national of the other State Party, Claims by either State Party against a national of the other State Party and Some Claims between State Parties. The Claims between two States are permissible only if they qualify as official claims as defined in the Claims Settlement Declaration.[492]

Since the Declarations did not expressly prohibit the claims brought by a State against nationals of the other State, Iran filed such claims before the Tribunal. The claims were against the U.S. Respondents who did not qualify as governmental entities. The United States was against Iran's interpretation of Claims Settlement

491 Claims Settlement Declarations, Article VII, para. 2 (19 January 1981).

492 Claims Settlement Declarations, Article II, para. 2 (19 January 1981).

Declaration. Consequently, Iran requested the Tribunal to decide whether the two Algerian Declarations had conferred jurisdiction on the Tribunal over claims by the Government of Iran against nationals of the United States. The Tribunal examined this issue in case number A/2. In this case, Iran stated that since the termination of all litigation between the Government of each party and the nationals of the other through binding arbitration is the purpose of the Tribunal, the Tribunal did have such jurisdiction.

At the beginning, the Tribunal confirmed its jurisdiction over questions regarding the interpretation of either of the two Algerian Declarations in accordance with Article VI paragraph 4 of the Claims Settlement Declaration.

Subsequently, regarding the main question the Tribunal pointed out all the jurisdictional provisions throughout the Declaration and concluded:

> "It can be easily seen that the parties set up very carefully a list of the claims and counter claims which could be submitted to the arbitral tribunal. As a matter of fact they knew well that such a Tribunal could not have wider jurisdiction than that which was specifically decided by mutual agreement."[493]

The Tribunal stated afterwards that the parties expressly mentioned the right of counterclaim for States against nationals of other States, which is normal and is admitted only in response to a claim and obviously does not mean, by analogy, that each State is allowed to submit claims against nationals of the other State.

c) *State versus state*

The claims brought by the States against each other are labeled as "official Claims" bases on Article II(2) of the Claims Settlement Declaration. It provides:

> "The Tribunal shall also have jurisdiction over official claims of the United States and Iran against each other arising out of contractual arrangements between them for the purchase and sale of goods and services."

Thus, the admissible claims brought by States against each other are limited to the sale and purchase of goods and therefore all cases submitted by Iranian Customs Administration against the United States were dismissed based on lack of jurisdiction.

As an example, on 15 January 1982 Iranian Customs Administration filed the case number B/2 seeking customs duties and charges it alleged are owed by the United States. The claim arose out of an arrangement whereby the Claimant

---

493 IUSCT Case No. A2 (DEC 1-A2-FT), (21 December 1981), in Pieter Sanders (ed.), Yearbook Commercial Arbitration, Vol. 8, (1983), p. 257.

allowed various goods to be temporarily imported into Iran free of the usual customs duties as part of the United States' exhibitions at the 1976, 1977 and 1978 International Trade Fairs and 1977 Machine Tool Exhibition. The obligations were independent of any contract and were under the letters of guarantee, which were issued by the United States Embassy in Tehran, which guaranteed that if the goods were not re-exported within a stipulated time governing Customs Regulations will be followed.[494]

In this case, the Tribunal pointed out that the guarantees are not contractual arrangements and even if they could be characterized as such, they were not for the purchase and sale of goods and services. From the Tribunal's viewpoint, they just constitute an assumption of administrative responsibility by the embassy to facilitate the importation of goods for exhibition at the various Tool and Trade Fairs.[495] Consequently, the Tribunal concluded that there is no other possible jurisdictional basis in the Claims Settlement Declaration for such claim.

d) Government-controlled entities

Government-controlled entities include all agencies and official organs of the State and corporations, which are operated under the State's control.

Even though the term "control" is defined under the Claims Settlement Declaration, the interpretation of this term has brought inconsistencies. Article VII of the Declaration defines Iran and United States in paragraphs 3 and 4. It includes the Government, any political subdivision of the State, and any agency, instrumentality, or entity controlled by the Government or any political subdivision thereof. This definition is beyond the customary notion of "State" and makes the jurisdiction of the Tribunal far broader than that possible under the customary law of State responsibility.[496]

As explained before, after the revolution in Iran and the upheaval of the crisis many foreign investors and contractors and also Iranians who didn't feel safe anymore left the country and abandoned their businesses. These abandoned entities

---

494 Iranian Customs Administration v. United States of America, IUSCT Case No. B2 (265-B2-2), Award, (13 November 1986), para. 1.

495 Iranian Customs Administration v. United States of America, IUSCT Case No. B2(265-B2-2), Award, (13 November 1986), para. 8.

496 Caron, David D., "The Basis of Responsibility: Attribution and Other Trans-Substantive Rules", in R. Lillich & D. Magraw (eds.), The Iran-United States Claims Tribunal: Its Contribution to the Law of State Responsibility, Irvington-on-Hudson, Transnational Publishers, (1998), p. 112.

were to be put on track again. Therefore, it was time for the Iranian Government to interfere and take control. The Government did this by various methods. For some cases it appointed managers only to run the companies without any decision-making power. The other way was appointing managers who had full authority to run the entities, but without taking over their properties. The other method used was the mechanism of *de jure* or *de facto* expropriation.[497]

Thus, we can see different degrees of influence of Government over entities that were owned by private persons. Based on Iran's point of view, the term "controlled entity" in the Claims Settlement Declaration would not encompass the entities, which underwent the State's control in involuntary conditions. Iran believed that the mere act of appointing managers could not make one entity fully a Government-controlled entity and therefore, the Government should not be held responsible for liabilities of such entities. It is similar to receivership under the U.S. legal system.

On the contrary, before the establishment of the Iran-United States Claims Tribunal, Iran had another approach in U.S. courts. Iran defended in the cases submitted by Americans that these entities belong to the Government and therefore enjoy sovereign immunity. Those submissions were used later by the American claimants against Iran and the Tribunal did also confirm that those entities fall within the realm of controlled entities.

From another angle and with the approach of finding the unique character of the Tribunal, it has to be mentioned that the Claims Settlement Declaration gave such broad jurisdiction to the Tribunal that allows it to deal with two categories of claims at the same time; public international law claims, and private municipal law claims. The former could be explained as a claim of a U.S. national alleging a breach of an international obligation of the government of Iran. In this sense, the Respondent is only the government of Iran and not the other Respondents listed in Article VII(3), whereas the latter are claims of a U.S. national alleging a breach of contract by an Iranian Government–owned corporation or a privately owned corporation, which underwent the control of government after the revolution of Iran. These claims could be brought against the whole range of Respondents in accordance with Article VII(3). Settling both of these claims is something unique and exciting about this Tribunal. Because of this distinction, the naming of the proper Respondent is also important. For the claims against a breach of public international law such as expropriation, the Respondent should be named

497 Khalilian, Khalil, "Iran-United States Claims Arbitration-Debates on Commercial and Public International Law", Trafford Publishing, (2012), p. 42.

as the Government of Iran. But there are examples in which the naming was not accurate. For example, in Fedders Corporation and Loristan Refrigeration case, the Claimant named only Loristan Refrigeration Industries and General Industrial Corporation as Respondents but as the claims was for expropriation and therefore it was an issue of international public law, the Claimant required to name the government of Iran and seek an amendment of its claim. The Tribunal stated:

> "The Tribunal notes that although the Statement of Claim referred directly only to Loristan and General, the wording of the Statement of Claim indicated clearly that a part of the claim alleged by the Claimant was based on the nationalization or taking of assets by Iran. Therefore it was clear from the Statement of Claim that Iran was intended to be a Respondent in this case."[498]

In similar situations, it would be necessary to amend the claim, but in this case there was a long debate in the Tribunal regarding this issue. However, the amendment was granted by the Tribunal and it explained further that:

> "...This interpretation of the Statement of Claim is confirmed by the fact that in its Reply the Claimant did not seek to add Iran as a Respondent; on the contrary, I assumed that Iran was already a proper Respondent. Consequently, the Tribunal holds that specifying Iran as a Respondent is a clarification of the Statement of Claim rather than an amendment of the Claim."[499]

aa) The notion of "control"

After a short glance at some basics about State responsibility we came to the conclusion that this Tribunal enjoys a broad Jurisdiction and settles even the claims against Government-controlled entities. Maybe the notion of "control" should now be explained in order to understand the critical points the Tribunal should take into account.

The Tribunal was faced often with the question whether the Respondents were controlled by the Government and whether the legislative or judicial branches of the Government could constitute this control. The answer to the latter question was affirmative. In Alfred Haber, *P.A. v. The Islamic Republic of Iran*, for example, the Islamic Republic of Iran Broadcasting (IRIB), which is the successor of National Iranian Radio and Television (NIRT), contends that

---

498 Fedders Corporation v. Loristan Refrigeration Industries, Decision No. DEC 51-250-3, (28 October 1986, Iran-U.S. Claims Tribunal Reports, Vol. 13, p. 98.

499 Fedders Corporation v. Loristan Refrigeration Industries, Decision No. DEC 51-250-3, (28 October 1986, Iran-U.S. Claims Tribunal Reports, Vol. 13, p. 98.

it is under the supervision of all three state organs and the executive branch does not have dominant control over it. Consequently, IRIB denies that it is a Government-controlled entity. But the Tribunal after a detailed survey in Iranian constitution concluded that the meaning of the term "Government" should be understood in the light of the common practice of international law and international legal document such as Claims Settlement Declaration that in our case regulate inter-State relationships and there is no wonder that the words "State" and "Government" are used as synonyms in such documents.[500] The Tribunal then added that:

> "...for the test of government control as defined in Article VII, paragraph 3, of the Claims Settlement Declaration, it is immaterial how the State distributes its authority among the organs of the government. Government control can be exercised (i) by the executive, the legislative or the judicial branch or (ii), as here by two or more of them jointly or (iii) by some other element of the State's structure within the definition of Article VII, paragraph 3, of the Claims Settlement Declaration.... Thus, the Tribunal does not accept IRIB's interpretation of government control under the Claims Settlement Declaration."[501]

bb) Date of control

The date on which the entity had to have been controlled by the government is not stated expressly in the Claims Settlement Declaration.[502] But it is well reasoned to consider the date of the Declarations (19 January 1981), as the Tribunal according to Article II(1) has only jurisdiction over claims if they are outstanding on that date. The cases before the Tribunal were often related to a time prior to the Declarations and therefore, in most decisions the Tribunal did not made reference to any specific date. The question came to attention in cases such as *Continental Grain Export Corporation v. Union of Consumers' Co-operatives* (EMKAN). In this case, the Tribunal found out that all the evidences show that no control existed prior to 19 January 1981. The earliest record is dated 20 October 1981 which describes the finding scheme for EMKAN. Therefore, the

---

500 Alfred Haber, P.A., a claim of less than US$250,000 presented by the United States of America v. The Islamic Republic of Iran, Award, IUSCT Case No. 10159 (437-10159-3), (4 September 1989), para. 16.

501 Alfred Haber, P.A., a claim of less than US$250,000 presented by the United States of America v. The Islamic Republic of Iran, Award, IUSCT Case No. 10159 (437-10159-3), (4 September 1989), para. 16–17.

502 Aldrich, George H., "The Jurisprudence of the Iran-United States Claims Tribunal", Clarendon Press. Oxford, (1996), p. 81.

Tribunal concluded that it has no jurisdiction over the Claimant's claims and the claim was dismissed.[503] Similarly, in *Shannon and Wilson, Inc. v. Atomic Energy Organization of Iran* (AEOI) case, which was a claim based on an agreement concluded between S&W and Energy Technology Consultants (Enertec) on 11 December 1977,[504] as the Tribunal was examining its jurisdiction over Enertec, it found out that:

> "The evidence indicates, however, that Enertec is a private stock company, incorporated in Tehran on 19 January 1978 no evidence has been adduced indicating that Enertec was controlled by AEOI or by the Government of the Republic of Iran at the time the Claim arose or on 19 January 1981 or, indeed, at any other time. The Tribunal therefore concludes that Enertec is not an entity controlled by the Government of Iran; accordingly, the Tribunal lacks jurisdiction over a claim against Enertec."[505]

Regarding the exact date of control, although the Tribunal in *Eastman Kodak Co. v. the Government of Iran* stated that the control might also have to be shown at the date the claim arose, but in *William Ray Hollyfield v. The Islamic Republic of Iran* in which the Claimant alleged that General Systems Company (GSC) failed to pay to the Claimant certain salary and benefits owed to him under an employment contract with GSC, a company allegedly controlled by Information Systems Iran (ISIRAN) and Iran, the Tribunal showed different approach. In this case, the Respondent challenged the Tribunal's jurisdiction based on that GSC is not a controlled entity of Iran in accordance with Article VII(3) of the Claims Settlement Declaration. It contended that GSC was always a private and independent company without any connection with the Government except performing services for ISIRIAN again as an independent contractor. In support of its arguments, it provided the Tribunal with Articles of Association showing that it was organized by two individuals, Dariush Mohazzebi and Parirokh Haji Otmishi.[506] On the contrary, the Claimant alleged that GSC is an entity controlled by ISIRAN and the Tribunal has already decided that it is under control

503 Continental Grain Export Corporation v. Union of Consumers' Co-operatives for Iranian Workers (EMKAN), Award, IUSCT Case No. 243-112-1, (6 August 1986), para. 10–11.

504 Shannon and Wilson, Inc. v. Atomic Energy Organization of Iran, Award, IUSCT Case No. 207-217-2, (5 December 1985), para. 1.

505 Shannon and Wilson, Inc. v. Atomic Energy Organization of Iran, Award, IUSCT Case No. 207-217-2, (5 December 1985), para. 12.

506 William Ray Hollyfield, a claim of less than U.S. $250,000 presented by the United States of America v. The Islamic Republic of Iran, Award, IUSCT Case No. 10087 (446-10087-2), (3 November 1989), para. 8-9.

of the Government of Iran. The Claimant also pointed out that in the contract between GSC and ISIRAN it is expressly provided that ISIRAN has the right to manage and control the work performed by GSC and its employees.[507] Further arguments were made by the Claimant regarding GSC being a controlled entity after February 1979. Though this arguments were made, "the Tribunal credits Mr. Mohazzebi's testimony and finds that GSC, while largely dormant as of 19 January 1981 for reasons both lack of funds and of computer software business, was not, as of that date, under the management or control of the Government of Iran or any Government-controlled entity."[508] So, the Tribunal unlike the former case considered the evidence of control in 1978 and 1979 and somehow implied that the only important date for examining this matter should be 19 January 1981.

Once again in *Arthur J. Fritz & Co. v. Sherkate Tavonie Sherkathaye Sakhtemanie*, the Tribunal stated that the question of control does not apply to a date later than the date of the Claims Settlement Declaration.[509]

cc) Other factors in relation to the notion of "control"

One of the primary sources for the Tribunal to find whether an entity is controlled by the Government of Iran was actually Iranian laws. In *Gruen Associates Inc. v. Iran Housing Co.*, the Tribunal had to find whether the Housing Company is "Iran" within the meaning of Article VII, paragraph 3 of the Declaration. The Claimant drew the Tribunal's attention to Article 7 of a law enacted in July 1979 amending the Law for the Formation of the Social Security Organization, which reads as follows:

> "As of the date of the enactment of this law, Bank Refah Kargaran and the Iran Housing Company are removed from the Ministry of Health and Welfare; and while preserving their judicial personality and their financial and administrative independence, they shall be administered under the supervision of the Social Security Organization in accordance with the charters which shall be approved by the Council of Ministers

507 William Ray Hollyfield, a claim of less than U.S. $250,000 presented by the United States of America v. The Islamic Republic of Iran, Award, IUSCT Case No. 10087 (446-10087-2), (3 November 1989), para. 11.

508 William Ray Hollyfield, a claim of less than U.S. $250,000 presented by the United States of America v. The Islamic Republic of Iran, Award, IUSCT Case No. 10087 (446-10087-2), (3 November 1989), para. 16.

509 Arthur J. Fritz & Co. v. Sherkate Tavonie Sherkathaye Sakhtemanie (Cooperative Society of Construction Companies) and The Government of the Islamic Republic of Iran, Award, IUSCT Case No. 426-276-2, (30 June 1989), para. 38.

> upon the recommendation of the High Council of the Organization. Until new charters are approved, the present charters and regulations of each of the above organizations remain effective."[510]

Therefore, the Tribunal concluded that a claim against the Iran Housing Company is a claim against Iran.[511]

Another factor, though less referred by the Tribunal, is the nature of activities performed by an entity.[512] In some cases, the Tribunal found the existence of control by examining the type of activity an entity performed alongside with other evidences. For example, in *Hyatt International Corp. v. The Government of the Islamic Republic of Iran*, the Tribunal cited the nature of activity of Alavi Foundation and the Foundation for the oppressed (Bonyad-e-Mostazafan), both established by the order of Imam Khomeini, among other reasons. Even though the agent of Iran has stated that Imam Khomeini in establishing the Foundation and appointing its Council and president has acted in his capacity as a religious leader and not in his governmental role, but the Tribunal believed that under the regime established by the Constitution of Iran an exercise of religious authority may also constitute an exercise of governmental authority.[513] Important for the Tribunal was that the functions of the foundations included holding of the properties confiscated by the Government and the management of them for the public purposes.[514]

Another apparent evidence that links an entity to the Government is the ownership of that entity. It can be accepted that a company 100 % owned by the Government is a Government-controlled entity. But Iran's argument at the Tribunal was that an indirect ownership through another entity could not fall

---

510 Official Gazette No. 10043, dated 25-5-1358 (16 August 1979) cited in Gruen Associates Inc. v. Iran Housing Company, Ministry of Health and Social Welfare, Government of the Islamic Republic of Iran, Award, IUSCT Case No. 61-188-2.

511 Gruen Associates Inc. v. Iran Housing Company, Ministry of Health and Social Welfare, Government of the Islamic Republic of Iran, Award, IUSCT Case No. 61-188-2.

512 Aldrich, George H., "The Jurisprudence of the Iran-United States Claims Tribunal", Clarendon Press. Oxford, (1996), p. 84.

513 Hyatt International Corporation, Hyatt Management Inc., International Project Systems Inc. v. The Government of the Islamic Republic of Iran, Bank Mellat (formerly known as Bank Omran), Alavi Foundation, Foundation for the Oppressed, Iran Touring and Tourism Organization, Award, IUSCT Case No. ITL 54-134-1, para. 17.

514 Hyatt International Corporation, Hyatt Management Inc., International Project Systems Inc. v. The Government of the Islamic Republic of Iran, Bank Mellat (formerly known as Bank Omran), Alavi Foundation, Foundation for the Oppressed, Iran Touring and Tourism Organization, Award, IUSCT Case No. ITL 54-134-1, para. 14.

within the meaning of paragraph 3 of Article VII. For instance, in *Economy Forms Corporation v. The Government of the Islamic Republic of Iran*, Mana and Sabir were entities, though indirect, under control of the Government. Mana was 100 % owned by the Industrial Development and Renovation Organization, all of whose shares in turn were owned by the Government of Iran and a few governmental organizations. Sabir, on the other hand, was owned by the Ministry of Energy.[515] The Tribunal rejects the position that the entities do not fall under Article VII(3) because they are not directly under control and stated:

> "First, no distinction is made in Article VII, paragraph 3 between direct and indirect control by the Government. Second, the separate juridical status of an entity two or more levels removed from the Government itself is no a sufficient basis from which to conclude that the entity conducts its operations free of the control of the Government. The Tribunal therefore holds that it has jurisdiction over both Mana and Sabir as controlled entities."[516]

Besides ownership, the Government appointing administrators for the entity could also be a factor for the Tribunal to trace the Government's control. The Tribunal has often expressed that the entity is under the Government's control whenever it was managed, administered, or supervised by persons appointed by the Government.[517] One example is *RayGo Wagner Equipment Co. v. Star Line Iran Co.* case. Despite of Star Line's objection, RayGo believed that Star Line is a Government-controlled entity. The Tribunal examined the situation and found that after the revolutionary events in Iran the company had not been run by its registered directors and the Tribunal found out, though without formal decree to this effect, that Star Line had been administered by persons who had been appointed by some public authority.[518] The Tribunal concluded that appointing the

---

515 Economy Forms Corporation v. The Government of the Islamic Republic of Iran; The Ministry of Energy; Dam & Water Works Constructions Co. ("SABIR); Sherkat Sakhtemani Mani Sahami Kass ("MANA"); and Bank Mellat, Award, IUSCT Case No. 55-165-1, para. 5.

516 Economy Forms Corporation v. The Government of the Islamic Republic of Iran; The Ministry of Energy; Dam & Water Works Constructions Co. ("SABIR); Sherkat Sakhtemani Mani Sahami Kass ("MANA"); and Bank Mellat, Award, IUSCT Case No. 55-165-1, para. 5.

517 Aldrich, George H., "The Jurisprudence of the Iran-United States Claims Tribunal", Clarendon Press Oxford, (1996), p. 84.

518 RayGo Wagner Equipment Company v. Star Line Iran Company, Award, IUSCT Case No. 20-17-3, (15 December 1982), para. 2.

persons for the administration of the company establishes *prima facie* evidence that Star Line Iran is controlled by the Government of Iran.[519]

In the another *RayGo Wagner* case against Iran Express Terminal Corporation, beside former factors, we can find another factor, which brought the Tribunal to conceive the fact that Star Line Iran was a Government-controlled entity. This factor is statements made by the entity, which could be used against it. In this case, while Express Terminal objected the jurisdiction of the Tribunal based on lack of Government's control on this corporation, RayGo mentioned a law suit before a United States Court, in which Express Terminal took the position that the court lacked jurisdiction over the claim raised against it because the company was administered by the Government of Iran and under the appropriate laws of the United States it was a sovereign entity and therefore immune from the jurisdiction of the United States courts.[520]

Apparently, the factors pertinent to finding of control are not an exhaustive list, but they could vary with regard to the situations. For example, examining the existence of "Control" in Iran's situation after the revolution was something unique that cannot be compared with in normal situations.

dd) No evidence of control

It is actually normal that in the post-revolution Iran, as a lot of companies were administered directly or indirectly by the Government, the cases in which the Tribunal holds a Respondent not controlled by the Government were relatively few.[521] In case the Tribunal found no evidence that an entity is controlled then it shall decide that it has no jurisdiction over the claim.

In *American Housing International Inc. v. Housing Cooperative Society of Officers of State General Gendarmerie* case, there was a long debate finding out whether Cooperative is controlled by the Government of Iran. While Claimant contended that the Cooperative is an entity controlled by the Government of Iran as defined by the Claims Settlement Declaration, Respondent argued that in fact the State General Gendarmerie itself is a political subdivision of Iran, or alternatively, an agency or instrumentality of the Government of Iran, but they

---

519 RayGo Wagner Equipment Company v. Star Line Iran Company, Award, IUSCT Case No. 20-17-3, (15 December 1982), para. 2.

520 RayGo Wagner Equipment Company v. Iran Express Terminal Corporation, Award, IUSCT Case No. 30-16-3, (18 March 1983), para. 3.

521 Aldrich, George H., "The Jurisprudence of the Iran-United States Claims Tribunal", Clarendon Press Oxford, (1996), p. 86.

added that the Cooperative has been established as a society of officers of Iranian Gendarmerie and based on its Articles of Association is controlled by company organs.[522] The Tribunal examined Articles of Association of the Cooperative as well as the Iranian Commercial Code. According to Article 20 of the Iranian Commercial Code, trading companies are of seven kinds, the seventh of which is "Producers and Consumers Cooperative Society." Based on the same code, all trading companies have juridical personality. More importantly, according to Article 589 of the Iranian Commercial Code:

> "The decisions of a juridical person are rendered by the authorities who, by virtue of the law or its Articles of Association, are entitled to do so."

Therefore, the Tribunal should have referred to Articles of Association of the Cooperative (AoA). According to Article 17 of the AoA, "the organs of the company consist of the General Assembly of the Shareholders, the Board of Directors, the managing director, and the inspectors of the company." Based on Article 34, the Board of Directors are to be selected by the General Meeting's Majority votes from amongst the shareholders. Duties, powers and responsibilities of the Board of Directors are also listed in Article 37 and envisage its full control over the Cooperative. Therefore, the Cooperative is not managed by the State Gendarmerie but by the shareholders of the Society.[523] Claimant submitted some evidence proving that the Government of Iran was involved with this society and gave assistance in different ways such as providing land and revising plans. But eventually the Tribunal believed that this much of Government's involvement would not constitute sufficient proof of governmental control over the Cooperative as it is required in Article VII(3) of the Claims Settlement Declaration. At the end, the Tribunal concluded that since the cooperative is not controlled by Iran, it does not fall within the meaning of Article VII(3) and therefore, the Tribunal has no jurisdiction over the Cooperative claim as against the cooperative itself.[524]

---

522 American Housing International Inc. v. Housing Cooperative Society of State General Gendarmerie, Bank Saderat Iran and The Government of the Islamic Republic of Iran, Award, IUSCT Case No. 117-199-3, (17 March 1984), para. 2.

523 American Housing International Inc. v. Housing Cooperative Society of State General Gendarmerie, Bank Saderat Iran and The Government of the Islamic Republic of Iran, Award, IUSCT Case No. 117-199-3, (17 March 1984), para. 3.

524 American Housing International Inc. v. Housing Cooperative Society of State General Gendarmerie, Bank Saderat Iran and The Government of the Islamic Republic of Iran, Award, IUSCT Case No. 117-199-3, (17 March 1984), para. 4.

A similar decision could be found in *Middle East Management and Construction Corporation v. the Government of the Islamic Republic of Iran*. The Claimant ("MEMCCO") is an American corporation. It filed its claims based on five separate contracts, one of which was between International Marketing and Distributing Company ("IMDICO") and the Cooperative of Workers of the Ministry of Roads and Transportation ("Housing Coop").[525] The Claimant contended that the Housing Coop was controlled by the Ministry of Roads and Transportation ("Ministry"). They brought up that the Minister had personally been involved in approving and agreeing to this project. The other reason expressed by the Claimant was that according to the Articles of Association of the Hosing Coop, the Ministry of Cooperatives and Rural Affairs had such power regarding the decisions of the Housing Coop, that the Housing Coop had to be considered and Government-controlled entity.[526] The Claimant contended in addition that the Ministry itself was involved to such a degree in this project that the contract is to be considered to have been concluded de facto with the Ministry or at least the Ministry is responsible for the obligations of the Housing Coop.[527]

On the contrary, the Respondents seemed to have a completely different approach. They contended that Housing Coop is private and non-governmental and has its own Articles of Association. It is neither an agent of a Ministry nor an entity controlled by it. The Tribunal did not accept the Claimant's arguments. For example, from the Tribunal's viewpoint a visit by the Minister to a prospective housing site are a kind of action rather supportive than with legal commitment. The Tribunal mentioned that the Housing Coop, not the Ministry, was party to the contract with IMDICO and there is no evidence proving that Housing Coop was acting as an agent for the Ministry. In addition, there is no evidence demonstrating a link between the Housing Coop and the Ministry of a type to suggest Ministerial control over the Housing Coop. Other factors approve this view such as the land was acquired privately and funding was not through the

525 Middle East Management and Construction Corporation v. The Government of the Islamic Republic of Iran, Award, IUSCT Case No. 202-292-2, (25 November 1985), para. 1.

526 Middle East Management and Construction Corporation v. The Government of the Islamic Republic of Iran, Award, IUSCT Case No. 202-292-2, (25 November 1985), para. 3.

527 Middle East Management and Construction Corporation v. The Government of the Islamic Republic of Iran, Award, IUSCT Case No. 202-292-2, (25 November 1985), para. 4.

Government.[528] Finally, the Tribunal concludes that the Claimant has failed to prove that the Housing Coop was controlled by the Government of Iran within the meaning of Article VII(3) of the Claims Settlement Declaration; thus, the claims based on a contract with the Housing Coop is not a claim against Iran as defined in that Article and is therefore not within the jurisdiction of the Tribunal.[529]

A lot more complicated case concerning this issue is *Arthur J. Fritz & Co. v. Sherkate Tavonie Sherkathaye Sakhtemanie* (Cooperative Society of Construction Companies). As it can be understood from the name of the company, it is a cooperative society consisting of construction companies, rather than of employees. In this case, the Claimant asserted that the Respondent (STSS) is an entity controlled by the government of Iran within the Article VII(3) of the Claims Settlement Declaration. As evidence, the Claimant mentioned the presence of a Revolutionary Public Prosecutor in STSS from July 1979 until September 1981, the fact that Iran was controlling a significant number of the Society's members and the way in which certain trucks were requisitioned from STSS by the Iranian Ministry of Roads and Transportation.[530] Fritz demonstrated his arguments by relying on the 1985 Report to the 15th Annual Assembly of STSS (the "Report"), which included references by STSS' Board of Directors to the involvement of the Prosecutor.[531] Important points from the Report shows that nearly all the inventory of the Society had been sold under the supervision of the representatives of the Revolutionary Public Prosecutor. No sale was made without the approval of the representative of the Islamic Revolutionary Public Prosecutor.

Furthermore, Fritz argued that based on the Report STTS' assets were managed entirely by the government. The Government interfered STTS' day-to-day

528 Middle East Management and Construction Corporation v. The Government of the Islamic Republic of Iran, Award, IUSCT Case No. 202-292-2, (25 November 1985), para. 10.

529 Middle East Management and Construction Corporation v. The Government of the Islamic Republic of Iran, Award, IUSCT Case No. 202-292-2, (25 November 1985), para. 12.

530 Arthur J. Fritz & Co. v. Sherkate Tavonie Sherkathaye Sakhtemanie (Cooperative Society of Construction Companies) and The Government of the Islamic Republic of Iran, Award, IUSCT Case No. 426-276-2, (30 June 1989), para. 23

531 Arthur J. Fritz & Co. v. Sherkate Tavonie Sherkathaye Sakhtemanie (Cooperative Society of Construction Companies) and The Government of the Islamic Republic of Iran, Award, IUSCT Case No. 426-276-2, (30 June 1989), para. 24.

operations to the extent that every act required its approval. Fritz added that the Prosecutor had an active role in the sale of STSS' assets and actively advanced the interests of the creditors controlled by the Government of Iran to the detriment of STSS' other creditors, including the Claimant.[532] Another evidence proving the Government's control is takeover of 79 of STSS' trucks by the Ministry, which according to Fritz was a unilateral decision by the Government and the money afterwards used to pay STTS' debts to the Government banks.[533] The Claimant asserted according to an affidavit of former chairman of STSS' Board of Directors that STSS is under government control as a result of its ownership structure. Based on said affidavit, many of major companies, of which STSS constituted, were assigned to the Poor People's Foundation that itself is a controlled entity.[534]

Iran though challenged the Tribunal's jurisdiction asserting that STSS is not a controlled entity, thus the claim is not attributable to Iran. Explaining this argument, Iran asserted that STSS is a cooperative society whose members are construction companies. It is a private company, which is officially incorporated and registered. The company has been managed in conformity with its Articles of Association, which provides that the General Assembly is STSS' highest authority and its powers include determining the company program and policy and appointing the Board of Directors.[535] In addition, the Board of Director is represented as the company's lawful representative. According to STSS's assertions, the company has always been run by the directors that had been elected by the Assembly, and representatives of Government-owned or Government-controlled member companies were never included. The majority members of STSS were private companies never affiliated to or controlled by the Government according to an affidavit showing that only 49 out of a total

532 Arthur J. Fritz & Co. v. Sherkate Tavonie Sherkathaye Sakhtemanie (Cooperative Society of Construction Companies) and The Government of the Islamic Republic of Iran, Award, IUSCT Case No. 426-276-2, (30 June 1989), para. 25.

533 Arthur J. Fritz & Co. v. Sherkate Tavonie Sherkathaye Sakhtemanie (Cooperative Society of Construction Companies) and The Government of the Islamic Republic of Iran, Award, IUSCT Case No. 426-276-2, (30 June 1989), para. 26.

534 Arthur J. Fritz & Co. v. Sherkate Tavonie Sherkathaye Sakhtemanie (Cooperative Society of Construction Companies) and The Government of the Islamic Republic of Iran, Award, IUSCT Case No. 426-276-2, (30 June 1989), para. 27.

535 Arthur J. Fritz & Co. v. Sherkate Tavonie Sherkathaye Sakhtemanie (Cooperative Society of Construction Companies) and The Government of the Islamic Republic of Iran, Award, IUSCT Case No. 426-276-2, (30 June 1989), para. 30.

237 members were Government-controlled.[536] In response to the assertion of the Claimant about the involvement of the prosecutor, the company explained that because of STSS' failure to settle its debts to certain Government-owned banks, mainly Bank Tejarat, the Prosecutor attached company's assets. As the delay in reopening of the premises has caused difficulties for member construction companies, STSS requested the Prosecutor to issue instructions for withdrawal of the aggression from the company's warehouse and workshop. According to Bank Tejarat's letter to the prosecutor, it seemed to support the request for lifting attachment so that the assets could be sold to pay off the Cooperative debts.

Regarding the appointing of the representatives for sale of the assets by the Prosecutor, STSS argued that it was only to supervise over the sale of the STTS' properties in order to pay its debts.[537] In addition, STSS tried to demonstrate that the company's members retained control. It pointed out that the members appointed a new Board of Directors, approved the 1979 financial statements and directors' report in August 1980 General Assembly and the fact that the General Assembly has been held every year in accordance with the law and its Articles of Association.[538] In any event, the Prosecutor's intervention ceased in the course of 1981, while under the Claims Settlement Declaration the Tribunal would have jurisdiction, control must have continued from a date prior to the signing date of the Claims Settlement Declaration to the date of the award.[539]

Before the Tribunal determined whether STSS was a controlled entity, it examined the STSS' statement regarding the date of control and as mentioned before according to the Tribunal's precedent, the question of control does not

---

536 Arthur J. Fritz & Co. v. Sherkate Tavonie Sherkathaye Sakhtemanie (Cooperative Society of Construction Companies) and The Government of the Islamic Republic of Iran, Award, IUSCT Case No. 426-276-2, (30 June 1989), para. 31.

537 Arthur J. Fritz & Co. v. Sherkate Tavonie Sherkathaye Sakhtemanie (Cooperative Society of Construction Companies) and The Government of the Islamic Republic of Iran, Award, IUSCT Case No. 426-276-2, (30 June 1989), para. 33.

538 Arthur J. Fritz & Co. v. Sherkate Tavonie Sherkathaye Sakhtemanie (Cooperative Society of Construction Companies) and The Government of the Islamic Republic of Iran, Award, IUSCT Case No. 426-276-2, (30 June 1989), para. 34.

539 Arthur J. Fritz & Co. v. Sherkate Tavonie Sherkathaye Sakhtemanie (Cooperative Society of Construction Companies) and The Government of the Islamic Republic of Iran, Award, IUSCT Case No. 426-276-2, (30 June 1989), para. 35.

apply to a date later than the date of the Claims Settlement Declaration, thus the assertion is without merit.[540]

The Tribunal afterwards found the STSS' assertions true concerning the company being controlled by its members based on its Article of Association. Though some of the members were Government-controlled companies, it was unlikely that after some members left between 1981 and 1986 and some other remained and were privately held in 1981, a sufficient number would have been Government-controlled in 1981 to contribute to a majority.[541]

The Tribunal stated that it is the Claimant's burden to disprove this inference and establish that the government indeed controlled enough of STSS' members. The Tribunal added that the fact that a minority of STSS' members attended its Assembly meetings does not compel the conclusion that Government-controlled members exercised inordinate authority over STSS at those meetings. Based on the lack of evidence of the activity of the Prosecutor after selling the assets, the Tribunal concluded his presence may have been a temporary measure; therefore, the prosecutor's actions may have been only the resolution of STSS' debt problems rather than the transfer of control.[542] The Claimant's main reliance on this argument was the 1985 report, while the Tribunal determined that the 1985 Report, in the absence of further evidence, does not satisfy the Claimant's burden of proof.[543] Eventually, the Tribunal stated that on the matter of STSS being an entity controlled by Iran, sufficient evidence has not been presented; therefore, the Tribunal dismissed the claim against STSS for lack of jurisdiction.

These cases compel the conclusion that detailed examinations have to be undertaken by the Tribunal to determine whether an entity is Government-controlled. In the foregoing case, despite of the Claimant's convincing arguments, the Tribunal found the evidence insufficient. That would be even more

540 Arthur J. Fritz & Co. v. Sherkate Tavonie Sherkathaye Sakhtemanie (Cooperative Society of Construction Companies) and The Government of the Islamic Republic of Iran, Award, IUSCT Case No. 426-276-2, (30 June 1989), para. 39.
541 Arthur J. Fritz & Co. v. Sherkate Tavonie Sherkathaye Sakhtemanie (Cooperative Society of Construction Companies) and The Government of the Islamic Republic of Iran, Award, IUSCT Case No. 426-276-2, (30 June 1989), para. 40.
542 Arthur J. Fritz & Co. v. Sherkate Tavonie Sherkathaye Sakhtemanie (Cooperative Society of Construction Companies) and The Government of the Islamic Republic of Iran, Award, IUSCT Case No. 426-276-2, (30 June 1989), para. 44.
543 Arthur J. Fritz & Co. v. Sherkate Tavonie Sherkathaye Sakhtemanie (Cooperative Society of Construction Companies) and The Government of the Islamic Republic of Iran, Award, IUSCT Case No. 426-276-2, (30 June 1989), para. 47.

complicated with respect to Iran, since at the time, due to the extraordinary situation, government's footprints could be traced in almost every company.

e) Dual nationals

Dual nationality is a status describing the person who is a national of two countries at a same time. This status could be established in different ways.[544] First, it has arisen when an individual was naturalized in one country at the same time their birth country, from which the individual has acquired his nationality *jus soli*, refused to release them and instead demanding their perpetual allegiance.[545] Dual nationality may also occur where states extracted duties from citizens and then extended protection to them.[546] The third cause of dual nationality was the result of the interplay of birthright citizenship rules of *jus soli* and *jus sanguinis*. As a result of increased migrations, many countries broadened their birthright citizenship to include not only the individuals born within the nation's border but also those born in other countries to citizen parents.[547]

The question of whether the nationals possessing both Iranian and American nationality are entitled to submit claims before the Tribunal has led to tremendous controversy.[548] Since many Iranians who have been naturalized in the United States were submitting claims against Iran and the lack of express provision in the Tribunal's rules concerning dual nationals, this became a major issue before the Tribunal. There is no addressing of an individual who is a citizen of both Iran and the United States in the Claims Settlement Declaration. As said before, the Tribunal was established with the aim of terminating all litigation between the parties; therefore, the Tribunal had to ascertain the status of the dual nationals.[549]

---

544 Magallona, Merlin M., "On Dual Allegiance and Dual Nationality", World Bulletin: Bulletin of the International Studies of the Philippines, Vol. 6, Issue. 1, (1990), pp. 1–6.

545 Peake, Jessica, "Diplomatic Protection for Dual Nationals: Effective Nationality or Non-Responsibility?", Trinity College Review, Vol. 10, (2007), p. 101.

546 Spiro, Peter J., "Dual Nationality and the Meaning of Citizenship", Emory Law Journal, Vol. 46, No. 4, (1997), p. 1418.

547 Spiro, Peter J., "Dual Nationality and the Meaning of Citizenship", Emory Law Journal, Vol. 46, No. 4, (1997), p. 1418.

548 Brower, Charles N.; Brueschke, Jason D., "The Iran-United States Claims Tribunal", Martinus Nijhoff Publishers, (1998), p. 32.

549 Note, "Claims of Dual Nationals in the Modern Era: The Iran-United States Claims Tribunal", Michigan Law Review, Vol. 83, No. 3, (1984), p. 598.

In Case number A18, which was submitted by Iran against the United States, the question before the Tribunal was exactly whether the Claims Settlement Declaration grants the Tribunal jurisdiction over claims against Iran filed by persons who during the relevant period which is from the date the claim arose until 19 January 1981 were Iranian citizens under the law of Iran and the United States under the law of the United States.

At first, the Tribunal pointed out that as the parties have agreed, the Algiers Declarations constitute a treaty under international law, and therefore it should be interpreted in accordance with Articles 31 and 32 of the Vienna Convention on the Law of Treaties. Based in said Articles the Tribunal has to interpret the relevant provisions of the Algiers Declarations in accordance with their ordinary meaning to be given to the terms of the treaty in their context and in the light of its object and purpose. The relevant provisions in this case are paragraph 1 of Article II and paragraph 1(a) of Article VII regarding the definition of nationals.

Iran's position was also that the text is clear and unambiguous but based on Iran's point of view, the ordinary meaning of the word "national" excludes dual nationals.

Based on Iran's position, jurisdiction of the Tribunal should be determined by reference to the Claims Settlement Declaration; particularly Article VII, paragraph 1(a). The parties intended the function of the Tribunal to be the adjudication of international claims on the basis of the exercise of diplomatic protection. Iran concluded that the said Article should be interpreted in accordance with rules of international law and read in a manner consistent with the customary international law relevant to the exercise of diplomatic protection.[550] Definition of the word "national" by "citizen" does not indicate that the parties are intended to depart from the traditional rule of diplomatic protection, which requires the aggrieved person to possess the nationality of the Claimant State according to that State's internal laws. Iran believed that dual nationality is an abnormal status and therefore cannot be considered within the ordinary meaning of the term "national".

Iran added that "… a treaty text can confer jurisdiction on an international tribunal only to the extent that it reflects the 'converging will' of the two States and that Iran, not recognizing dual nationality could not be presumed to

550 The Islamic Republic of Iran v. The United States of America, Decision, IUSCT Case No. A18 (DEC 32-A18-FT), (6 April 1984), Journal of International Arbitration, Vol. 1, Issue. 2, (1984), p. 173.

have accepted such jurisdiction when the Claims Settlement Declaration was signed."[551]

In support of this interpretation, Iran brought some additional points. Requirements of ownership and control of corporations in Article VII, paragraph 1(b) should also apply to natural person and this will justify Iran's approach on dual nationality. Iran also stressed that under the rules of interpretation in international law in the event of any doubt, a provision submitting a State to the jurisdiction of an international tribunal should be construed restrictively. This principle cannot be counter-balanced by the rule of interpretation that suggests all language should have a "useful effect", because Article VII, paragraph 1(a) would still have its useful effect without inclusion of dual nationals.

Iran believed that an interpretation, which provides for jurisdiction over the claims of dual nationals, would violate the equality of States, which is the main basis of the rule of non-responsibility and is the recognized principle to be applied in this context.[552]

Iran pointed out that the exercise of diplomatic protection under international law prohibits claims by persons who possess the nationality of both the Claimant and respondent states and this prohibition finds its evidence in traditional sources of international law. Iran contends that State practice has traditionally supported this approach and even the American practice has only changed since the Second World War, thus such a recent alteration should be disregarded. Iran's point of view finds support in writings of various prominent legal scholars.

United States also believed that the Article is clear and does not need further interpretations. However, it maintains that the definition of "national" by reference to citizenship under national law was intended to make this clear that nationals, including dual nationals are all entitled to bring claims in the Tribunal. The United States believed when interpretation is necessary the Tribunal should resort to international law that would result in an interpretation, which would

---

551 The Islamic Republic of Iran v. The United States of America, Decision, IUSCT Case No. A18 (DEC 32-A18-FT), (6 April 1984), in Pieter Sanders (ed.), Yearbook Commercial Arbitration, Vol. 10, (1985), p. 203.

552 The Islamic Republic of Iran v. The United States of America, Decision, IUSCT Case No. A18 (DEC 32-A18-FT), (6 April 1984), Journal of International Arbitration, Vol. 1, Issue. 2, (1984), p. 174.

make the determination of jurisdiction, depends on the dominant and effective nationality of each dual national claimant.[553]

As interpreted by the United States, the correct reading of the paragraph 1(a) of Article VII of the Claims Settlement Declarations would be that a national of Iran means a natural person who is a citizen of Iran under Iranian law, and a national of the United States means a natural person who is a citizen of the United States under the law of the United States. It added that the ordinary meaning of "United States citizen" includes a citizen who is a dual national. The United States pointed out that the meanings of "citizen" and "national" are different in international legal usage. While "citizenship" stresses the application of municipal law, "nationality" stresses the application of state membership and is determined with reference to international law.[554]

Moreover, the United States opposed Iran's interpretation of Article VII, paragraph 1(a) and found it in contradiction with its plain meaning. Iran reads the provision disjunctively to conclude that a national means a "citizen of Iran *or* a citizen of the United States *but not of both.*" The United States believed that this interpretation makes something out of the declaration that the parties did not agree upon.

In addition, the parties have established exclusions of certain claimants from the jurisdiction of the Tribunal very clearly; therefore, creating another exclusion would not be logical. If their will was to exclude dual nationals they would have done so expressly as in Article XVII of the Treaty of Amity. The United States added that the exact language used in Article VII, paragraph 1(a), by its use in such modern practice, and has long been understood to include dual nationals.

United States finds the assumption of Iran that the Claims Settlement Declaration must be consistent with customary international law pertaining to the exercise of diplomatic protection not correct. Therefore, the clauses of a treaty must be precisely followed even in the case of deviation from general rules of international law.

United States added that if customary law is to be applied, the Tribunal should in each case examine whether the nationality is dominant and effective because the principle of effective nationality has long been applied to resolve conflicts

553 The Islamic Republic of Iran v. The United States of America, Decision, IUSCT Case No. A18 (DEC 32-A18-FT), (6 April 1984), Journal of International Arbitration, Vol. 1, Issue. 2, (1984), p. 175.

554 The Islamic Republic of Iran v. The United States of America, Decision, IUSCT Case No. A18 (DEC 32-A18-FT), (6 April 1984), Journal of International Arbitration, Vol. 1, Issue. 2, (1984), p. 175.

of nationality in international arbitration.[555] The older theory of absolute non-responsibility, which held States absolutely non-responsible for the claims of persons who were nationals of both the claiming and respondent states, is no longer applicable. The United States listed the grounds on which this theory has been criticized: "that it is an inaccurate oversimplification of the body of precedents; that it is based on a theoretically true, but in practice false, assumption that such claimants would otherwise enjoy the protection of two nations; that it gives inequitably undue weight to municipal laws providing for nationality on the basis of *jus sanguinis* or restricting voluntary expatriation; and that it requires international tribunals to abstain from international law determinations of the nationality of the claimants, and thereby harms nationals of States whose nationality laws make it impossible or difficult to change nationality and punishes them because of nominal and possibly irrelevant ties to the respondent state. As a consequence of such criticisms, the absolute non-responsibility theory has been rejected in favor of determinations of effective nationality in the major post-war international precedents."[556]

Eventually, the United States contends that some Iranian approaches regarding citizenship are contrary to the human rights of the claimants as set forth in the Universal Declaration of Human Rights such as Iran's legal restrictions on voluntary expatriation or automatic imposition of citizenship on certain persons such as the children of Iranian men who were born in the United States.[557]

---

555 The Islamic Republic of Iran v. The United States of America, Decision, IUSCT Case No. A18 (DEC 32-A18-FT), (6 April 1984), Journal of International Arbitration, Vol. 1, Issue. 2, (1984), p. 176.

556 The Islamic Republic of Iran v. The United States of America, Decision, IUSCT Case No. A18 (DEC 32-A18-FT), (6 April 1984), Journal of International Arbitration, Vol. 1, Issue. 2, (1984), p. 176.

557 Article 988 of the Iranian Civil Code states:

Iranian national cannot abandon their nationality except on the following conditions:

That they have reached the full age of 25.

That the Council of Ministers has allowed their renunciation of their Iranian nationality.

That they have previously undertaken to transfer, by some means or other, to Iranian nationals, within one year from the date of renunciation of their nationality, all the rights that they possess on landed properties in Iran or which they may acquire by inheritance although Iranian laws may have allowed the possession of the same properties in the case of foreign nationals.

The wife and children of the person who renounces his nationality according to this Article do not lose their Iranian nationality, whether the children are minors of

On the contrary, the Tribunal deemed that the text could not be considered as so clear and unambiguous and definitely needs further analysis. The Tribunal believed that definition of "nationals" as "citizens" in the Claims Settlement Declaration was not an adequate way to raise the issue of dual nationality. The Tribunal shows its approach by commenting on both parties' arguments, stating:

> "In view of the formal, recorded position of the United States with respect to claims by dual nationals, that is, that a State is not required to recognize a claim asserted against it by another State on behalf of an individual possessing the nationality of both States, unless such individual has a closer and more effective bond with the claimant State, it would be expected that, if the United States wished to propose a different rule which ignored the relative closeness of ties, it would have done so more clearly. With respect to the additional Iranian argument, the Vienna Convention does not require any demonstration of a 'converging will' or of a conscious acceptance by each Party of all implications of the terms to which it has agreed. It is the 'terms of the treaty in their context and in the light of its object and purpose' with which the Tribunal is to be concerned, not the subjective understanding or intent of either of the Parties."[558]

Consequently, as paragraph 3(c) of Article 31 of the Vienna Convention directs the Tribunal to take into account any relevant rules of international law applicable in the relations between the parties, and as there is a considerable body of law and legal literature, the Tribunal concludes that the applicable rule of international law is that of dominant and effective nationality.[559]

---

age, unless the permission of the Council of Ministers allows them to renounce their nationality, and

That they have completed their national military service.

Article 989 of the same code states:

In case any Iranian subject acquired foreign nationality after the solar year 1280 (1901-1902) without the observance of the provisions of law, his foreign nationality will be considered null and he will be regarded as an Iranian national.

Nevertheless, all his landed properties will be sold under the supervision of the local Public Prosecutor and the proceeds will be paid to him after the deduction of the expenses of sale. In addition, he will be disqualified to attain the position of Cabinet Minister or Assistant Minister or of membership of the Legislative Assemblies, Provincial and District Councils and Municipal Councils, or any other governmental positions.

558 The Islamic Republic of Iran v. The United States of America, Decision, IUSCT Case No. A18 (DEC 32-A18-FT), (6 April 1984), in Pieter Sanders (ed.), Yearbook Commercial Arbitration, Vol. 10, (1985), p. 203.

559 The Islamic Republic of Iran v. The United States of America, Decision, IUSCT Case No. A18 (DEC 32-A18-FT), (6 April 1984), Journal of International Arbitration, Vol. 1, Issue. 2, (1984), p. 177.

The Tribunal has also defined its method to determine the dominant and effective nationality, which could be seen in *Morteza Khatami v. the Government of the Islamic Republic of Iran* case. The Tribunal states that in order to find the stronger ties it should consider all relevant factors, such as the Claimant's habitual residence, center of interests, family ties, participation in public life and other evidence of attachment.[560]

In this case, the Tribunal showed its support of the doctrine of dominant and effective nationality. But the Tribunal did not come up with an adequate justification that why this doctrine should be the preferred standard. The Tribunal mainly articulated the inadequacies of the principles underlying the older doctrine of state non-responsibility.[561]

In order to have a better consideration of what the Tribunal did, we briefly examine these two doctrines and their results and eventually discuss whether the Tribunal's choice had less inequitable consequences.

aa) Doctrine of state non-responsibility

Based on this theory in international law, international claims belong only to one State, no matter who suffered the actual harm. Actually, international claim was defined as "… a demand of one government upon another through diplomatic channels or an international tribunal, for redress for acts or omissions for which the respondent government is contended responsible under international law or provisions of a treaty."[562] Based on this theory, an individual does not have a right to seek redress for a wrong inflicted by another nation but may only go through diplomatic protection which would be again inseparable from nationality.

The issues regarding nationality are regulated by municipal and not international law and lack of a uniform international law to determine nationality has led to the peculiarity of dual nationality.[563] This theory does not support dual nationality, since a State cannot fully protect a national against another State of which that individual is a citizen.[564] According to Borchard, one of the supporters of this doctrine:

560 Morteza Khatami v. The Government of the Islamic Republic of Iran, Award, IUSCT Case No. 767 (562-767-3), (13 December 1994), para. 24.

561 Note, "Claims of Dual Nationals in the Modern Era: The Iran-United States Claims Tribunal", Michigan Law Review, Vol. 83, No. 3, (1984), p. 600.

562 Nielsen, Fred Kenelm, "International Law Applied to Reclamations, J. Bryne, (1933), p. 55.

563 Note, "Claims of Dual Nationals in the Modern Era: The Iran-United States Claims Tribunal", Michigan Law Review, Vol. 83, No. 3, (1984), p. 601.

564 An endorsement of this Theory could be seen in Article 4 of the Hague Convention (Convention on Certain Questions Relating to the Conflict of Nationality Laws, 12 April 1930):

> "The principle generally followed [by international tribunals] has been that a person having dual nationality cannot make one of the countries to which he owes allegiance a defendant before an international tribunal In other words, a person cannot sue his own government in an international court, nor can any other government claim on his behalf."[565]

It has been also argued that accepting dual nationality would lead us to deny the sovereign equality. Because where both nationalities are valid, permitting one State to represent one national against his other State would be giving greater effect to one of the nationalities. Generally speaking, the school of State non-responsibility has arisen in connection with the resolution of such dual nationality problems and supports the principle of equality, which is based on the sovereign equality of States.[566]

This theory seems to be unsatisfactory especially where an individual is a dual national of both Claimant and Respondent states; according to this theory, neither States would be able to exercise diplomatic protection on his behalf, thus in certain situations the results of this doctrine would be inequitable.[567] This dual national person would have no form of redress for injuries caused by one of the States and it's a situation similar to statelessness.

One of the most influential international arbitral decisions, the *Nottebohm* case, regarding dual nationals also endorsed the doctrine of dominant and effective nationality.[568]

bb) Doctrine of dominant and effective nationality

Since dual nationality causes problems for both dual national themselves and their sovereigns, many attempts have been undertaken to limit the incidence of

---

A State may not afford diplomatic protection to one of its nationals against a State whose nationality such person also possesses.; See also Article 16(a) of the Harvard Draft Convention on Responsibility of States for Damage done in their Territory to the Person or Property of Foreigners (1929):

A state is not responsible if the person injured or the person on behalf of whom the claim is made was or is its own national.

565 Borchard, Edwin M., "The Diplomatic Protection of Citizens Abroad or the Law of International Claims", The Banks Law Publishing Co., (1916), p. 588.

566 Leigh, Guy I.F., "Nationality and Diplomatic Protection", International and Comparative Law Quarterly, Vol. 20, (1971), p. 460.

567 Peake, Jessica, "Diplomatic Protection for Dual Nationals: Effective Nationality or Non-Responsibility?", Trinity College Review, Vol. 10, (2007), p. 104.

568 Nottebohm Case (Liechtenstein v. Guatemala), (second phase), Judgment of April 6th, 1955: ICJ Reports, (1955), p. 4.

dual nationality.[569] The courts have also focused on solving the problems that dual nationality creates.

The principle of effective nationality dates back to 1834 and the *James Louis Drummond Case*.[570] In that case, the criterion of habitual residence was offered by court in order to determine an individual's effective nationality. This decision was a great step at the time. The essence of this doctrine is that in case of conflict between two governments regarding the nationality of a dual national claimant, the nationality of its habitual residence at the time that the claim arose should prevail over his other nationality.[571] Not just his habitual residence is the key but the court would pay attention also to the special circumstances of each case to determine which of the dual national's citizenships is dominant.[572] According to this doctrine, the choice of one State over the other based on the individual's stronger attachments cannot infringe the equality of the two States.[573] Another explanation of this Doctrine is declaring the fact that this is an international Tribunal, which is entitled to recognize a nationality as validly acquired at the domestic level or to determine the legal status of that nationality at the international level. The point is that a nationality granted at the domestic level cannot be recognized and given effect automatically on the international plane. Therefore, once a State applies to an international tribunal, it is then on the international plane. From that moment it is the international law, which determines the international effect of the State's act and not its domestic law.[574] The Tribunal is to examine the existence of the genuine connection between the national and the said State, as it is said in the *Nottebohm*'s case: "But the issue which the court must decide is not one which pertains to the legal system of Liechtenstein. It does

569 Scott, Bieler I., "Dual Nationality, Dominant Nationality and Federal Diversity Jurisdiction (Notes)", Washington and Lee Law Reviews, Vol. 38, Issue. 1, (1981), p. 78.

570 James Louis Drummond Case 2 Knapp, PC Rep 295; 12 Eng Rep 492, available at: http://www.geocities.ws/englishreports/12ER492.pdf (accessed on 1 May 2016).

571 Rode, Zvonko R., "Dual Nationals and the Doctrine of Dominant Nationality", The American Journal of International Law, Vol. 53, No. 1, (1959), p140.

572 Scott, Bieler I., "Dual Nationality, Dominant Nationality and Federal Diversity Jurisdiction (Notes)", Washington and Lee Law Reviews, Vol. 38, Issue. 1, (1981), p. 81.

573 Aghahosseini, Mohsen, "Claims of Dual Nationals and the Developments of Customary International Law – Issues Before the Iran-United States Claims Tribunal", Developments in International Law, Vol. 59, Martinus Nijhoff Publishers, (2007), p. 1.

574 Aghahosseini, Mohsen, "Claims of Dual Nationals and the Developments of Customary International Law – Issues Before the Iran-United States Claims Tribunal", Developments in International Law, Vol. 59, Martinus Nijhoff Publishers, (2007), p. 76.

not depend on the law or on the decision of Liechtenstein whether that State is entitled to exercise its protection, in the case under consideration. To exercise protection, to apply to the court, is to place oneself on the plane of international law. It is international law which determine whether a State is entitled to exercise protection and to seize the Court."[575] It became clearer when the Court added that the naturalization was performed by Liechtenstein in line with its domestic jurisdiction, so the question would be whether such an act has an international effect.[576] Thus, the Court had to determine whether the naturalization conferred on Nottebohm can be invoked against Guatemala so that Liechtenstein is entitled to exercise its protection in favor of Nottebohm against Guatemala. The Nottebohm case is of great importance, since it is one of the main resources in discussing the effective nationality doctrine. In this case, it is pointed out that it is plausible that international law leaves it to each State to establish the rules governing the grant of its own nationality and the reason is that the fact of diversity of demographic conditions had made it impossible to reach any general agreement on the rules concerning nationality. While setting out the nationality rules are left to each State, the rules are not entitled to recognition by another State, unless it has acted in conformity with this general aim of making the legal bond of nationality accord with the individual's genuine connection with the State.[577] By this means, the Court concluded that it should examine whether the nationality granted to Nottebohm is real and effective. In order to determine this matter, the duty of the Tribunal is to find stronger factual ties between the people concerned with one of the States whose nationality is involved. In doing so, there are many factors that should be taken into account such as the habitual residence, center of interests, family ties, attachment shown by him for a given country, participation in public life. The importance of each factor differs from one case to another.[578] ICJ after investigating the said factors found that the naturalization of Nottebohm was not based on any real prior connection with Liechtenstein nor did it alter the way of his living. The lacking of genuineness was a fact pointed out

575 Nottebohm Case (Liechtenstein v. Guatemala), International Court of Justice, (6 April 1955), p. 20.
576 Nottebohm Case (Liechtenstein v. Guatemala), International Court of Justice, (6 April 1955), p. 21.
577 Nottebohm Case (Liechtenstein v. Guatemala), International Court of Justice, (6 April 1955), p. 22.
578 Nottebohm Case (Liechtenstein v. Guatemala), International Court of Justice, (6 April 1955), p. 22.

by the Court. Thus, Guatemala is under no obligation to recognize a nationality granted in such circumstances.[579]

cc) Tribunal's approach on the standing of dual nationals

The issue of dual nationality is one of the most vexing questions of modern international claims practice and the role of the Iran-United States Claims Tribunal is very important since it has some 130 cases of dual nationality on its docket.[580]

Dual nationals in the case of this Tribunal had acquired their dual nationality by different means. Some of them were Iranian who were born in Iran and went to study abroad and were later naturalized in the United States. The less in number were those, who were born with sole United States nationality and later acquires Iranian nationality as a result of a marriage to Iranian nationals. Additionally, there were the children of Iranian and the United States' parents who acquired both nationalities because of the operation of the laws of Iran and the United States. All that those people had in common was the possession of financial interests in Iran. The types and amount of these interests were different.

In order to understand the background of the Tribunal's decision on the issue of dual nationality, it's important to study some features of Iran and the United States' laws on nationality. The Iranian law on nationality is generally based on the *jus sanguinis* rule, but it could also be gained liberally.[581] The Iranian law does not

---

579 Nottebohm Case (Liechtenstein v. Guatemala), International Court of Justice, (6 April 1955), p. 26.

580 Aghahosseini, Mohsen, "Claims of Dual Nationals and the Developments of Customary International Law – Issues Before the Iran-United States Claims Tribunal", Developments in International Law, Vol. 59, Martinus Nijhoff Publishers, (2007), p. 2.

581 Article 976:

The following persons are considered to be Iranian

All persons residing in Iran except those whose foreign nationality is established; the foreign nationality of such persons is considered to be established if their documents of nationality have not been objected to by the Iranian Government.

Those born in Iran or outside whose fathers are Iranian.

Those born in Iran of unknown parentage.

Persons born in Iran of foreign parents, one of whom was also born in Iran.

Persons born in Iran of a father of foreign nationality who have resided at least one more year in Iran immediately after reaching the full age of 18; in other cases their naturalization as Iranian will be subject to the stipulations for Iranian naturalization laid down by the law.

Every woman of foreign nationality who marries an Iranian husband.

Every foreign person who has obtained Iranian nationality.

recognize dual nationality. This non-recognition is not stated expressly though it could be perceived from other Articles such as Article 986 of the Iranian Civil Code which states the possibility of a non-Iranian woman who has become an Iranian national by virtue of her marriage to a national of Iran, to revert to her former nationality after the divorce or death of her husband. Furthermore, this refusal can be seen also in Articles 988 and 989, as before mentioned.

On the other hand, the United States law is based on the rule of *jus soli*, but it also recognizes *jus sanguinis*. The Fourteenth Amendment (1868) stated that all persons born in the United States and subject to United States jurisdiction automatically acquire United States citizenship. The reflection could be seen today in § 301 (a) of the Immigration and Nationality Act of 1952.[582] In contradiction to the Iranian law, the law of the United States does not prohibit the dual

---

Note- Children born of foreign diplomatic and consular representatives are not affected by clause 4 and 5 of this Article.

Naturalization is also prescribed by Article 979:

Persons can obtain Iranian nationality if they:

Have reached the full age of 18.

Have resided five years, whether continuously or intermittently, in Iran.

Are not deserters from military service.

Have not been convicted in any country of non-political major misdemeanors or felonies.

In the case of Clause 2 of this Article, the period of residence in foreign countries in the service of the Iranian Government will be considered as residence in Iran.

582 Article 301 considered following persons as nationals of United States:

a person born in the United States, and subject to the jurisdiction thereof;

a person born in the United States to a member of an Indian, Eskimo, Aleutian, or other aboriginal tribe: Provided, that the granting of citizenship under this subsection shall not in any manner impair or otherwise affect the right of such person to tribal or other property;

a person born outside of the United States and its outlaying possessions of parents both of whom are citizen of the Unites States and one of whom has had a residence in the United States or one of its outlaying possessions, prior to the birth of such person;

a person born outside of the United States and its outlaying possessions of parents one of whom is a citizen of the United States who has been physically present in the United States or one of its outlaying possessions for a continuous period of one year prior to the birth of such person, and the other of whom is a national, but not a citizen of the United States;

a person born in an outlaying possession of the Unites States of parents one of whom is a citizen of the United States who has been physically present in the United States or one of its outlaying possessions for continuous period of one year at any time prior to the birth of such person;

nationality; however, it does not approve it. This is how the U.S. Department of State explained the U.S. policy on dual nationality:

> "While recognizing the existence of dual nationality, the U.S. Government does not encourage it as a matter of policy because of the problems it may cause…"[583]

As stated before, the issue of dual nationality has once brought before the Tribunal in form of an interpretative case (A/18). At the same time chamber two were hearing three cases regarding this issue.

The *Esphahanian v. Bank Tejarat* case was the first case that the Tribunal has decided in favor of a dual national. In this case, Esphahanian who was an Iranian and naturalized American submitted a claim against Bank Tejarat for the amount of a cheque dishonored by the Iranian's bank, predecessor of Bank Tejarat. The Bank objected based on the fact that he is still Iranian since the requirements for the renunciation of the Iranian nationality had not been met.[584]

The Tribunal held in the Applicable part of the award that in this case it should resort to Article VII(1) of the Declaration which defines "national" of Iran or of the United States. The Tribunal stated:

> "Both parties agree that the Tribunal's task to determine whether Esphahanian's claim is within its jurisdiction as a claim of a national of the United States within the meaning of these articles. Since the Claim Settlement Declaration and the General Declaration together constitute a Treaty under international law, we are guided in interpreting

---

a person of unknown parentage found in the United States while under the age of five years, until shown, prior to his attaining the age of twenty-one years, not to have been born in the United States;

a person born outside the geographical limits of the United States and its outlying possessions of parents one of whom is an alien, and the other a citizen of the United States who, prior to the birth of such person, was physically present in the United States or its outlying possessions for a period or periods totaling not less than five years, at least two of which were after attaining the age of fourteen years: Provided …

a person born before noon (Eastern Standard Time) May 24, 1934, outside the limits and jurisdiction of the United States of an alien father and a mother who is a citizen of the United States who, prior to the birth of such person, had resided in the United States.

583 U.S. Department of State, 7 FAM 081 (CT: Con-106; 06-06-2005), available at https://fam.state.gov/searchapps/viewer?format=html&query=dual%20nationality&links=DUAL,NATION&url=/FAM/07FAM/07FAM0080.html#M081 (accessed on 2 May 2006)

584 Nasser Esphahanian v. Bank Tejarat, Award, IUSCT Case No. 157 (31-157-2), (29 March 1983), in Pieter Sanders (ed.), Yearbook Commercial Arbitration, Vol. 9, (1984), p. 273.

> them by Articles 31 and 32 of the Vienna Convention on the Law of Treaties of May 23, 1969."[585]

This is a statement that has repeated many times at the beginning of the Tribunal's award. The Tribunal explained that the Declarations are recognized as Treaties; therefore, their interpretations should be in accordance with the Vienna Convention.

Both parties expressed that the text is clear and unambiguous but each of them reached a different outcome. Esphahanian argues that it applies to all nationals of the United States and dual nationals are also nationals of the United States. On the contrary, the Bank argues that since Iran does not recognize dual nationality, it does not seem that Iran accepted it either when the Declaration was signed.

The Tribunal did not accept any of these arguments and stated that Claimant's interpretation leads to such an absurd outcome, where permits dual nationals to submit claims against wither Government or both. At the same time, the Tribunal believed that the simple fact that Respondent asserted with respect to non-recognition of dual nationality by Iran is not by itself dispositive. This approach was implied also by 1955 Treaty of Amity between Iran and the United States by providing certain exceptions regarding dual nationals.[586]

After this explanation made by the Tribunal, it concluded that based on considerable body of law, precedents and legal literature, the applicable rule of international law is that of dominant and effective nationality. Reaching this conclusion, the Tribunal has reviewed a considerable number of legal precedents such as *Canevaro* case (Italy and Peru), *Nottebohm* case (Liechtenstein and Guatemala) that demonstrated the approval of the International Court of Justice in the search for the real and effective nationality.[587]

In addition, the Tribunal also mentioned the Advisory Opinion of 11 April 1949 of International Court of Justice referred to the "ordinary practice whereby a State, does not exercise protection on behalf of one of its nationals against a State which regards him as its own national." The Institute of International

---

585 Nasser Esphahanian v. Bank Tejarat, Award, IUSCT Case No. 157 (31-157-2), (29 March 1983), in Pieter Sanders (ed.), Yearbook Commercial Arbitration, Vol. 9, (1984), p. 273.

586 Nasser Esphahanian v. Bank Tejarat, Award, IUSCT Case No. 157 (31-157-2), (29 March 1983), in Pieter Sanders (ed.), Yearbook Commercial Arbitration, Vol. 9, (1984), p. 273.

587 Nasser Esphahanian v. Bank Tejarat, Award, IUSCT Case No. 157 (31-157-2), (29 March 1983), in Pieter Sanders (ed.), Yearbook Commercial Arbitration, Vol. 9, (1984), p. 275.

Law also adopted the same approach during its meeting of 1965. Moreover, the Tribunal referred to the 1930 Hague Convention, which provides in its Article 4 that:

> "A State may not afford diplomatic protection to one of its nationals against a State whose nationality such person also possesses."[588]

The same Convention states in Article 5 that:

> "Within a third State, a person having more than one nationality shall be treated as if he had only one. Without prejudice to the application of its law in matters of personal status and of any connections in force, a third State shall, of the nationalities which any such person possesses, recognize exclusively in its territory either the nationality of the country in which he is habitually and principally resident, or the nationality of the country with which in the circumstances he appears to be in fact most closely connected."[589]

Above all, the Tribunal was convinced that the application of dominant and effective nationality is even supported by the general structure of the Algiers Accords.[590]

The Tribunal reminded the parties that shortly after the seizure of 52 U.S. nationals in the United States' Embassy in Tehran, a great number of plaintiffs obtained court attachments from the U.S. courts. Due to the effectiveness of establishment of this Tribunal and its purpose to resolve all the litigation, the United States forced it nationals to submit their Claims in this Tribunal and dissolved their attachments. One of those dissolved attachments was for Esphahanian. After expressing these facts, the Tribunal brought three conclusions regarding the application of dominant and effective nationality to demonstrate the truth of its statement about the structure of Algiers Declarations.

First, the Tribunal mentioned that the creation of this Tribunal by Iran and the United States was not a typical exercise of diplomatic protection of nationals. In other words, it is not a Tribunal in which the State seeks redress for its nationals or on behalf of them. As an example, the Tribunal stressed that in this case the Government of the United States is not a party to the arbitration of claims of the

588 Article 5 of The Convention on Certain Questions Relating to The Conflict of Nationality Laws, The Hague, (12 April 1930).

589 Article 4 of The Convention on Certain Questions Relating to The Conflict of Nationality Laws, The Hague, (12 April 1930).

590 Nasser Esphahanian v. Bank Tejarat, Award, IUSCT Case No. 157 (31-157-2), (29 March 1983), in Pieter Sanders (ed.), Yearbook Commercial Arbitration, Vol. 9, (1984), p. 277.

United States nationals, not even in the small claims where it acts as counsel for those nationals.[591]

Second, the scope of the responsibility of either States are far broader than usual because based on the definition of Iran and the United States in the Claims Settlement Declaration, they include agencies, instrumentalities and entities controlled by the State. This more than normal liability is also more than usual in cases of diplomatic espousal of claims, where the States are to pay compensation for their own violation of international law.[592]

Eventually, the Tribunal asserted that this is a Tribunal, which is established as a substitution of national courts. Similar to the national courts, the Tribunal could also confront the conflict of nationality law and since there is no *lex fori* binding on it, the parties should have known that the Tribunal would have no choice but to apply the dominant and effective nationality.[593]

Consequently, based on these arguments the Tribunal concluded that it "has jurisdiction (a) over claims against Iran by dual Iran-United States nationals when the dominant and effective nationality of the Claimant is that of the United States and (b) over claims against the United States by dual Iran-United States nationals when the dominant and effective nationality of the Claimant is that of Iran."[594]

The only exception could be seen in the caveat added by the Tribunal showing the precedent for denying jurisdiction on equitable grounds in case of fraudulent use of nationality. For example, where an individual disguises his dominant or effective nationality in order to obtain some benefits with his secondary nationality, which otherwise would not be available to him.[595]

---

591 Nasser Esphahanian v. Bank Tejarat, Award, IUSCT Case No. 157 (31-157-2), (29 March 1983), in Pieter Sanders (ed.), Yearbook Commercial Arbitration, Vol. 9, (1984), p. 277.

592 Nasser Esphahanian v. Bank Tejarat, Award, IUSCT Case No. 157 (31-157-2), (29 March 1983), in Pieter Sanders (ed.), Yearbook Commercial Arbitration, Vol. 9, (1984), p. 277.

593 Nasser Esphahanian v. Bank Tejarat, Award, IUSCT Case No. 157 (31-157-2), (29 March 1983), in Pieter Sanders (ed.), Yearbook Commercial Arbitration, Vol. 9, (1984), p. 278.

594 Nasser Esphahanian v. Bank Tejarat, Award, IUSCT Case No. 157 (31-157-2), (29 March 1983), in Pieter Sanders (ed.), Yearbook Commercial Arbitration, Vol. 9, (1984), p. 278.

595 In the caveat the Tribunal referred to Flegenheimer Case (20 September 1958), Reports of International Arbitral Awards, Vol. XIV, pp. 327–390.

The important step in this case and other similar cases for the Tribunal would be to determine the effective nationality by finding the closest connection and bonds of an individual with a country. In this case, the Tribunal found Esphahanian's contacts with United States so close. Proofs of it are his residence in the United States since 1946, serving in U.S. armed forces, becoming a citizen in 1958, his marriage to an American woman, having American children who speak no Farsi and attended only American schools. He bought four residences in America and all of his investments were there except for a limited period of time (1970–1978). Since he was naturalized as a U.S. citizen, he paid taxes and voted in elections even during the time that he was outside the United States.[596]

Esphahanian's contacts with Iran were also considerable. He had some relatives in Iran whom he visited. He retained his Iranian passport and had his principal residence there for nearly nine months of each of the years 1970–1977. He lived there with his family and the children attended American school in Tehran during that time. There was a proof before the Tribunal that his American employer wanted him to work in number of countries within the Middle East and also paid for his expenses. There is also adequate evidence to demonstrate the fact that virtually all of the fund used to purchase the check in question were acquired legitimately from activities which were not related to Esphahanian's Iranian nationality.

The Tribunal further pointed out that based on Iranian law a national is able of renunciation of Iranian nationality but as a result he could enter Iran only once to sell or transfer his properties. Thus, Esphahanian had no way but using his Iranian passport. There is an evidence also proving that the visa stamps of all countries other than Iran and one Lebanese and one Saudi Arabian visa are all in his American passport.

Therefore, the Tribunal concluded that:

> "On the basis of these facts, the Tribunal concludes that Esphahanian's dominant and effective nationality at all relevant times has been that of the United States, and the funds at issue in the present claim are related primarily to his American nationality, not his Iranian nationality. With the exceptions of his use of an Iranian passport to enter and leave Iran and his nominal ownership of stock on behalf of his employer, all of his actions relevant to this claim could have been done by a non-Iranian. The Tribunal holds that the Claimant, Nasser Esphahanian, is a national of the United States within the

596 Nasser Esphahanian v. Bank Tejarat, Award, IUSCT Case No. 157 (31-157-2), (29 March 1983), in Pieter Sanders (ed.), Yearbook Commercial Arbitration, Vol. 9, (1984), p. 278.

> meaning of the Claims Settlement Declaration and that the Tribunal has jurisdiction to decide his claim against Bank Tejarat."[597]

Clearly, we see in this case and in what we saw in A/18 case the Tribunal chose the application of the dominant and effective nationality role. But the other matter is whether the Tribunal's justifications are convincing enough or not. In A/18 case, the Tribunal referred to customary international law. This act is also allowed by Vienna Convention but according to the applicable law rules of this Tribunal only after that there is no answer in the parties' agreement and that the rule of international law should be applicable in the relations between the parties. But there are no such explanations to be found in the Tribunal's awards and decisions. Choosing from two rival rules, the rule of non-responsibility and the rule of dominant nationality is not an easy task. Since some interpretation rules require international tribunals to take international law into account only if it is applicable in the relations between the parties and this means that international tribunal should have the consent of the parties on that matter, which the Tribunal did not have from Iran. As Iran stated that no matter what the customary international law is, the parties did not agree upon authorizing the Tribunal to settle the claims of dual nationals of Iran and the United States in the Tribunal.[598]

From another angle, the other justification for the Tribunal's reference to the dominant and effective nationality rule is to take a step toward the development of this rule parallel to the progressive trend in international law, the rights of individuals *vis-à-vis* States. This fact is revealed in Case No. A/18 of the Tribunal, in which the Tribunal after discussing The Hague Convention, precedents and legal literature all in favor of the dominant and effective nationality rule, added:

> "This trend toward modification of the Hague Convention rule of non-responsibility by search for the dominant and effective nationality is scarcely surprising as it is consistent with the contemporaneous development of international law to accord legal protections to individuals, even against the State of which they are nationals."[599]

---

597 Nasser Esphahanian v. Bank Tejarat, Award, IUSCT Case No. 157 (31-157-2), (29 March 1983), in Pieter Sanders (ed.), Yearbook Commercial Arbitration, Vol. 9, (1984), p. 279.

598 Aghahosseini, Mohsen, "Claims of Dual Nationals and the Developments of Customary International Law – Issues Before the Iran-United States Claims Tribunal", Developments in International Law, Vol. 59, Martinus Nijhoff Publishers, (2007), p. 253.

599 The Islamic Republic of Iran v. The United States of America, Decision, IUSCT Case No. A18 (DEC 32-A18-FT), (6 April 1984), p. 11.

In the section of legal literature, the Tribunal conferred a great number of component lawyers in support of the rule of dominant nationality, while the minority referred also to a great number of authorities that endorsed the rule of non-responsibility.[600] Notwithstanding the objections regarding the way the Tribunal conceptualized its theory and of course the lack of explanations on this matter, one could not decline the remarkable effort of the Tribunal to interactively consider and evaluate plenty of factors in one case alone. This was an exceptional attempt, which is going to be repeated in other arbitral tribunals.

As we witnessed, proving the nationality is a relatively easy task, while proving the nationality being dominant and effective is an elaborate task which requires heated deliberation.

It is important to mention once again that two dates are of great importance before the Tribunal on determining the matter of dominant and effective nationality. One is 19 January 1981 (when Claims Settlement Declaration was signed) and the other is the date of acquiring the nationality, which must be some time before the date on which the claim arose. Besides this time span that should be evaluated, the events throughout the Claimant's life prior to the accrual of the nationality is of importance. Lack of these characters was the main reason of the rejection of many cases before the Tribunal. As in the *Malek* case, the Tribunal pointed out that even though this period of time is decisive for the Tribunal's jurisdiction, it is not the only matter to be considered in order to determine if the United States (or Iranian as the case may be) nationality of a Claimant is his "dominant and effective nationality" at the relevant time. In order to establish what the dominant and effective nationality is at the date the claim arose, it is required to examine the events of the Claimant's life preceding this date. That would include the entire life of the Claimant from birth and all the factors that reflect the reality and the sincerity of the choice of national allegiance he claims to have made, are relevant.[601]

600 See Dissenting Opinion of the Iranian Arbitrators in Case A-18 Concerning the Jurisdiction of the Tribunal over Claims presented by Dual Iranian-United States Nationals against the Government of Iran.

601 Reza Said Malek v. The Government of the Islamic Republic of Iran, Interlocutory Award, IUSCT Case No. 193, (ITL 68-193-3), (23 June 1988), para. 14.

2) The *Ratione Materiae* jurisdiction of the Tribunal

a) *Article II of the Claims Settlement Declaration and the Undertakings*

The *Ratione Materiae* Jurisdiction is pointed out by Article II of the Claims Settlement Declaration and paragraph 2-B of the Undertakings:

> Article II:
> An international arbitral tribunal (the Iran-United States Claims Tribunal) is hereby established for the purpose of deciding claims of nationals of the United States against Iran and claims of nationals of Iran against the United States, and any counterclaim which arises out of the same contract, transaction or occurrence that constitutes the subject matter of that national's claim, if which claims and counterclaims are outstanding on the date of this Agreement, whether or not filed with any court, and rise out of debts, contracts (including transactions which are the subject of the letters of credit or bank guarantees), expropriations or other measures affecting property rights, excluding claims described in Paragraph 11 of the Declaration of the Government of Algeria of January 19, 1981, and claims arising out of the actions of the United States in response to the conduct described in such paragraph, and excluding claims arising under a binding contract between the parties specifically providing that any disputes thereunder shall be within the sole jurisdiction of the competent Iranian courts, in response to the Majlis position.

The Tribunal shall also have jurisdiction over official claims of the United States and Iran against each other arising out of contractual arrangements between them for the purchase and sale of goods and services.

The Tribunal shall have jurisdiction, as specified in paragraphs 16–17 of the Declaration of the Government of Algeria of 19 January 1981, over any dispute as to the interpretation or performance of any provision of that Declaration.

This Article describes the jurisdiction of the Tribunal in general. It provides for nearly all types of disputes that could be brought before a tribunal especially in international investment field. The subject-matter jurisdiction of the Tribunal and the personal jurisdiction sometimes overlap as we try to describe them. As an example, in previous section when we explained the jurisdiction of the Tribunal over the Governments of Iran and the United States, it is naturally required to explain the type of the dispute, which is under the Tribunal's jurisdiction. That was partly entering into the realm of the subject-matter jurisdiction of the Tribunal, which cannot be avoided.

In addition to the Article II of the Claims Settlement Declaration, paragraph 2-B of the Undertaking mentions also the aspects of the Tribunal's subject-matter jurisdiction. This paragraph states:

"(B) To retain U.S. $1.418 billion in the Escrow Account for the purpose of paying the unpaid principal of and interest owing, of any, on the loans and credits referred to in Paragraph (a) after application of the U.S. $3.667 billion and on all other indebtedness held by United States banking institutions of, or guaranteed by, the Government of Iran, its agencies, instrumentalities or controlled entities not previously paid, and for the purpose of paying disputed amounts of deposits, assets, and interest, if any, owing on Iranian deposits in U.S. banking institutions. Bank Markazi and the appropriate United States banking institutions shall promptly meet in an effort to agree upon the amounts owing. In the event of such agreement, the Bank Markazi and the appropriate banking institutions shall certify the amount owing to the Central Bank of Algeria which shall instruct the bank of England to credit such amount to the account, as appropriate, of the Bank Markazi or of the Federal Reserve Bank of New York in order to permit payment to the appropriate banking institution. In the event that within 30 days any U.S. banking institution and the Bank Markazi are unable to agree upon the amounts owed, either party may refer such dispute to binding arbitration by such international arbitration panel as the parties may agree, or failing such agreement within 30 additional days after such reference, by the Iran-United States Claims Tribunal. The presiding officer of such panel or tribunal shall certify to the Central Bank of Algeria the amount, if any, determined by it to be owed, whereupon the Central Bank of Algeria shall instruct the Bank of England to credit such amount to the account of the Bank Markazi or of the Federal Reserve Bank of New York in order to permit payment to the appropriate banking institution. After all disputes are resolved either by agreement of by arbitration award and appropriate payment has been made, the balance of the funds referred to in this Paragraph (B) shall be paid to Bank Markazi."

b) The Iranian-forum clause decision

As we read in the Claims Settlement Declaration, there are three exclusions of the Tribunal's jurisdiction, which are claims arising out of Iran's seizure of 52 U.S. citizens and their subsequent detention, actions by the United States in response to the seizure and claims "arising under a binding contract between the parties specifically providing that any disputes thereunder shall be within the sole jurisdiction of the competent Iranian courts in response to the Majlis position."[602] The former exclusion is the one that we are going to discuss further because this issue has initiated some arguments concerning the applicable law of the Tribunal that we will analyze later.

The arguments basically originated in different positions of Iran and the United States regarding the enforceability of choice of forum clauses. Since the effect of this exclusion was not clear enough, the Tribunal selected nine test cases

---

602 Claims Settlement Declarations, Article II, para. 1, (19 January 1981).

in order to provide the chambers with guidance for the future cases. These cases were presenting a total of 19 different cases before the three chambers.[603]

The argument began as the United States alleged that the said exclusion only works under three conditions. Firstly, claim should have arisen under a contract. This means that the exclusion does not apply to the claims based on expropriation, tort or any other non-contract claims. Secondly, the contract should have provided that any dispute thereunder would be subject to the sole jurisdiction of the Iranian Courts. This condition rules that a certain forum should be specified; Iranian courts in our case. Furthermore, that particular forum should be given a sole jurisdiction. As an outcome, the contracts that provided the jurisdiction of Iranian courts for the resolution of not all but some of the disputes shall not be excluded. The third condition asserts that the contractual choice of forum should be binding. That seemed to be the hardest condition, as the United States maintained that the Tribunal was to determine this matter autonomously. It went further and the United States contended that the Tribunal should not enforce an Iranian choice of forum clause because the Iranian courts and legal system has been affected by a fundamental change and actually they are not the same as those stipulated under the contracts.[604]

On the other hand, Iran believed that instead of referring to the exclusions pointed out in Article II(1), one should first of all consider that principally state contract claims are under the Jurisdiction of the courts of that State. The jurisdiction of the State remains unless there is another specification. As in all of the contracts involving Iranian state enterprises such a choice of forum clause was exclusively providing for the jurisdiction of Iranian courts, the United States' argument was redundant and should not be accepted.

On the one hand the position of the United States is very narrow and it would be really hard to meet the said requirements. Iran's position, on the other hand, was rather broad. Any claim could be beyond the jurisdiction of the Tribunal only if it was based on a contract providing for the jurisdiction of Iranian over the claims, even if it was in a very general phrase.[605]

603 Stein, Ted L., "Jurisprudence and Jurists' Prudence: The Iranian-Forum Clause Decisions of the Iran-U.S. Claims Tribunal", The American Journal of International Law, Vol. 78, (1984), p. 3.

604 Badaruddin, Schandor S., "Choice of Law Decisions in the Iran U.S. Claims Tribunal", Emory International Law Review, Vol. 4, (1990), pp. 172–173.

605 Berglin, R. Håkan, "Treaty Interpretation and the Impact of Contractual Choice of Forum Clauses on the Jurisdiction of International Tribunals: The Iranian Forum Clause Decisions of the Iran-United States Claims Tribunal", Texas International Law Journal, Vol. 21, (1985–1986), p. 41.

Now that we have discussed the position of both parties, we should take a look to the nine test cases and see how the Full Tribunal analyzed them. The awards all started after a quotation of the exclusion provision of Article II(1) of the Claims Settlement Declaration that stated:

> "Chamber (1, 2 or 3) of the Tribunal gas relinquished to the Full Tribunal jurisdiction over this case for the limited purpose of deciding whether claims therein arising out of contracts containing provisions for the settlement of disputes fall within the scope of the abovementioned provision of the Claims Settlement Declaration."

The cases were to send back to the chambers after the decision on clauses had been made. The Chambers continued the proceedings.

Some of these nine case included more than one contract and therefore, more than one forum clause. It was the total of 19 different clauses to deal with.[606]

As mentioned before, for considering the Article II exclusions, certain requirements have to be met. In order to avoid repetition, instead of explaining each case separately, the Tribunal's view on each requirement will be discussed.

aa) Binding contract

The considerations regarding this issue in the cases decided by the full Tribunal were almost similar. They reveal the fact that the Tribunal finds the word "binding" ambiguous. This ambiguity is resulted from different intentions of the parties at the phase of negotiations.

It has been also argued that the word "binding" was brought to the text in order to distinguish two different types of contract in Iranian law; binding contracts and revocable contracts. But it also seems not to be the case, because the Tribunal had indicated that the word "binding" was originally proposed by the American negotiators and was not derived from the said distinction in Iranian law.

A long debate on this issue is reflected in *T.C.S.B, Inc. v. Iran* case. This case was based on two contracts; Mali Abad Contract and BHRC Contract. The Claimant tried different arguments in order to prove that the case does not fall within the scope of the forum clause exclusion. The BHRC Contract contained a provision, which reads:

606 "Interlocutory awards Nos. 1-9 in cases Nos. 6, 51, 68, 121, 140, 159, 254, 293 and 466 (decision on forum selection clauses), Yearbook Commercial Arbitration, Pieter Sanders (ed.), Vol. VIII, (1983), p. 282–283.

> "All disputes arising out of this subcontract, or the interpretation and understanding of its provisions between the parties, which cannot be settled through amicable negotiations or correspondence, shall first be referred to a committee composed of a representative of each of the Employer, Housing Organization, and Subcontractor. In case no agreement can be reached or if one of the parties does not agree with the judgment of the majority of the committee, the dispute will be settled according to the laws of Iran by reference of it to competent courts of Iran."[607]

The wording of this clause seems to fulfill the Article II requirements and exclude the case from the Tribunal's jurisdiction. United States, however, argued that it does not fulfill the requirements and cannot be considered as a binding commitment to the sole jurisdiction of Iranian courts because of the fundamental changes that have occurred in Iran since the conclusion of this contract.

The Tribunal, on the other hand, did not accept this approach and stated:

> "It is not generally the task of this Tribunal, or of any arbitral tribunal, to determine the enforceability of choice of forum clauses in contracts. If the parties wished the Tribunal to determine the enforceability of contract clauses specifically providing for the sole jurisdiction of Iranian courts, it would be expected that they would do so clearly and unambiguously. Thus, the Tribunal would be reluctant to assume such a task in the absence of a clear mandate to do so in the Algiers Declaration."[608]

The Tribunal believed that the wording of Claims Settlement Declaration (binding contract) was intended to refer to the contract as a whole and not only to its forum selection clause. The Tribunal recognized the possibility to interpret the word "contract" as only a clause in a contract. However, the Tribunal believed, should the parties meant to refer specifically to an enforceable forum selection clause providing for the sole jurisdiction of Iranian court, had they agreed on such interpretation. Eventually, the Tribunal found such wording ambiguous and felt obliged to go beyond the text and look for other evidence.[609]

---

607 T.C.S.B., Inc. v. Iran, Interlocutory Award, IUSCT Award No. ITL 5-140-FT, (5 November 1982), Part. III.

608 T.C.S.B., Inc. v. Iran, Interlocutory Award, IUSCT Award No. ITL 5-140-FT, (5 November 1982), Part. III; Stone & Webster Overseas Group, Inc. v. National Petrochemical Company, Razi Chemical Company (formerly Shahpur Chemical Company Limited), Interlocutory Awards, IUSCT Awards No. ITL 8-293-FT, (5 November 1982), Part. II.

609 T.C.S.B., Inc. v. Iran, Interlocutory Award, IUSCT Award No. ITL 5-140-FT, (5 November 1982), Part. III; Stone & Webster Overseas Group, Inc. v. National Petrochemical Company, Razi Chemical Company (formerly Shahpur Chemical Company Limited), Interlocutory Awards, IUSCT Awards No. ITL 8-293-FT, (5 November 1982), Part. II.

Therefore, the Tribunal stated that there is not adequate evidence of two governments agreeing on a meaning for the word "binding." But at the same time the United States pointed out the negotiations at the drafting phase, which shows the intent of the Americans. The former Deputy Secretary of State, Warren Christopher, said that United States would insist on the word "binding" and this would describe "the importance of the new term."

Nevertheless, the Tribunal said:

> "…if the words 'binding contract' were to be interpreted as referring to the binding character of the entire contract, this would leave the Tribunal with a vicious circle since, e.g., in case of a contention that the contract is invalid as a result of fraud, the Tribunal would have to go into the merits of the case in order to find out whether it has jurisdiction but would at the same time not be entitled to go into the merits until it has been established that it has jurisdiction. Thus, neither of the two possible interpretations gives any sensible meaning to the word 'binding' in the present context. Therefore, the Tribunal concludes that this word is redundant."[610]

These considerations were all almost identical in cases 2-52, 4-121, 5-140 and 8-293. The Tribunal in these cases included that it has no jurisdiction over the claims based on the contracts in each case.

bb) Specifically providing

The next test that the Tribunal ran to decide whether a case should fall under the exclusion of Article II was to determine if the forum clause specifically provides for the jurisdiction of the Iranian courts. The Tribunal's interpretation could be seen in four of the nine test cases.

Case number 1-6 was based on a contract (the "TAVANIR Contract") signed between Gibbs & Hill Iran, an alleged affiliate of Gibbs & Hill, Inc., and Respondent TAVANIR (Iran Power Generation and Transmission Company) for engineering, consulting and construction monitoring services in connection with the implementation of electrical transmission systems. This contract included the following clause:

> "All disputes that may arise between the parties hereto over this Contract or the interpretation of its contents, that cannot be settled through negotiation or correspondence in an amicable manner, shall first be referred to a committee consisting of the highest authority of the Client (or his Deputy) and the Consulting Engineer for Settlement,

610 T.C.S.B., Inc. v. Iran, Interlocutory Award, IUSCT Award No. ITL 5-140-FT, (5 November 1982), Part. III.

> and in case they fail to settle the dispute in accordance with this Contract and current regulations, the dispute shall be settled through courts according to Iranian law."[611]

In this case, the Claimant contended that this Article does not specify any competent Iranian courts nor does it confer upon any court, Iranian or otherwise, sole jurisdiction, as required by Article II of the Claims Settlement Declaration. But Respondents believed that the Treaty provisions conferring jurisdiction of the Tribunal should be interpreted in a restrictive manner. The Tribunal stated:

> "Article II, paragraph 1, of the Claims Settlement Declaration excludes from the jurisdiction of the Tribunal claims arising under contracts which *specifically* provide for the sole jurisdiction of the competent Iranian courts. The TAVANIR Contract does not contain any provision, which unambiguously restricts jurisdiction to the courts of Iran. Consequently, this article does not with sufficient clarity fulfill the requirements laid down in the exclusion clause of Article II, paragraph 1, of the Claims Settlement Declaration."[612]

Therefore, the Tribunal pointed out that Article 24 of TAVANIR Contract only provides that disputes, failing settlement between the parties, shall be solved through court proceedings and Iranian law should govern them, notwithstanding of the courts that deals with them.[613]

Another Award demonstrating this matter is Award No. 7-254, which dealt with contracts concluded between Zokor International as Claimant and the Government of Iran and Societe du Chemin de Fer Urbain de Teheran et de sa Banlieue (METRO) as Respondents. The Claim was based on METRO's alleged failure to perform its obligations pursuant to the contracts. Regarding the dispute settlement issue Article 45 of the Contract was stipulated:

---

611 Article 24 of TAVANIR Contract (23 November 1977).

612 Gibbs & Hill, Inc. v. Iran Power Generation and Transmission Company ("TAVANIR") of the Ministry of Energy of the Government of Iran, Atomic Energy Organization of Iran ("AEOI") of the Ministry of Energy of the Government of Iran, Ministry of Energy of the Government of Iran, Iranians' Bank, Bank Tejarat East Taleghani, The International Bank of Iran and Japan, Interlocutory Award, IUSCT Award No. ITL 1-6-FT, (5 November 1982), Part. II.

613 Gibbs & Hill, Inc. v. Iran Power Generation and Transmission Company ("TAVANIR") of the Ministry of Energy of the Government of Iran, Atomic Energy Organization of Iran ("AEOI") of the Ministry of Energy of the Government of Iran, Ministry of Energy of the Government of Iran, Iranians' Bank, Bank Tejarat East Taleghani, The International Bank of Iran and Japan, Interlocutory Award, IUSCT Award No. ITL 1-6-FT, (5 November 1982), Part. II.

> "Should a dispute arise between the Manufacturer and the Employer, whether related to the execution of the contractual works or about the interpretation of the Articles of the contract, general conditions of the contract and other contractual documents, and if the dispute is not resolved in an amicable way, the same shall be referred to competent judicial authorities and courts and shall be resolved in accordance with the laws in force in Iran unless there is a convention between the Imperial Government and the Government of the country of the Manufacturer."

Similar to the previous case, the Claimant contended that this article does not *specifically* provide for the sole and exclusive jurisdiction of Iranian courts, because it does not mention that all disputes arising under the contract shall be submitted to Iranian courts. However, the Respondent asserted that the Treaty provisions conferring jurisdiction on the Tribunal should be interpreted in a restrictive manner. The Respondent's point is that Iran's agreement to submit disputes to arbitration before the Tribunal should not be extended beyond what clearly has been intended by the two Governments. Besides, Respondents contended that the dispute settlement provision is an integral part of the contracts, while these contracts do not provide for reference of disputes to judicial other than the judicial of Iran, hence these must be considered to have sole jurisdiction over the disputes.[614]

But Article 45 does not seem to fulfill the conditions made by Article II, paragraph 1, of the Claims Settlement Declaration, which excludes from the jurisdiction of the Tribunal only claims arising under contracts, which specifically provide for the sole jurisdiction of the competent Iranian courts. Therefore, the Tribunal held, since Article 45 of the instant contracts does not fall within the exclusion clause of the forum clause, it cannot exclude the Tribunal from its jurisdiction based on those contracts. [615]

Another case dealing with the same issue is the one between T.C.S.B. Inc. and Iran, which is based on two contracts concluded between the U.S. Claimant and the Housing Organization of Iran. The first Contract ("the Mali Abad" Contract) concerned services in connection with the construction of a planned community of apartment houses in Iran. The Mali Abad contract contained a dispute resolution provision that reads as follows:

---

614 Zokor International Inc. v. the Government of the Islamic Republic of Iran, Societe du Chemin de Fer Urbain de Teheran et de sa Banlieue ("METRO"), Interlocutory Award, IUSCT Award No. ITL 7-254-FT, (5 November 1982).

615 Zokor International Inc. v. the Government of the Islamic Republic of Iran, Societe du Chemin de Fer Urbain de Teheran et de sa Banlieue ("METRO"), Interlocutory Award, IUSCT Award No. ITL 7-254-FT, (5 November 1982).

> "All disputes arising out of this contract, or the interpretation and understanding of its provision between the parties, which cannot be solved and settled through amicable negotiations or correspondence, shall first be referred to a committee composed of three representatives of the Plan and Budget Organization, the [Housing] Organization and the Consulting Engineer [T.C.S.B.]. In case no agreement can be reached or if one of the parties to the contract does not submit to the judgment of the majority of the committee, the dispute will be settled according to the laws of Iran and if necessary by arbitration or by reference to competent courts."[616]

The contract also stated that the laws of the Imperial Government of Iran should govern the contract in every respect.

In this respect the Tribunal found that the Mali Abad Contract does not fall within the scope of the forum clause exclusion contained in Article II, paragraph 1, of the Claims Settlement Declaration. The Tribunal explained that jurisdiction of the tribunal would only then be excluded under Article II, paragraph 1 of the Claims Settlement Declaration, where the contract specifically provides for the sole jurisdiction of the competent Iranian courts. To that end, in this case, the Mali Abad contract refers to arbitration as an alternative to court proceedings, without mentioning any particular courts. Therefore, the Tribunal believed that sufficient clarity to meet the exclusion's requirements is lacking and such article in Mali Abad contract does not exclude the jurisdiction of the Tribunal.[617]

cc) Any disputes

The other test the Tribunal ran in order to determine whether the dispute settlement clause fulfills the Claims Settlement Declaration's requirements is that the provisions should cover "any disputes".

As the first example Case No. 4-121 will be mentioned, which is between a U.S Claimant, George W. Drucker, Jr. and Foreign Transaction Company, Insurance Company of Iran, National Grain and Sugar and Tea Organization as Respondents. This case deals with five contracts. The first claim, which is based on the Rice Contract, is for payment for a quantity of rice delivered by South Gulf Trading and Shipping Co. Ltd. ("South Gulf"). The Claimant alleged that this company is to be 60% owned by him. However, the Respondent objected

---

616 T.C.S.B., Inc. v. Iran, Interlocutory Award, IUSCT Award No. ITL 5-140-FT, (5 November 1982), Part. II;

617 T.C.S.B., Inc. v. Iran, Interlocutory Award, IUSCT Award No. ITL 5-140-FT, (5 November 1982), Part. II.

the Tribunal's jurisdiction, asserting that the claim arises from the Rice Contract confers jurisdiction upon competent Iranian courts.[618]

The dispute settlement provision in this contract reads as follows:

> "Any dispute arising from the execution of this agreement, if not settled amicably, shall be resolved through the Iranian legal authorities."

This is the translation to be found in Claimant's memorial. The one filed by the Respondent, however, is:

> "Any dispute arising from the performance of this contract, not settled amicably, shall be settled by reference to the legal authorities of Iran. The Respondents contended that 'Iranian legal authorities' is equivalent to 'the competent Iranian courts.'"

Apart from other arguments, Claimant brought up that the forum selection clause is required to cover "any disputes" under that contract but the Rice Contract fails to meet with this requirement because it only applies to the disputes arising from execution or performance of the contract. It, for example, does not cover disputes arising from interpretation.[619]

The Tribunal addressed this issue by examining the wording "any dispute arising from the execution" or "from the performance". The question would be whether such wordings fall within the exclusion clause. To that end the Tribunal noted:

> "It is true that the wording here to some extent may appear to limit the scope of Article 14. It could be argued that disputes concerning the interpretation or validity of the contract were not covered by it, such disputes would fall outside the scope of the article only if they did not arise out of performance or non-performance of the contract. It is in practice often difficult if not possible to draw a demarcation line between disputes concerning the performance of the parties' contractual obligations, on the one hand, and the interpretation or validity of the agreement on the other hand; disputes of the former kind will often inevitably entail questions of interpretation or validity, and disputes of the latter kind usually arise from performance. Abstract questions of interpretation or validity not arising from performance might form the basis for requests for declaratory judgments, but those would hardly be disputes under the contract. In view of this, the

618 George W. Drucker, Jr. v. Foreign Transaction Co., Insurance Company of Iran, National Grain, Sugar and Tea Organization, Interlocutory Award, IUSCT Award No. ITL 4-121-FT, (5 November 1982), Part. II.

619 George W. Drucker, Jr. v. Foreign Transaction Co., Insurance Company of Iran, National Grain, Sugar and Tea Organization, Interlocutory Award, IUSCT Award No. ITL 4-121-FT, (5 November 1982), Part. II.

> Tribunal holds that the scope of Article 14 of the Rice Contract is sufficiently broad so as to meet the requirement of the exclusion provision in this respect."[620]

The Tribunal, however, reached a different conclusion in award No. 6-159, which is the outcome of a claim based on a number of agreements between the U.S. Claimants and Iranian military authorities. Under one of these contracts ("the Peace Sceptre Contract"), the Claimant was required to provide equipment and services in connection with the installation of certain facilities at two air bases in Iran. The Following provisions could be found in Articles 9 and 11 of the Contract:

> "All disputes and differences between the two parties arising out of interpretation of the Contract or execution of the Works which cannot be settled in a friendly way, shall be settled in accordance with the rules provided by the Iranian laws, via referring to the competent Iranian Courts.

The Governing law of this contract is the Iranian law. This contract is subject to the Laws of the Imperial Government of Iran in every respect."[621]

Similar to the previous case the Claimants contended that the clause does not cover all disputes as required by Claims Settlement Declaration, because its scope is expressly limited to the interpretation of the contract and the execution of the works.[622]

The Tribunal this time agreed with the Claimant and stated that the Claims Settlement Declaration's exclusion applies only where the contractual choice of Iranian courts covers all claims that may arise under the contract. However, in this contract the jurisdiction of Iranian courts is solely with respect to disputes arising from the interpretation of the contract and execution of works and, therefore, it cannot be considered as comprehensive enough to exclude the Tribunal's

---

620 George W. Drucker, Jr. v. Foreign Transaction Co., Insurance Company of Iran, National Grain, Sugar and Tea Organization, Interlocutory Award, IUSCT Award No. ITL 4-121-FT, (5 November 1982), Part. II.

621 Ford Aerospace & Communications Corporation, Aeronutronic Overseas Services Inc. v. The Air Force of the Islamic Republic of Iran, The Ground Forces of the Islamic Republic of Iran, The Ministry of National Defense of the Islamic Republic of Iran, Bank Markazi and the Government of Iran, Interlocutory Award, IUSCT Award No. ITL 6-159-FT, (5 November 1989), Introduction.

622 Ford Aerospace & Communications Corporation, Aeronutronic Overseas Services Inc. v. The Air Force of the Islamic Republic of Iran, The Ground Forces of the Islamic Republic of Iran, The Ministry of National Defense of the Islamic Republic of Iran, Bank Markazi and the Government of Iran, Interlocutory Award, IUSCT Award No. ITL 6-159-FT, (5 November 1989).

jurisdiction in favor of Iranian courts.[623] Consequently, the Tribunal made its decision stating that this Article in the contract does not exclude the Tribunal from jurisdiction over claims based on the said contract.

dd) Sole jurisdiction

The fourth test to run by the Tribunal is to determine if the provision mentions the choice of forum as a "sole jurisdiction". This matter has been discussed in almost all of the test cases.

Case No. 8-293 between Stone & Webster Overseas Group as Claimant and National Petrochemical Company and Razi Chemical Company as Respondents deals with a number of contracts.

According to the first Contract ("the Construction Contract"), Stone & Webster Construction Company undertook to provide certain services in connection with the expansion of a fertilizer complex in Iran. Following dispute settlement clause was in the contract:

> "All disputes arising out of or in connection with this Agreement, any performance or non-performance thereof, or the consequences of any of the foregoing shall be settled by a competent Court of Law of Iran."[624]

The Tribunal decided that this provision fulfills the requirements of Article II, paragraph 1, of the Claims Settlement Declaration. Consequently, the Tribunal has no jurisdiction over the claims to the extent that they are based on the Construction Contract.

The next Claim in the same case was based on the FOB Contract and the Services Agreement. This contract ("the FOB Contract") was concluded between Stone and Webster Engineering Limited, another alleged subsidiary of the Claimant, and the Respondent Razi Chemical Company in 1974. Its dispute settlement provision reads as follows:

> "All disputes arising out of or in connection with this Agreement, any performance or non-performance thereof, or the consequences of any of the foregoing shall be settled

623 Ford Aerospace & Communications Corporation, Aeronutronic Overseas Services Inc. v. The Air Force of the Islamic Republic of Iran, The Ground Forces of the Islamic Republic of Iran, The Ministry of National Defense of the Islamic Republic of Iran, Bank Markazi and the Government of Iran, Interlocutory Award, IUSCT Award No. ITL 6-159-FT, (5 November 1989), Introduction.

624 Stone & Webster Overseas Group, Inc. v. National Petrochemical Company, Razi Chemical Company (formerly Shahpur Chemical Company Limited), Interlocutory Awards, IUSCT Awards No. ITL 8-293-FT, (5 November 1982), Part. II.

> by arbitration. The arbitration shall take place in Paris. The dispute will be submitted to three arbitrators, two of whom shall be appointed one by each of the parties and the third one (who shall be a national of a country other than the U.K., U.S.A., or Iran) by the former two. In the event that either of the parties, although duly requested in writing, shall fail within sixty days to designate its arbitrator, or in the event that the said arbitrator shall fail within sixty days to designate such third arbitrator, such arbitrator shall be appointed by the International Chamber of Commerce upon the application of either party. The arbitrators shall determine their own procedure and governing law in pursuance of the basic rules and regulations of the International Chamber of Commerce. The award to be rendered shall be final and conclusive and binding upon all the parties without any right to appellate or other review. Judgment upon the award rendered by the arbitrators may be entered in any Court having jurisdiction thereof and in any event the parties agree to submit jurisdiction of any court in France to enter judgment on said award…"[625]

In 1978, the parties concluded a further contract ("the Services Agreement") for engineering services to be performed in Iran. This Contract had an arbitration clause, which reads as follows:

> "Any disputes arising between the parties under or in connection with this Agreement shall be settled by the parties hereto by amicable agreement. In the event of failure to achieve such amicable agreement within a reasonable time the dispute shall be finally settled by arbitration in Paris, France, under Commerce in Paris by one or more arbitrators appointed in accordance with such rules. The arbitration proceedings and all papers sent or presented in connection therewith shall be in the applicable language hereof. The arbitration decision shall be rendered as soon as possible and shall be final, binding on both parties hereto and judgment upon the award of the arbitrators may be entered in any court having jurisdiction thereof. The arbitration shall be in lieu of any other remedy, recourse to Courts of Law being excluded other than for enforcement of arbitral awards."[626]

The Tribunal pointed out that neither of the above articles fulfills the requirements of Article II, paragraph 1, of the Claims Settlement Declaration, since they do not provide for jurisdiction of the Iranian courts.

---

625 Stone & Webster Overseas Group, Inc. v. National Petrochemical Company, Razi Chemical Company (formerly Shahpur Chemical Company Limited), Interlocutory Awards, IUSCT Awards No. ITL 8-293-FT, (5 November 1982), Part. II.

626 Stone & Webster Overseas Group, Inc. v. National Petrochemical Company, Razi Chemical Company (formerly Shahpur Chemical Company Limited), Interlocutory Awards, IUSCT Awards No. ITL 8-293-FT, (5 November 1982), Part. III.

Another test case that has dealt with this issue is case No. 9-466 between Dresser Industries as Claimant and the Government of the Islamic Republic of Iran and the National Iranian Oil Company as Respondents.

This case is based on a contract concluded in 1977 between the parties for the purchase of various compressors. The Arbitration Clause of the contract reads as follows:

> "23.1 Any disputes arising from the execution or interpretation of the provisions of the Conditions or Purchase Order which cannot be solved by mutual agreement shall upon written notice of one party to the other be settled by an arbitration board consisting of three arbitrators. Each of the parties shall appoint one arbitrator. The two arbitrators before proceeding to arbitration shall appoint a third arbitrator who shall be the president of the arbitration board.
> 23.2 If one of the parties does not appoint its arbitrator or does not advise the other party of the appointment made by it within one month of the institution of the proceeding, the other party shall have the right to apply to the President of the Supreme Court of Iran for such appointment."[627]

After considering these provisions, the Tribunal concluded that even though Iranian law provides for a degree of control by the Iranian courts over the arbitral process, such limited control does not deprive the arbitrators of their jurisdiction. Consequently, this limited jurisdiction conferred by Iranian Law on the courts with regard to arbitration could not be considered as sole jurisdiction of the Iranian Courts required by Article II, paragraph 1, of the Claims Settlement Declaration. For these reasons, the Tribunal held that the abovementioned articles do not fall within the scope of the forum clause exclusion contained in Article II, paragraph 1, of the Claims Settlement Declaration.[628]

A more detailed discussion over this matter could be read in Case No. 1-6 that we already mentioned its first contract (TAVANIR) under the second test (specifically providing). Now we are going to discuss the second contract (the AEOI Contract), which was concluded between Gibbs & Hill Iran and Respondent AEOI in 1977, regarding the design and review of a nuclear plant.

The relevant provisions in this contract are Articles 12 and 13, which provide as follows:

---

627 Dresser Industries, Inc. v. The Government of the Islamic Republic of Iran; The National Iranian Oil Company, Interlocutory Award, IUSCT Award No. ITL 9-146-FT, (5 November 1982).

628 Dresser Industries, Inc. v. The Government of the Islamic Republic of Iran; The National Iranian Oil Company, Interlocutory Award, IUSCT Award No. ITL 9-146-FT, (5 November 1982).

> "Article 12- Laws and Regulations
> The Contractor in the fulfillment of its obligations shall comply with all relevant laws, regulations and other official provisions in Iran and other countries in which the Contractor performs services for AEOI.
> This Agreement shall be governed by and construed in accordance with the applicable laws of Iran.
> Article 13- Settlement of Disputes
> Any disputes, disagreements or questions which might arise between the parties in connection with interpretation of any provision of this Agreement or the compliance or non-compliance therewith, which cannot amicably be settled by the parties shall be settled by arbitration laws of Iran."[629]

On the one hand, Claimant contended that Article 13 does not fulfill the requirements of Article II, paragraph 1, of Claims Settlement Declaration, since it provides for arbitration and not for jurisdiction of the Iranian courts.

On the other hand, Respondents contended that the reference to the arbitration laws of Iran is equivalent to the jurisdiction of the Iranian courts. Because based on the Iranian Code of Civil Procedure, the arbitral process, the arbitral award and the enforceability of it are under control of the Iranian courts. Respondents added that based on Iranian law, an arbitration clause considered as a submission of the dispute to the Iranian judicial system of which the arbitral process forms a part.[630]

Claimant, however, argued that arbitration is not equivalent to court proceedings under the laws of Iran any more than under most other domestic laws. Furthermore, Iranian law does not provide for an appeal to the courts on the merits of an arbitration award and Article 13 of the contract does not preclude arbitration from being held in a country other than Iran.[631]

---

629 Gibbs & Hill, Inc. v. Iran Power Generation and Transmission Company ("TAVANIR") of the Ministry of Energy of the Government of Iran, Atomic Energy Organization of Iran ("AEOI") of the Ministry of Energy of the Government of Iran, Ministry of Energy of the Government of Iran, Iranians' Bank, Bank Tejarat East Taleghani, The International Bank of Iran and Japan, Interlocutory Award, IUSCT Award No. ITL 1-6-FT, (5 November 1982), Part. III.

630 Gibbs & Hill, Inc. v. Iran Power Generation and Transmission Company ("TAVANIR") of the Ministry of Energy of the Government of Iran, Atomic Energy Organization of Iran ("AEOI") of the Ministry of Energy of the Government of Iran, Ministry of Energy of the Government of Iran, Iranians' Bank, Bank Tejarat East Taleghani, The International Bank of Iran and Japan, Interlocutory Award, IUSCT Award No. ITL 1-6-FT, (5 November 1982), Part. III.

631 Gibbs & Hill, Inc. v. Iran Power Generation and Transmission Company ("TAVANIR") of the Ministry of Energy of the Government of Iran, Atomic Energy Organization

We see that there is an extreme difference between the parties' approach on this issue. But toward which view is the Tribunal leaning?

The Tribunal considered arbitration as an alternative to litigation in courts and stated, recourse to arbitration as an alternative to litigation would not be necessarily equal to sole jurisdiction of any court.

The Tribunal explained that in certain circumstances Iranian law provides for a certain control by Iranian courts over the arbitral process, including the appointment of arbitrators in cases where the parties fail to designate their arbitrator, the issuance of a writ of execution for enforcement of the award, and jurisdiction to nullify an award on specific grounds (Articles 635, 662 and 665 of the Iranian Code of Civil Procedure). However, such control similar to those in most law systems does not undermine arbitration, nor ignores its character, which provides a final settlement outside of courtrooms. In particular, Iranian courts have to decline jurisdiction over claims covered by an arbitration clause, the arbitrators are not bound to observe the rules of court procedure (Article 657 of the Iranian Code of Civil Procedure), and according to the Iranian Procedural Law (Article 665 of the Iranian Code of Civil Procedure) the arbitral award can be declared null and void by the courts only on specific grounds.[632]

Based on reasons mentioned above, the Tribunal decided that the provision provides for a limited jurisdiction and does not fulfill the requirements pointed out by Article II, paragraph 1, of the Claims Settlement Declaration; therefore, the provision does not exclude the Tribunal from jurisdiction over claims based on the said contract.

ee) The competent Iranian courts

This is the final test in order to determine the exclusion of the Tribunal's jurisdiction, with which was dealt only in one of the nine test cases. We have already

of Iran ("AEOI") of the Ministry of Energy of the Government of Iran, Ministry of Energy of the Government of Iran, Iranians' Bank, Bank Tejarat East Taleghani, The International Bank of Iran and Japan, Interlocutory Award, IUSCT Award No. ITL 1-6-FT, (5 November 1982), Part. III.

632 Gibbs & Hill, Inc. v. Iran Power Generation and Transmission Company ("TAVANIR") of the Ministry of Energy of the Government of Iran, Atomic Energy Organization of Iran ("AEOI") of the Ministry of Energy of the Government of Iran, Ministry of Energy of the Government of Iran, Iranians' Bank, Bank Tejarat East Taleghani, The International Bank of Iran and Japan, Interlocutory Award, IUSCT Award No. ITL 1-6-FT, (5 November 1982), Part. III, para. 3.

reported case No. 4-121. The claim was based on a Contract ("the Rice Contract") and its disputes settlement clause provides as follows:

> "Any dispute arising from the performance of this contract not settled amicably, shall be settled by reference to the Iranian legal authorities."

The different ways of interpretation of "the Iranian legal authorities" led to arguments. Based on the Respondent's position this phrase is equivalent to "the competent Iranian Courts," while the Claimant saw it as an extremely broad expression, which could be describing any Iranian Government official or body and not necessarily the competent Iranian courts.

The Tribunal, however, did not express the same view. The Tribunal explained:

> "…it can be assumed that the contracting parties when referring disputes to be settled by 'legal authorities' intended this expression to cover such bodies or authorities that exist within the legal system for the purpose of resolving commercial disputes. Therefore, the scope of the expression 'legal authorities' in the present context cannot be so wide as to cover governmental or other official bodies or agencies not dealing with disputes settlement. Nor would it be reasonable to read into Article 14 a reference to settlement through arbitration; such an interpretation would not be compatible with the word 'authorities' which indicates a body enjoying the status emanating from the State. In view of this, the Tribunal considers that 'legal authorities' must be understood to have the same meaning as 'courts', a term that itself includes administrative as well as judicial tribunals."[633]

IV) The substantive applicable law of the Tribunal

There are in general two areas in which the determination of an applicable law comes to mind. One is the law that should govern the proceedings and the other is the substantive law, which is to be applied in different issues in a case. The latter issue is governed by the UNCITRAL rules as provided by Article III of the Claims Settlement Declaration:

> "Members of the Tribunal shall be appointed and the Tribunal shall conduct its business in accordance with the arbitration rules of the United Nations Commission on International Trade Law (UNCITRAL) except to the extent modified by the Parties or by the Tribunal to ensure that this Agreement can be carried out. The UNCITRAL rules for appointing members of three-member tribunals shall apply *mutates mutandis* to the appointment of the Tribunal."

---

633 George W. Drucker, Jr. v. Foreign Transaction Co., Insurance Company of Iran, National Grain, Sugar and Tea Organization, Interlocutory Award, IUSCT Award No. ITL 4-121-FT, (5 November 1982), Part. II.

However, the principal matter that we aim to discuss in this study is the applicable substantive law. In this regard, we should refer to Article V of the Claims Settlement Declaration.

Article V of the Claims Settlement Declaration stipulates a way to determine the applicable law, which is quite different with what we normally see in other arbitration rules. This article provides:

> "The Tribunal shall decide all cases on the basis of respect for law, applying such choice of law rules and principles of commercial and international law as the Tribunal determines to be applicable, taking into account relevant usages of the trade, contract provisions and changes circumstances."

This range of freedom definitely has some special grounds. In this case it could be easily understood that the unique situation and the strained political relationship between Iran and the United States at the time of the Algiers negotiations kept the negotiators away from being able to reach an agreement on a detailed choice of law rule. It was very hard for the two parties to agree on any system of law to govern the claims.[634]

The freedom that this article has bestowed upon the Tribunal in determining the choice of law is extraordinary. Even the Tribunal itself admitted the broadness of Article V and found that an interpretation would be necessary sometimes. Chamber one stated:

> "It is difficult to conceive of a choice of law provision that would give the Tribunal greater freedom in determining case by case the law relevant to the issues before it. Such freedom is consistent with, and perhaps almost essential to, the scope of the tasks confronting the Tribunal, which include not only claims of a commercial nature, such as involved in the present case, but also claims involving alleged expropriations or other public acts, claims between the two Governments, certain claims between banking institutions, and issues of interpretation and implementation of the Algiers Declarations. Thus the Tribunal may find it necessary to interpret and apply treaties, customary international law, general principles of law and national laws, 'taking into account relevant usages of the trade, contract provisions and changed circumstances', as Article V directs."[635]

634 Crook, John R., "Applicable Law in International Arbitration: The Iran-U.S. Claims Tribunal Experience", The American Journal of International Law, Vol. 83, (1989), p. 281.

635 CMI International, Inc. v. Ministry of Roads and Transportation and the Islamic Republic of Iran, IUSCT Award, Award No. 99-245-2, (27 December 1983), Part B., para. 1.

It is worthy to mention that the system employed by the Claims Settlement Declaration aims to cover both commercial arbitration as well as investment arbitration. To that effect the applicable law regime is designated to deal, on the one hand, with international disputes arising from breach of customary international law or breach of conventional obligation, such as breach of the Treaty of Amity, and, on the other hand, with disputes of a rather private law nature arising from breaches of contracts between a national of Iran or the United States and the other Government or an entity or enterprise of that Government.[636]

1) The origin of Article V of the Claims Settlement Declaration

It seems that Article V of the Claims Settlement Declaration is derived from Article 15 of the 1899 Hague Convention for the Pacific Settlement of the International Disputes, which reads as follows:

> "International arbitration has for its object the settlement of differences between State by judges of their own choice, and on the basis of respect for law."[637]

The similarities between this article and Article V of the Claims Settlement Declaration are apparent. This position could be related to the more influential approach in the nineteenth century, which was aimed to keep the arbitrators from deciding the cases based on non-legal grounds.[638]

2) The tribunal's fundamental obligation

In order to analyze Article V of the Claims Settlement declaration, it is appropriate to divide it into two main parts. The first part lays down a basis for the Tribunal in order to determine the applicable law. Thus, the first obligation according to the first part of Article V is that the Tribunal is obliged to decide "on the basis of respect for law." This is a very broad stipulation that led to many arguments on various subjects. For example, based on this very sentence of Article V, the United States argued that the Tribunal is not authorized to decide *ex aequo et bono* or act as an *amiable compositeur.*

---

636 Mohebi, Mohsen, "The International Law Character of the Iran-United States Claims Tribunal", Kluwer Law International, (1998), p. 112.

637 Article 15 of the Convention for the Pacific Settlement of International Disputes (Hague I) (29 July 1899).

638 Crook, John R., "Applicable Law in International Arbitration: The Iran-U.S. Claims Tribunal Experience", The American Journal of International Law, Vol. 83, (1989), p. 281.

Generally, tribunals have to adjudicate the disputes on the basis of law, unless they are expressly allowed by the parties to decide the case *ex aequo et bono.* Therefore, it's been said:

> "… arbitration on the basis of law is the principle, but *amiable compositeur* is the exception."[639]

This rule has been recognized by most of the arbitration rules, such as Article 38(2) of the Statute of International Court of Justice[640] and Article 42(3) of the ICSID Convention.

The Tribunal, however, referred to the language of Art. 33(2) UNCITRAL rules, which allows the Tribunal to decide *ex aequo et bono* only in case of parties' agreement, which has not been happened in the Tribunal's history.[641] It is worth to add that UNCITRAL rules were modified, to be applied by the Tribunal.[642] By the modifications, the first paragraph of the original UNCITRAL Rule No. 33 was replaced by Article V of the Claims Settlement Declaration and the second paragraph was modified as follows:

> "The Tribunal shall decide *ex aequo et bono* only if the arbitrating parties have expressly and in writing authorized it to do so." And, the third paragraph of Article 3 was completely deleted."[643]

---

639 Mohebi, Mohsen, "The International Law Character of the Iran-United States Claims Tribunal", Kluwer Law International, (1998), p. 116.

640 Article 38(2) of the Statute of International Court of Justice:
"This Provision shall not prejudice the power of the court to decide a case ex aequo et bono, if the parties agree thereto."

641 Lagergren, Gunnar, "Iran-United States Claims Tribunal", The Dalhousie Law Journal, Vol. 13, (1990), p. 511.

642 Caron, David D.; Caplan, Lee M., "The UNCITRAL Arbitration Rules, A Commentary", Oxford University Press, Second Edition, (2013), p. 128–129.

643 Article 33 of the 1976 UNCITRAL Rules provides:
The arbitral tribunal shall apply the law designated by the parties as applicable to the substance of the dispute. Failing such designation by the parties, the arbitral tribunal shall apply the law determined by the conflict of laws rules which it considers applicable.
The arbitral tribunal shall decide as amiable compositeur or ex aequo et bono only if the parties have expressly authorized the arbitral tribunal to do so and of the law applicable to the arbitral procedure permits such arbitration.
In all cases, the arbitral tribunal shall decide in accordance with the terms of the contract and shall take into account the usages of the trade applicable to the transaction.

It has been criticized that permitting the Tribunal to make decisions *ex aequo et bono* would be inconsistent with Article V of the Claims Settlement Declaration, which requires all the decisions to be on the basis of "respect for law."[644]

In a broader view, there are two types of arbitration; one is based on law and legal principles, under which, the Tribunal has to apply rules of law, notwithstanding their source. It is important that based on this type of arbitration the tribunal could not base its decision on equity. In other words, the Tribunal is not permitted to decide *ex aequo et bono*.

As mentioned before, in almost all arbitration rules the important issue is to decide the case based on law. Arbitration on the basis of law is the principle, while an *ex aequo et bono* decision could be rendered only where an expressed agreement has been made by both parties and, therefore, is an exception. But in the case of this Tribunal it has been argued that the main purpose of Article V of the Claims Settlement Declaration was to prevent the Tribunal to decide *ex aequo et bono*.

But it should be noted, even though the mutual agreement of parties for authorizing a decision *ex aequo et bono* has not happened, the Tribunal as Legergren reports, "...has often referred with regard to procedural matters to its 'inherent power', and with regard to substantive matters to 'equity', 'fairness' and 'justice'."[645]

The Tribunal's decisions confirm this report. For example, in Benjamin R. Isaiah, which is a case concerning dishonor of a check, the Tribunal referred to equity and stated:

> "In any event, the Tribunal believes that it would be inequitable for such a bank to be able to escape liability to the beneficial owner of the funds represented by such a dishonored check and retain the funds to which the bank has no claim."[646]

The Tribunal even mentioned the other possible arguments but eventually stated:

> "While it might be argued that Iranian law must be applied to this claim on the ground that the act giving rise to the unjust enrichment took place at least partly in Iran, and that the enrichment occurred there, it might also be argued that this is unnecessarily

644 Stewart. David P.; Sherman, Laura B., "Developments at the Iran-United States Claims Tribunal: 1981-1983", in The Iran-United States Claims Tribunal edited by Richard B. Lillich, University Press of Virginia, (1984), p. 16.

645 Lagergren, Gunnar, "Iran-United States Claims Tribunal", The Dalhousie Law Journal, Vol. 13, (1990), p. 511.

646 Benjamin R. Isaiah v. Bank Mellat (as successor to international Bank of Iran), IUSCT Award, Award No. 35-219-2, (30 March 1983), Part. IV

> restrictive in view of the fact that the dishonored check was drawn on a New York bank and much of the underlying transaction occurred outside Iran."[647]

Thus, based on this considerations and the freedom given to the Tribunal by Article V of the Claims Settlement Declaration, the Tribunal is free to apply general principles of law in a case such as this, while there is no reason to believe the result would be different if only Iranian law were applied.[648]

But this is not exactly the same as deciding *ex aequo et bono*. What the Tribunal did in abovementioned case was more of a reference to general principles of law. It does not make any difference if those principles are based on equity or not but the point is they still remain in the circle of "respect for law" as said by Article V of the Claims Settlement Declaration.

It should also be noted that there is also another technical problem for the Tribunal to decide *ex aequo et bono*. The Constitution of the Islamic Republic of Iran has a principle concerning resolving the disputes related to public and state property, which reads as follows:

> "Article 139
> The settlement of claims relating to public and State property or the referral thereof to arbitration is in every case dependent on the approval of the Council of Ministers, and the Assembly must be informed of these matters. In cases where one party to the dispute is a foreigner, as well as in important cases that are purely domestic, the approval of the Assembly must also be obtained. Law will specify the important cases intended here."

Majlis, the parliament of Iran, approved only the Act of 14 January 1981, under which the disputes between Iran and the United States are to be settled by arbitration and as deciding *ex aequo et bono* is an exception to the rule, there is no approval on decision *ex aequo et bono* from parliament of Iran and in general it was constitutionally impossible for Iran to accept this matter.[649]

An example would be the *Starrett Housing Corporation v. the Government of Iran*.

In this case, the Tribunal was to determine whether there had been a taking of the Claimant's property by the Government of the Islamic Republic of Iran, and if positive, how it is going to be compensated. In order to do that, the Tribunal

647 Benjamin R. Isaiah v. Bank Mellat (as successor to international Bank of Iran), IUSCT Award, Award No. 35-219-2, (30 March 1983), Part. IV

648 Benjamin R. Isaiah v. Bank Mellat (as successor to international Bank of Iran), IUSCT Award, Award No. 35-219-2, (30 March 1983), Part. IV

649 Mohebi, Mohsen, "The International Law Character of the Iran-United States Claims Tribunal", Kluwer Law International, (1998), p. 119.

had to examine the valuation of the taken property rights. Starrett Housing Corporation is the parent company of a group of subsidiary corporations engaged in construction and development projects.[650] The involvement of this corporation in Iran began in 1974 pursuant to the series of agreements regarding a program for the construction of a residential community on then-unimproved land adjacent to northwest of Tehran. Based on certain requirements in Iran for foreign nationals to secure permits to own land, Starrett assigned the Basic Project Agreement to an Iranian subsidiary, Shah Goli Apartment Company ("Shah Goli"). The Tribunal found that the valuation of the property rights requires advice from an expert, because of all the complicated accounting matters. In spite of a number of problems facing the experts reaching their valuation specially failures of the parties to submit documents within the time limit prescribed by the expert, the Tribunal received a very detailed expert opinion. The next step for the Tribunal was to determine two points; firstly, the appropriate standard of compensation based on the applicable law and secondly, the weight that should be given to the expert opinions.[651] Based on the Treaty of Amity between Iran and the United States, the Claimants are entitled to receive a "just" compensation, which represents the full equivalent of the property taken at the time of the taking. The Tribunal stated that the Starrett Construction was a wholly owned subsidiary of N&B Unternehmensberatung, a German company, which was in turn wholly owned by Starrett Housing International, Inc. The wording of the Treaty of Amity governs not only "property" of nationals but also "interests in property," and this phrase, based on the Tribunal's view, is broad enough to encompass indirect ownership of property rights held through a subsidiary that is not a U.S national.[652]

Regarding the second issue, we should note that the use of experts is foreseen by Article 27, paragraph 1, of the Tribunal Rules, which authorize the Tribunal to "appoint one or more expert to report it, in writing, on specific issues to be determined by the Tribunal." In determining the weight of the Report, the Tribunal

650 Starrett Housing Corporation, Starrett Systems, Inc., Starrett Housing International, Inc. v. The Government of the Islamic Republic of Iran, Bank Markazi Iran, Bank Omran, Bank Mellat, IUSCT Award No. 314-24-1, (14 August 1987), para. 1.

651 Starrett Housing Corporation, Starrett Systems, Inc., Starrett Housing International, Inc. v. The Government of the Islamic Republic of Iran, Bank Markazi Iran, Bank Omran, Bank Mellat, IUSCT Award No. 314-24-1, (14 August 1987), para. 260.

652 Starrett Housing Corporation, Starrett Systems, Inc., Starrett Housing International, Inc. v. The Government of the Islamic Republic of Iran, Bank Markazi Iran, Bank Omran, Bank Mellat, IUSCT Award No. 314-24-1, (14 August 1987), para. 261.

considered a number of factors. The Tribunal found that the impartiality is evident in the Report.[653] In addition, the Report was meticulous and comprehensive which led to the substantial value of the whole work. The Tribunal found out that the written evidence in the record confirms that the expert fully carries out the procedures that he described.[654] The Tribunal also had the opportunity to question the Expert and gather some clarifications regarding the Report at the Hearing held pursuant to Article 27, paragraph 4, of the Tribunal Rules.[655] To a large extent, the Tribunal accepted the Report prepared by the Expert. At some points it seemed necessary for the Tribunal to determine the matters by considering what a hypothetical reasonable businessman would have done. Therefore, the Tribunal felt obliged to exercise its discretion to "determine equitably" the amount involved.[656] On this matter, the Tribunal also cited some of the cases concerning this principle.[657] All of these cases show the Tribunal's approach regarding a decision *ex aequo et bono*. But we should admit that the Tribunal does not decide on this basis regularly and freely and for such decision the Tribunal is required to demonstrate that this is nothing but what the parties had desired. In fact, maybe we could say that the Tribunal does not decide *ex aequo et bono*, as it actually is, but sometimes the Tribunal goes through a method quite similar to it, which should be taken into consideration.

---

653 Starrett Housing Corporation, Starrett Systems, Inc., Starrett Housing International, Inc. v. The Government of the Islamic Republic of Iran, Bank Markazi Iran, Bank Omran, Bank Mellat, IUSCT Award No. 314-24-1, (14 August 1987), para. 265.

654 Starrett Housing Corporation, Starrett Systems, Inc., Starrett Housing International, Inc. v. The Government of the Islamic Republic of Iran, Bank Markazi Iran, Bank Omran, Bank Mellat, IUSCT Award No. 314-24-1, (14 August 1987), para. 267.

655 Starrett Housing Corporation, Starrett Systems, Inc., Starrett Housing International, Inc. v. The Government of the Islamic Republic of Iran, Bank Markazi Iran, Bank Omran, Bank Mellat, IUSCT Award No. 314-24-1, (14 August 1987), para. 270.

656 Starrett Housing Corporation, Starrett Systems, Inc., Starrett Housing International, Inc. v. The Government of the Islamic Republic of Iran, Bank Markazi Iran, Bank Omran, Bank Mellat, IUSCT Award No. 314-24-1, (14 August 1987), para. 339.

657 Economy Froms Corp. v. Islamic Republic of Iran, Award No. 55-165-1, p. 21, (14 June 1983); Sola Tiles, Inc. v. The Government of the Islamic Republic of Iran, award No. 298-317-1, para. 65, (22 April 1987); William J. Levitt v. Islamic Republic of Iran, Award No. 297-209-1, para. 48, (22 April 1987); Thomas Earl Payne v. The Government of the Islamic Republic of Iran, Award No. 245-335-2, para. 37, (8 August 1986).

3) Determination of the substantive applicable law

According to Article V, there are a range of different possibilities for determining the applicable law, as the Article states: "…applying such choice of law rules and principles of commercial and international law as the Tribunal determines to be applicable..."

It becomes clear that the Tribunal should apply choice of law rules and also commercial and international law. Besides the Tribunal has to pay attention to some other rules, as the Article mentions: "…taking into account relevant usages of the trade, contract provisions and changed circumstances."

It is also important to consider two different languages that have been used for each section. The first part sounds more peremptory, while the second part is less imperative.

Now we are going to explain each of the possibilities step by step. As we mentioned, all of the sources are not to be referred at the same time necessarily and they display different levels of importance.

a) Contract

Even though there is no reference to the parties' choice of law in the Claims Settlement Declaration, in contrast to almost all other arbitration rules, the Tribunal's caseload shows that in a great number of disputes, the terms of parties' contracts have played a primary role.

Normally, the first rule on applicable law in almost every set of arbitration rules is the parties' agreement. All other methods of determining the applicable law, therefore, come after mentioning the primary rule of party autonomy.

Surprisingly, this is not the case in Claims Settlement Declaration. Article V does not mention parties' choice of law at all. The rule begins with the freedom of the Tribunal to determine the choice of law. However, this is natural that one of the very first methods exercised by tribunals is to find the applicable law by searching for the parties' intentions, which sometimes can be determined by the terms of the contract. Article V of the Claims Settlement Declaration also states that the tribunal should take "relevant usages of the trade, contract provisions and changed circumstances" into account.

It should be noted that solely a reference to a contract does not prevent the Tribunal from reaching to law systems because basically every contract lives in a legal system and cannot be separated from it.[658] The consequence of this fact

---

658 Crook, John R., "Applicable Law in International Arbitration: The Iran-U.S. Claims

would be that the Tribunal would need a reference in order to interpret or implement the terms of the agreement. In such situations, the Tribunal rather refers to general principles than to a national law.

aa) Payment

Regarding payment issues, the Tribunal found it unnecessary to refer to a certain national law. Almost all the law systems have considered the requirement of payment for goods, thus the Tribunal could easily refer to the practice of the parties without being bound to refer to a national law system. There were a considerable number of cases concerning goods or services that were shipped or provided without the payment being received. Some of these cases were simple though huge sums were involved. As an example, the Claimant R. J. Reynolds Tobacco Company requested an amount of U.S. $36,294,667.66 plus interest from the Iranian Tobacco Company ("ITC").

Another types of claims in the workload of the Tribunal, another effect of Islamic revolution in Iran, were those concerning disrupted performance. In such cases, the Tribunal mainly looked into the terms of contracts. To demonstrate the Tribunal's method of procedure on these sorts of cases, an example would be helpful.

In *Richard D. Harza v. Iran* case, the claims were based on a contractual relationship between Harza International Engineering Company as the consulting engineer on two groups of dam projects in the Khuzestan province, two projects on the Karun River and four projects on the Marun River, and KWPA (Khuzestan Water and Power Authority). In this case, two projects on the Karun River were constructed but none of the projects on the Marun River proceeded beyond the planning phase.[659] The Tribunal, in this case, had to cope with complex facts in order to find out whether the claim for payment is legitimate or if Iran's counterclaim has stronger base. Iran believed that the preconstruction program was poor and unsatisfactory. As the counterclaim was comprised of complicated engineering matters, the Tribunal employed engineering experts. Iran has counterclaimed that the remedial works completed concerning damages

Tribunal Experience", The American Journal of International Law, Vol. 83, (1989), p. 288.

659 Richard D. Harza, John A. Scoville, George E. Pabich v. the Islamic Republic of Iran Water and Power Authority, SEA-MAN-PACK Company, LTD., S.G. Services Company, IUSCT Award, Award No. 232-97-2, (2 May 1986), para. 5.

allegedly stemming from the discovery during construction of a clay seam in the right abutment.[660]

The Tribunal was trying to achieve the standards of good engineering, based on which it could determine the acceptability of the preconstruction operations and explorations. To that end, the Tribunal raised the question whether Harza International carried out the preliminary investigations, as required by the contract, by using its best technical knowledge and according to the best accepted standards.

bb) Performance

Once again, the Tribunal referred to a term in the contract concluded between the parties and aimed to find out whether it has been duly performed.

To explain the case more clearly, a geological accident (anomaly) was discovered in the right abutment of the dam, which was an area roughly 130 meters long with a maximum width of 20 meters of clay, water and air solution features. A detailed exploration even showed that this anomaly contained one large mainly clay-filled cavity that its existence allegedly should have been hidden during the preconstruction phase.

The expert's findings however stated as follows:

> "Mr. Kerisel found no evidence that Harza International had concealed the existence of the geological accident. He also found out that all of the remedial works recommended by Harza International and implemented by KWPA were necessary and in accordance with industry practices and standards then prevailing."[661]
>
> "Mr. Kerisel, however, expressed the view that the investigation program was not as extensive as it should have been."[662]

Eventually, the Tribunal concludes that issues discussed by Mr. Kerisel and Claimants are of engineering matter, for which the evidence provides no clear technical or professional standards, therefore there is a legit expectation that the experts would differ thereon. Consequently, the Tribunal asserted that Harza

---

660 Richard D. Harza, John A. Scoville, George E. Pabich v. the Islamic Republic of Iran Water and Power Authority, SEA-MAN-PACK Company, LTD., S.G. Services Company, IUSCT Award, Award No. 232-97-2, (2 May 1986), para. 88.

661 Richard D. Harza, John A. Scoville, George E. Pabich v. the Islamic Republic of Iran Water and Power Authority, SEA-MAN-PACK Company, LTD., S.G. Services Company, IUSCT Award, Award No. 232-97-2, (2 May 1986), para. 92.

662 Richard D. Harza, John A. Scoville, George E. Pabich v. the Islamic Republic of Iran Water and Power Authority, SEA-MAN-PACK Company, LTD., S.G. Services Company, IUSCT Award, Award No. 232-97-2, (2 May 1986), para. 94.

International fulfilled its contractual standard of performance with regard to the pre-construction exploration program.[663]

As mentioned before, there are plenty of complex cases concerning the issue of performance. Another example is *Minnesota Mining and Manufacturing Company v. Iran*. The Claimant in this case was Minnesota Mining and Manufacturing Company that raised a claim against Government and State of Iran, Ministry of Housing and Urban Development, Ministry of Health, Darou Pakhsh, Ministry of Defense, and Iranian Navy. Moreover, Abol-Hassan Diba & Co. LTD. ("Diba"), Arme Joint Stock Private Company ("Arme") and Polyacryl Iran Corporation ("Polyacryl") were three entities, which were not specifically named as Respondents in the Statement of Claim but whose interest was stated in the Statement of Defense.[664] This case is comprised of three claims of the Claimant or its subsidiary 3M Middle East for goods and services. The largest one is concerning a contract between 3M Middle East and Arme for application of a special deck coating substance to a portion of the Tehran Sports Stadium.[665] Arme and the Ministry of Housing, on the other hand, asserted counterclaims alleging 3M Middle East's defective performance. In response, the Claimant contended that the work was completed, all defects were remedied and AFFA as the project engineer approved the project as required under the Contract.[666]

The Claimant refers to the Contract in respect of performance and states:

> "...the Contract states the certification of completion by AFFA is conclusive on Arme, "any statement by Purchaser [Arme] to the contract notwithstanding." The Claimant argues that AFFA's approval of the repair work and recommendation that Arme and the Ministry of Housing pay the full amounts due precludes Arme or the Ministry of

---

663 Richard D. Harza, John A. Scoville, George E. Pabich v. the Islamic Republic of Iran Water and Power Authority, SEA-MAN-PACK Company, LTD., S.G. Services Company, IUSCT Award, Award No. 232-97-2, (2 May 1986), para. 99.

664 Minnesota Mining and Manufacturing Company v. The Islamic Republic of Iran, Ministry of Housing and Urban Development, Arme Construction Company, Abol-Hassan DiBa & Co. Ltd., and Polyacryl Iran Corporation, IUSCT Award, Award No. 343-423-3, (18 December 1987), para. 1.

665 Minnesota Mining and Manufacturing Company v. The Islamic Republic of Iran, Ministry of Housing and Urban Development, Arme Construction Company, Abol-Hassan Diba & Co. Ltd., and Polyacryl Iran Corporation, IUSCT Award, Award No. 343-423-3, (18 December 1987), para. 22.

666 Minnesota Mining and Manufacturing Company v. The Islamic Republic of Iran, Ministry of Housing and Urban Development, Arme Construction Company, Abol-Hassan Diba & Co. Ltd., and Polyacryl Iran Corporation, IUSCT Award, Award No. 343-423-3, (18 December 1987), para. 57.

> Housing from now alleging that defects were in existence which detract from 3M Middle East's rights under the Contract. The Ministry of Housing has confirmed that AFFA's "determination [was] dispositive and binding on the parties under the contract."[667]

Regarding the counterclaim, the Tribunal found the letter issued by the AFFA not the kind of "Acceptance Certificate" required by the Contract. However, the Tribunal stated:

> "Nevertheless, as a statement by AFFA it is clearly dispositive as to the issue of whether the work to be performed under the Contract was ultimately completed to AFFA's satisfaction. Accordingly the Tribunal finds that the full service price specified in the Contract is payable."[668]

cc) Existence of contract

Apart from payment and performance issues, in some cases the Tribunal was confronted with the basic question of whether a contract existed between the parties at the first place. It is interesting that in some cases the Tribunal did not find a contract.[669]

As an example, in *Sea-Land Service v. Iran*, the Claimant is a corporation registered under the laws of Delaware engaged in the international transportation by water. The Respondent is the Ports and Shipping Organization ("PSO"), which is the governmental instrumentality in Iran. The Sea-Land claimed that is was deprived by PSO of the right to continued use of a containerized cargo facility constructed and operated by it as the port of Bandar Abbas in Iran, which led to losses.[670] One of the theories, on which this claim is based, is the breach of the contract (the "Facility Agreement" dated 28 November 1976) between PSO and ILB (an Iranian transportation company) for the provision of a parcel of

---

667 Minnesota Mining and Manufacturing Company v. The Islamic Republic of Iran, Ministry of Housing and Urban Development, Arme Construction Company, Abol-Hassan Diba & Co. Ltd., and Polyacryl Iran Corporation, IUSCT Award, Award No. 343-423-3, (18 December 1987), para. 58.

668 Minnesota Mining and Manufacturing Company v. The Islamic Republic of Iran, Ministry of Housing and Urban Development, Arme Construction Company, Abol-Hassan Diba & Co. Ltd., and Polyacryl Iran Corporation, IUSCT Award, Award No. 343-423-3, (18 December 1987), para. 76.

669 Crook, John R., "Applicable Law in International Arbitration: The Iran-U.S. Claims Tribunal Experience", The American Journal of International Law, Vol. 83, (1989), p. 290.

670 Sea-Land Service, Inc. v. The Government of the Islamic Republic of Iran, Ports and Shipping Organization, IUSCT Award, Award No. 135-33-1, (20 June 1984), part. I.

land at Bandar Abbas for the construction of a container terminal and the right to operate it. Sea-Land contended that it is legit to enforce the contract since ILB was acting as its agent with PSO's knowledge, or, as an alternative, that it was a third-party beneficiary of the contract by the common intention of both parties. Sea-Land further argued that ILB by entering into a second contract with Sea-Land ("Preferential Use Agreement") on 18 April 1977 was actually acting as an agent for PSO.[671]

The Tribunal believed that the Facility Agreement should be governed by Iranian law, since both parties were Iranian and the subject matter was a parcel of land in Bandar Abbas port. To that end, the Tribunal had to consider the relevant provisions of the Iranian Civil Code.

So explain Articles 196, 231 and 662 the agency theory in Iranian Law:

> "Article 196
> Anyone who enters into a transaction does so for himself, unless when entering into the transaction he expressly provides for the contrary, or unless the contrary is subsequently proved. When entering into a transaction for himself, however, anyone can make provision for the benefit of a third party."
> "Article 231
> Transactions and contracts are only binding on the two parties concerned or their legal substitutes except in cases coming under Article 196."
> "Article 662
> An attorney ship must not be given except for a matter, which the principal himself is entitled to engage in; and the attorney must be a person who has the capacity to execute that matter."
> Based on above-mentioned articles, the named party to the contract, which is ILB in this case, must be considered as a principle not as an agent, unless there is evidence to the contrary."

Article 196 also would govern for the Tribunal to determine if there is a third-party beneficiary. This article requires an express mention of such a beneficiary in the contract. Such an expression could not be found in the contract. To this end, the Tribunal stated was there any kind of relationship between Sea-Land and PSO, be it direct or indirect, it would have been reflected in the original Facility Agreement. However, it is indicated that ILB was the one who obtained the license over the land by virtue of the Facility Agreement. Five months later and at the same time parties entered into the Agency Agreement, Sea-Land

671 Sea-Land Service, Inc. v. The Government of the Islamic Republic of Iran, Ports and Shipping Organization, IUSCT Award, Award No. 135-33-1, (20 June 1984), part. I.

secured the right to use the parcel of land, as it was entering into the Preferential Use Agreement with ILB.

The Preferential Use Agreement acknowledged that, the license was produced by ILB Container for the uses and purposes of Sea-Land Service, Inc. and it substantially amounted to a sub-license by ILB to Sea-Land of the right to develop, improve and use the land provided that Sea-Land Service at all times complies with the provisions of such license, and/or such license is not revoked, limited or restricted in any way by the Iranian Port and Shipping Organization or any other Iranian governmental authority. The Tribunal believed that it did not, however, transfer any interest in the land itself, which was to remain in ILB.[672]

The Tribunal entered into a detailed discussion concerning the existence of the contract, considering the Iranian Law and eventually denied the claims insofar as they were based on contracts.[673]

Sometimes it is challenging for the tribunals even to determine whether a contract exists or not. As we saw in the aforesaid case, after an extended examination, the Tribunal found no contract, while the Dissenting Opinion manifests a whole different analysis. Holtzmann believed that Sea-Land Service actually entered into contracts with PSO. Even though the majority thought that there was a broad understanding between Sea-Land and PSO, they held that this never "crystallized" into an enforceable contract and was not a sufficiently "clear contractual formula." He also believed that the majority denied the claim according to the failure of the underlying agreements to meet their own formalistic concept regarding the duty of businessmen to create a binding contractual relationship. Through this argument, the majority ignored documents and testimony that clearly defined the contracts and it misapplied the applicable law on formation of contracts.[674]

---

672 Sea-Land Service, Inc. v. The Government of the Islamic Republic of Iran, Ports and Shipping Organization, IUSCT Award, Award No. 135-33-1, (20 June 1984), part. II(A)(i)(b), para. 9.

673 Sea-Land Service, Inc. v. The Government of the Islamic Republic of Iran, Ports and Shipping Organization, IUSCT Award, Award No. 135-33-1, (20 June 1984), part. II(A)(i)(b), para. 10.

674 Opinion of Howard M. Holtzmann Dissenting as to Award on the Claims and Concurring as to Dismissal of Counterclaims, Sea-Land Service, Inc. v. The Government of the Islamic Republic of Iran, Ports and Shipping Organization, IUSCT Award, Award No. 135-33-1, (20 June 1984), part. I.

In addition, he believed that taking into account the subsequent actions of the parties, it would not be easily imaginable that the parties had not been relying upon the existence of enforceable contracts.

It is very complicated in this case to determine whether there was an actual contract or not, but applying the Iranian law, one should also take into account the other provisions of Civil Code concerning the contracts. As Holtzmann pointed out that based on the Civil Code of Iran, In the absence of a written contract, any words used in verbal negotiation, any sign or gesture indicating the consent of the parties and acts such as handing over or taking delivery of any goods or property will be sufficient.

> "Article 193
> A transaction may be created by an act which indicates intention and consent, such as taking delivery or handing over unless in circumstances excepted by law."

This article supports Holtzmann's opinion and also the fact that the Tribunal has to put a lot into examining the contracts as a part of applicable law and at the same time a document that should be construed under the applicable law.

dd) Interpretation

In a similar vein, it is essential for the Tribunal to make the correct interpretation of a contract. Each tiny detail could play an enormous role in the course of interpretation and various interpretations could cause very different outcomes. The role of those tiny details turns bolder in huge cases. An example would demonstrate this fact clearly.

On 18 January 1982, the Claimant, International Systems & Controls Corporation ("ISC"), filed a Claim claiming between U.S. $102 million and U.S. $125 million approximately, plus interest and costs against the Industrial Development and Renovation Organization ("IDRO"), Iran Wood and Paper Industries ("IWPI"), Mazandaran Wood and Paper Industries ("MWPI") and the Islamic Republic of Iran. The claim was basically based on four contracts entered into between Stadler Hurter Limited ("SHL"), incorporated in Canada, its subsidiary Stadler Hurter Worldwide ("SHW"), incorporated in Bermuda, and IDRO during 1973 and 1974. The projects were about industrial plants and related equipment for the utilization of forest products in Gilan and Mazandaran.[675]

---

675 International Systems & Controls Corporation v. Industrial Development and Renovation Organization of Iran, Iran Wood and Paper Industries, Mazandaran Wood and Paper Industries and The Islamic Republic of Iran, IUSCT Award, Award No. 256-439-2, (26 September 1986), paras. 1-4.

Based on the Statement of Claim, ISC asserted five claims claiming that the Respondents breached the Gilan and Mazandaran contracts by failing to pay progress billings as they became due, by refusing, despite SHL's readiness, to authorize resumption of work following the cessation of force majeure conditions in April 1979 and by failing in the light of the circumstances to terminate the contracts in accordance with their termination clauses.

The important turning point in this case is the SHL's Proposal in Bankruptcy, dated 31 October 1979. This Proposal was drafted based on Canadian law and appointed Paul Bertrand as Trustee. It was amended on 9 January 1980. The related paragraphs of the Proposal are paragraphs 8 and 9, which provide as follows:

> "The Trustee shall be vested with all the powers of a trustee under Section 14 of the Bankruptcy Act, and in particular shall have the right to incur obligations, borrow money and give security on any of the free property of the Company by mortgage, hypothec, charge, assignment, pledge or otherwise, such obligations and money borrowed to be discharged and repaid with interest out of the property of the Company in priority to the claim of the creditors."
> "That to secure and guarantee the execution of the foregoing Proposal, the Company does hereby pledge, cede, transfer, assign and convey to the Trustee in trust for and on behalf of the creditors all its property wherever situated and all such property that may be acquired by it or devolve upon it during the term of this Proposal together with such powers in or over or in respect of property as might have been exercised by it for its own benefit, the whole in the manner and to the extent as if the undersigned was a bankrupt and the Trustee herein were vested with its assets as same is defined under Section 47 of the Bankruptcy Act."[676]

These paragraphs have led to uncertainty about whether the Tribunal has jurisdiction over the claims or not. As the Respondents contended, one of the fundamental requirements of Article VII(2) of the Claims Settlement Declaration[677]

---

676 International Systems & Controls Corporation v. Industrial Development and Renovation Organization of Iran, Iran Wood and Paper Industries, Mazandaran Wood and Paper Industries and The Islamic Republic of Iran, IUSCT Award, Award No. 256-439-2, (26 September 1986), para. 56.

677 Article VII(2) of the Claims Settlement Declaration provides:
"'Claims of nationals' of Iran or the United States, as the case may be, means claims owned continuously, from the date on which the claims arose to the date on which this Agreement enters into force, by nationals of that State, including claims that are owned indirectly by such nationals through ownership of capital stock or other proprietary interests in juridical persons, provided that the ownership interests of such nationals, collectively, were sufficient at the time the claim arose to control the corporation or

is that the beneficial interest in the claim must be owned by the Claimant but the Claimant argued that this proposal did not deprive SHL or ISC of beneficial ownership of the claim.[678]

Under Canadian law, after the creditors of SHL are paid off, all remaining assets, if any, should be returned to SHL. On this ground, the Claimant contended that SHL, therefore, retains a continuing ownership interest in such assets. It also submitted an expert opinion.[679]

In determining whether the Tribunal has jurisdiction, the Tribunal noted that it does not aim to interpret the domestic laws of Quebec and Canada, but since both parties have agreed and admitted that the proposal is actually a contract between the debtor and his creditors and it gives the debtor as much or as little freedom over his actions as is agreed upon in such contract.[680] Therefore, the Tribunal has to determine what the parties have agreed to and consider whether the debtor divested itself under the contract of the ownership of the claims brought before the Tribunal and put an end to its ownership, even though it could revert subsequently.[681]

The Tribunal found the wording of paragraph 9 of the proposal unambiguous and stated:

> "This wording is unambiguous in that SHL thereby conveyed "all its property" to the Trustee, who then held the same "in trust for and on behalf of the creditors." The Trustee was given the legal ownership of all the company's property wherever situated, the

---

other entity, and provided, further, that the corporation or other entity is not itself entitled to bring a claim under the terms of this Agreement."

678 International Systems & Controls Corporation v. Industrial Development and Renovation Organization of Iran, Iran Wood and Paper Industries, Mazandaran Wood and Paper Industries and The Islamic Republic of Iran, IUSCT Award, Award No. 256-439-2, (26 September 1986), paras. 61,62.

679 International Systems & Controls Corporation v. Industrial Development and Renovation Organization of Iran, Iran Wood and Paper Industries, Mazandaran Wood and Paper Industries and The Islamic Republic of Iran, IUSCT Award, Award No. 256-439-2, (26 September 1986), para. 64.

680 International Systems & Controls Corporation v. Industrial Development and Renovation Organization of Iran, Iran Wood and Paper Industries, Mazandaran Wood and Paper Industries and The Islamic Republic of Iran, IUSCT Award, Award No. 256-439-2, (26 September 1986), para. 77.

681 International Systems & Controls Corporation v. Industrial Development and Renovation Organization of Iran, Iran Wood and Paper Industries, Mazandaran Wood and Paper Industries and The Islamic Republic of Iran, IUSCT Award, Award No. 256-439-2, (26 September 1986), para. 78.

> beneficial owners of the said property expressly being the creditors of the company. At that time, therefore, SHL no longer retained any legal or beneficial interest in its claims since all those claims were assigned as part of the property of SHL. The fact that at some time in the future SHL would be entitled to the remaining assets, if any, is irrelevant. By contract, though the Proposal, SHL transferred the ownership of its claims to the Trustee."[682]

The Tribunal also believed that a potential future interest could not be considered as an existing interest and, therefore, could not meet the requirement of continuous ownership based on the Claims Settlement Declaration.[683] Consequently, the Tribunal concluded that the continuous ownership of the claims until 19 January 1981 has not been proved. In reaching this decision, the Tribunal has also contemplated various decisions of the previous cases.[684] The cases presented thus far supports the fact that contracts are of very important role in the Tribunal's decision-making process. It is interesting to note that a small deviation in Interpretation of a single paragraph of a contract could cause a significant discrepancy between the potential outcomes. In the mentioned case, the Tribunal concludes that it has no jurisdiction over the claim so it stops examining further. Therefore, at times interpretation may largely influence on the outcome of a dispute. It is relevant for the drafters to take these kinds of decisions of the tribunals into account to avoid the potential problems and raise the chance of a smooth trial.

ee) Termination

It is also worth noting that in terms of determining the applicable law and its correlation with contracts, the issue of contract termination gains importance. As indicated before, sometimes the Tribunal avoids explaining the process of

---

682 International Systems & Controls Corporation v. Industrial Development and Renovation Organization of Iran, Iran Wood and Paper Industries, Mazandaran Wood and Paper Industries and The Islamic Republic of Iran, IUSCT Award, Award No. 256-439-2, (26 September 1986), para. 80.

683 International Systems & Controls Corporation v. Industrial Development and Renovation Organization of Iran, Iran Wood and Paper Industries, Mazandaran Wood and Paper Industries and The Islamic Republic of Iran, IUSCT Award, Award No. 256-439-2, (26 September 1986), para. 82.

684 Phelps Dodge Corp. et al. v. The Islamic Republic of Iran, IUSCT Award, Award No. 217-99-2, (19 March 1986); Foremost Tehran Inc. et al. V. The Government of the Islamic Republic of Iran, IUSCT Award, Award No. 220-37-1, (11 April 1986); International Technical Products v. The Islamic Republic of Iran, IUSCT Award, Award No. 196-302-3, (28 October 1985).

determining the applicable law and simply proceed in accordance with the contract provisions regarding termination.[685] As described by Crook, the Tribunal put up a degree of resistance to find termination on account of breach, despite of the existence of factual evidence in its support. Thus, a number of claims concerning lost profits have been denied.[686]

This can be illustrated by several well-known cases such as cases originated from the nationalization of the oil industry of Iran and the contracts between NIOC and the members of the Consortium, namely, the Sale and Purchase Agreement ("SPA"). In this regard, 11 claims were filed with the Tribunal (Cases No. 72 to 81 and 150) all based on alleged breaches, repudiation and expropriation of the SPA on the part of NIOC and Iran.[687] The review of these cases alone needs a lot of delicate discussions that is apart from the aim of this study. The aim here is only to draw the attention to the conclusions made by the Tribunal. Even though the Claimants pointed out various arguments in order to prove the breach of the SPA agreement, the Tribunal took another approach. Thereby the Tribunal tried to manifest that the Agreement has been terminated. It actually examines the possibility of termination in different periods of time. Regarding the functionality of the Agreement between 1975 and 1978, the Tribunal was close to enunciate the termination, where it stated:

> "In view of these fact, the Tribunal finds difficult to accept, without qualification, the proposition that the SPA was operative at the end of 1978. Actually, a number of its most important provisions were replaced by ad hoc agreements, or even de facto ones, often reluctantly and only implicitly accepted by one party or the other. At the same time, the conduct of the parties does not allow the Tribunal to conclude that the Agreement was frustrated or otherwise terminated at this time. A series of its provisions continues to be performed according their terms, and the ad hoc arrangements substituted for those provisions can only be construed as informal amendments to this Agreement."[688]

---

685 Crook, John R., "Applicable Law in International Arbitration: The Iran-U.S. Claims Tribunal Experience", The American Journal of International Law, Vol. 83, (1989), p. 291.

686 Crook, John R., "Applicable Law in International Arbitration: The Iran-U.S. Claims Tribunal Experience", The American Journal of International Law, Vol. 83, (1989), p. 291.

687 Mobil Oil Iran Inc. and Mobil Sales and Supply Corporation v. Government of the Islamic Republic of Iran and National Iranian Oil Company, IUSCT Partial Award, Award No. 311-74-3, (14 July 1987), para. 24.

688 Mobil Oil Iran Inc. and Mobil Sales and Supply Corporation v. Government of the Islamic Republic of Iran and National Iranian Oil Company, IUSCT Partial Award, Award No. 311-74-3, (14 July 1987), para. 111.

One step further would be found in the Tribunal's statement concerning the time between December 1978 and March 1979:

> "It is not disputed that the Claimants withdrew OSCO's expatriate personnel in late December and early January 1979 because of the civil disturbances associated with the revolutionary movements. It is also common ground that oil production as well as oil exports were severely disturbed during this time and for some time were completely terminated."[689]

The Tribunal actually based this decision on the intent of both parties demonstrated in their further negotiations in regard to compensate the claimant's rights under the SPA Agreement.

Similar method was taken by the Tribunal in *Whittaker Corp v. Iran* case to conclude that the parties have terminated their contracts. The Tribunal stated:

> "The telex of 27 February 1979 offered MIO the choice either to take delivery on the condition that Bank Markazi transfer funds to Bank of America and extend the letter of credit, or to cancel the Contract if delivery was no longer desired ....The Tribunal finds that MIO accepted the offer to cancel the Contract by its telex of 26 May 1979 informing the Claimant that the goods were no longer needed. The last sentence of this telex stating "[w]e will contact you for our future needs" indicated that MIO considered the Contract cancelled."[690]

Both the claim and the counterclaim were dismissed by the Tribunal based on the communication took place between the parties.

a) National law

National law, or in investment arbitrations, the law of the contracting state is a source of law, which is gradually losing its importance. As it was explained in ICSID part, it seems that nowadays the tribunals prefer to refer to international law rather than national law. In other words, it has been a steady decrease in the number of reference to the national law in international arbitration. This is because of the fact that the tribunals are more eager to decide cases based on parties' common understandings. There are plenty of examples demonstrating same national rules, which are now also known as international law. Therefore,

---

689 Mobil Oil Iran Inc. and Mobil Sales and Supply Corporation v. Government of the Islamic Republic of Iran and National Iranian Oil Company, IUSCT Partial Award, Award No. 311-74-3, (14 July 1987), para. 112.

690 Whittaker Corporation (Bermite Division) v. The Islamic Republic of Iran, The Iranian National Defense Industries Organization, IUSCT Award, Award No. 301-286-1, (27 April 1987), para. 25.

there is a path toward the primacy of international law over national law. But before expanding this conclusion to all tribunals, one should also mention that the process could seem different based on the nature of the tribunal, in which the case is being decided. For example, for territorialized tribunals, the doctrine of party autonomy is respected by the national arbitration law of the tribunal's judicial seat, while the same thing would be respected by first sentence of Article 42(1) of the ICSID Convention or Article V of the Iran-United States Claims Settlement Declaration.[691] As previously mentioned regarding the ICSID rules, in many instances national law was selected over international law. In ICSID cases, we have experienced that many factors may justify the primary of national law's application, such as party agreement of its application or the fact of State sovereignty and control over foreign investors. Applicable law clauses are usually even not negotiable in cases of ordinary contracts with State parties. By contrast, in extraordinary contracts where States are involved and costly investments and risks are at stake, the law of the sovereign would not be accepted as whole and to all aspects of the contract.[692] Nevertheless, it seems, there is no fix rule to give one of these a primacy but depending all conditions under which a case is decided, the result may vary. A review of the awards of Iran-United States Claims Tribunal reveals that it leans toward not referring to national law as much and instead tries to make reference to non-national principles. Crook's clear explanation reads as follows:

> "The Tribunal has typically avoided reference to national systems of law as the source of controlling rules, instead, it has regularly applied non-national principles derived from the parties' contracts, general principles of law or public international law."[693]

The Tribunal has even disregarded the parties' agreed choice of law in order to avoid referring to the national law. This is not to be seen only in one award of the Tribunal but through many examples. Apparently, the Tribunal does not have a consistent precedent on this matter. To demonstrate this issue, CMI International case has been referred to several times. The Tribunal provides:

---

691 Kjos, Hege Elisabeth, "Investor-State Arbitration-The Interplay Between National and International Law", Oxford University Press, (2013), p. 158.

692 Westberg, John A., "The Applicable Law Issue in International Business Transactions with Government Parties-Rulings of the Iran-United States Claims Tribunal", ICSID Review-Foreign Investment Law Journal, Vol. 2, p. 475.

693 Crook, John R., "Applicable Law in International Arbitration: The Iran-U.S. Claims Tribunal Experience", The American Journal of International Law, Vol. 83, (1989), p. 279.

"With respect to the assessment of damages, the Tribunal considers its main task to be determining what are the losses suffered by the Claimant and to award compensation therefor. Our search is for justice and equity, even in cases where arguably relevant national laws might be designed to further other and doubtless quite legitimate goals. In present case, conclusions from those adopted by the Tribunal (except with respect to accounting for profits on resales, which will be discussed below), the Tribunal prefers to analyze damage-related questions in accordance with general principles of law, rather than by reference to the code as incorporated in the statutory law of Idaho."[694] The other example of disregarding the applicable law could be seen in awards of interest. In the case raised by Iran in Parguin Private Join Stock Company and the United States the Tribunal reaffirmed its previous standing and stated:

"Arguments based on the American law prohibiting interest in awards against the United States such as those of the Respondent in this Case were raised by the United States in Atomic Energy Organization of Iran and United States of America, Award No. 24-B7-1 (15 August 1986). There the Tribunal stated:

It has been the practice of the Tribunal to award interest, when claimed and due, to compensate for damages suffered due to delay in payment, whether the contract in question provides for it or not and notwithstanding general choice of law provisions.

In conformity with this precedent, the Tribunal holds that the law of the Contract is not applicable to the payment of interest and that there is no circumstance in this case justifying a departure from its practice."[695]

Similarly, in *Gould Marketing Inc.* case concerning the termination of the contract as a result of frustration, although the contract provided that the American law (California) is applicable, the Tribunal applied general principles of law in deciding the consequences.[696] The Tribunal has even mentioned that a rule of domestic law is not binding on an international Tribunal.[697]

694 CMI International, Inc. v. Ministry of Roads and Transportation and the Islamic Republic of Iran, IUSCT Award, Award No. 99-245-2, (27 December 1983), Part. B, Para. 1.

695 Parguin Private Joint Stock Company, a Claim of less than US$ 250,000, presented by The Islamic Republic of Iran v. The United States of America, IUSCT Award, Award No. 275-12783-3, (15 December 1986), para. 32.

696 Gould Marketing, Inc. as successor to Hoffman Export Corporation v. Ministry of Defence of The Islamic Republic of Iran, IUSCT Award, Award No. 136-49/50-2, (22 June 1984), Part. B(1).

697 Alan Craig v. Ministry of Energy of Iran; Water Engineering service (MAHAB); Khuzestan Water and Power Authority (KWPA); Khadamat Iran-Zemin Engineering Consultant Services Company (KIZ), IUSCT Award, Award No. 71-346-3, (2 September 1983), Part. IV(1)(b).

In conclusion, one could say that in modern arbitration we are distancing from the need to refer to the conflicts of law rules. The task of the arbitrators is far greater than using a simple method to find one system of law of a single State to refer to. This is also why the drafters have modified the UNCITRAL rules on this matter and discarded the obligation to refer to conflicts of law rules. Commenting on the UNCITRAL modifications, Bellet stated:

> "It would have been extremely awkward for these arbitrators to choose between Iranian law and American law. With tensions running high, it was worth avoiding such choices, particularly in cases where the parties alleged political or economic coercion in the execution of the certain contracts. In this way claimants and their opponents were practically always in agreement not to invoke any rigid conflicts of law rules."[698]

These examples all show the reluctance of the Tribunal to apply the national law and how it leans toward applying general principles of law, public international law and the rules derived from the contract provisions.

b) General principles of law

In deciding the cases, one of the most referred sources by the Tribunal is the general principles of law. As the awards of the Tribunal are widely accessible, the Tribunal's jurisprudence has provided the scholars and the practitioners in field of international arbitration with a substantial body of general principles for the first time.[699]

Using general principles is the main way of the Tribunal applying rules, which are common to both Iranian and American parties. In other words, it counts as another means for the Tribunal to achieve justice and equity, bearing in mind that these rules could assist the Tribunal dealing with contracts between parties from different legal systems. The necessity of employing general principles of law by the Tribunal also results from insufficient attention given by the parties to choice of law clauses while drafting their contracts.[700] Even when the Tribunal is applying the rules agreed on by the parties, general principles of law is a great complement which could be selected by either parties or arbitrators.

---

698 Bellet, Pierre, "Foreword", Law & Policy in International Business, Vo. 16, (1984), p. 673.

699 Hanessian, Grant, "'General Principles of Law' in the Iran-U.S. Claims Tribunal", Columbia Journal of Transnational Law, Vol. 27, (1988–1989), p. 311.

700 For detailed discussion on choice la law clauses in international contracts see: Lowe, James R., "Choice of Law Clauses in International Contracts: A Practical Approach", Harvard International Law Journal, Vol. 12, (1971).

At first glance, "general principles of law" reminds us of Article 38(1)(c) of the Statute of the International Court of Justice, which introduced "general principles of civilized nations" as a source of public international law. As the definition of general principles and its general examples are already explained in ICSID part of this study, in this part focus will be on the jurisprudence of the Tribunal on this issue.

The sources of the Tribunal's Jurisprudence on general principles are of great importance. The most utilized source by the Tribunal is the comparative analysis of legal systems. The Tribunal has obviously referred to principles derived from the laws of Iran and the United States. Moreover, as an almost great part of Iranian law has its roots in French law, the Tribunal has also referred to that in a number of cases. Not only the said legal systems have been referred to, but the Tribunal beside taking into account the major legal systems has referred to special national laws where there was a relevant connection. For example, referring to the German law, where one of the parties to the contract was German.

As an example, the DIC of Delaware case illustrates the matter clearly. In this case, the Tribunal, while examining the existence of a contract, refers to Iranian law and conclude a widely accepted general principle. The Tribunal explained that based on Iranian civil code, where the concerned value is over 500 Rials and the contract is not in writing, oral or written testimony would not provide required proof. In this case, the Tribunal asserted that it seems acceptance of part performance can be proof of the contract, where Claimants rely on contemporaneous documents which demonstrated the understanding reached with TRC. The tribunal added:

> "Moreover, although the governing law of the contract itself must be taken to be that of Iran, each forum applies its own procedural and evidentiary rules to the disputes before it, and it is arguable that the type of evidence admissible to establish a contract is a procedural or evidentiary matter. Under Article V of the Claims Settlement Declaration the Tribunal must look to "principles of commercial and international law" for guidance. It is widely accepted by municipal systems of law that one can prove the existence of an enforceable oral contract through evidence demonstrating part performance. See, e.g., II K. Zweigert & H. Kotz, An Introduction to Comparative Law: The Institutions of Private Law 40-41, 48-50 (1977). Such a principle must be taken to constitute a general principle of law. Moreover, it could be argued that, by its conduct, TRC is estopped to assert the nonexistence of the contract." [701]

---

701 DIC of Delaware, Inc., Underhill of Delaware, Inc. v. Tehran Redevelopment Corporation, The Government of The Islamic Republic of Iran, IUSCT Award, Award No. 176-255-3, (26 April 1985), Part. B(1).

In the same case, discussing damages, the Tribunal also referred to French law and concluded that the termination of the contract does not preclude a damage remedy.[702]

Harnischfeger Corp. case is an example of the reference to the German law. In this case, Harnischfeger Corporation ("Harnco") filed a Statement of Claim containing seven separate claims again the Ministry of Roads and Transportation ("MORT" or "MRT"). The Industrial Development and Renovation Organization of Iran ("IDRO") and Machine Sazi Arak ("MSA"). The claims were revolving around purchase and delivery of crane machinery, as well as to alleged breaches of a Technical Service Agreement. The claim was actually an indirect claim on behalf of Harnco's West German subsidiary, Harnischfeger GmbH. In this case again, the Tribunal tries to examine whether an agreement has been reached and whether essential elements that their lack could lead the Tribunal to consider the contract null from the beginning exist. The Tribunal found out that the communications between parties indicates that by the time the order were given by MSA, Mort had not given its consent to the contemplated MORT/Harnco Agreement yet.[703] The Tribunal dismissed claims six and seven because of the lacking evidence showing MORT ever entered into such agreement, which is basically the essential condition to implement such agreement. The Tribunal believed it is a generally accepted principle that a party relieve from liability where an essential error has been made with respect to the conditions, upon which a party has initially entered into agreement. It eventually states:

> "Even though in the present case the reasons indicated above would not necessarily render the agreement null from the beginning, the Tribunal holds that it would be contrary to good faith (cf. § 242 on "Treu und Glauben" in the German Civil Code) to allow Harnco to rely on that agreement against MSA afterwards when it is known that the essential conditions on which the conclusion of that agreement was based never materialized. Accordingly, Claims Six and Seven are dismissed also against MSA."[704] 82-93 (1977).

702 DIC of Delaware, Inc., Underhill of Delaware, Inc. v. Tehran Redevelopment Corporation, The Government of The Islamic Republic of Iran, IUSCT Award, Award No. 176-255-3, (26 April 1985), Part. B(2).

703 Harnischfeger Corporation v. Ministry of Roads and Transportations, Development and Renovation Organization of Iran, Machine Sazi Pars, IUSCT Award, Award No. 175-180-3, (26 April 1985), Part. B(ii).

704 Harnischfeger Corporation v. Ministry of Roads and Transportations, Development and Renovation Organization of Iran, Machine Sazi Pars, IUSCT Award, Award No. 175-180-3, (26 April 1985), Part. B(ii).

As it is apparent, the Tribunal relied on general principles of law, which according to the explanations, have been derived from the German law or in other words, the source expressed by the Tribunal is the German legal system.

As the case clearly demonstrated, the Tribunal does not limit itself to the Iranian and American legal system but it goes further and gets help from any element which connects it to a source of general principles of law in order to be able to decide based on equity. It can be easily comprehended from the decisions of the Tribunal that the Tribunal has mostly used its great freedom in determining the applicable in a very cautious way. As explained, the Tribunal has avoided the national laws even at the times that they have been chosen as applicable law. One could say that the result would be the same applying the national laws, but for such Tribunal providing a magnificent deposit of legal precedent on international commercial arbitration, it was a vital step.

Despite the Tribunal's effort to base its decision on general principles in order to produce the most appropriate and just results, contradicting opinions are to be found as well. In the abovementioned case, Judge Mosk had a whole different opinion, which is illustrated in his dissenting opinion. He stated:

> "I respectfully dissent from the Final Award because I believe that the Claimant is entitled to damages for the breaches of contracts by MSA. In my opinion the Tribunal has, by utilizing theories that are not based on appropriate legal principles and were not raised by the parties, erroneously concluded that MSA is not liable for its breaches of contracts."[705]

Regarding choice of law issue, however, he did not oppose the fact of utilizing general principles but how the Tribunal reached whatever legal principles. He also did recognize that it is not always necessary to discuss the source of law utilized because it is not always possible or at least it would be so difficult when there are not only one but multiple jurisdictions involved. He particularly stated that it could be very complicated for the Tribunal to obtain a consensus on the appropriate source of legal principles.

In addition to the comparative municipal law, which the Tribunal employed to conclude general principles of law, *Lex Mercatoria* was another source. It should be pointed out that general principles of law and *Lex Mercatoria* are two

---

705 Harnischfeger Corporation v. Ministry of Roads and Transportations, Development and Renovation Organization of Iran, Machine Sazi Pars, Dissenting Opinion of Richard M. Mosk from Final IUSCT Award, Award No. 175-180-3, (26 April 1985).

different terms with some similarities. In other words, *Lex Mercatoria* could be considered as a set of rules founded on international trade usages, standard clauses and contracts, uniform laws, general principles of law and international instruments.[706] Therefore, *Lex Mercatoria* has a wider character than general principles of law; however, there is still a wide divergence between the existing definitions of *Lex Mercatoria*.[707]

Apart from the meaning and sources of the *Lex Mercatoria*,[708] the focus in this study is on the usage of this source by the Tribunal. As an example, the Tribunal refers toArticles 4 and 6 of the "Uniform Rules for the Collection of Commercial Paper" adopted by the International Chamber of Commerce in *Granite State Machine Co.* case.[709]

Similar to reference to national general principles of law, the Tribunal has also referred to the general principles, which stemmed from public international law.

Two of the most referred general principles by the Tribunal are unjust enrichment and force majeure that can be illustrated by following awards.

---

706 Lew, Julian D M.; Mistelis, Loukas A.; Kröll, Stefan, "Comparative International Commercial Arbitration", Kluwer Law International, The Hague/London/New York, (2003), p. 454.

707 On *Lex Mercatoria* see: Berger, Klaus Peter, "The Creeping Codification of the Lex Mercatoria", Kluwer Law International, The Hague/London/Boston, (1999).

708 Dalhuisen has provided the following hierarchy of *lex mercatoria* (Dalhuisen, Jan H., "Legal Orders and Their Manifestation: The Operation of the International Commercial and Financial Legal Order and Its Lex Mercatoria", Berkeley Journal of International Law, Vol. 24, (2006), p. 180.):

fundamental legal principle;

mandatory custom;

mandatory uniform treaty law (to the extent applicable under its own scope definition and in its own territory);

the contract (or party autonomy in matters at the free disposition of the parties);

directory custom;

directory uniform treaty law (to the extent applicable under its own scope definition and in its own territory);

general principles largely derived from comparative law, uniform treaty law (even where not directly applicable or not sufficiently ratified), ICC Rules and the like; and

residually, domestic laws found through conflict of laws rules.

709 Granite State Machine Co., Inc. v. The Islamic Republic of Iran, Bank Markazi Iran, Bank Saderat Iran, IUSCT Award, Award No. 18-30-3, (15 December 1982), Part. IV.

aa) Unjust enrichment

Unjust enrichment is an old principle first enunciated by Romans, which is referred in both common law and civil law countries.[710] This principle refers to a situation, where a party is unjustifiably enriched without any legal ground. No matter the enrichment occurs through performance by another or in any other manner at the expense of another party, the enriched party is obliged to render restitution to the disadvantaged party.[711]

The Tribunal referred to unjust enrichment and quantum meruit, especially in cases, where the other means of recovery were unavailable and on the other hand, for the Tribunal not to award compensation would be inequitable.[712] When a valid contract already exists, the Tribunal would refer to that instead of referring to the general principles. However, the Tribunal can always complement its justifications with such principles. It should be maintained that the theory of unjust enrichment is to be distinguished from another reasons, based on which a Claimant could have the right to restitution, such as an agreement, a civil wrong, a crime and continuing ownership.[713] Therefore, we should differentiate the claims which are based on a contractual promise from the claims that could be fitted in unjust enrichment category.

In many cases, the Tribunal was involved with the claims of unjust enrichment. The Tribunal takes also the jurisdictional issues into account while dealing with unjust enrichment claims. It is important for such claims, not to be based on a contract. The Jurisprudence of the Tribunal demonstrates that Tribunal would refuse the unjust enrichment claim, when it is an alternative to a contract-based claim and the Tribunal has already refused the principle claim based on lack of jurisdiction.[714]

The Tribunal in *Ultrasystems Inc.* case cited unjust enrichment for the first time. The Claimant, Ultrasystems Inc., was a corporation organized under the laws of the State of California of the United States of America. Isiran (Information Systems Iran) and Ultrasystems entered into a contract whereby Ultrasystems

---

710 Gallo, Paolo, "Unjust Enrichment: A Comparative Analysis", The American Journal of Comparative Law, Vol. 40, (1992), p. 431.

711 Trans-lex.org, Principle No. IX.1-Basic rule. (Accessed on 30 November 2016).

712 Brunetti, Maurizio, "The Lex Mercatoria in Practice: The Experience of the Iran-United States Claims Tribunal", Arbitration International, Vol. 18, (2002), p. 368.

713 Burrows, Andrew, "A Restatement of the English Law of Unjust Enrichment", Oxford University Press, (2012), p. 25.

714 Dames and Moore v. The Islamic Republic of Iran, IUSCT Award, Award No. 97-54-3, (20 December 1983).

provided certain services, in 1976. As the contract terminated after its performance in 1977, they entered into a second contract. Based on this contract Ultrasystems should act as a consultant and provide certain personnel. Isiran in return had to make the payments based on a prescribed schedule. One of the claims was based on an unpaid invoice submitted by Ultrasystems charging Isiran for consulting and other work related to the contract. Evidence showed that the work was performed at Isiran's request but Isiran denied receiving the invoice, even though it accepted that the work was performed.

In this case, the Tribunal without any detailed explanations concluded:

> "We think it is likely that the invoice was sent and received, but remained unpaid as part of the general break in contractual relations. Nevertheless, the request for work, and the performance provided pursuant to that request, rendered Isiran liable at least in quantum meruit, without regard to the Contract."[715]

Regarding this award of the Tribunal, some points should be noted. Firstly, the Tribunal discussed the issue under the jurisdiction section and it eventually held that without regard to the contract, the claim could be justified under quantum meruit. Secondly, in this Award the Tribunal has not exactly cited the "unjust enrichment" theory yet, but it used "quantum meruit." Quantum meruit means "as much as he deserved" or "reasonable remuneration or value."[716] Quantum meruit was mostly used in common law and with reference to the theory of quasi-contract or implied contract. Implied contract is defined as an obligation imposed by law that is a result of the conduct of the parties or a special relationship between them or because one of them would otherwise be unjustly enriched. This is a definition provided by *Black's Law Dictionary*. This theory, however, has been rejected in favor of unjust enrichment.[717]

The first award, in which the Tribunal actually cited "unjust enrichment" for the first time was *Benjamin R. Isaiah v. Bank Mellat*.[718] The claim was in regard to a dishonored check drawn by the International Bank of Iran on the Chase Manhattan Bank. The Respondent brought some defenses on the merits.

---

715 Ultrasystems Inc. v. The Islamic Republic of Iran and Information Systems Iran, IUSCT Award, award No. 89-84-3, (7 December 1983).

716 Birks, Peter, "Unjust Enrichment", Oxford University Press, Second Edition, (2005), p. 287.

717 Burrows, Andrew, "A Restatement of the English Law of Unjust Enrichment", Oxford University Press, (2012), p. 25.

718 Benjamin R. Isaiah v. Bank Mellat (as successor to International Bank of Iran), IUSCT Award, Award No. 35-219-2, (30 March 1983).

In addition, it contended that the Tribunal has no jurisdiction over this case because the said check was not payable to the Claimant but to another person, whose nationality was not established. The Respondent asserted that actually the check was supposed to be paid to Farkash, an affiliate of the Claimant, who was an Israeli. On the contrary, the Claimant believed that Isaiah was the "owner and holder" of the check dated 2 January 1979 and the fact that it was not paid due to the expropriation of the assets and properties of the Bank by the Government of Iran.[719] The payment, therefore, refused by Chase Manhattan Bank in New York on 10 January was due to insufficient funds.

Discussing jurisdictional matters, the Tribunal stated as Isaiah's claim is based on a dishonored check, whose payee is an Israeli national, therefore, Isaiah could not pursue the claim directly, notwithstanding his beneficial interest, because at the time the claim arose, he was not the holder of the check. This is in accordance with Article VII(2) of the Claims Settlement Declaration, which provides that a claim must be owned continuously by nationals of the same State from the date it arose until the date the Declaration entered into force. Since the endorsement of the check from Farkash to Isaiah was subsequent to the date the claim arose, the requirements of said Article could not be satisfied. Hence, the Tribunal stated that it does not have jurisdiction over a claim by Isaiah as an alleged holder in due course on the check itself.[720]

Isaiah, however, asserted that he has a claim against the bank for unjust enrichment. He explains that the bank was given funds, of which he was the beneficial owner and that the bank has retained the amount for its own benefit and to his detriment.[721] He added that the check was not an ordinary check but a bank check, which was purchased by the Karayesh Co., the drawer of which was the predecessor of Bank Mellat. He concluded that in this situation and the dishonor of the bank check, which is an extremely rare occurrence, the claim may be made by the beneficial owner of the funds (Isaiah) against the bank for unjust enrichment.[722]

---

719 Benjamin R. Isaiah v. Bank Mellat (as successor to International Bank of Iran), IUSCT Award, Award No. 35-219-2, (30 March 1983), Part. II.

720 Benjamin R. Isaiah v. Bank Mellat (as successor to International Bank of Iran), IUSCT Award, Award No. 35-219-2, (30 March 1983), Part. III.

721 Benjamin R. Isaiah v. Bank Mellat (as successor to International Bank of Iran), IUSCT Award, Award No. 35-219-2, (30 March 1983), Part. III.

722 Benjamin R. Isaiah v. Bank Mellat (as successor to International Bank of Iran), IUSCT Award, Award No. 35-219-2, (30 March 1983), Part. III.

The Tribunal mentioned it is a novel claim but it is only acceptable if it can be proved. The Tribunal eventually held that it has jurisdiction over the claim for unjust enrichment.

The Tribunal has recourse against the Bank for the retained funds. Discussing this matter, the Tribunal resorted to restitutionary theories such as "unjust enrichment" and "enrichissement sans cause," which are to be found in the laws of many countries.

The relevant one is the Iranian law, which explains this theory in Articles 301 and 303 of the Civil Code as follows:

> Article 301:
> "Anyone who intentionally or inadvertently acquires goods to which he has no claim, is bound to deliver such goods to the actual owner."
> Article 303:
> "Anyone who receives any property without any right is responsible for the actual property and for any profits that may accrue thereto, whether or not he is aware of his having no right to the property."

Furthermore, the Tribunal referred to International Law and mentioned that unjust enrichment is also an important element of state responsibility. Since it is an extremely rare situation, where the bank checks are dishonored, the Tribunal was unaware of any precedent holding a drawer bank of dishonored check liable to the beneficial owner of the funds based on unjust enrichment. Nonetheless, the Tribunal considered it as inequitable for such a bank to retain the funds and avoid the liability.[723] Consequently, based on the principle of "unjust enrichment," the Tribunal awarded the amount of the check.

It should be noted that the concept of unjust enrichment is one most often used general principle by the Iran-US Tribunal. As in said award, the Tribunal emphasized that it was a general principle of law, every time it applied it. This is a pertinent way for the Tribunal to reach justice and equity, especially where the other rules would not necessarily end to a just result.[724]

723 Benjamin R. Isaiah v. Bank Mellat (as successor to International Bank of Iran), IUSCT Award, Award No. 35-219-2, (30 March 1983), Part. IV.

724 Wühler, Norbert, "Application of General Principles of Law", in Albert Jan van den Berg (ed.), Planning Efficient Arbitration Proceedings: The Law Applicable in International Arbitration, ICCA Congress Series, Vol. 7, Kluwer Law International, (1996), p. 559.

The Tribunal explained the conditions regarding the application of this principle in *Sea-Land Service, Inc. v. the Islamic Republic of Iran* case.[725] Sea-Land is the Claimant in this case, which is a corporation registered under the laws of Delaware in the United States and engaged in the international transportation by water of containerized cargo. Ports and Shipping Organization (PSO) was a governmental entity in Iran, which was in charge of administration and control of the Iranian port facilities. Since the background of this case has been explained before, now we are going to only focus on the issues regarding unjust enrichment and the insight of the Tribunal.

One of the arguments rendered by Sea-Land was that PSO or the Government was unjustly enriched at the expense of Sea-Land and it should be compensated accordingly. The Tribunal explained the concept thoroughly in this case. Based on the Tribunal's explanations, there should be conditions already existing for the Tribunal to recourse to this principle:

> "There are several instances of recourse to the principle of unjust enrichment before international tribunals. There must have been an enrichment of one party to the detriment of the other, and both must arise as a consequence of the same act or event. There must be no justification for the enrichment, and no contractual or other remedy available to the injured party whereby he might seek compensation from the party enriched."[726]

In most of the cases, the Tribunal has referred to unjust enrichment as a general principle to award compensation. As we mentioned before, in Isaiah case the Tribunal awarded U.S. $380,000, as the amount of the check. In Sea-Land case, the Tribunal awarded U.S. $750,000 and indicated it as an "approximation" of compensation.[727] In Morrison-Kundsen, the Tribunal awarded compensation again based on quantum meruit.[728]

---

725 Sea-Land Service, Inc. v. The Government of the Islamic Republic of Iran, Ports and Shipping Organization. IUSCT Award, Award No. 135-33-3, (20 June 1984).

726 Sea-Land Service, Inc. v. The Government of the Islamic Republic of Iran, Ports and Shipping Organization. IUSCT Award, Award No. 135-33-3, (20 June 1984), Part. II(A)(v).

727 On the measure of damages See Sea-Land Service, Inc. v. The Government of the Islamic Republic of Iran, Ports and Shipping Organization. IUSCT Award, Award No. 135-33-3, (20 June 1984) and the Separate Opinion of Judge Holtzmann.

728 Morrison-Knudsen Pacific Limited v. The Ministry of Roads and Transportation and The Islamic Republic of Iran, IUSCT Award, Award No. 143-127-3, (13 July 1983), Part. III(2). For more examples on unjust enrichment see: Schlegel Corporation on behalf of Schlegel Lining Technology GMBH v. National Iranian Copper Industries Company, IUSCT Award, Award No. 295-834-2, (27 March 1987); Futura Trading

Apart from the awards rendered based on the principle of unjust enrichment, the Tribunal has refused in many cases the claim of unjust enrichment. As mentioned before, the Tribunal has mentioned some conditions for the claim based on unjust enrichment.

One of the common examples is where the case is based on a contract, in which an Iranian forum clause was incorporated and the Tribunal accordingly had to dismiss the claim for lack of jurisdiction.[729]

Dealing with contract issues and unjust enrichment claims are not as similar as it may seem. At first glance, one could be of the opinion that in case of an existed contract there could be no chance for an unjust enrichment claim to be accepted but the Tribunal has proved the contrary.

In the Mobil case, the first claim was related to the recovery of capital advances made by the Trading Companies "by way of prepayment for crude oil to be purchased by them," according to the terms of Article 11.B of the Agreement. The recovery of these advances by way of set off, as paragraph D of the Agreement provided, was actually impossible on the ground that the Agreement was terminated and the oil purchases were interrupted. However, these facts could not result in the Claimant not being recovered. Therefore, the Tribunal stated whatever the cause of the termination and breaches of contract, the advances themselves established the right to reimbursement. Since the Tribunal found that there is no legal justification for NIOC to retain the advances, it concluded that NIOC would be unjustly enriched in case such advances were retained.[730]

Based on the Tribunal's discussion, we can conclude that the possibility to bring an unjust enrichment claim is possible even when the case is generally based on a contract. The details regarding the order of events should be always

---

Incorporated v. Khuzestan Water and Power Authority, IUSCT Award, Award No. 183-325-3, (19 August 1985); W. Jack Buckamier v. The Islamic Republic of Iran, Isiran/Army, Tehran Redevelopment Corporation, Bank Mellat, Hejrat Branch (formerly Iran-Arab Bank), IUSCT Award, Award No. 528-941-3, (6 March 1992); Oil Field of Texas, Inc. v. The government of the Islamic Republic of Iran, National Iranian Oil Company, Oil Service Company of Iran, IUSCT Interlocutory Award, Award No. ITL 10-43-FT, (7-8 December 1982).

729 For an opposite view see: Dissenting Opinion of Judge Richard Mosk, Dames & Moore v. The Islamic Republic of Iran, The Atomic Energy Organization of Iran, The National Iranian Steel Company, The Iranian Medical Center and The National Iranian Gas Company, IUSCT Award, Award No. 97-54-3, (20 December 1983).

730 Mobil Oil Iran Inc. and Mobil Sales and Supply Corporation v. Government of the Islamic Republic of Iran and National Iranian Oil Company, IUSCT Partial Award, Award No. 311-74-3, (14 July 1987), para. 54.

taken into account in such cases, as in said case one could say that there was debts existed prior to the contract.[731] Thus, the awards rendered by the Tribunal, some accepting and others dismissing the unjust enrichment claims when a contract exists should not be considered as an inconsistency in Tribunal's jurisprudence.

As mentioned above, for the principle of unjust enrichment to be accepted by the Tribunal it is important that the enrichment has been already identified at the outset since it is an essential element of the definition of unjust enrichment principle. The question here would be how the Tribunal examines whether enrichment has in fact taken place. This issue is illustrated in Flexi-Van Leasing case. The case arose out of alleged lease agreements involving marine transport equipment between the Claimant and two companies, Star Line and Iran Express Lines, Claimant's allegations were controlled by the Government of Iran. The Claimant, therefore, alleged that the control of the Government caused the companies to breach and repudiate their lease agreements. Flexi-Van thus claimed for a recovery for the value of the contract rights, which were expropriated by the Government of Iran. Alternatively, the Claimant contended that in any event, this claim is also supportable on three other grounds especially the theory of unjust enrichment. It alleged that the Government has been unjustly enriched by the retention and use of Flexi-Van's equipment. On the other hand, the Government refused that it has been enriched at all. The Government of Iran asserted that all the assets of Iran Express were destroyed by Iraqi army during the war on the port of Khorramshahr. Therefore, the Government alleged that it is not enriched by nor is it liable for the loss of equipment that could have belonged to Flexi-Van.[732]

On deciding this aspect of the case, the Tribunal first mentioned unjust enrichment as a concept accepted by different legal systems of the world, including Iran and the United States. The Tribunal also stressed, "The benefit obtained by the enriched party is an indispensable element of the remedy of unjust enrichment."[733] After discussing the importance of the theory and its characteristics, the Tribunal started to study the case to determine whether it is compatible with this principle, meaning whether the Tribunal would be able to identify every essential element of unjust enrichment theory in *Flexi-Van* case. In doing so,

731 Aldrich, George H., "The Jurisprudence of the Iran-United States Claims Tribunal", Clarendon Press. Oxford, (1996), p. 405.

732 Flexi-Van Leasing, Inc. v. The Government of the Islamic Republic of Iran, IUSCT Award, Award No. 259-36-1, (11 October 1986), Part. I(2).

733 Flexi-Van Leasing, Inc. v. The Government of the Islamic Republic of Iran, IUSCT Award, Award No. 259-36-1, (11 October 1986), Part. II(3)(e).

the Tribunal expressed that even though enrichment is an inherent part of this principle, in this case there is no "beneficial gain" for the Tribunal to find. Therefore, the Tribunal stated that the remedy of unjust enrichment is not available. The Claim of Flexi-Van regarding the Government of Iran being unjustly enriched was mainly based on Maass's affidavit. Allegedly, the containers were used by private persons or companies so the Government could have not been benefited from them. Maass gave, however, not a detailed report and nothing as to the number of containers he observed. The Tribunal, thus, stated that it is not capable to determine the amount of enrichment, if any, only based on one affidavit, which was very general and imprecise.[734] Therefore, the Tribunal dismissed the claim for unjust enrichment, which seems a just decision in this case. It would be improper for the Tribunal to base its decision on such vague statement.

Above are some of the arguments regarding the issue of unjust enrichment, one of the most cited general principles by the Tribunal, which are of course not exclusive and there is also a great deal of theoretical discussions in dissenting opinions of the mentioned awards.

bb) Force majeure

Considering the background of Iran's political situation at that time and the Iran's Islamic revolution, force majeure is one of the most referred general principles cited by both parties and the Tribunal itself. This was added to the fact that the Tribunal had a tendency to analyze the contract termination issues in a way other than finding a breach either by the respondent Government or its controlled entities.[735] Referring to the general principles, especially force majeure was relatable in the case of Iran-US disputes.

Before we illustrate the Tribunal's approaches toward force majeure, it would be helpful to first define the principle and note its characteristics. Force majeure is widely accepted as a general principle of law.[736] It could be found under Article

734 Flexi-Van Leasing, Inc. v. The Government of the Islamic Republic of Iran, IUSCT Award, Award No. 259-36-1, (11 October 1986), Part. II(3)(e).

735 Crook, John R., "Applicable Law in International Arbitration: The Iran-U.S. Claims Tribunal Experience", The American Journal of International Law, Vol. 83, (1989), p. 293.

736 See generally: Konarski, Hubert, "Force Majeure and Hardship Clauses in International Contractual Practice", International Business Law Journal, (2003), pp. 405–428; Schwenzer, Ingeborg, "Force Majeure and Hardship in International Sales Contracts", Victoria University of Wellington Law Review, Vol. 39, (2009), pp. 709–726.

79 of the United Nations Convention on Contracts for the International Sale of Goods (CISG), Article 7.1.7 of the UNIDROIT Principles of International Commercial Contracts (UPICC). Similar provisions are to be found in model contract clauses of International Chamber of Commerce (ICC) and Article 8:108 of the Principles of European Contract Law (PECL). This principle is explained similarly through various provisions, for example, Article 79(1) of the CISG states:

> "Non-performance by a party is excused if that party proves that the non-performance was due to an impediment beyond its control and that is could not reasonably be expected to have taken the impediment into account at the time of the conclusion of the contract or to have avoided or overcome it or its consequences."

Basically, this principle could be categorized as one of the exemptions for non-performance, which is addressed by significant private "soft law" codifications of contract law principles beside the national law systems.[737]

However, there are distinctions in juridical status of force majeure in common law and civil law countries. While in civil law countries, force majeure is traditionally part of the contract law, which refers to an unforeseen and unavoidable event, in common law countries, it is recognized as excusing tort liability for injuries caused by an act of god, and thus it is not ruled under contract law.[738]

This French term literally means "a superior force." According to *Black's Law Dictionary*, force majeure is "an event or effect that can be neither anticipated nor controlled."

The Tribunal has consistently mentioned that events in Iran in late 1978 to mid-1979 established force majeure conditions. However, the Awards have evidenced the Tribunal has different approaches on this issue. In other words, in some awards force majeure has stronger consequences than the others. In some cases, it could authorize the contract's termination and in others it does not bring such consequence.

The principle of force majeure came up first in *Gould Marketing v. Ministry of National Defense of Iran* case, without the issue being explicitly mentioned by the

---

737 See generally: Brunner, Christoph, "Force Majeure and Hardship under General Contract Principles-Exemption for Non-Performance in International Arbitration", Kluwer Law International, The Netherlands, (2009); Ewan McKendrick, "Force Majeure and Frustration of Contract", Lloyds of London Press Ltd, (1991).

738 Hanessian, Grant, "'General Principles of Law' in the Iran-U.S. Claims Tribunal", Columbia Journal of Transnational Law, Vol. 27, (1988-1989), p. 332.

parties.[739] There are awards, like the said one, in which the Tribunal employed a rather general and expansive view. The Tribunal sometimes found this principle sufficient to terminate the contract without it being invoked by the parties. In *Gould* case, the arguments of both parties was aimed for proving the other parties' breach of contract.

The Tribunal explains the situation in Iran as follows:

> "It remains the Tribunal's task to determine from the facts what was the legal situation between the parties at the time performance ceased. By December 1978, strikes, riots and other civil strikes in the course of the Islamic Revolution had created classic force majeure conditions at least in Iran's major cities. By "force majeure" we mean social and economic forces beyond the power of the state to control through the exercise of due diligence. Injuries caused by the operation at such forces are therefore not attributable to the state for purposes of its responding for damages. Similarly, as between private parties, one party cannot claim against the other for injuries suffered as a result of delays in or cessation of performance during the time force majeure conditions prevail, unless the existence of these conditions is attributable to the fault of the respondent party."[740]

According to the Tribunal's explanations, force majeure was sufficient to justify the non-performance by both parties. The Tribunal considered the situation in Iran as "classic force majeure conditions."

This was not the only approach employed by the Tribunal. Evidently, the Tribunal on some cases has dealt differently with this issue. In other words, the Tribunal sometimes acts more strictly and cautiously and analyzes certain factual circumstances in order to determine the possible consequences of force majeure. One of the most important examples of the said view is illustrated in Sylvania case.[741] Even though both Claimant and Respondent had ceased the performance of the Contract by 15 February 1979 and referred to the force majeure conditions, it should be noted that this principle is an exception to the obligation to perform, thus the Tribunal saw the requirement to prove the relating conditions for each party who has invoked it. Therefore, the Tribunal holds that the Respondent should provide the Tribunal with sufficient evidence showing

739 Gould Marketing, Inc. as successor to Hoffman Export Corporation v. Ministry of Defense of The Islamic Republic of Iran, IUSCT Interlocutory Award, Award No. ITL 24-49-2, (27 July 1983).

740 Gould Marketing, Inc. as successor to Hoffman Export Corporation v. Ministry of Defense of The Islamic Republic of Iran, IUSCT Interlocutory Award, Award No. ITL 24-49-2, (27 July 1983), Part. III.

741 Sylvania Technical Systems, Inc. v. The Government of the Islamic Republic of Iran, IUSCT Award, Award No. 180-64-1, (27 June 1985).

that the force majeure conditions continued to exist until and beyond mid-July 1979 and prevented it from performing its obligations in accordance with the Contract. The Tribunal has admitted that it is very difficult to exactly determine the force majeure conditions, however it held:

> "It might even be doubtful whether such a general determination would be possible, because the question of force majeure has to be seen, and may well be answered differently, in relation to every specific contractual obligation. But we do hold that there is insufficient proof in this case to support the Respondent's contention that conditions over which it had no control continued to and beyond 16 July 1979 and still prevent it even from making contractual payments and releasing letters of credit."

After reading this award and comparing it with the one discussed before, we could clearly see the distinction between two approaches. The first view was more general and expansive, while the second was aiming to consider more details and special situations in different time spans. The Tribunal seemed to adopt the second approach afterwards.[742]

Therefore, the number of cases, in which the Tribunal has found that the contracts were ultimately been terminated due to force majeure, remains small. In cases, where the Tribunal does not determine the necessary conditions of force majeure as ground of contract termination, it considers other contract provisions. The American Bell International Inc. ("ABII") case would be an illustrative example. This case was in connection with a ten-year plan to modernize the civilian and military telecommunications system of Iran ("Seek Switch Program"). The Claim was based on Respondent's alleged failure to make payments due based on two contracts and the alleged expropriation of certain Claimant's funds.[743] The Respondent, on the other hand, denied the Claimant's contentions and submitted several counterclaims based on alleged contract

742 For more examples see: American Bell International, Inc. v. The Islamic Republic of Iran, The Ministry of Post, Telegraph and Telephone of the Islamic Republic of Iran, and The Telecommunications Company of Iran, IUSCT Award, Award No. 225-48-3, (19 September 1986); Exxon Research and Engineering Company v. National Iranian Oil Company, Bank Markazi Iran, and The Government of Iran, IUSCT Award, Award No. 308-155-3, (9 June 1987); Amco International Finance Corporation v. The Government of the Islamic Republic of Iran, National Iranian Oil Company, National Petrochemical Company and Kharg Chemical Company Limited, IUSCT Award, Award No. 310-56-3, (14 July 1987).

743 American Bell International, Inc. v. The Islamic Republic of Iran, The Ministry of Post, Telegraph and Telephone of the Islamic Republic of Iran, and The Telecommunications Company of Iran, IUSCT Award, Award No. 225-48-3, (19 September 1986), Para. 1.

breaches by Claimant.[744] To some extent, the problems resulted from some discussions concerning the level of ABII's work force required in Iran. Based on the contract, the work force was to increase significantly. As the growth stopped, ABII protested calling that "arbitrary" and a violation of the contract but it also conceived that based on Iran's current situation its role would be more limited. However, the CEO of ABII called the situation a "partial termination" of the contract.[745] According to the contract, Iran was allowed to order ABII to reduce its work force and ABII was entitled to be compensated for the costs associated with the termination or partial termination of the contract. At the time the parties were negotiating intervening events prevented them from completing the negotiation process. Respondents argued as the work ceased due to the special political situation namely the Islamic revolution of Iran and not due to termination or other acts, the contract does not provide for the payment of the termination cost to Claimant. On the contrary, the Claimant strongly believed that it is entitled to its termination costs, still if the termination was based on force majeure.[746] The Tribunal found Article 18 of the contract inapplicable, since neither of parties referred to it as a ground of termination. The alternative ways for termination costs could be found under paragraph 10 of Appendix 3, which provides that "reimbursement of any costs incurred by the Contractor as a result of conditions or events described in the following articles will be paid by the Employer to the Contractor."[747] The Tribunal noted, however, that it does not mean that force majeure has no consequence at all. There is still a part attributable to force majeure and the fact that it prevented the parties from negotiating financial consequences. But the important point in this case and other similar cases it that the Tribunal stated:

---

744 American Bell International, Inc. v. The Islamic Republic of Iran, The Ministry of Post, Telegraph and Telephone of the Islamic Republic of Iran, and The Telecommunications Company of Iran, IUSCT Award, Award No. 225-48-3, (19 September 1986), Para. 2.

745 American Bell International, Inc. v. The Islamic Republic of Iran, The Ministry of Post, Telegraph and Telephone of the Islamic Republic of Iran, and The Telecommunications Company of Iran, IUSCT Award, Award No. 225-48-3, (19 September 1986), Para. 34.

746 American Bell International, Inc. v. The Islamic Republic of Iran, The Ministry of Post, Telegraph and Telephone of the Islamic Republic of Iran, and The Telecommunications Company of Iran, IUSCT Award, Award No. 225-48-3, (19 September 1986), Para. 51.

747 American Bell International, Inc. v. The Islamic Republic of Iran, The Ministry of Post, Telegraph and Telephone of the Islamic Republic of Iran, and The Telecommunications Company of Iran, IUSCT Award, Award No. 225-48-3, (19 September 1986), Para. 52.

> "Thus force majeure, although not the ultimate cause to which claimant's termination costs can be attributed, created conditions which made it impossible for Claimant to recover what it was entitled to under the contract. Unlike those situations in which costs are directly attributable to force majeure, this does not reflect the allocation of risks as contemplated by contract 138, but rather is a consequence of a situation unforeseen in the contract. In such circumstances the determination of the rights and liabilities of the parties is subject to the Tribunal's equitable discretion, using the contract as a framework and reference point."[748]

Therefore, the Tribunal should take a number of issues into account. The Tribunal had to consider that force majeure had a direct effect on some events while it could be only attributed directly in other cases. For example, some of the ABII employees left Iran just because of force majeure. Although this event falls outside the contract's framework, but still the event is directly attributable to force majeure. However, in case the negotiating process was interfered, force majeure indirectly resulted in costs for ABII. Consequently, there would be no compensation for termination costs, which are attributable to force majeure, namely the costs with respect to departure of persons. Provisions of the contract gave the Claimant the choice between termination of the contract or bearing the risk of the costs and he chose the former. The Tribunal clarified its argument by stating that in cases, where the contract does not contain a force majeure clause or such clause is not invoked, the guiding rule with respect to costs attributable to force majeure would be "the loss must lie where it falls."[749]

With respect to the latter situation concerning force reductions, the Tribunal strongly believed that ABII was entitled to recover the costs. This is based on the contract contemplating that in every virtually conceivable situation, ABII was entitled to recover the costs but in case of force majeure not resulting in termination. Since this is the case, ABII is actually entitled to the termination costs. These are all in accordance with the contract the Tribunal has even maintained that it is even its task to reach an outcome as close as possible to the contractual stated:

> "It is the Tribunal's task to reach a result which as closely as possible corresponds to the contractual scheme. Therefore, in determining the amount of the costs caused by the

748 American Bell International, Inc. v. The Islamic Republic of Iran, The Ministry of Post, Telegraph and Telephone of the Islamic Republic of Iran, and The Telecommunications Company of Iran, IUSCT Award, Award No. 225-48-3, (19 September 1986), Para. 54.

749 American Bell International, Inc. v. The Islamic Republic of Iran, The Ministry of Post, Telegraph and Telephone of the Islamic Republic of Iran, and The Telecommunications Company of Iran, IUSCT Award, Award No. 225-48-3, (19 September 1986), Para. 56.

fore reductions the Tribunal finds it in the circumstances proper to proceed from the definition of termination costs in Contract 138."[750]

Reviewing this case shows the great dedication of the Tribunal finding and applying general principles. There is actually a sub-principle that the Tribunal has been referring to and that is "the loss must lie where it falls" in cases, where the contract does not have any provisions on force majeure.

Furthermore, we could clearly see how the Tribunal engaged itself with the details in comparison with the former case discussed above. This approach is the one the Tribunal seemed to adopt. The Tribunal focused mainly on determining remedies, which could lead to readjust benefits and eventually a fair outcome rather than being overly engaged determining the substantive law.[751]

cc) Other principles

There are many other concepts, especially those relating to contract issues, that the Tribunal has referred to as general principles of law. Some of them are already explained throughout this study. The issues are mainly with respect to formation of contract, find a contract, confirm or deny the existence of contract, performance, interpretation, and contract remedies. These subjects are however not exclusive. There are issues, which can be sometimes categorized under national law as well. For example, in several cases on existence of contracts, the Tribunal has referred to a principle contemplating the parties could not deny the contract after they already confirmed it by their action. In other words, when a party conducts in a way, which confirms the existence of the contract, he cannot deny it afterwards. An example would be part performance of an oral contract, which is illustrated in *Delaware* case at the beginning of general principles of law section.

Regarding interpretation, the Tribunal in *CBA International v. Iran* pointed out that the contracts should be interpreted by reading the text as a whole. The Tribunal explained this principle as follows:

"According to the most fundamental principle of interpretation, the Article in question must be presumed to be capable of being given meaning and effect as the expression of the common intention of the Parties. If one of the words used gives rise to ambiguity,

---

750 American Bell International, Inc. v. The Islamic Republic of Iran, The Ministry of Post, Telegraph and Telephone of the Islamic Republic of Iran, and The Telecommunications Company of Iran, IUSCT Award, Award No. 225-48-3, (19 September 1986), Para. 59.

751 Hanessian, Grant, "'General Principles of Law' in the Iran-U.S. Claims Tribunal", Columbia Journal of Transnational Law, Vol. 27, (1988-1989), p. 337.

> such ambiguity must be resolved in favor of the interpretation most likely to give sensible effect to the Article taken as a whole."[752]

The Tribunal, furthermore, applied general principles that requires parties to perform their contract with due diligence. In *General Dynamics v. Iran*, the Tribunal expressed that under general principles of law, the parties should perform their contract obligations satisfactorily and with due diligence and negligence would amount to a breach of contract.[753]

After studying the Tribunal's view on general principles of law, it should be noted that how exceptional it is to see this source of law resolving the most complicated legal disputes between two countries with such different cultural, political and juridical systems; however, it could not be expected from the general principles of law to answer all possible questions.

c) Public international law

Public international law is a source, which has been applied by the Tribunal in a relatively small number of cases. However, since the Tribunal normally has not explained and justified its choice of law, it is sometimes difficult to distinguish a sole source of law, to which the Tribunal has referred. Furthermore, the Tribunal mostly refers to two or more sources at the same time, even when the outcome would be the same in case of using only one source.

The role of the Tribunal becomes bolder when its uniqueness is being considered. As the Tribunal has a very special instance in both national and international law matters, considering its jurisdiction, it is important to distinguish the claims by their nature. This is illustrated in the new level of claims that nationals of Iran or the United States have the right to submit a claim against the other Government. The nature of these claims could make them rest upon public international law or private law.[754] As discussed at the beginning of this chapter, there were some arguments especially from the Iranian side that such

---

752 CBA International Development Corporation v. The Government of Iran, IUSCT Award, Award No. 115-928-3, (16 March 1984), Part. III.

753 General Dynamics Corporation and General International Corporation v. The Islamic Republic of Iran, The Government of the Islamic Republic of Iran and the Navy of the Islamic Republic of Iran, IUSCT Award, Award No. 123-283-3, (13 April 1984), Part. IV(3).

754 Crook, John R., "Applicable Law in International Arbitration: The Iran-U.S. Claims Tribunal Experience", The American Journal of International Law, Vol. 83, (1989), p. 300.

claims come before the Tribunal only through diplomatic espousal by the United States. The basis of such an argument was that the Tribunal is a subject to public international law and consequently it requires respecting the applicable rules to diplomatic protection and espousal. The Tribunal has consistently refused such arguments.[755]

A great deal of Tribunal's contributions is with respect to expropriation claims. The Tribunal has done a tremendous amount of work in this section of law so that in almost every subsequent expropriation related work afterwards a reference to the Tribunal's awards is nearly impossible. Therefore, studying the Tribunal's jurisprudence on such claims requires a separate study. An example could be the cases involved with the 1955 Treaty of Amity between Iran and the United States. Even though the International Court of Justice had confirmed the enforceability of this Treaty in 1979, the Iranian parties refused its effect with respect to the events of 1978–1980. The Tribunal has referred to customary international law as the source of applicable standards on the issues regarding expropriation. The standard of compensation ruled by the Treaty of Amity was something that has consistently applied by the Tribunal only that the Tribunal justified it in different ways. For example, the Tribunal named it as *lex specialis* while deciding the *INA Corp. v. Iran* case and stated:

> "Moreover, for the purpose of this case we are in the presence of a *lex specialis*, in the form of the Treaty of Amity, which in principle prevails over general rules."[756]

In this case, as the parties did not make any arguments against the validity of the Treaty of Amity, the Tribunal assumed that it has remained valid. The standard under the Treaty of Amity required full compensation while based on other standards it could be reduced to partial compensation. There were debates in respect to the standard of compensation based on customary international law. The Tribunal, however, in Amco case stated that both the Treaty and customary international law require "just" compensation, which reflect at a minimum a full equivalent of the expropriated property.

With respect to this issue, Article IV, paragraph II of the Treaty of Amity reads as follows:

---

755 More explanations and examples on the Tribunal's view on diplomatic protection can be found under "dual nationals" section.

756 INA Corporation v. The Government of the Islamic Republic of Iran, IUSCT Award, Award No. 184-161-1, (12 August 1985), Part. II.

> "Property of nationals and companies of either High Contracting Party, including interests in property, shall receive the most constant protection and security within the territories of the other High Contracting Party, in no case less than that required by international law. Such property shall not be taken except for a public purpose, nor shall it be taken without the prompt payment of just compensation. Such compensation shall be in an effectively realizable form and shall represent the full equivalent of the property taken; and adequate provision shall have been made at or prior to the time of taking for the determination and payment thereof."

The Tribunal believes that "just compensation" could be understood as equal to the full value of the expropriated assets and it is confirmed by Article IV of the Treaty of Amity. The more detailed discussion on this issue could be seen in the Award and also the concurring opinion of Judge Brower on the same award.[757] It should be noted that on this issues three chambers of the Tribunal employed quite different approaches.

International law plays a role again when the Tribunal has to interpret treaties. This issue has come up at different points in this study. A full Tribunal was considered in the Algiers Accords in order to decide the Treaty interpretation cases, known as interpretive cases.

Furthermore, the relevance of the Vienna Convention is doubtless. The Tribunal has regularly referred to this convention as a rule of interpretation in general. As Article 31(1) of the Vienna Convention states:

> "1. A treaty shall be interpreted in good faith in accordance with the ordinary meaning to be given to the terms of the treaty in their context and in the light of its object and purpose."

And then again at the third paragraph of same Article:

> "3. There shall be taken into account, together with the context:
> (a) Any subsequent agreement between the parties regarding the interpretation of the treaty or the application of its provisions;
> (b) Any subsequent practice in the application of the treaty which establishes the agreement of the parties regarding its interpretation;
> (c) Any relevant rules of international law applicable in the relations between the parties."

Based on this very paragraph the Tribunal has based one of its important arguments. As we explained in the section of "dual nationality", the Tribunal has employed the rule

757 Amco International Finance Corporation v. The Government of the Islamic Republic of Iran, National Iranian Oil Company, National Petrochemical Company and Kharg Chemical Company Limited, IUSCT Award, Award No. 310-56-3, (14 July 1987).

of "dominant and effective nationality", which is a relevant rule of international law in accordance with paragraph 3 of Article 31 of the Vienna Convention.[758]

d) *Changed circumstances*

"Changed circumstances" is actually not an independent source compared to other sources discussed above. The ground that we discuss this principle under a separate title is that Article V of the Claims Settlement Declaration directly names it. This principle justifies the termination of contract in situations involving sensitive governmental contracts.[759]

It seems that reference to "changed circumstances" by the Claims Settlement Declaration is resulted from the negotiations concerning Iranian forum clauses. It could be the intent of the United States negotiators in order to prevent the Tribunal from considering forum clauses considering the political upheaval in Iran. Most of the United States' arguments in cases involving Iranian forum clauses revolve around the tremendously changed circumstances in Iran during and after the revolution to the extent that the judicial system has become totally different and it wouldn't be fair for the claims to be settled in an Iranian forum.[760]

Despite of how reasonable this argument could sound, it is also been said that the real intent of the drafters could not be discovered and "the Tribunal has thus far declined to comment on what constitute 'changed circumstances'."[761]

---

758 Crook, John R., "Applicable Law in International Arbitration: The Iran-U.S. Claims Tribunal Experience", The American Journal of International Law, Vol. 83, (1989), p. 305.

759 Crook, John R., "Applicable Law in International Arbitration: The Iran-U.S. Claims Tribunal Experience", The American Journal of International Law, Vol. 83, (1989), p. 298.

760 More explanations and examples are to be found under the "The Iranian-Forum Clause Decisions" section.

761 Bellet, Pierre, "Foreword", Law & Policy in International Business, Vo. 16, (1984), p. 672.

Conclusion

In this study, we tried to cover the most important issues relating to applicable law, particularly applicable substantive law, in two forums namely ICSID and Iran-United States Claims Tribunal. This study would not seem complete unless we point out the highlights that could lead us to benefiting from all the facts and information that we have put in current order so far. However, the first step would always be reiterating the preliminary questions that we had in mind in order to navigate this concluding remarks in a more comprehensible way.

The very first issue that every reader could come up with is the reason that we choose these two arbitration forums in particular. Why ICSID and Iran-United States Claims Tribunal? What makes them enough noteworthy for us to choose them as a basis for a comparison? It should be noted that comparison itself is not the ultimate goal. Nor is the mere explanation of the rules that these forums have worked thereunder. But the primary goal is to find out the characteristics that gradually become precedents. It does not always matter how similar and comparable the functions of tribunals are in order for them to affect one another. The cases don't have to simply reflect the same subject matter to become eligible for having an effect on the cases after them. Sometimes some unique circumstances in the background of an arbitration tribunal or any other tribunal makes it so unique and distinctive mainly in a special issue, that other tribunals regardless of how similar they are to the former tribunal, could not help but to look into the first tribunal's decision. It is never an uncomplicated task for a tribunal to carry out a deep and fundamental research on every single issue that it is facing. It is neither plausible nor right. Right in the sense, that the said tribunal would never reach those detailed conclusions that a tribunal would have come up with, which its only or almost primary focus was to examine each and every aspect of that special issue. Dual nationality would be a notable example here. Not every tribunal or generally arbitration institution would have to deal with this issue on a regular basis. Therefore, the most pertinent way that comes to mind is to utilize the experience of the tribunals that deal with the issue thoroughly and have actually become some sort of precedent maker. We can even take a step further and say this is exactly one of the rationales behind the necessity of precedents to begin with. Precedents are great to be referred as a strong backup to tribunals' decisions but it is not their only role. They facilitate the process of rendering a decision for the tribunals on the issues that those tribunals are not normally dealing with or matters that are secondary to the genuine field of their cases.

The increasing reference to the international case law demonstrates the need for acquiring a systematic approach for numerous practical questions. Recent developments in the field of international investment arbitration reaffirm this approach.

Given this summary, we could grasp the relevancy of the choice of ICSID and Iran-United States Claims Tribunal in this study. ICSID's growing workload manifests its success in the field of investment arbitration. It has provided both investors and host states with an acceptable level of efficiency and confidentiality. In other words, ICSID mirrors the world of international investment arbitration, hence it could be a great base for us to examine the special legal matters in the light of its jurisprudence. On the other hand, the Iran-United States Claims Tribunal, which has already done most of its job successfully, appears to be completely different from ICSID as to its limited jurisdiction, unique function and special background. The purposes of these tribunals are entirely different but one cannot ignore the legal implications of their awards and decisions. As we can see, the Iran-United States Claims Tribunal's awards and decisions are among most cited ones especially on certain subjects. That is due to the uniqueness of this Tribunal, which is different with *ad hoc* Tribunals, more concentration on special subjects on an almost regular basis that leads to higher quality of its outcome.

There is not just the quantity of certain awards rendered from a tribunal that grants it a precedential weight. Other factors have also a role to play. When we take a look at the definition of precedent at the first place, we find that, for example, there should be a similarity of issues between the previous and ongoing cases. It should be noted precedent in our case, namely in international law is not the one used in common law system known as "stare decisis." The difference lies on the function and power of previous decisions. Generally, there is no binding precedent in international law as it is in common law. However, that does not make it any less important. Precedent in broader terms equips judges and arbitrators with pertinent guidance; therefore, as ICJ also confirms, it is not binding but it does not mean that it's not precedent any more.

Given the above terms, the precedent in relation to our study is not binding but it should be persuasive to even be considered in the world of investment arbitration. Hence, consistency is of essence. In addition, the standing of the Tribunal should be considered for the relevance of the potential precedent that may be drawn by it.

Another factor that makes Iran-United States Claims Tribunal an attractive forum is the wide diversity of cases that it has covered by now. This adds to its significant role of being a potential source for useful precedent. It has even been said "the Tribunal has produced more international law than any other law-making body in the history of mankind."[762]

When we think deeper, to find the relevancy we have to consider whether the two tribunals in question apply the same law. Even on this level Iran-United States Claims Tribunal has been well considered as a pertinent option. Since we examined several ICSID and Iran-US Claim Tribunal's decision through this study, it became apparent that they both tend to rely more on international law rather than domestic. The determination process and their rationalization could be different at some points due to the unique political background behind the Iran-United States Claims Tribunal. However, the outcome is very similar. While we were clarifying the applicable law rules in these tribunals, their case law demonstrated that both ICSID and Iran-United States Claims Tribunal rely more on international law principles than other available sources. No matter how different their rules on determining the applicable are and the greater freedom that the Iran-United States Claims Tribunal enjoys in comparison to ICSID, ultimately the tribunals tend to base their decisions and justifications on international law for many reasons. That alone helps to assure consistency and brings out referable precedent for the tribunals dealing with whatever subject in future. It does not only facilitate the process of rendering an award for the arbitrators but it also greatly affects how the other subjects to an international arbitration process would feel and trust the arbitral procedure. Compared to other traditional means of dispute resolution, arbitration and other alternative methods are still fresh. Therefore, in order to make it even more attractive, it should be able to build trust. But how could it be done? Given the numerous aspects of arbitration, this question can have countless answers. In regard to our current study, which focuses on applicable law, a relevant point would be anticipation. The more the parties could foresee the process of their potential arbitration case clearer more likely it becomes for them to consider this means of dispute resolution. It is a logical fact in general that the more we already know about a certain matter and the more we could anticipate the future occurrences concerning that matter, the better we could trust it. The exact same scenario exists in real arbitration world. Applicable law issue is of essence, since different approaches on this matter could reverse the outcome of a case and it is unsurprising that the parties feel more motivated to submit their case to arbitration, when they know that there is more likely that their case is going to be reviewed under international law rules. It is

762 Judge Abraham D. Sofaer, Legal adviser to the U.S. State Department for many years during the Iran-United States Claims Tribunal activity.

also in law practitioners' favor to ground their case relying on the international rule and strengthen their arguments based on the rich precedent that is available for all members of the arbitration world.

While studying Iran-US Claim Tribunal, we observed how the Tribunal sometimes insisted on applying the general principles of law, which not only reinforce the power of these rules but also demonstrate how flexible and reliable they are that a tribunal with a high level of trickiness and sensibility, given the very special situation between Iran and the United States at that time period could easily employ them. Iran-United States Claims Tribunal is a clear example of the power of international rules, where the parties are at a point, in which not even the simplest negotiation between them seems doable. General principles of international law are sometimes akin to a compromise. The parties in our case would do everything in their power to avoid each other's domestic rules. This is true even if there is a direct reference to one country's domestic laws. The opposing party, as we saw in several examples before, would choose a path only to prove that law is not applicable.

Empirical researches show that ICSID had an extensive reliance on Iran-United States Claims Tribunal's precedents.[763] The Iran-US Tribunal, for example, provides any tribunal a wealth of experience on expropriation as one of the most important issues in investment arbitration.

These two dispute resolution institutions are genuinely different. Their jurisdictional scope, backgrounds, origins and rules may seem even incomparable. ICSID was established by many States with its significant purpose of resolving investment dispute, while the Iran-United States Claims Tribunal convened by two States, namely Iran and the United States of America to generally resolve all the disputes, which resulted after the Islamic revolution in Iran. As we reviewed, ICSID tribunals resolve cases in accordance with ICSID's own rules, whereas The Hague Tribunal has employed a revised version of UNCITRAL rules. Therefore, it is reasonable for the ICSID convention to be different given the fact that it has been tailored to meet typical requirements of an investment dispute. Despite of these differences, both institutions have also had several common legal issues relating to the field of international investment.

Adjudicating the disputes would be possible only after clear determination of the law, which is to be applied. This is actually one of the preliminary and most

763 Drahozal, Christopher R.; Gibson, Christopher S., "Iran-United States Claims Tribunal Precedent in Investor-State Arbitration", Journal of International Arbitration, Vol. 23, Issue. 6, (2006), p. 536.

important steps for any tribunal to take. In two chapters, we mainly discussed the rule of determining the applicable substantive law under ICSID and Iran-United States Claims Tribunal, namely Article 42(1) of ICSID Convention and Article V of the Claims Settlement Declaration. If we start to point out the differences between these two articles, the first issue that comes to mind is the less specific nature of the one under Claims Settlement Declaration. The tone of Article V sounds less of a command and more of a suggestion and as a result the greater freedom it bestows upon the arbitrators. However, this could not be merely accounted as the exact intention of the negotiators. As we reviewed the background of Iran-United States Claims Tribunal in Chapter 2, we saw the very exceptional circumstances, under which this Tribunal was established. Given these circumstances, which caused almost complete lack of diplomatic relations between Iran and the United States in addition to incompatible ideologies, which have been clearly mirrored in the history of the negotiations, it was almost impossible for the parties to reach a consensus on several matters including the applicable law. Thus, the more general the rules were the more chance existed that the Tribunal will be successfully established. These rules at least are testimony to the flexibility of arbitration under even most challenging circumstances. In contrast to Claims Settlement Declaration, the Washington convention adopted a more precise set of rules in order to determine the applicable law. Similar to many other arbitration rules, its primary principle on applicable law is the agreement made by the parties. In simple words, under ICSID Convention the first step would be to examine whether or not the parties have made an agreement regarding the applicable law. The answer of this preliminary question would lead the Tribunal to the next level. An affirmative answer leads to the simplest situation. On the contrary, when the parties neither made an agreement prior to the arbitration nor are able to agree on the applicable law after submitting the case, the situation would be more complicated. However, the ICSID Convention has foreseen this probability and accordingly laid down pertinent rules. The primary principle of parties' agreement is nothing new or unique. ICC and UNCITRAL have also very similar approaches in addition to the numerous domestic laws on arbitration, which have adopted the UNCITRAL model rules. This rule indicates party authority, which is a vital principle in international arbitration. The applicable law rule under the Claims Settlement Declaration on the other hand is notably broad. Despite we described the ICSID applicable law rules as specific but that description would be significant when we start to compare the rules with ones under Claims Settlement Declaration. Generally, ICSID rules also provide a great freedom for the decision makers and even allow them to decide entirely on the basis of general principles of international law without reference to national legal rules. According to Article V of the Claims Settlement Declaration, the arbitrators are not even obliged to honor the parties' agreements. The only requirement for the Tribunal is to decide on the basis of respect for law. Throughout the process, the Tribunal has a wide choice of sources and it has the freedom of choosing the one it determines to be applicable. Besides, in accordance with the said Article, while the Tribunal determines the choice of law, it should take three points into account; namely relevant usages of the trade, contract provisions and changed circumstances. As we discussed in the relevant chapter, this Article could not be drafted any wider. It does not even stipulate that the Tribunal should or may decide based on these three points, but it utilizes "taking into account." This verb does not imply any level of obligation. As a matter of fact, taking a rule into account and applying it cannot be considered as the same. Consequently, the Tribunal is free to choose the substantive rules from whatever sources and through whatever mechanism, which could even add to the complexities the Tribunal confronted with at the time.

Despite all these dissimilarities between the applicable law rules under ICISID and Iran-United States Claims Tribunal's rules, there are some important legal questions relating this issue that they share. They even seem to have common approaches on several issues. Whether the national law or international law should be given the primacy. While discussing the ICSID rules on applicable law, we mentioned several awards with the main task to answer this very question in light of Article 42(1) of the ICSID Convention. One view was regarding a two-step approach or supplementary character of international law, which has been explained in many ICSID awards in decisions. International law should be used according to this view in two instances; first, when there is a lacuna in regard to the host state law and second, where the law of the host state needs to be corrected by the international law because of existing conflicts between them. Therefore, international law acts as a controller of national law. The primacy of international law was not only considered where the parties had not reached an agreement in respect to applicable law, but it also applied, where a set of national rules was chosen. Therefore, the debate is not limited to the second sentence of Article 42(1), which authorizes the Tribunal to determine the applicable law in absence of parties' agreement and international law and the law of host state are among the choices. Choice of national law by the parties does not mean that international law would not be applied anymore.

The attempt to find the ICSID tribunals' views on applicable law and finding the stronger interpretation of Article 42(1) is a lot easier than doing the same thing based on Iran-United States Claims Tribunal's jurisprudence. The vagueness resulted from the way Article V was drafted. It is genuinely complicated for the Tribunal to even attempt to interpret Article V; therefore, the Iran-US panels have rarely spent time justifying their applicable law choices.

In spite of the fact that there is no such thing as primary authority of the parties to determine the applicable law, the Tribunal's most common source of law has been the contract provisions. The primacy of international law over national law has not only been supported by ICSID tribunals, but Iran-United States Claims Tribunal has also recognized it. This Tribunal has shown reluctance to refer to national laws and applied general principles of law instead even where parties had agreed to a national law in contract. This tendency to apply the rules of international law sometimes stemmed from the Tribunal trying to avoid Iranian or American laws that may become conflicting. Therefore, we can conclude that based on several ICSID and Iran-United States Claims Tribunal's award they commonly expressed that in resolving international disputes, general principles of law should be prioritized over national laws. This view is not totally consistent when it comes to cases where the parties have expressly chosen the applicable law in their contracts.

These facts all reflect how great the importance of international law, especially general principles of international law, are in the process of international arbitration. The experience of these two tribunals is very promising to the evolution of international dispute resolution and arbitration in particular. It demonstrates that there is a tool existing as guidance and correctional power to avoid potential injustices that may result from applicable national laws in international reality. This is actually one of the points of general principles of law being a vital part of many existing arbitration rules and as a matter of fact, it could not serve its purpose without being given the primacy over national laws.

While certainly the freedom granted to the Iran-United States Claims Tribunal by the Claims Settlement Declaration with respect to determination of applicable law is extraordinary, it does not mean that there is no limit to the Tribunal's discretion. There are still some issues as we noted in this study that the Tribunal is required to have parties' express agreement prior to employing a decision such as rendering a decision *ex aequo et bono*. The ICSID Convention has delivered its attitude toward this issue very clearly through the third paragraph of Article 42. Since there is no such specification in Claims Settlement Declaration, it leaves us no way but referring to the main principle, which is laid down by Article V, under which the Tribunal has to decide on the basis of respect for law. This very stipulation leads to many arguments condemning the Tribunal's power to decide *ex aequo et bono*. It has been contested against the power of Tribunal to decide *ex aequo et bono* noting that it would be inconsistent with Article V and its main purpose.

These arguments are mainly based on older beliefs, where the proponents of arbitration believed that once a dispute is given to an arbitral tribunal and *ex aequo et bono* is utilized as a method of resolving the dispute, it practically means that the entire applicable law system would be completely disregarded and could lead to subjectivity. This argument has had its strength even until recent past. The fact is however the method of *ex aequo et bono* is proved to be very practical, expeditious and cost efficient especially compared to interpreting various laws in an environment replete with mutual distrust. The mutual uncertainty that actually rooted in parties being unsure about the court system as well as the laws of that country. With that being said, the method of *ex aequo et bono* could be considered as a perfect solution, which is available to the parties upon their agreement. There are many situations, in which it is impossible for the parties or even decision makers to have access to a crystalized interpretation of a local law. However, this method might not be a panacea for all potential applicable law challenges that the parties may face in future, it definitely should be considered as a baseline action in cases, in which this method may seem pertinent.

Alongside the issues regarding applicable law, the Iran-United States Claims Tribunal's workload is also worthy of review given the diverse variety of legal matters that it covers; however, discussing every aspect of its contributions would not fit into this work. While we focus on choice of law questions raised throughout the tribunal's proceedings, we come across several substantive issues such as the status of dual nationalities, the potency of choice of forum clauses and identifying government-controlled entities. These are controversial issues that resulted in long debates that add significantly to the corpus of international arbitration.

Finally, it should be noted that although The Hague tribunal may have failed to provide a comprehensive and detailed interpretation of what Article V really means or at least has not attempted to do, the awards and decisions rendered by the Tribunal are evidently not only in line with the main purposes of the Claims Settlement Declaration but they remarkably contribute to the international arbitral procedures. To that end, effective functioning of the Iran-United States Claims Tribunal despite facing adversities and the significant amount of rich precedent it added to the reservoir of international arbitration by it is a testimony to its success and reflects the reliability of this means of dispute resolution.

Bibliography

Aghahosseini, Mohsen, "Claims of Dual Nationals and the Developments of Customary International Law – Issues Before the Iran-United States Claims Tribunal", *Developments in International Law*, Vol. 59 (2007).

Ajibo, Collins C., "The Governing Law in Investor-State Arbitration: The BIT, International Law, and Choice of Law Clause", *International Arbitration Law Review*, Vol. 6 (2015), 125.

Aldrich, George H., "The Jurisprudence of the Iran-United States Claims Tribunal", Clarendon Press Oxford, Oxford (1996).

Alvik, Ivar, "Contracting with Sovereignty: State Contracts and International Arbitration", Hart Publishing, Oxford and Portland, Oregon (2011).

Atsegbua, Lawrence, "International Arbitration of Oil Investment Disputes: The Severability Doctrine and Applicable Law Issues Revisited", *African Journal of International and Comparative Law*, Vol. 5, Issue. 3 (1993), 634.

Badaruddin, Schandor S., "Choice of Law Decisions in the Iran U.S. Claims Tribunal", *Emory International Law Review*, Vol. 4 (1990), 157.

Banifatemi, Yas, "The Law Applicable in Investment Treaty Arbitration", in Katia Yannaca-Small (ed.), *Arbitration under International Investment Agreements, a Guide to the Key Issues*, Oxford University Press, Oxford (2010), 191.

Basedow, Jürgen, "The Law of Open Societies: Private Ordering and Public Regulation of International Relations: General Course on Private International Law", Leiden/Boston, Martinus Nijhoff Publishers (2013).

Bellet, Pierre, "Foreword", *Law & Policy in International Business*, Vol. 16 (1984), 667.

Belohlávek, Alexander J., "Application of Law in Arbitration, Ex aequo et Bono and Amiable Compositeur", *Czech (& Central European) Yearbook of Arbitration*, Vol. 3 (2013), 25.

Ben Hamida, Walid, "Two Nebulous ICSID Features: The Notion of Investment and the Scope of Annulment Control – Ad Hoc Committee's Decision in Patrick Mitchell v. Democratic Republic of Congo", *Journal of International Arbitration*, Vol. 24, Issue. 3 (2007), 287.

Berger, Klaus Peter, "The Creeping Codification of the Lex Mercatoria", Kluwer Law International, The Hague/London/Boston (1999).

Berglin, R. Håkan, "Treaty Interpretation and the Impact of Contractual Choice of Forum Clauses on the Jurisdiction of International Tribunals: The Iranian

Forum Clause Decisions of the Iran-United States Claims Tribunal", *Texas International Law Journal*, Vol. 21 (1985–1986), 39.

Birks, Peter, "Unjust Enrichment", Oxford University Press, Second Edition (2005).

Bjorklund, Andrea K, "Mandatory Rules of Law and Investment Arbitration", *American Review of International Arbitration*, Vol. 18 (2007), 175.

Blessing, Marc, "Mandatory Rules of Law versus Party Autonomy in International Arbitration", *Journal of International Arbitration*, Vol. 14, Issue. 4 (1997), 23.

Borchard, Edwin M., "The Diplomatic Protection of Citizens Abroad or the Law of International Claims", The Banks Law Publishing Co., New York (1916).

Bowett, "State Contracts with Aliens", *British Yearbook of International Law*, Vol. 5, Issue 1 (1988), 49.

Bray, Devin; Bray, Heather L., "International Arbitration and Public Policy", JurisNet LLC, Huntington, New York (2014).

Broches, Aron, "Convention on the Settlement of Investment Disputes between States and Nationals of Other States of 1965 Explanatory Notes and Survey of Its Application", in Albert Jan van den Berg (ed.), *Yearbook Commercial Arbitration*, Vol. 18 (1993), 626.

Broches, Aron, "Observation on the Finality of ICSID Awards", *ICSID Review-Foreign Investment Law Journal*, Vol. 6 (1991), 231.

Broches, Aron, "On the Finality of Awards: A Reply to Michael Reisman", *ICSID Review-Foreign Investment Law Journal*, Vol. 8 (1993), 92.

Broches, Aron, "Selected Essays- World Bank, ICSID, and Other Subjects of Public and Private International Law", Martinus Nijhoff Publishers, Dordrecht (1994).

Broches, Aron, "The Convention on the Settlement of Investment Disputes between States and Nationals of Other States", *Collected Courses of the Hague Academy of International Law*, Vol. 136, Brill Nijhoff, Leiden/Boston (1972), 331.

Brower, Charles N., "The Iran-United States Claims Tribunal: Its Genesis, Structure, Organization, Jurisdiction and History", *Collected Courses of the Hague Academy of International Law*, Vol. 224 (1990), 123.

Brower, Charles N.; Brueschke, Jason D., "The Iran-United States Claims Tribunal", Martinus Nijhoff Publishers, Den Haag (1998).

Brunetti, Maurizio, "The Lex Mercatoria in Practice: The Experience of the Iran-United States Claims Tribunal", *Arbitration International*, Vol. 18 (2002), 355.

Brunner, Christoph, "Force Majeure and Hardship under General Contract Principles-Exemption for Non-Performance in International Arbitration", Kluwer Law International, The Netherlands (2009).

Burrows, Andrew, "A Restatement of the English Law of Unjust Enrichment", Oxford University Press (2012).

Caron, David D., "Reputation and Reality in the ICSID Annulment Process: Understanding the Distinction Between Annulment and Appeal", *ICSID Review-Foreign Investment Law Journal*, Vol. 7 (1992), 21.

Caron, David D., "The Basis of Responsibility: Attribution and Other Trans-Substantive Rules", in R. Lillich & D. Magraw (eds.), *The Iran-United States Claims Tribunal: Its Contribution to the Law of State Responsibility*, Irvington-on-Hudson, Transnational Publishers (1998).

Caron, David D.; Caplan, Lee M., "The UNCITRAL Arbitration Rules, A Commentary", Oxford University Press, Second Edition, Oxford (2013).

Cherian, Joy, "Investment Contracts and Arbitration-The World Bank Convention on the Settlement of Investment Disputes", A.W. Sijthoff-Leyden, Leiden (1975).

Chetterjee, C., "The Reality of The Party Autonomy Rule In International Arbitration", *Journal of International Arbitration*, Vol. 20, Issue. 6 (2003), 539.

Christopher, Warren; Mosk, Richard M., "The Iranian Hostage Crisis and the Iran-U.S, Claims Tribunal: Implications for International Dispute Resolution and Diplomacy", *Pepperdine Dispute Resolution Law Journal*, Vol. 7, Issue. 2 (2007), 165.

Chukwumerije, Okezie, "Choice of Law in International Commercial Arbitration", Quorum Books, Westport, CT (1994).

Comeaux, Paul E.; Kinsella, N. Stephen, "Reducing Political Risk in Developing Countries: Bilateral Investment Treaties, Stabilization Clauses, and MIGA & OPIC Investment Insurance", *New York Law School Journal of International and Comparative Law*, Vol. 15 (1994), 1.

Croff, Carlo, "The Applicable Law in an International Commercial Arbitration: Is It Still a Conflict of Laws Problem?", *International Lawyer*, Vol. 16 (1982), 613.

Crook, John R., "Applicable Law in International Arbitration: The Iran-U.S. Claims Tribunal Experience", *The American Journal of International Law*, Vol. 83, Issue. 2 (1989), 278.

De Vries, Henry P., "International Commercial Arbitration: A Contractual Substitute for National Courts", *Tulane Law Review*, Vol. 57 (1982), 42.

Delaume, George R., "Convention on the Settlement of Investment Disputes Between States and Nationals of Other States", *International Lawyer*, Vol. 1, Issue. 1 (1966), 64.

Delaume, George R., "How to Draft an ICSID Arbitration Clause", *ICSID Review-Foreign Investment Law Journal*, Vol. 7, Issue. 1 (1992), 168.

Diehl, Alexandra, "The Core Standard of International Investment Protection-Fair and Equitable Treatment", Kluwer Law International, Alphen aan den Rijn (2012).

Dolzer, Rudolf; Schreuer, Christoph, "Principles of International Investment Law", Oxford University Press, Oxford (2008).

Dolzer, Zayar, "The Iranian Revolution Past, Present and Future", available at www.iranchamber.com (accessed on 15 May 2016).

Drahozal, Christopher R.; Gibson, Christopher S., "Iran-United States Claims Tribunal Precedent in Investor-State Arbitration", *Journal of International Arbitration*, Vol. 23, Issue. 6 (2006), 521.

Engle, Rachel, "Party Autonomy in International Arbitration: Where Uniformity Gives Way to Predictability", *The Transnational Lawyer*, Vol. 15, Issue. 2 (2002), 323.

Ewan McKendrick, "Force Majeure and Frustration of Contract", Lloyds of London Press Ltd, London (1991).

Feldman, Mark B., "The Annulment Proceedings and the Finality of ICSID Arbitral Awards", *ICSID Review-Foreign Investment Law Journal*, Vol. 2, Issue. 1 (1987), 85.

Fenyvesi, Jósef Bulcsú, "Application of International Law as Applicable Law under the First Sentence of Art 42(1) of the ICSID Convention", *Jura: A Pecsi Tudomanyegytem Allam- es Jogtudomanyi Karanak tudomanyos lapja*, Vol. 2005, Issue. 1 (2005), 61.

Gaillard, Emmanuel, "The Extent of Review of the Applicable Law in Investment Treaty Arbitration", in: *Annulment of ICSID Awards*, E. Gaillard and Y. Banifatemi (eds.), Juris Publishing, New York (2004).

Gaillard, Emmanuel; Banifatemi, Yas, "The Meaning of 'and' in Article 42(1), Second Sentence, of the Washington Convention: The Role of International Law in the ICSID Choice of Law Process", *ICSID Review-Foreign Investment Law Journal*, Vol. 18, Issue. 2 (2003), 375.

Gallo, Paolo, "Unjust Enrichment: A Comparative Analysis", *The American Journal of Comparative Law*, Vol. 40, Issue. 2 (1992), 431.

Gouran, Hafiz; Khosla, Aditi, "The Choice of Law in ICSID Arbitration in Relation to Investment Disputes", *Vindobona Journal of International Commercial Law & Arbitration*, Vol. 16 (2012), 35.

Hanessian, Grant, " 'General Principles of Law' in the Iran-U.S. Claims Tribunal", *Columbia Journal of Transnational Law*, Vol. 27 (1988–1989), 309.

Hertz, Michael F., "The Hostage Crisis and Domestic Litigation: An Overview", in *The Iran-United States Claims Tribunal*, Richard B. Lillich (ed.), University Press of Virginia, Charlottesville (1984).

Hirsh, Moshe, "Between Fair and Equitable Treatment and Stabilization Clause: Stable Legal Environment and Regulatory Change in International Investment Law", *Journal of World Investment & Trade*, Vol. 12, Issue. 6 (2011), 297.

History of ICSID Convention, ICSID Publication, Volume. I–IV (2006).

Jacob, Kenneth S., "Reinvigorating ICSID with a New Mission and with Renewed Respect for Party Autonomy", *Virginia Journal of International Law*, Vol. 33 (1992), 123.

Juenger, Friedrich K., "Conflict of Laws, Comparative Law and Civil Law: The Lex Mercatoria and Private International Law", *Louisiana Law Review*, Vol. 60 (2000), 1133.

Kahn, Phillipe, "The Law Applicable to Foreign Investments: The Contribution of the World Bank Convention on the Settlement of Investment Disputes", *Indiana Law Journal*, Vol. 44, Issue. 1 (1968), 27.

Khalilian, Khalil, "Iran-United States Claims Arbitration-Debates on Commercial and Public International Law", Trafford Publishing, United States (2012).

Kjos, Hege Elisabeth, "Investor-State Arbitration-The Interplay Between National and International Law", Oxford University Press, Oxford (2013).

Koh, Harold Hongju, "Why Transnational Law Matters", *Penn State International Law Review*, Vol. 24, Issue. 4 (2006), 745.

Konarski, Hubert, "Force Majeure and Hardship Clauses in International Contractual Practice", *International Business Law Journal*, Issue. 4 (2003), 405.

Lagergren, Gunnar, "Iran-United States Claims Tribunal", *The Dalhousie Law Journal*, Vol. 13 (1990), 505.

Lauterpacht, Hersch, "The Function of Law in the International Community", Archon Books, London (1966).

Leigh, Guy I. F., "Nationality and Diplomatic Protection", *International and Comparative Law Quarterly*, Vol. 20 (1971), 453.

Levin, Morris J., "Party Autonomy: Choice-of-Law Clauses in Commercial Contracts", *The Georgetown Law Journal*, Vol. 46 (1957–1958), 260.

Lew, Julian D. M.; Mistelis, Loukas A.; Kröll, Stefan, "Comparative International Commercial Arbitration", Kluwer Law International, The Hague/London/New York (2003).

Lew, Julian D. M., "Applicable Law in International Commercial Arbitration – A Study in Commercial Arbitration Awards", Oceana Publications, INC., New York (1978).

Lillich, Richard B., "The Iran-United States Claims Tribunal 1981–1983", University Press of Virginia, Charlottesville (1984).

Livingstone, Mia Louise, "Party Autonomy in International Commercial Arbitration: Popular Fallacy or Proven Fact?", *Journal of International Arbitration*, Vol. 25, Issue. 5 (2008), 259.

Lorenzen, Ernest G., "Validity and Effects of Contracts in the Conflict of Laws (Part 1)" *Yale Law Journal*, Vol. 30 (1920–1921), 565.

Lorenzen, Ernest G., "Validity and Effects of Contracts in the Conflict of Laws (Part 2)", *Yale Law Journal*, Vol. 30 (1921), 655.

Lowe, James R., "Choice of Law Clauses in International Contracts: A Practical Approach", *Harvard International Law Journal*, Vol. 12 (1971), 1.

Lowenfeld, Andreas F., "The ICSID Convention: Origins and Transformation", *Georgia Journal of International and Comparative Law*, Vol. 38 (2009), 47.

Magallona, Merlin M., "On Dual Allegiance and Dual Nationality", *World Bulletin: Bulletin of the International Studies of the Philippines*, Vol. 6, Issue. 1 (1990), 1.

Mann, Frederick A., "The Proper Law of Contracts Concluded by International Persons", *British Year Book of International Law*, Vol. 35 (1959), 34.

Martin, Antoine P., "Stability in Contemporary Investment Law: Reconsidering the Role and Shape of Contractual Commitments in Light of Recent Trends", *Manchester Journal of International Economic Law*, Vol. 10, Issue. 1 (2013), 38.

Mason, Josephine K., "Arbitral & Judicial Decision: The Role of Ex Aequo Et Bono in International Border Settlement: A Critique of the Sudanese Abyei Arbitration", *American Review of International Arbitration*, Vol. 20 (2010), 519.

Mayer, Pierre, "Mandatory Rules of Law in International Arbitration", *Arbitration International*, Vol. 2, Issue. 4 (1986), 274.

Mohebi, Mohsen, "The International Law Character of the Iran-United States Claims Tribunal", Kluwer Law International, Den Haag (1998).

Moses, Margaret L., "The Principles of International Commercial Arbitration", Cambridge University Press, Second Edition, Cambridge (2012).

Nelson, Annalise, "Investments in the Deep Freeze? Stabilization Clauses in Investment Contracts", Kluwer Arbitration Blog (2011).

Note, "Claims of Dual Nationals in the Modern Era: The Iran-United States Claims Tribunal", *Michigan Law Review*, Vol. 83, Issue. 3 (1984), 571.

Paulsen, Monrad G.; Sovern, Michael I., "Public Policy in the Conflict of Laws", *Columbia Law Review*, Vol. 56, Issue. 7 (1956), 969.

Peake, Jessica, "Diplomatic Protection for Dual Nationals: Effective Nationality or Non-Responsibility?", *Trinity College Review*, Vol. 10 (2007), 98.

Peter, Wolfgang, "Arbitration and Renegotiation of International Investment Agreements", Kluwer Law International, Den Haag (1995).

Pinsolle, Philippe, "The Annulment of ICSID Awards", *The Journal of World Investment & Trade*, Vol. 1, Issue. 1 (2000), 243.

Pirrwitz, Bjorn, "Annulment of Arbitral Awards under Article 52 of the Washington Convention on the Settlement of Investment Disputes between States and Nationals of Other States", *Texas International Law Journal*, Vol. 23, Issue. 1 (1998), 73.

Reed, Lucy; Paulsson, Jan; Blackaby, Nigel, "Guide to ICSID Arbitration", Kluwer Law International, Den Haag (2004).

Reisman, W. Michael, "The Breakdown of the Control Mechanism in ICSID Arbitration", *Duke Law Journal*, Issue 4 (1989), 739.

Reisman, W. Michael, "The Regime for Lacunae in the ICSID Choice of Law Provision and the Question of Its Threshold", *ICSID Review- Foreign Investment Law Journal*, Vol. 15, Issue. 2 (2000), 362.

Reisman, W. Micheal, "International Non-Liquet: Recrudescence and Transformation", *International Lawyer*, Vol. 3, Issue. 4 (1969), 741.

Reisman, W. Michael, "Repairing ICSID's Control System: Some Comments on Aron Broches' 'Observations on the Finality of ICSID Awards' ", *ICSID Review-Foreign Investment Law Journal*, Vol. 7, Issue. 1 (1992), 196.

Rode, Zvonko R., "Dual Nationals and the Doctrine of Dominant Nationality", *The American Journal of International Law*, Vol. 53, Issue. 1 (1959), 139.

Rowat, Malcolm D., "Multilateral Approaches to Improving the Investment Climate of Developing Countries: The Cases of ICSID and MIGA", *Harvard International Law Journal*, Vol. 33, Issue. 1 (1992), 103.

Rubino-Sammartano, Mauro, "Amiable Compositeur (Joint Mandate to Settle) and Ex Bono et Aequo (Discretional Authority to Mitigate Strict Law): Apparent Synonyms Revisited", *Journal of International Arbitration*, Vol. 9, Issue. 1 (1992), 5.

Schatz, Sylvia, "The Effect of the Annulment Decision in Amco v. Indonesia and Klöckner v. Cameroon on the Future of the International Center for the Settlement of Investment Disputes", *American University International Law Review*, Vol. 3, Issue 2 (1988), 481.

Schreuer, C., "Jurisdiction and Applicable Law in Investment Treaty Arbitration", *McGill Journal of Dispute Resolution*, Vol. 1 (2014), 1.

Schreuer, C., "The ICSID Convention: A Commentary", Cambridge University Press, Cambridge (2009).

Schreuer, Christoph H., "The ICSID Convention—A Commentary", Cambridge University Press, Second Edition, Cambridge (2009).

Schreuer, Christoph, "Decisions Ex Aequo et Bono Under the ICSID Convention", *ICSID Review—Foreign Investment Law Journal*, Vol. 11, Issue. 1 (1996), 1.

Schreuer, Christoph, "From ICSID Annulment to Appeal Halfway Down the Slippery Slope", *The Law and Practice of International Courts and Tribunals*, Vol. 10, Issue. 2 (2011), 211.

Schreuer, Christoph, "ICSID Annulment Revisited", *Legal Issues of Economic Integration*, Vol. 30, Issue. 2 (2003), 103.

Schwartz, Eric A., "Finality at What Cost? The Decision of the Ad Hoc Committee in Wena Hotels v. Egypt", in: *IAI International Arbitration Series; Annulment of ICSID Awards*, E. Gaillard and Y. Banifatemi (eds.), Juris Publishing, New York (2004), 43.

Schwenzer, Ingeborg, "Force Majeure and Hardship in International Sales Contracts", *Victoria University of Wellington Law Review*, Vol. 39, Issue. 4 (2009), 709.

Scott, Bieler I., "Dual Nationality, Dominant Nationality and Federal Diversity Jurisdiction (Notes)", *Washington and Lee Law Reviews*, Vol. 38, Issue. 1 (1981), 77.

Sever, Jay R., "Comment: The Relaxation of Inarbitrability and Public Policy Checks on U.S. and Foreign Arbitration: Arbitration Out of Control?", *Tulane Law Review*, Vol. 65 (1991), 1661.

Shihata, Ibrahim F. I.; Parra, Antonio R., "Applicable Substantive Law in Disputes between States and Private Foreign Parties: The Case of Arbitration under the ICSID Convention", *ICSID Review*, Vol. 9, Issue. 2 (1994), 182.

Silberman, Linda; Franco Ferrari, "Getting to the Law Applicable to the Merits in International Arbitration and the Consequences of Getting It Wrong", *Conflict of Laws in International Arbitration*, Vol. 7, Issue. 26 (2010), 257.

Spiro, Peter J., "Dual Nationality and the Meaning of Citizenship", *Emory Law Journal*, Vol. 46, Issue. 4 (1997), 1411.

Stein, Ted L., "Jurisprudence and Jurists' Prudence: The Iranian-Forum Clause Decisions of the Iran-U.S. Claims Tribunal", *The American Journal of International Law*, Vol. 78, Issue. 1 (1984), 1.

Steindl, Barbara Helene, "ICSID Annulment vs. Set Aside by State Courts-Compared to ICSID ad hoc Annulment Committees, Is It the State Courts That Are Now More Hesitant to Set Aside Awards?", *Yearbook on International Arbitration*, Vol. 4 (2015), 181.

Stewart. David P.; Sherman, Laura B., "Developments at the Iran-United States Claims Tribunal: 1981 1983", in *The Iran-United States Claims Tribunal*, Richard B. Lillich (ed.), University Press of Virginia, Charlottesville (1984), 5.

Tetley, William Q. C., "Vita Food Products Revisited (Which Parts of the Decision Are Good Law Today?)", *McGill Law Journal*, Vol. 37 (1992), 292.

Thomas, J. Christopher; Harpeet, Kaur, "Applicable Law under International Investment Treaties", *Singapore Academy of Law Journal*, Vol. 26 (2014), 975.

Timmer, Laurens J. E., "Manifest Excess of Powers as a Ground for the Annulment of ICSID Awards", *The Journal of World Investment & Trade*, Vol. 14, Issue. 5 (2013), 775.

Timmer, Laurens J. E., "The Meaning of 'Investment' as a Requirement for Jurisdiction Ratione Materiae of the ICSID Centre", *Journal of International Arbitration, Kluwer Law International*, Vol. 29, Issue. 4 (2012), 363.

Trekman, Leon, "Ex Aequo et Bono: Demystifying an Ancient Concept", *Chicago Journal of International Law*, Vol. 8, Issue. 2 (2007–2008), 621.

Triebel, Volker, "The Choice of Law in Commercial Relations: A German Perspective", *International and Comparative Law Quarterly*, Vol. 37 (1988), 935.

Waincymer, Jeff, "International Commercial Arbitration and the Application of Mandatory Rules of Law", *Asian International Arbitration Journal*, Vol. 5, Issue.1 (2009), 1.

Weintraub, Russel J., "Functional Developments in Choice of Law for Contracts", *Recueil des Cours*, Vol. 187 (1984), 239.

Westberg, John A., "The Applicable Law Issue in International Business Transactions with Government Parties-Rulings of the Iran-United States Claims Tribunal", *ICSID Review-Foreign Investment Law Journal*, Vol. 2, Issue. 2 (1987), 473.

Wise, Krysta, "Islamic Revolution of 1979: The Downfall of American-Iranian Relations", *Southern Illinois University Carbondale, Legacy*, Vol. 11, Issue. 1 (2011), 1.

Wühler, Norbert, "Application of General Principles of Law", in Albert Jan van den Berg (ed.), *Planning Efficient Arbitration Proceedings: The Law Applicable in International Arbitration, ICCA Congress Series*, Vol. 7, Kluwer Law International, Alphen aan den Rijn (1996), 553.

Zhang, Mo, "Party Autonomy and Beyond: An International Perspective of Contractual Choice of Law", *Emory International Law Review*, Vol. 20, Issue. 2 (2006), 511.

STUDIEN ZUM VERGLEICHENDEN UND INTERNATIONALEN RECHT

Herausgeber: Bernd von Hoffmann (†), Erik Jayme, Heinz-Peter Mansel, Christine Budzikiewicz, Michael Stürner, Karsten Thorn und Marc-Philippe Weller

Band 1 Ferdinand Henke: Die Datenschutzkonvention des Europarates. 1986.

Band 2 Peter Czermak: Der express trust im internationalen Privatrecht. 1986.

Band 3 Peter Kindler: Der Ausgleichsanspruch des Handelsvertreters im deutsch-italienischen Warenverkehr. Eine rechtsvergleichende und kollisionsrechtliche Untersuchung. 1987.

Band 4 Wilhelm Denzer: Stellung und Bedeutung des Engineers in den FIDIC-Bauvertragsbedingungen. 1988.

Band 5 Marijan-Maximilian Lederer: Die internationale Enteignung von Mitgliedschaftsrechten unter besonderer Berücksichtigung der französischen Enteignungen 1982. 1989.

Band 6 Rainer Esser: Klagen gegen ausländische Staaten. 1990.

Band 7 Chang Jae-Ok: Auf dem Weg zu einer Materialisierung des Immateriellen? Personen-, Persönlichkeitsschutz und Geldersatz des immateriellen Schadens in rechtsvergleichender Hinsicht am Beispiel des koreanischen und japanischen Zivilrechts unter besonderer Berücksichtigung des deutschen Rechts. 1990.

Band 8 Paul-Frank Weise: Lex mercatoria. Materielles Recht vor der internationalen Handelsschiedsgerichtbarkeit.1990.

Band 9 Werner Born: Der Auftrittsvertrag für Musikgruppen im Bereich der Rock- und Popmusik. 1990.

Band 10 Ralf Erich Jürgens: IPR und Verfassung in Italien und in der Bundesrepublik Deutschland. 1990.

Band 11 Rainer Gildeggen: Internationale Schieds- und Schiedsverfahrensvereinbarungen in Allgemeinen Geschäftsbedingungen vor deutschen Gerichten. 1991.

Band 12 Klaus Grabinski: Die kollisionsrechtliche Behandlung des Durchgriffs bei rechtlich verselbständigten Unternehmen in privater oder öffentlicher Hand. 1991.

Band 13 Dieter Stummel: Konkurs und Integration. Konventionsrechtliche Wege zur Bewältigung grenzüberschreitender Insolvenzverfahren. 1991.

Band 14 Joachim Güntzer: Die Rechtsstellung des Geschäftsführers im spanischen Aktienrecht. Die Neuregelung des spanischen Aktienrechts nach dem Beitritt Spaniens zur EG. 1991.

Band 15 Sabine Isenburg-Epple: Die Berücksichtigung ausländischer Rechtshängigkeit nach dem Europäischen Gerichtsstands- und Vollstreckungsübereinkommen vom 27.9.1968. Untersuchungen zum Anwendungsbereich von Art. 21 EuGVÜ unter schwerpunktmäßiger Behandlung der Frage nach der Bestimmung eines europäischen Streitgegenstandsbegriffs. 1992.

Band 16 Ulrich Nickl: Die Qualifikation der culpa in contrahendo im Internationalen Privatrecht. 1992.

Band 17 Theo Rauh: Leistungserschwerungen im Schuldvertrag. Eine rechtsvergleichende Untersuchung des englischen, US-amerikanischen, französischen und deutschen Rechts unter besonderer Berücksichtigung der gerichtlichen Praxis. 1992.

Band 18 Bernadette Chaussade-Klein: Vorvertragliche "obligation de renseignements" im französischen Recht. 1992.

Band 19 Josef Sievers: Verbraucherschutz gegen unlautere Vertragsbedingungen im französischen Recht. Vom Code civil zum "Code de la consommation" – die Entstehung eines Sonderprivatrechts für Verbraucher. 1993.

Band 20 Achim Schäfer: Grenzüberschreitende Kreditsicherung an Grundstücken, unter besonderer Berücksichtigung des deutschen und italienischen Rechts. 1993.

Band 21 Eugenio Hernández-Breton: Internationale Gerichtsstandsklauseln in Allgemeinen Geschäftsbedingungen. Unter besonderer Berücksichtigung des deutsch-südamerikanischen Rechtsverkehrs (dargestellt am Beispiel Argentinien, Brasilien und Venezuela). 1993.

Band 22 Ingo Reng: Unterhaltsansprüche aufgrund nichtehelicher Lebensgemeinschaft – Internationales Privatrecht und ausländisches materielles Recht. 1994.

Band 23 Stefanie Roloff: Die Geltendmachung ausländischer öffentlicher Ansprüche im Inland. 1994.

Band 24 Katharina Ludwig: Der Vertragsschluß nach UN-Kaufrecht im Spannungsverhältnis von Common Law und Civil Law. Dargestellt auf der Grundlage der Rechtsordnungen Englands und Deutschlands. 1994.

Band 25 Malte Diesselhorst: Mehrparteienschiedsverfahren. Internationale Schiedsverfahren unter Beteiligung von mehr als zwei Parteien. 1994.

Band 26 Manfred Kost: Konsensprobleme im internationalen Schuldvertragsrecht. 1995.

Band 27 Wolff-Heinrich Fleischer: Das italienische Wettbewerbsrecht und die Probleme des selektiven Parfümvertriebs unter Berücksichtigung der Rechtslage in Frankreich und Deutschland. 1995.

Band 28 Angelika Fuchs: Lateinamerikanische Devisenkontrollen in der internationalen Schuldenkrise und Art. VIII Abschn. 2 b) IWF-Abkommen. 1995.

Band 29 Jacques Matthias Aull: Der Geltungsanspruch des EuGVÜ: "Binnensachverhalte" und Internationales Zivilverfahrensrecht in der Europäischen Union. Zur Auslegung von Art. 17 Abs. 1 S. 1 EuGVÜ. 1996.

Band 30 Hartmut Ost: EVÜ und fact doctrine. Konflikte zwischen europäischer IPR-Vereinheitlichung und der Stellung ausländischen Rechts im angelsächsischen Zivilprozeß. 1996.

Band 31 Stefan Wagner: Die Testierfähigkeit im Internationalen Privatrecht. 1996.

Band 32 Wolfgang Jakob Hau: Positive Kompetenzkonflikte im Internationalen Zivilprozeßrecht. Überlegungen zur Bewältigung von *multi-fora disputes*. 1996.

Band 33 Markus Schütz: UN-Kaufrecht und *Culpa in contrahendo*. 1996.

Band 34 Volker Geyrhalter: Das Lösungsrecht des gutgläubigen Erwerbers. Ein "vergessener" Kompromiß und die Auswirkungen auf das heutige deutsche

Recht unter besonderer Berücksichtigung des internationalen Sachenrechts. 1996.

Band 35 Andreas Kramer: Abwicklungsstörungen bei Kaufverträgen. Die Lieferung vertragswidriger Sachen im deutschen und italienischen Recht. 1996.

Band 36 Petra Krings: Erfüllungsmodalitäten im internationalen Schuldvertragsrecht. 1997.

Band 37 Tonja Gaibler: Der rechtsgeschäftliche Irrtum im französischen Recht. 1997.

Band 38 Dirk Otto: Rechtsspaltung im indischen Erbrecht. Bedeutung und Auswirkungen auf deutsch-indische Nachlaßfälle. 1997.

Band 39 Gregor W. Decku: Zwischen Vertrag und Delikt. Grenzfälle vertraglicher und deliktischer Haftung dargestellt am Beispiel der Berufs- und Expertenhaftung zum Schutze des Vermögens Dritter im deutschen und englischen Recht. 1997.

Band 40 Gregor W. Decku: Zwischen Vertrag und Delikt. Grenzfälle vertraglicher und deliktischer Haftung dargestellt am Beispiel der Berufs- und Expertenhaftung zum Schutze des Vermögens Dritter im deutschen und englischen Recht. 1997.

Band 41 Ulrike Höpping: Auswirkungen der Warenverkehrsfreiheit auf das IPR unter besonderer Berücksichtigung des Internationalen Produkthaftungsrechts und des Internationalen Vertragsrechts. 1997.

Band 42 Helene Boriths Müller: Die Umsetzung der europäischen Übereinkommen von Rom und Brüssel in das Recht der Mitgliedstaaten. Dargestellt am Beispiel Deutschlands und Dänemarks. 1997.

Band 43 Bernd von Hoffmann / Myong-Chang Hwang (eds.): The Public Concept of Land Ownership. Reports and Discussions of a German-Korean Symposium held in Seoul on October 7-9, 1996. 1997.

Band 44 Oliver Heeder: Fraus legis. Eine rechtsvergleichende Untersuchung über den Vorbehalt der Gesetzesumgehung in Deutschland, Österreich, der Schweiz, Frankreich und Belgien unter besonderer Berücksichtigung des Internationalen Privatrechts. 1998.

Band 45 Heinrich Schütt: Deliktstyp und Internationales Privatrecht. Dargestellt an grenzüberschreitenden Problemen der Arzthaftung. 1998.

Band 46 Axel Steiner: Die stillschweigende Rechtswahl im Prozeß im System der subjektiven Anknüpfungen im deutschen Internationalen Privatrecht. 1998.

Band 47 Martina Schulz: Der Eigentumsvorbehalt in europäischen Rechtsordnungen. Rechtsvergleichende Untersuchung des deutschen, englischen und französischen Rechts unter besonderer Berücksichtigung von Erweiterungen und Verlängerungen. 1998.

Band 48 Karin Dreher: Die Rechtswahl im internationalen Erbrecht. Unter besonderer Berücksichtigung des italienischen IPR-Reformgesetzes N. 218 vom 31. Mai 1995. 1999.

Band 49 Giuliano Gabrielli: Das Verhältnis zwischen der Anfechtung wegen Eigenschaftsirrtums und den Gewährleistungsansprüchen im deutschen, österreichischen und italienischen Recht. 1999.

Band 66 Jochen Nikolaus Schlotter: Erbrechtliche Probleme in der Société Privée Européenne. IPR-Harmonisierung im einheitlichen Europäischen Rechtsraum. 2002.

Band 67 Konrad Ost: Doppelrelevante Tatsachen im Internationalen Zivilverfahrensrecht. Zur Prüfung der internationalen Zuständigkeit bei den Gerichtsständen des Erfüllungsortes und der unerlaubten Handlung. 2002.

Band 68 Tobias Bosch: Die Durchbrechungen des Gesamtstatuts im internationalen Ehegüterrecht. Unter besonderer Berücksichtigung deutsch-französischer Rechtsfälle. 2002.

Band 69 Ursula Philipp: Form im amerikanischen Erbrecht. Zwischen Formalismus und harmless error. 2002.

Band 70 Christian Stefan Wolf: Der Begriff der wesentlich engeren Verbindung im Internationalen Sachenrecht. 2002.

Band 71 André Fomferek: Der Schutz des Vermögens Minderjähriger. Ein Vergleich des deutschen und des englischen Rechts unter Berücksichtigung des schottischen und irischen Rechts. 2002.

Band 72 nicht erschienen

Band 73 Markus Dreißigacker: Sprachenfreiheit im Verbrauchervertragsrecht. Der Verbraucher im Spannungsfeld zwischen kultureller Identität und Privatautonomie. 2002.

Band 74 Vassiliki Myller-Igknay: Auskunftsansprüche im griechischen Zivilrecht. Auswirkungen im deutsch-griechischen Rechtsverkehr sowie im deutschen internationalen Privat- und Verfahrensrecht. 2003.

Band 75 Stefan Bruinier: Der Einfluss der Grundfreiheiten auf das Internationale Privatrecht. 2003.

Band 76 Nika Witteborg: Das gemeinsame Sorgerecht nichtverheirateter Eltern. Eine Untersuchung im soziologischen, rechtsgeschichtlichen, verfassungsrechtlichen, rechtsvergleichenden und internationalen Kontext. 2003.

Band 77 Peter Stankewitsch: Entscheidungsnormen im IPR als Wirksamkeitsvoraussetzungen der Rechtswahl. 2003.

Band 78 Jan Wilhelm Ritter: Euro-Einführung und IPR unter besonderer Berücksichtigung nachehelicher Unterhaltsverträge. Eine Untersuchung mit Blick auf das deutsche, französische und schweizerische Recht. 2003.

Band 79 Wolf Richard Herkner: Die Grenzen der Rechtswahl im internationalen Deliktsrecht. 2003.

Band 80 Ira Ditandy: Internationale Zuständigkeit. Neuregelung durch die LOPJ 1985. Vergleich mit dem europäischen Vorbild und Auswirkungen auf das spanische internationale Zivilverfahrensrecht. 2003.

Band 81 Andrea Verena Schefold: Werbung im Internet und das deutsche Internationale Privatrecht. 2004.

Band 82 Klaus Herkenrath: Die Umsetzung der Richtlinie 93/13/EWG über missbräuliche Klauseln in Verbraucherverträgen in Deutschland, dem Vereinigten Königreich, Frankreich und Italien. Auswirkungen nationaler Umsetzungstechniken auf dem Harmonisierungserfolg. 2003.

Band 83 Alexander Thünken: Das kollisionsrechtliche Herkunftslandprinzip. 2003.

Band 84 Barbara v. Daumiller: Die Rechtswahl im italienischen internationalen Erbrecht: und ihre Auswirkungen im deutsch-italienischen Rechtsverkehr. 2003.

Band 85 Robert Mödl: Macht, Verantwortlichkeit und Zurechnung im Konzern. Eine rechtsvergleichende Untersuchung auf der Grundlage des deutschen, spanischen und US-amerikanischen Rechts. 2003.

Band 86 Ursula Kerpen: Das Internationale Privatrecht der Persönlichkeitsrechtsverletzungen. Eine Untersuchung auf rechtsvergleichender Grundlage. 2003.

Band 87 Barbara Ploeckl: Umgangsrechtsstreitigkeiten im deutsch-französischen Rechtsverkehr. Bestehende internationale und nationale Regelungen und der geplante *europäische Besuchstitel*. 2003.

Band 88 Katrin Wannemacher: Die Außenkompetenzen der EG im Bereich des Internationalen Zivilverfahrensrechts. Der räumliche Anwendungsbereich des Art. 65 EGV am Beispiel der EuGVO und der EheVO. 2003.

Band 89 Maren B. Eilinghoff: Das Kollisionsrecht der ungerechtfertigten Bereicherung nach dem IPR-Reformgesetz von 1999. 2004.

Band 90 Patrick Niehr: Die zivilprozessuale Dokumentenvorlegung im deutsch-englischen Rechtshilfeverkehr nach der deutschen und der englischen Prozessrechtsreform. 2004.

Band 91 Anna Christina Gördes: Internationale Zuständigkeit, Anerkennung und Vollstreckung von Entscheidungen über die elterliche Verantwortung. Die VO(EG) Nr. 1347/2000, ihre geplanten Änderungen und das Verhältnis beider zum Minderjährigen- und Kinderschutzabkommen. 2004.

Band 92 Martin Rädler: Rechtsbehelfe des Käufers eines Unternehmens oder einer unternehmerischen Beteiligung gegen den Verkäufer im deutschen und französischen Recht. 2004.

Band 93 Marc-Yngve Dietrich: Rechtsstellung und Beteiligung der Gläubiger im französischen Insolvenzverfahren. 2004.

Band 94 Katia Niemann: Die rechtsgeschäftliche und organschaftliche Stellvertretung und deren kollisionsrechtliche Einordnung. Deutschland und England im Vergleich. 2004.

Band 95 Daniel Ludwig: Neuregelungen des deutschen Internationalen Insolvenzverfahrensrechts. Eine Untersuchung unter vergleichender Heranziehung der Europäischen Insolvenzver-ordnung. 2004.

Band 96 Cordelia Faulenbach: Der gemeinschaftsrechtliche Vorbehalt im europäischen Wettbewerbsrecht. Die Herkunftslandanknüpfung der E-Commerce-Richtlinie unter dem Einfluss der Grundfreiheiten. 2004.

Band 97 Ulf Dörner: Der Vertragsgerichtsstand nach dem Protokoll von Buenos Aires. 2004.

Band 98 Martin Schmidhuber: Verhaltenskodizes im nationalen und grenzüberschreitenden elektronischen Geschäftsverkehr. Zur Frage der Integration der Selbstregulierung durch Private in die staatliche Rechtsordnung. 2004.

Band 99 Florian Kienle: Die fehlerhafte Banküberweisung im internationalen Rechtsverkehr. Unter besonderer Berücksichtigung des Artikels 4A US Uniform Commercial Code. 2004.

Band 100 Thomas Alexander Brandt: Die Adoption durch eingetragene Lebenspartner im internationalen Privat- und Verfahrensrecht. 2004.

Band 101 Florian Pulkowski: Subunternehmer und Internationales Privatrecht. Der Subunternehmer als Quasi-Verbraucher im Europäischen Kollisionsrecht. 2004.

Band 102 Ulrich Becker: Grundrechtsschutz bei der Anerkennung und Vollstreckbarerklärung im europäischen Zivilverfahrensrecht. Bestimmung der Grenzen für die Einführung eines europäischen Vollstreckungstitels. 2004.

Band 103 Thomas Badelt: Aufrechnung und internationale Zuständigkeit unter besonderer Berücksichtigung des deutsch-spanischen Rechtsverkehrs. 2005.

Band 104 Florian D. Wagner: Vorvertragliche Aufklärungspflichten im internationalen Franchising. Zur Harmonisierung von Delikts- und Vertragsstatut im internationalen Privatrecht unter besonderer Berücksichtigung der Franchise-Gesetzgebung des US-Bundesstaates Kalifornien. 2005.

Band 105 Vera Heine: Die Umsetzung der *EG-Richtlinie über missbräuchliche Klauseln in Verbraucherverträgen* im englischen und deutschen Recht. 2005.

Band 106 Alexander Franz: Überregionale Effektentransaktionen und anwendbares Recht. Eine kollisionsrechtliche Untersuchung unter besonderer Berücksichtigung der Vorschrift des § 17 a DepotG. 2005.

Band 107 Hanna-Maria Uhlenbrock: Gesetzliche Regelungen für nichteheliche Lebensgemeinschaften in Deutschland und Frankreich. Ein Vergleich des Unterhaltsrechts bei der eingetragenen Lebenspartnerschaft und beim Pacte civil de Solidarité. 2005.

Band 108 Katrin Stieß: Anknüpfungen im internationalen Urheberrecht unter Berücksichtigung der neuen Informationstechnologien. 2005.

Band 109 Hendrik Otto: Der gesetzliche Abschlussprüfer im italienischen Recht. Eine rechtsvergleichende Untersuchung unter besonderer Berücksichtigung der zivilrechtlichen Haftung. 2005.

Band 110 Frauke Stuphorn: Bankhaftung für Kreditauskünfte im deutschen und französischen Recht. 2005.

Band 111 Nina Fürer: Die zivilrechtliche Haftung für Raucherschäden. 2005.

Band 112 Giovanni B. Barillà: *Contratto autonomo di garanzia* e *Garantievertrag*. Categorie civilistiche e prassi del commercio. 2005.

Band 113 Timo Torz: Gerichtsstände im Internationalen Insolvenzrecht zur Eröffnung von Partikularinsolvenzverfahren. 2005.

Band 114 Martina Schmid: Die Grenzen der Auslegungskompetenz des EuGH im Vorabentscheidungsverfahren nach Art. 234 EG. Dargestellt am Beispiel der überschießenden Richtlinienumsetzung. 2005.

Band 115 Stephan Lesage-Mathieu: Dispositives Kollisionsrecht im prozessualen Kontext. 2005.

Band 116 Jürgen Görtz: Die subjektiven Grenzen der Rechtskraft US-amerikanischer Urteile. 2005.

Band 117 Vera Hoppe: Die Einbeziehung ausländischer Beteiligter in US-amerikanische class actions. Unter Berücksichtigung des Class Action Fairness Act 2005. 2005.

Band 118 Silke Pütz: Parteiautonomie im internationalen Urhebervertragsrecht – Eine rechtsdogmatische und rechtspolitische Betrachtung der Grenzen freier Rechtswahl im internationalen Urhebervertragsrecht unter besonderer Berücksichtigung des neuen deutschen Urhebervertragsrechts. 2005.

Band 119 Alice Nieroba: Die europäische Rechtshängigkeit nach der EuGVVO (Verordnung (EG) Nr. 44/2001) an der Schnittstelle zum nationalen Zivilprozessrecht. 2006.

Band 120 Jan Kayser: Alternative Formen gerichtlicher und außergerichtlicher Streitbeilegung im deutschen und französischen Zivilprozess. Les modes alternatifs judiciaires et extrajudiciaires de résolution des conflits en procédure civile allemande et française. 2006.

Band 121 Mirko Ehrich: Der internationale Anwendungsbereich des deutschen und französischen Rechts gegen irreführende Werbung. Freie Wahl von Form und Mittel, Rom II und Herkunftslandprinzip. 2006.

Band 122 Daniel Thelen: Die Haftung des Sekundärschädigers für Gewalttaten anderer im US-amerikanischen Deliktsrecht ausgehend von dem Problem rechtsextremistisch motivierter Gewalttaten. 2006.

Band 123 Anne Winterling: Die Entscheidungszuständigkeit in Arbeitssachen im europäischen Zivilverfahrensrecht. 2006.

Band 124 Sarah Gerling: Die Gleichstellung ausländischer mit inländischen Vollstreckungstiteln durch die Verordnung zur Einführung eines Europäischen Vollstreckungstitels für unbestrittene Forderungen. Im Vergleich zum bisherigen Recht und zur Rechtslage in den USA. 2006.

Band 125 Christian Bank: Präventivmaßnahmen börsennotierter Gesellschaften zur Abwehr feindlicher Übernahmeversuche in Deutschland und Großbritannien. Eine rechtsvergleichende Untersuchung des deutschen und britischen Rechts unter Berücksichtigung der Europäischen Übernahmerichtlinie. 2006.

Band 126 Christian Weis: Kaufrechtliche Gewährleistung und Garantievergabe in Deutschland und Spanien. Unter besonderer Berücksichtigung des Unternehmenskaufs. 2006.

Band 127 Emilio Maus Ratz: Der Nacherfüllungsanspruch nach UN-Kaufrecht. Im Lichte der deutschen, spanisch-mexikanischen und US-amerikanischen Rechtswissenschaft. 2006.

Band 128 Constanze Jacobs: Die Sachmängelgewähr im deutschen und belgischen Kaufrecht nach Umsetzung der Verbrauchsgüterkauf-Richtlinie. 2006.

Band 129 Ulrike Teichert: Lückenfüllung im CISG mittels UNIDROIT-Prinzipien – Zugleich ein Beitrag zur Wählbarkeit nichtstaatlichen Rechts. 2007.

Band 130 Sascha Reichardt: Internationale Zuständigkeit im Gerichtsstand der unerlaubten Handlung bei Verletzung europäischer Patente. 2006.

Band 131 Bilgehan Cetiner: Die Sachmängelhaftung des Verkäufers im UN-Kaufrecht und im neuen deutschen Schuldrecht. Eine rechtsvergleichende Studie. 2006.

Band 132 Jan Streer: Die Umsetzung der Verbrauchsgüterkaufrichtlinie im englischen Recht durch die Sale and Supply of Goods to Consumer Regulations 2002. 2007.

Band 133 Kathrin Wannenmacher: Einstweilige Maßnahmen im Anwendungsbereich von Art. 31 EuGVVO in Frankreich und Deutschland: Eine Betrachtung ausgesuchter Verfahren des einstweiligen Rechtsschutzes im internationalen Zivilverfahrensrecht – gerichtliche Zuständigkeit, Anerkennung und Vollstreckung. 2007.

Band 134 Wim Kreytenberg: Die individuelle Schwerpunktbestimmung internationaler Schuldverträge nach der Ausweichklausel des Artikel 4 Absatz 5 Satz 2 EVÜ. Ein Beitrag zur Förderung von Rechtssicherheit und Einzelfallgerechtigkeit im europäischen Kollisionsrecht der Schuldverträge. 2007.

Band 135 Nikolaus Geiben: Der Vorvertrag im Internationalen Privatrecht. Unter besonderer Berücksichtigung des Immobilienerwerbs im portugiesischen und brasilianischen Recht. 2007.

Band 136 Predrag Maksimovic: Der Kapitalschutz im europäischen, serbischen und deutschen Recht der Gesellschaft mit beschränkter Haftung. 2007.

Band 137 Alexander Rathenau: Die Anwendung des EuGVÜ durch portugiesische Gerichte unter Berücksichtigung des autonomen internationalen Zivilverfahrensrechts. 2007.

Band 138 Matthias Creydt: Die Besicherung von Weltraumvermögenswerten. Ein neues einheitliches internationales Sicherungsrecht und dessen Vergleich zum US-amerikanischen Mobiliarsicherungsrecht. 2007.

Band 139 Oliver Borkhardt: Registerpublizität und Kollisionsrecht besitzloser Mobiliarsicherheiten nach dem neuen Art. 9 UCC. 2007.

Band 140 Jens Engelmann-Pilger: Deliktische Haftung für das Fehlverhalten Dritter im Common Law. 2007.

Band 141 Bastian Rotmann: Der Schutz des Dritten in der europäischen Mobiliarzwangsvollstreckung. Eine rechtsvergleichende Untersuchung vor dem Hintergrund der Verordnung (EG) Nr. 805/2004 zur Einführung eines Europäischen Vollstreckungstitels für unbestrittene Forderungen. 2007.

Band 142 Oliver Ratzel: Die Präklusion isolierter Unterhaltsverfahren durch den ausländischen Scheidungsverbund. Zugleich ein Beitrag zur internationalen Verbundszuständigkeit im Lichte der Quellenveränderung. 2007.

Band 143 Bettina Maria Stade: Die Konstitutionalisierung des Zivilprozessrechts in Spanien und Deutschland vor dem Hintergrund der Europäisierung des Zivilprozessrechts. 2007.

Band 144 Julia El-Bitar: Der deutsche und der französische Kulturgüterschutz nach der Umsetzung der Kulturgüterrückgaberichtlinie. Eine materiellrechtliche und kollisionsrechtliche Untersuchung. 2007.

Band 145 Aris Kaschefi: Sachmängelhaftung im französischen Kaufrecht vor und nach Umsetzung der Verbrauchsgüterkaufrichtlinie. Mit rechtsvergleichenden Hinweisen zum deutschen Recht unter besonderer Berücksichtigung von Weiterfressersachverhalten. 2007.

Band 146 Isabel Roth: Die internationale Zuständigkeit deutscher Gerichte bei Persönlichkeitsrechtsverletzungen im Internet. 2007.

Band 147 Theresa Wilhelmi: Das Weltrechtsprinzip im internationalen Privat- und Strafrecht. Zugleich eine Untersuchung zu Parallelitäten, Divergenzen und Interdependenzen von internationalem Privatrecht und internationalem Strafrecht. 2007.

Band 148 Alice Halsdorfer: Privat- und kollisionsrechtliche Folgen der Verletzung von Kulturgüterschutznormen auf der Grundlage des UNESCO-Kulturgutübereinkommens 1970. 2008.

Band 149 Thomas Müller-Froelich: Der Gerichtsstand der Niederlassung im deutsch-amerikanischen Rechtsverkehr. Eine Untersuchung zu Fragen der Entscheidungs- und Anerkennungszuständigkeit. 2008.

Band 150 Christopher Luhn: Privatautonomie und Inhaltskontrolle von Eheverträgen. Ein kritischer Vergleich des deutschen und des australischen Rechts mit Bezügen zum Internationalen Privatrecht. 2008.

Band 151 Kristin Kohler: Die grenzüberschreitende Verbraucherverbandsklage nach dem Unterlassungsklagengesetz im Binnenmarkt. 2008.

Band 152 Dorothee Maria Kaulen: Die Anerkennung von Gesellschaften unter Artikel XXV Abs. 5 S. 2 des deutsch-US-amerikanischen Freundschafts-, Handels- und Schifffahrtsvertrags von 1954. 2008.

Band 153 Birka Vanessa Stroschein: Parteizustellung im Ausland. Eine systemvergleichende Untersuchung des Gemeinschafts- und Staatsvertragsrechts unter Einbeziehung des deutschen, französischen, englischen und US-amerikanischen Zustellungsrechts. 2008.

Band 154 Nancy Gruschinkse: Das europäische Kollisionsrecht der Aufrechnung unter besonderer Beachtung des Insolvenzfalles. 2008.

Band 155 Hans-Christian Frick: Sprachrisiko im Zeitalter des Ethnomarketings. US-amerikanische Erfahrungen und europäische Rechtsentwicklung. 2009.

Band 156 Stephan Mangold: Verbraucherschutz und Kunstkauf im deutschen und europäischen Recht. 2009.

Band 157 Robert Beier: Die gesetzlichen Rechte des überlebenden Ehegatten nach dem deutschen und spanischen Kollisionsrecht. Unter besonderer Berücksichtigung der *viudedad aragonesa*. 2009.

Band 158 Julia-Marie Oppermann: Internationale Handelsschiedsgerichtsbarkeit und Verjährung. 2009.

Band 159 Stephan Boese: Strukturprinzipien im Gläubigerschutz. Eine rechtsvergleichende Untersuchung zur GmbH und zur englischen Limited Company. 2009.

Band 160 Thomas Rosa: Das Kaufrecht nach dem Zivilgesetzbuch der Tschechischen und Slowakischen Republik. Eine rechtsvergleichende Darstellung im Lichte des deutschen Bürgerlichen Gesetzbuches. 2009.

Band 161 Roland Weis: Rechnungslegungspflichten von EU-Scheinauslandsgesellschaften im Land ihrer tatsächlichen wirtschaftlichen Betätigung. Insbesondere im Hinblick auf in Deutschland tätige englische Limiteds. 2009.

Band 162 Henning Frase: "Leoninische Vereinbarungen" und Ergebnisbeteiligungspflicht im deutschen und italienischen Gesellschaftsrecht. Zum *patto leoni-*

no des italienischen Rechts und möglichen Entsprechungen im deutschen Recht. 2010.

Band 163 Christiane Tödter: Europäisches Kindschaftsrecht. Nach der Verordnung (EG) Nr. 2201/ 2003. 2010.

Band 164 Edda Gampp: *Perpetuatio fori internationalis* im Zivilprozeß und im Verfahren der freiwilligen Gerichtsbarkeit. 2010.

Band 165 Mei Wu: Die Reform des chinesischen Beweisrechts vor dem Hintergrund deutscher und US-amerikanischer Regelungsmodelle. 2010.

Band 166 Corina Leimert: Stand und Entwicklung des italienischen Rechts der Unternehmenszusammenschlüsse (gruppi di società / gruppi di imprese). 2010.

Band 167 Kasim Özen: Die Scheidungsgründe im türkischen Zivilgesetzbuch. 2010.

Band 168 Helena Isabel Maier: Marktortanknüpfung im internationalen Kartelldeliktsrecht. Eine internationalzuständigkeits- und kollisionsrechtliche Untersuchung unter Einbeziehung rechts-vergleichender Überlegungen zum englischen Recht. 2011.

Band 169 Thomas Spernat: Die gleichgeschlechtliche Ehe im Internationalen Privatrecht. Unter besonderer Berücksichtigung des Einflusses des EG-Vertrags. 2011.

Band 170 Max Johann Lipsky: Statutenwechsel im italienischen Sachenrecht – Auswirkungen auf den Im- und Export von Mobiliarsicherheiten. Eine Untersuchung der rechtlichen Beständigkeit dinglicher Kreditsicherheiten im deutsch-italienischen Rechtsverkehr. 2011.

Band 171 Silvia Karolina Seilstorfer: Die Umsetzung der Verbrauchsgüterkaufrichtlinie in Portugal mit rechtsvergleichenden Hinweisen zum deutschen Recht. 2011.

Band 172 Stephan Georg Knöchel: Anerkennung französischer Urteile mit Drittbeteiligung. Eine Untersuchung der Anerkennung von Drittbindungswirkungen nach der EuGVVO und autonomem deutschem Recht. 2011.

Band 173 Kristina Menzel: Vollstreckungsschutz zugunsten privater Altersvorsorge. Eine rechtsvergleichende Untersuchung zum deutschen und schweizerischen Recht. 2011.

Band 174 Manuela Krach: Scheidung auf Mexikanisch. Das materielle Recht der Scheidung im Mehrrechtsstaat Mexiko unter Berücksichtigung von Eheschließung und Ehewirkungen. 2011.

Band 175 Vanessa Sofia Wagner: Verkehrsschutz beim redlichen Erwerb von GmbH-Geschäfts-anteilen. Ein Vergleich des Rechts für Gesellschaften mit beschränkter Haftung in Deutschland, England und Italien. 2011.

Band 176 Alexander Swienty: Der Statutenwechsel im deutschen und englischen internationalen Sachenrecht unter besonderer Betrachtung der Kreditsicherungsrechte. 2011.

Band 177 Kathrin Süß: Streitbeilegungsmechanismen im Verbraucherrecht. Unter besonderer Berücksichtigung der australischen Rechtsordnung. 2011.

Band 178 Efe Direnisa: Die materielle Rechtskraft im deutschen und türkischen Zivilverfahrensrecht. 2012.

Band 179 Julia Faenger: Leistungsunabhängige Nebenpflichten zum Schutz des Integritätsinteresses im deutschen und französischen Recht. Eine rechtsvergleichende Betrachtung ausgehend von den Rücksichtspflichten des § 241 Abs. 2 BGB. 2012.

Band 180 Dorothea Heine: Das Kollisionsrecht der Forderungsabtretung. UNCITRAL-Abtretungs-konvention und Rom I-Verordnung. 2012.

Band 181 Lisa B. Möll: Kollidierende Rechtswahlklauseln in Allgemeinen Geschäftsbedingungen im internationalen Vertragsrecht. 2012.

Band 182 Jutta Jasmin Uusitalo: Einbeziehung von AGB im unternehmerischen Geschäftsverkehr zwischen Deutschland und Finnland. 2012.

Band 183 Darya Alikhani Chamgardani: Der Allgemeine Teil des iranischen Schuldvertragsrechts. Im Spannungsverhältnis zwischen rezipiertem französischen und traditionellem islamischen Recht. 2013.

Band 184 Volker Anton: Aktuelle Entwicklungen des Bankgeheimnisses im Rechtsvergleich unter besonderer Berücksichtigung seiner exterritorialen Wirkungen. Deutschland, Luxemburg, Österreich, Schweiz und Liechtenstein. 2013.

Band 185 Charlotte Wilhelm: Die Regelung der Geld- und Warenkreditsicherheiten nach dem deutschen Recht im Vergleich zum Draft Common Frame of Reference (DCFR). 2013.

Band 186 Michael Nehmer: Erbunwürdigkeit und Elternunterhalt im Internationalen Privatrecht. Eine historisch-rechtspolitische Betrachtung. 2013.

Band 187 Pınar Şamiloğlu-Riegermann: Türkisches und deutsches Vertragshändlerrecht im Rechtsvergleich. 2014.

Band 188 Elvan Er: Realsicherheiten des türkischen Mobiliarsachenrechts. Eine Darstellung des geltenden türkischen Rechts unter vergleichender Berücksichtigung des deutschen und schweizerischen Kreditsicherungsrechts. 2014.

Band 189 Maya Mandery: Party Autonomy in Contractual and Non-Contractual Obligations. A European and Anglo-Common Law perspective on the freedom of choice of law in the Rome I Regulation on the law applicable to contractual obligations and the Rome II Regulation on the law applicable to non-contractual obligations. 2014.

Band 190 Gregor Nikolas Rutow: Rechtsvergleich über die Zulässigkeit von Haftungsausschlüssen, Haftungsbeschränkungen und pauschaliertem Schadensersatz in einzelnen arabischen Rechtsordnungen. 2014.

Band 191 Christoph Rödter: Das Gesellschaftskollisionsrecht im Spannungsverhältnis zur Rom I- und II-VO. Eine Untersuchung zur Reichweite des Gesellschaftsstatuts in Abgrenzung zu den Kolligionsregeln der Rom I- und II-VO. 2014.

Band 192 Melanie Kaspers: Die gemischten und verbundenen Verträge im Internationalen Privatrecht. 2015.

Band 193 Tong Xue: Parteiautonomie im chinesischen Internationalen Privatrecht. Am Beispiel der Rechtswahl im Internationalen Vertrags-, Delikts-, und Sachenrecht. 2016.

Band 194 Martin Metz: US-Menschenrechtsklagen und Neoterritorialismus. 2017.

Band 195 Matthias A. Sauter: Mitveräußerungspflichten im deutschen und italienischen Recht. 2018.

Band 196 Daniel Brauner: Die Anwendungsbereiche von CISG und PR CESL im Vergleich. 2018.

Band 197 Christina Bohländer. MAC-Klauseln in Unternehmenskaufverträgen nach US-amerikanischem und deutschem Recht. 2018.

Band 198 Steven Leunert. Die Verteidigungsmechanismen des Haftenden im Internationalen Produkthaftungsrecht der Rom II-Verordnung. 2018.

Band 199 Niki Nozari: Applicable Law in International Arbitration – The Experience of ICSID and Iran-United States Claims Tribunal. 2019.

www.peterlang.com

www.ingramcontent.com/pod-product-compliance
Ingram Content Group UK Ltd.
Pitfield, Milton Keynes, MK11 3LW, UK
UKHW021831100926
8556IPUK00004B/279

9 783631 775042